Asia's Reckoning

RICHARD McGREGOR

Asia's Reckoning

The Struggle for Global Dominance

ALLEN LANE
an imprint of
PENGUIN BOOKS

ALLEN LANE

UK | USA | Canada | Ireland | Australia
India | New Zealand | South Africa

Allen Lane is part of the Penguin Random House group of companies
whose addresses can be found at global.penguinrandomhouse.com.

First published in the United States of America by Viking, an imprint of Penguin Random House LLC 2017
First published in Great Britain by Allen Lane 2017
001

Photograph credits
Insert page 1 (top): Getty Images / Archive Photos / FPG; 2 (top, bottom), 3 (top), 4 (bottom),
5 (bottom): Getty Images / Bettmann; 3 (middle): Getty Images / Hulton Archive / David Hume Kennerly;
3 (bottom): Getty Images / Ullstein Bild; 4 (top), 5 (top): Getty Images / Gamma-Rapho/ Kurita Kaku;
6 (top): Getty Images / Sygma / Jacques Langevin; 6 (bottom): Getty Images / Sankei Archive;
7 (top): Getty Images / Getty Images News / Koichi Kamoshida; 7 (bottom), 10 (top),
16 (bottom): Getty Images / The Asahi Shimbun; 8 (top): Getty Images / Hulton Archive / Cynthia Johnson;
8 (bottom): Getty Images / AFP; 9 (middle), 13 (bottom): Getty Images / Getty Images
News / Pool; 9 (bottom): Getty Images / Bloomberg; 10 (bottom): Getty Images / AFP / Kazuhiro Nogi;
11 (top): Getty Images / AFP / STR; 11 (bottom): Getty Images / AFP / Yoshikazu Tsuno;
12 (top): Getty Images / AFP / Toru Yamanaka; 12 (bottom): Getty Images / AFP / Paul J. Richards;
13 (top): Getty Images / AFP / Hoang Dinh Nam; 14 (top): Getty Images / Visual China Group / VCG;
14 (bottom): Getty Images / AFP / Liu Jin; 15 (top): AP Images / Xinhua / Ding Lin;
15 (bottom): Getty Images / AFP / Greg Baker; 16 (top): Getty Images / AFP / Kimimasa Mayama

Map illustration by Jeffrey L. Ward

Printed in Great Britain by Clays Ltd, St Ives plc

A CIP catalogue record for this book is available from the British Library

ISBN: 978–0–241–24808–9

www.greenpenguin.co.uk

MIX
Paper from
responsible sources
FSC   FSC® C018179
www.fsc.org

Penguin Random House is committed to a
sustainable future for our business, our readers
and our planet. This book is made from Forest
Stewardship Council® certified paper.

Contents

Map   viii

Preface   xi

Introduction   1

POSTWAR

CHAPTER ONE: China, Red or Green   19

THE SEVENTIES

CHAPTER TWO: Countering Japan   41

CHAPTER THREE: Five Ragged Islands   55

THE EIGHTIES

CHAPTER FOUR: The Golden Years   77

CHAPTER FIVE: Japan Says No   98

THE NINETIES

CHAPTER SIX: Asian Values   123

CHAPTER SEVEN: Apologies and Their Discontents   144

THE TWENTY-FIRST CENTURY

CHAPTER EIGHT: Yasukuni Respects   169

CHAPTER NINE: History's Cauldron   190

CHAPTER TEN: The Ampo Mafia   212

CHAPTER ELEVEN: The Rise and Retreat of Great Powers   230

CHAPTER TWELVE: China Lays Down the Law   248

CHAPTER THIRTEEN: Nationalization   267

CHAPTER FOURTEEN: Creation Myths   289

CHAPTER FIFTEEN: Freezing Point   309

Afterword   333

Acknowledgments   353

Notes   357

Index   383

To Kath, Angus, and Cate

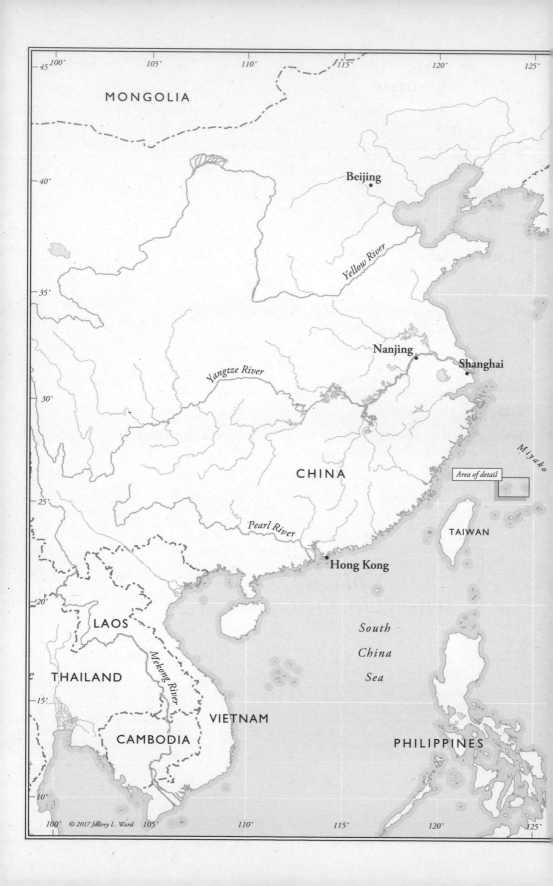

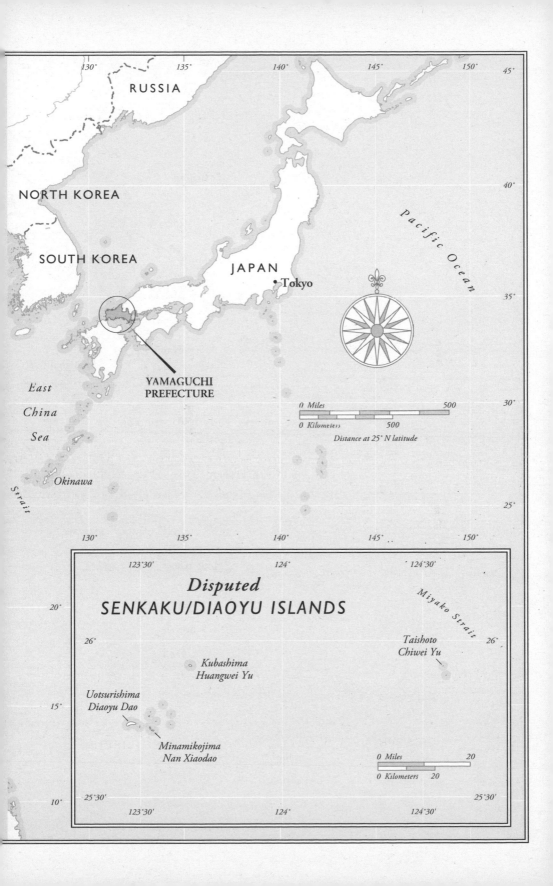

RUSSIA

NORTH KOREA

SOUTH KOREA

JAPAN

• Tokyo

Pacific Ocean

East China Sea

Okinawa

Strait

YAMAGUCHI
PREFECTURE

0 Miles 500
0 Kilometers 500
Distance at 25° N latitude

130° 135° 140° 145° 150°
45°
40°
35°
30°
25°

Disputed
SENKAKU/DIAOYU ISLANDS

Miyako Strait

Kubashima
Huangwei Yu

Taishoto
Chiwei Yu

Uotsurishima
Diaoyu Dao

Minamikojima
Nan Xiaodao

0 Miles 20
0 Kilometers 20

123°30' 124° 124°30'
20°
26° 26°
15°
25°30' 25°30'
10°
123°30' 124° 124°30'

Preface

There is no shortage of scenarios in which America's postwar world comes under challenge and starts to crack. It could take the form of a draining showdown with Islamist radicals in the Middle East, a conflict with Russia that engulfs Europe, or a one-on-one superpower naval battle with China. Soon after his election, Donald Trump finished his first conversation as president-elect with Barack Obama at the White House fretting about the threat from a nuclear-armed North Korea.

In daily headlines, the jousting between China and Japan can't compete with the medieval violence of ISIS or the outsize antics of Vladimir Putin or threats from tyrants like Kim Jong Un. The rivalry between the two countries has festered, by some measures, for centuries, giving it a quality that lets it slip on and off the radar. After all, China and Japan, according to the conventional wisdom, are at their core practical nations with pragmatic leaders.

The two countries, along with Taiwan, South Korea, and Southeast Asia, sit at the heart of the global economy. The iPhones, personal computers, and flat-screen televisions in electronic shops around the world; most of the mass-produced furniture and large amounts of the cheap clothing that fill shopping centers in the United States, Europe, and the United Kingdom; a vast array of industrial goods that consumers are scarcely aware of, from wires and valves to machine parts and the like—all of them, one way or another, are sourced through the supply chains anchored by Asia's two giants. With so much at stake, how could they possibly come to blows?

China and Japan's thriving commercial ties, one of the largest two-way trade relationships in the world, though, have failed to forge a closer political bond. In recent years, the relationship has taken on new and dangerous dimensions for both countries, and for the United States as well, an ally of Japan's that it has signed a treaty to defend. Far from exorcising memories of the brutal war between them that began in the early 1930s and lasted more than a decade, Japan and China are caught in a downward spiral of distrust and ill will. There has been the occasional thawing of tension and the odd uptick in diplomacy in the seventy years since the end of the war. Men and women of goodwill in both countries have dedicated their careers to improving relations. Most of these efforts, however, have come to naught.

Asia's version of the War of the Roses is being fought on multiple battlefields: on the high seas over disputed islands; in capitals around the world as each tries to convince partners and allies of the other's infamy; and in the media, in the relentless, self-righteous, and scorching exchanges over the true account and legacy of the Pacific War. The clash between Japan and China on this issue echoes a conversation between two Allied prisoners of war in Richard Flanagan's garlanded novel set on the Burma Railway in 1943, *The Narrow Road to the Deep North*. "Memory is the true justice, sir," a soldier says to his superior officer, explaining why he wants to hold on to souvenirs of their time in a Japanese internment camp. "Or the creator of new horrors," the officer replies.

In Europe, an acknowledgment of World War II's calamities helped bring the Continent's nations together in the aftermath of the conflict. In east Asia, by contrast, the war and its history have never been settled, politically, diplomatically, or emotionally. There has been little of the introspection and statesmanship that helped Europe to heal its wounds. Even the most basic of disagreements over history still percolate through day-to-day media coverage in Asia more than seventy years later, in baffling, insidious ways. Open a Japanese newspaper in 2017, and you might read of a heated debate about whether Japan invaded China, something that is only an issue because conservative Japanese still insist that their country was fighting a war of self-defense in the 1930s and 1940s. Peruse the state-controlled press in China, and you will see the Communist Party drawing legitimacy from its heroic defeat of Japan, though in truth, Chiang Kai-shek's Nationalists carried the burden of fighting the invaders, while the Communists mostly preserved their strength in hinterland hideouts. Scant recognition is given to the United States, who fought the Japanese for years before ending the conflict with two atomic bombs.

Although the United States and Japan are for the moment firm allies, the trilateral relationship among Washington, Tokyo, and Beijing has been fraught and complex in ways that are little understood and appreciated, often even inside the countries themselves. Each of the three, China, Japan, and the United States, at different times has tried to use one of the others to gain an ascendancy in regional diplomacy in the last century. Each at different times has felt betrayed by the others. All have tried to leverage their relations with one of the others at the expense of the third. In that respect, the relationship is like a geopolitical version of the scene in the movie *Reservoir Dogs* in which a trio of antagonists all simultaneously point guns at one another, creating a circle of dangerous, cascading threats.

In the east Asian version of this scenario, the United States has its arsenal trained on China. China, in turn, menaces Japan and the United States. In ways that are rarely noticed, Japan completes the triangle with its hold over the United States. If Tokyo were to lose faith in Washington and downgrade its alliance or trigger a conflict with Beijing, the effect would be the same: to upend the postwar system. In this trilateral game of chicken, only one of the parties needs to fire its weapons for all three to be thrown into war. Put another way, if China is the key to Asia, then Japan is the key to China, and the United States the key to Japan.

I left Tokyo for Hong Kong and China in 1995 after a five-year posting as a newspaper correspondent, soon after Japan's then prime minister issued a heartfelt apology for the war. At the time, I remember feeling relieved that the issue seemed to have finally been put to rest. The history wars, though, far from ending, were just getting started. Over the ensuing two decades, under pressure from the Chinese Communist Party and abetted by Japanese revisionists, the same old issues have remained stuck on the front lines of regional politics.

Like east Asia more generally, the story of Japan and China is one of stunning economic success and dangerous political failure. China in particular has a whiff of the Balkans, where many young people have a way of vividly remembering wars they never actually experienced. A sense of revenge, of unfinished business, lingers in the system.

It may not require a war, of course, to deliver the last rites for Pax Americana. Washington could simply turn its back on the world under an isolationist president, a president, in other words, who simply did what

Donald Trump promised to do on the campaign trail. America could also slip into unruly decline, with a weaker economy resulting in bits of empire, no longer financially sustainable, dropping off here and there.

Alternatively, of course, Pax Americana in Asia could survive, with a resilient U.S. economy and refreshed alliances robust enough to hold off an indebted and internally focused China. Indeed, it is unlikely that the United States will leave the region quietly. As Michael Green, a former U.S. government official, notes, over more than a century in the Asia-Pacific, Washington has beaten back quests for regional dominance "from the European powers, Imperial Japan and Soviet Communism."

The specter of a renewed Sinocentric order in Asia, though, is upending the regional status quo for good, whatever path the United States might take. Geopolitically, the three countries have increasingly become two, with Japan aligning itself more tightly with the United States than at any time in the seven decades–plus since the war. China, too, has changed. Once, Beijing begrudgingly accepted America's Asian alliances as a tool to keep the Soviets at bay and stabilize the region. Since the end of the cold war, its attitude has shifted, from frustration with America's enduring military footprint in Asia to outright rejection of the alliances as "cold war relics" that threaten China's security. As its power has grown, China has begun building a new regional order, with Beijing at the center in place of Washington. The battle lines are clear. For decades, the United States has set its forward defensive line against rival hegemons in the region in different places before establishing it firmly along and around the Japanese archipelago, where it stands today.

Asia's Reckoning traces the evolution of the three-way relationship among China, Japan, and the United States since the war, through the geopolitical about-turns, clashing personalities, commercial rivalries, trade disputes, and the never-ending scramble for the high ground on history. The story of the decades since then can be pieced together with greater clarity these days, thanks to troves of fresh U.S. documents detailing Washington's ties with Tokyo and Beijing—some released officially, others obtained through Freedom of Information Act requests, and still others stolen and then dumped on the Internet by WikiLeaks. Tokyo's diplomatic archives contain the transcripts of conversations between Japanese and Chinese leaders, and many other insights, unavailable even a few years ago.

In China, the historical record is more tightly guarded, with information seeping out through official channels and the few crevices in the system. Access to government and party records has been restricted further since Xi Jinping came to power. The Foreign Ministry's archives closed altogether in 2013 for three years, before being reopened in late 2016 with access to a limited set of documents. The archives were supposedly shut for a "system upgrade," but in Tokyo many pointed to another reason—the publication of embarrassing documents about Chinese territorial claims uncovered there by a right-wing Japanese newspaper.

There is only one subject area in which access to the archives has expanded in China: for material relating to Japanese wartime atrocities. Elsewhere, though, memoirs of retired officials and compendiums of old documents that contain much material from the Chinese perspective turn up in local bookshops (sometimes only briefly, before they are taken off the shelves). Like anyone who has tried reporting on China, I am thankful for them all.

ASIA'S RECKONING

Introduction

In June 2013, soon after Xi Jinping ascended to power, Barack Obama invited the new Chinese leader to what Washington billed as an informal, shirtsleeve summit. With a handful of advisers, the two leaders sat down for a private dinner prepared by a local celebrity chef at a resort in the sunbaked desert in Palm Springs, California. The following morning, they strolled through the grounds of Sunnylands, the two-hundred-acre former Annenberg estate, built by prominent Republican donors at the corner of Bob Hope and Frank Sinatra drives in Rancho Mirage. With its desert chic, Sunnylands had qualities that appealed to the White House as much as they had in the 1960s, when it was a haunt for show business's famous Rat Pack. Free from the weighty protocol of superpower summits, Obama wanted to put Xi at ease, to build the kind of relationship he had never enjoyed with Xi's predecessor, Hu Jintao.

In his decade in charge of China, a period during which the country's economy expanded fourfold into the world's second largest and its military emerged as a formidable power, Hu had been a frustratingly bloodless interlocutor. Few world leaders who met with him came away with a sense of the man and his ambitions for China. Once, when tired before a meeting, Obama joked to his aides that he was going "to do a Hu Jintao" to get through the encounter. Longevity in office neither amplified Hu's personality nor brought him out of his shell. He seemed to shrink as Chinese power grew, sticking to scripted speeches and stymieing any attempts at genuine interaction.

Xi would prove to be radically different, a decisive leader willing to take risks to crush opponents at home and challenge rivals abroad. No one made any jokes, in Washington or elsewhere, about dozing off in Xi's presence. But in his first outing in the United States as Communist Party chief and president, Xi did not depart dramatically from the style of his predecessor. Obama's advisers later described the meeting as an invest-ment, a word that conveyed a touch of disappointment. Xi's steely talk-ing points, which concerned Beijing's attempts to reform its economy and maintain peace and stability in the Asia-Pacific, were familiar to anyone who had met Hu.

There was only one moment at Sunnylands when Xi veered off script, when the conversation turned to Japan. His mood darkened as he began denouncing China's neighbor in such strong terms that Obama felt he needed to remind Xi that Japan was a friend and an ally of America's. The U.S. president raised his two hands above his head like a stop sign, as if he were a schoolteacher calling his class to order, a signal for Xi to temper his tirade and bring it to an end.

On one level, Xi's visceral anger toward Japan is easily explained. In late 2012, Tokyo had nationalized a ragtag group of small islands that lay between Taiwan and Okinawa, reigniting a long-running territorial dis-pute with Beijing. The rocky outcrops, known as the Senkakus by the Japanese and the Diaoyus by China, are claimed by both countries. The Politburo had nominated Xi to manage Beijing's response to Tokyo's ac-tion at an acutely delicate moment, just months before he was due to take over party leadership. Few issues are more fraught within the CCP than issues of territorial sovereignty, perhaps matched only by Japan itself. The two in combination are treacherous.

Most accounts of Sino-Japanese relations paint the two countries' differences as the inevitable, inexorable result of Japan's invasion and occupation of China in the 1930s and through World War II until To-kyo's surrender in August 1945, followed by an extended squabble over responsibility for the conflict. Alternatively, their clash is depicted as a traditional great-power contest, with an ascending superpower, China, running up against a now weaker rival competing to dominate the Asia-Pacific. A third template takes a longer view, one of a China bent on rebuilding the ascendancy the celestial kingdom enjoyed in Asia in im-perial times. None of these templates alone, however, captures the tan-gled emotions and complex psychology of the Sino-Japanese relationship, nor the contemporary geopolitical dimensions of their enmity. The tensions between China and Japan have a long tail that extends way beyond Xi's anger over a few islands.

For centuries, China had been both the Athens and the Rome of east Asia, an empire that established a template of cultural, political, and institutional values and structures that permeated the region. Japan's script, its merit-based bureaucracy, hierarchical social relations, and exam-intense education system—all of which remain embedded in the country's twenty-first-century way of life and governing institutions—originated in China.

In small, striking ways, the Japanese can display an authentic affinity with their Chinese heritage. In early 2016, at a farewell reception for a senior Japanese diplomat in Washington, each guest, including the Chinese ambassador, Cui Tiankai, was given a copy of a poem as he or she departed. Penned by the diplomat in whose honor the reception was held, the poem, which celebrated the seasonal blooming of cherry blossoms in Washington, was written in Chinese characters in the style of revered Tang dynasty poets. The gift was an homage to the enduring influence of Chinese culture, and to contemporary education in Japan, where schoolchildren still learn the art of classical Chinese poetry. Printed on pink paper, it was also a gesture that no people other than the Japanese could pull off with such expertise and grace.

The histories of modern Japan and China have much in common as well. Both were forcibly opened in the nineteenth century at the point of a gun wielded by an imperialist West. In the century that followed, they both battled to win the respect of the intruders who considered themselves racially superior to Asians. Far from displaying solidarity with each other, the two nations went in different directions: Japan modernized rapidly, while China disintegrated. Ever since, they have struggled to find an equilibrium of their own. If one country was ascendant, the other was subordinate. Through multiple wars, colonial subjugation, diplomatic reconciliation, and flourishing trade, each has at different times imposed the hierarchies that typify its own institutions on the other. Japan and China have demanded the West treat them as equals, but they have rarely managed to do so with each other.

In the words of a Japanese historian, the two countries have developed an "interdependence and autonomy, mutual respect and suspicion, attraction and repulsion, and admiration and condescension" toward each other. For all the periodic talk of their shared Asian identity, they have not hesitated to seek help from outsiders for support in their conflicts. Within their elites, the divisions are deeply personal as well.

From the high point of seemingly amicable relations from the late 1970s until the mid-1980s, a corrosive mutual antipathy has gradually become embedded within their ruling parties and large sections of the public. In turn, seemingly unavoidable political divisions—driven on the surface by constant demands from China for Japan to apologize for its wartime conduct and Japanese hostility to such pressure—have eroded trust and strengthened hyper-nationalists in both countries. China's economic rise and Japan's relative decline have only reinforced this trend. In both capitals, the domestic tail now wags the diplomatic dog as often as the other way around.

What once seemed impossible and then merely unlikely is no longer unimaginable: that China and Japan could, within coming decades, go to war. If they do, they will not be fighting on their own.

The Chinese often quote an ancient idiom when speaking about Japan: two tigers cannot live on one mountain. The phrase succinctly conveys how many Chinese view their competition with Japan to be the dominant indigenous power in Asia as a zero-sum game. The idiom, however, does not convey the larger contest afoot in the region. Standing between these two nations, and alongside Tokyo, is Washington, the predominant power in Asia from the moment the United States and its allies defeated Japan in the Pacific War.

Ever since, the United States has maintained military bases in east Asia, which, on the face of it, would seem to be imperial overreach of the most overbearing kind. With its sprawling armed footprint, Pax Americana has nonetheless had a stunning upside in the region, underwriting an explosion in wealth not matched in the world since the Industrial Revolution. Since the 1950s, Japan, and then South Korea, Taiwan, and China, were able to put bitter political and historical enmities aside to pursue economic growth. Southeast Asian nations followed in their wake, transforming a region only half a century ago typified by colonialism, conflict, and poverty into one of growth, prosperity, and power.

It was no wonder, then, that Obama surveyed the Asia-Pacific region with relative approval as he prepared to depart office in late 2016. In contrast with the religious extremism and primeval violence of the Middle East, postwar east and Southeast Asia had during his lifetime been distinguished largely by an explosion of material wealth and ambition. The people of Asia, Obama observed, don't begin their days "thinking about how to kill Americans."

The man who replaced him, Donald Trump, ran for the White House with a darker view of Asia's renaissance. Indeed, Pax Americana had become so much a part of the status quo in Washington that Trump's campaign-trail assaults on the country's long-standing bipartisan Asia policy seemed to take place almost in a vacuum. Trump criticized Japan and South Korea for free riding on U.S. security and said both countries should acquire nuclear weapons if they wished to reduce their reliance on Washington. On trade, he singled out China and Japan for cheating Americans, in league with the domestic Visigoths of globalization, Wall Street and big business. Trump tapped ruthlessly into grassroots anger by hammering what is perhaps the most potent critique of Pax Americana: not only has the United States protected Asia's flourishing economies; it has opened the American market to their exports in ways they would never reciprocate. As Trump's chief strategist, Stephen Bannon, a man accused of promoting white supremacist movements, put it, "The globalists gutted the American working class and created a middle class in Asia."

China's rise, or more accurately its reemergence, has only raised the stakes in east Asia for Trump and whoever might come after him in the White House. When the United States and its Western allies debated how to confront the threat posed by the radical Islamic State from 2014 onward, they didn't pause to factor in the impact of any armed conflict on the self-styled caliphate's GDP, let alone oil prices. China and Japan, by contrast, are global powers, with the world's second- and third-largest economies, backed by robust, advanced militaries. Along with South Korea and Taiwan, they sit at the nexus of the tightly integrated seaborne trade network that sustains global business and U.S. consumption. Any clash between China and Japan would not be a simple spat between neighbors. A single shot fired in anger could trigger a global economic tsunami, engulfing political capitals, trade routes, manufacturing centers, and retail outlets on every continent.

That scenario, in turn, underpins a second paradox. While keeping the peace, the U.S. presence in east Asia has at the same time papered over serial diplomatic failures in the region. Seven decades into Pax Americana, all of the frozen-in-the-1950s fault lines buried during the decades of high-speed growth are resurfacing. China and Taiwan, for all their tens of billions in two-way trade and deepening personal interaction, have drifted further apart than ever politically. The Korean peninsula remains divided along cold war contours and bristling with conventional and nuclear armory. The Sino-Japanese rivalry overflows with bitterness and mistrust, despite a bilateral business relationship that is one of the most valuable in the world.

The governments and people of east Asia may not wake up "thinking about how to kill Americans," in Obama's words, North Korea aside. Increasingly, however, they are bumping up against one another in fresh and perilous ways. Far from allowing the United States to simply pack up and go home, as Trump suggested in his campaign, Asia's success has only magnified the dangers of an American drawdown. "It is not only true that China changed the status quo by getting strong," said Yan Xuetong, one of China's most prominent hawks, "but also America and Japan changed the status quo by getting weak."

Entangled with the travails of an overstretched U.S. empire, unresolved regional enmities, and intensifying military competition is a story of the rise and fall and rise of the great powers of Asia. The about-turn in perceptions of Japan—from a colossus poised for world domination to a nation in seemingly inexorable decline in the space of two decades—has few parallels in modern history. The same applies, in reverse, to China.

In 1990, at the peak of Japan's bubble economy, twice as many Americans viewed Japanese economic power as a threat to U.S. interests as they did the Soviet military, according to one mainstream poll. During that period, prominent security hawks and senior CIA analysts also considered Japan's techno-nationalism a danger to U.S. security. Since 1990, the U.S. economy has tripled in size in nominal terms, and China's output has increased nearly thirty-fold. Over the same period, Japan has grown by just over 23 percent. The psychological impact of such a reversal is profound. "If you are number one in the class and one day your friend takes your place," said Yuji Miyamoto, a former Japanese ambassador to China, "how do you think you would feel?"

Likewise, the rapid rise of China is without precedent. China has grown faster, and for longer, than the other Asian tigers and now far overshadows the economies of Japan, South Korea, and Taiwan combined. Unlike those countries, China is neither an ally nor a security partner of the United States. If China surpasses the U.S. economy in size, which it is on track to do by about 2025, it will be the first time since the early nineteenth century that the world's largest economy will be non–English speaking, non-Western, and nondemocratic. China claims to be a status quo power, but everything about it—its economic clout, territorial claims, and political DNA, forged by vengeful anticolonial, antiforeign sentiment, primarily against Japan and the United States—suggests it wants to dominate the region rather than adapt to the American-made world. In the words of the Australian strategist Hugh White, "This is a people with a sense of their past greatness, recent humiliation, present achievement and future supremacy. It's a potent mix."

In parallel with these trends, the pragmatism Beijing once displayed toward the presence of the U.S. military in Asia is receding. After the Obama administration announced its pivot to Asia, Dai Bingguo, who was Hu Jintao's chief foreign policy adviser, had a sharp rejoinder for his then counterpart, Hillary Clinton. "Why don't you pivot out of here?" he said.

The rivalry between the United States and China is there for all to see. To set the United States and Japan against each other might seem strange by contrast, given the two nations' enduring ties. The U.S.-Japan security treaty has been upgraded and expanded numerous times since the United States formally committed to defend Japan in 1960 and was given military bases and ports in Japan in return. The accord survived an early wave of opposition in Japan, the Vietnam War, long and bitter trade disputes, racial insults on both sides, and the end of the cold war, which had provided the initial geopolitical rationale for the alliance. In the words of one scholar, the pact has lasted longer than any treaty between great powers "since the 1648 Peace of Westphalia."

Washington originally saw the alliance as a way to ensure Japan was on its side in the cold war and, later, stayed in sync with the United

States' broader global strategy. For Tokyo, according to the Japan scholar Kenneth Pyle, the security pact was an "unpleasant reality" imposed on the nation after the war, but one it cleverly and cynically made the best of. Tokyo largely left foreign and defense policy to Washington and in the meantime pursued helter-skelter economic development as the prime objective of national policy. The United States, meanwhile, has shifted its rationale for its presence in east Asia. When Henry Kissinger first went to China in 1971, he reassured Zhou Enlai that U.S. bases in the region were there to keep a lid on the Japanese. Washington now asserts that they are there to defend against China and North Korea. Both statements, at the time they were made, were probably true.

Some of Japan's misgivings about the agreement have long been out in the open. The left wing always opposed the U.S. alliance as an impingement of sovereignty and a dangerous enmeshment with militarized capitalism. Less well appreciated is the antipathy toward the United States harbored by Japanese conservatives, who also happen to be the alliance's greatest supporters. Apart from losing the war, a hard core of conservatives including Shinzō Abe carry a lengthy list of grievances against the United States: the war crimes tribunal, which they brand as "victor's justice"; the pacifist constitution written by General Douglas MacArthur's occupation and imposed on Japan; the harping on history by a country that dropped two atomic bombs on Japan; and the hectoring for decades for the Japanese economy to somehow become more like that of the United States. Such impositions, for conservatives, have undermined Japan's dignity and independence.

George Kennan, the renowned strategist, called Japan's partnership with the United States "an unnatural intimacy," born of conflict and agony between two very different countries, which, over time, developed into a close relationship of its own. This intimacy, if that is what in fact it is, has been hard won. A remarkable number of senior American officials, from Henry Kissinger to James Baker to Robert Zoellick, have not hidden their dislike for dealing with Tokyo. Brent Scowcroft, a hard-nosed veteran of America's national security establishment, interacted with all manner of recalcitrant and brutal governments and leaders in his years at the top in the White House. Yet in his authorized biography, Scowcroft called Japan "probably the most difficult country" the United

States had to deal with: "I don't think we understood the Japanese and I don't think the Japanese understood us."

A Chinese friend, trying to describe how Americans view east Asia, came up with a disarmingly simple formula: "The Americans like the Chinese, but they don't like China. They like Japan, but don't like the Japanese." At first blush, this assessment may seem at odds with endemic U.S.-China tensions, not to mention jarring for those Americans and Japanese who have formed close friendships over decades of cooperation. It is also true that however much any foreign officials liked their Chinese counterparts, the strictures of the party state made genuine friendship all but impossible. Nonetheless, this characterization of the relationship, as crass as it sounds, neatly encapsulates the competing strategic and emotional strands of trilateral ties. The Japanese have always been paranoid that the United States and China are natural partners—big, boisterous continental economies and military superpowers that wouldn't hesitate to bypass Tokyo in a flash, if only they could find a way to do so.

The territorial disputes, the enduring cold war strains, and China's demand for respect and fear of containment all help explain the region's diplomatic tensions. So, too, does geopolitics, which is the furnace for Sino-Japanese rivalry. But there is something else that stokes the fires—the wildly varying and persistently manipulated memories of the Sino-Japanese wars in Asia and their unresolved aftermath.

The history of China and Japan relations since the late nineteenth century, when the two countries first fought a war, has long had a dominant story line. Japan encroached on Chinese territory, demanding and then taking bits of land here and there before eventually launching a full-scale invasion and occupation in the 1930s. Tens of millions of Chinese soldiers and civilians were left dead in the conflict. After its defeat and surrender in 1945, so the narrative goes, Tokyo prevaricated endlessly about apologizing to China and making good for the damage wrought by its armies.

The first part of the story line is true. From the late nineteenth century onward, Japan did set out to dismember China. Although the precise numbers of casualties are still debated, the Nanjing Massacre is not an invention, as some prominent Japanese gratingly insist. Japan committed atrocities, used forced labor from its colonies to support the war effort, and oversaw the recruitment of the so-called comfort women for brothels for their soldiers.

The history of the history wars, however, is more complex, with many twists and turns that are lost in today's shrill headlines. When there was much soul-searching in Japan about the war during the 1950s and 1960s, for example, Beijing had no interest in seeking an apology and reparations. By the time China, now richer and stronger, decided that Japanese remorse should become a permanent fixture of bilateral relations, Tokyo had come to view such demands as little more than self-serving politics. In the process, history disputes have become a huge obstacle to a genuine postwar settlement.

The rage expressed in China toward Japan these days over history, though, is the tip of a much larger iceberg. Beyond the noise, Beijing's core problem is not with the details of the war but with the diplomatic deals that were agreed to settle it. In Washington's and Tokyo's eyes, the San Francisco Treaty of 1951 forms the foundation of the east Asian postwar order. Engineered by John Foster Dulles as President Dwight Eisenhower's personal emissary, the treaty ended the U.S. occupation, reestablished Japan as a sovereign nation, fixed it as a security partner for the United States, and gave the country space to rebuild itself into a modern, prosperous nation. The treaty also laid the basis for Japan's gradual rapprochement with other former wartime foes in Southeast Asia and Australia.

For Beijing, far from being the foundation of a new regional order, the San Francisco Treaty overturned it. Chinese scholars use a different template for the region, something that is largely overlooked in Washington, where Pax Americana is the natural order of things. Their reference point is the declarations of Allied leaders in Cairo in 1943 and in Potsdam in July 1945, weeks before the end of the war. The so-called Three Great Allies—the United States, the United Kingdom, and China (in the form of the Republic of China)—set the terms at these meetings for Japan's unconditional surrender. In the process, as Chinese politicians, historians, and activists have begun to argue more forcibly in recent years, Japan was consigned to a permanently subordinate role in the region.

Beijing favors Potsdam, because it disarmed Japan, restored the territories Tokyo had seized in the previous century, and confirmed China's great-power status. It discards San Francisco, by contrast, because the treaty enshrines the U.S.-Japan security alliance and the American military presence in east Asia. China was represented at Cairo in the form of the then-Nationalist government, but not at San Francisco. As Xi told the visiting Pentagon chief, Leon Panetta, in late 2012, "The international community must not allow Japan to attempt to negate the results of the World Anti-Fascist War, or challenge the postwar international order." The notion that Japan should sit inert in east Asia, enduring a kind of life sentence as a result of having lost the war, absurd as it is, is given much credence in China, from top leaders to popular political culture. One of the chapters of the mid-1990s nationalist bestseller on the mainland, *The China That Can Say No,* is titled "In Some Respects, to Do Nothing Is Japan's Contribution to the World!"

China, Japan, and the United States have been tangled together in many different ways, in theory as well as in practice. In the late 1980s, Zbigniew Brzezinski, Jimmy Carter's national security adviser and a fixture in Washington's diplomatic debates, called for a kind of condominium between the United States and Japan he dubbed "Amerippon." Brzezinski argued that the two dominant nations should foster a "more cooperative, politically more intimate, economically more organized partnership." Two decades later, the historian Niall Ferguson and the economist Moritz Schularick coined an equally awkward neologism, "Chimerica," to describe a marriage of convenience between the U.S. and Chinese economies, one that spent while the other saved but that together drove global growth. Brzezinski's timing was badly off, as the U.S.-Japan alliance developed deep cracks over trade in the late 1980s. Three years after his initial article, Ferguson backtracked as well, observing that Chimerica's brief marriage was "headed for divorce."

There is a third possible tie-up, rarely mentioned, that has its own specially minted label as well. In his 1977 novel, *Full Disclosure,* the late *New York Times* columnist William Safire conjured up a fictional alliance between the "Far Eastern powers." The term Safire invented probably requires a campus-style trigger warning before being uttered in public these days because of its racial overtones. He called the alliance the "Chi-Japs," a play on the popular cold war shorthand for the CCP in the United States, the "ChiComs" (pronounced "ChaiComs"). The novel's plot was fantastical, pitting the "ChiJaps" against a U.S.-Soviet alliance. Safire nonetheless unwittingly hit upon a mostly hidden neuralgic point in Washington. Just as Beijing rails against "Amerippon" and Tokyo is anxious about "Chimerica," U.S. officials at different times have fretted that China and Japan could team up to reduce Washington's role in east Asia or exclude it altogether.

The notion of Asian unity got a bad name in the 1930s, when it was used as a high-minded fig leaf for Japanese territorial ambitions. The Great East Asia Co-prosperity Sphere was just Tokyo's version of Western colonialism, only nastier. The idea was revived from the late 1970s and 1980s onward, this time benevolently, as the region's economies, led by Japan, began to expand and prosper, and loose regional political institutions grew up around them. Lee Kuan Yew, Singapore's founding father and longtime leader, gave the idea a philosophical luster, promoting the revival of what he called "Asian values." Conveniently styled as a throwback to Confucian notions of harmony and hierarchy, and blended with modern, mercantilist industrial policy, the notion touched a chord in a region where many saw the United States as a meddling interloper that had overstayed its welcome.

However attractive in theory, Asian unity has always foundered in practice. Absent the United States, China has the size, ambition, wealth, and military might to play a dominant role in the region for decades to come, and the mind-set as well. Trump's election in late 2016 and the isolationist rhetoric that helped him across the finish line only strengthened Beijing's hand. But old hierarchical habits die hard in Asia. China was never enthusiastic about building up Asian institutions while Japan was the region's largest economy. Likewise, Japan's enthusiasm for the Asian project diminished once China replaced it as the region's dominant power.

The fear of a big nation dominating and intimidating a smaller one is only one part of the equation. The nature of the Chinese Communist Party is rarely factored in when calibrating the country's diplomacy, but that is an oversight. The party is like the Swiss army knife of politics, with a blade for every function fixed firmly to its core metal spine. One blade handles policy, another personnel, and others the military, business, education, overseas Chinese, the media, and so on. The sharpest blade combines a number of functions that cumulatively add up to what Xi Jinping has called "the China Dream." According to this credo, Xi aims to make China a prosperous and proud nation, matching success at home with a resurrection abroad. In truth, they go together. The party cannot succeed at home unless it is seen to prevail overseas.

For a Chinese strategist plotting to sabotage the United States in the region, there is surely no better way to do so than pulling Tokyo even partially out of Washington's orbit. Certainly China has the leverage to do so, with its huge market for consumer and capital goods far outstripping any growth in U.S. trade offers. Within Japan, there has also always been a sizable constituency in favor of tying the knot with Beijing as the foundation for a Pan-Asian union.

Just imagine the seismic impact if America's so-called "unsinkable aircraft carrier in the Pacific," as Japan became known, set sail west. Pax Americana in Asia, and possibly around the world, would crumble. The prospect is not as ludicrous as Safire's novel made it sound, nor were U.S. concerns that it might happen. When the administration of Yukio Hatoyama announced out of the blue in Beijing in September 2009 that Japan wanted to reduce its dependence on the United States and create a "sea of fraternity" in Asia, Washington went into a tailspin.

But instead of seducing Japan, China has radiated hostility and more toward its neighbor. Cui Tiankai, the senior Foreign Ministry official who served as ambassador in Tokyo and Washington, framed the issue with deceptive simplicity as "whether Japan can accept a powerful China." Once Japan "solved this problem in its mind, all the other problems can be solved easily." Such invocations, as reasonable as they sound, don't capture the dominant view of Chinese diplomacy. Defeating Japan, according to a Chinese scholar who canvassed the views of officialdom in Beijing, is only the first step in establishing Beijing as the dominant power in Asia. China's victory doesn't have to be won on the battlefield, "but has to be politically and psychologically accepted by Japan and witnessed by the region."

China's increasingly dismissive view of Japan—a country that it no longer regards as a real competitor—is more than just a reminder that the party is not a good vehicle for diplomacy, an art that demands grace, flexibility, an appreciation of your counterpart's position, and the ability to make concessions. It also plays into the widespread conviction that Beijing is engaged in a monumental exercise of historical restitution. In this scenario, China is not so much trying to build a new Asian community as reinstating the old tributary system that prevailed in much of the region until about two hundred years ago, in which smaller, lesser countries acquiesced in Chinese dominance in return for the hegemon's goodwill.

Certainly, many Japanese believe this is Beijing's default mind-set. "In east Asia we have no tradition of relations between independent sovereign states in a kind of Westphalian system," Hidehiro Konno, a former senior official at Japan's powerful Trade Ministry, observed. "It's in [China's] DNA, and their DNA will dictate to them to behave more and more like an old Chinese empire." Put another way, Tokyo does accept the reality of a powerful China. Its response has been to draw closer to the United States. But what kind of United States is Japan reliant on?

The first time Donald Trump mulled running for the presidency, in the late 1980s, he complained incessantly about the unfairness of the U.S.-Japan security pact. He repeated similar charges in 2016. "You know we have a treaty with Japan where if Japan is attacked, we have to use the full force and might of the United States," Trump said at a rally in Iowa, a rural state he would go on to win. "If we're attacked, Japan doesn't have to do anything. They can sit home and watch Sony television, OK?" By 2016, of course, Sony was getting out of the TV business, because the company couldn't compete against cheaper manufacturers in China and South Korea. More to the point, by the time he was running for the White House, Trump was wrong about the security relationship as well.

For decades, Washington's message to Tokyo on defense, not unlike Trump's in the 1980s and on the campaign trail three decades later, had been simple: "Do more." In 2015, Shinzō Abe, Japan's prime minister, changed the postwar military equation by getting a constitutional reinterpretation through parliament to give Japan's military greater leeway. Now, if there ever is a war involving the United States, Abe's reforms mean that Japan can fight alongside it, whether it is directly attacked or not. The irony of this change is palpable. Having thrown off many of the shackles of the postwar era, it is now Tokyo that is increasingly insisting that Washington "do more" to fend off China.

Before Trump's election, just about any scenario for the United States in east Asia assumed there would be broad continuity for the core elements of past policy, including trade liberalization and a commitment to alliances. In his campaign, Trump shouted from the rooftops an opposing view, in favor of trade barriers and every country fending for itself. Far from "doing more," Trump's America wants to do less, which leaves Japan out on a dangerous limb. Tokyo cannot turn to China to replace Washington as a security guarantor. In all likelihood, Japan would have to go nuclear itself, an event that would mark a definitive end to the postwar era in east Asia.

While Trump upended many domestic and diplomatic articles of faith on the way to the White House, to the horror of the foreign policy establishment, the foundations of the Pax Americana began to shift from the moment Richard Nixon and Henry Kissinger embraced China in 1971, helping pave the way for Beijing's eventual return to the wider world. China was emboldened, and Japan, in turn, felt betrayed. Nearly half a century later, the three countries have developed a profound interdependence alongside strategic rivalries, profound distrust, and historical resentment.

In recent years, as China has become more powerful, scholars have cited the need to learn the lessons of the so-called Thucydides trap, the conflict that arises when an established power is challenged by a rising rival. Washington, however, might do just as well to examine another geostrategic dilemma identified by the same general-cum-historian of ancient Greece as it charts a course through the tangle of Sino-Japanese relations. It is dangerous to build an empire, Thucydides warned. It is more dangerous to let it go.

POSTWAR

CHAPTER ONE

China, Red or Green

You cannot be asked to apologize every day, can you? It is not good for a nation to feel constantly guilty, and we can understand this point.

—Mao Zedong to Japanese delegation, 1954

On a Saturday morning in California in late August 1971, Henry Kissinger greeted Tokyo's ambassador to the United States, Nobuhiko Ushiba, in his office in the "western White House," Richard Nixon's sprawling Spanish-style retreat in San Clemente, on the Pacific coast south of Los Angeles. The meeting took place just six weeks after the first of two seismic surprises sprung by the White House on America's closest ally in Asia—the secret opening with Communist China. Then, just a week before Ushiba's arrival, Nixon announced the United States would go off the gold standard, upending in one swoop the bedrock of the postwar economic order and sending countries like Japan scrambling to buy dollars. "We had a surprise announcement for you on July 15 and another surprise on August 15," Kissinger wryly told the ambassador. "I promise you there will not be another one on September 15."

Kissinger liked Ushiba about as much as he liked most other Japanese officials whom he dealt with, which was to say very little. Kissinger's trip to Beijing, and his hours of conversation with Mao Zedong and his premier, Zhou Enlai, had only confirmed his views. His discussions with Mao, and Zhou in particular, Kissinger reported back to Nixon, were the "most searching, sweeping and significant I have ever had in government." Compared with his exchanges with the sophisticated

19

philosopher-kings in Beijing, with whom Kissinger felt as if he were remaking the world, his interactions with Tokyo seemed trivial, perennially bogged down in the minutiae of trade battles, like a long-running dispute over Japanese textile exports. Even an invitation from Ushiba to dine at the embassy filled him with dread. "Every time the Japanese ambassador has me to lunch," the German-born Kissinger once complained, "he serves Wiener schnitzel."

The August meeting had been called to mend fences with the Japanese, but all of Kissinger's frustrations about dealing with Tokyo tumbled out anyway. "I don't know where the textile negotiations stand; they bore me," Kissinger told Ushiba. "With Japan, we always talk textiles instead of the direction of the next ten years." The conversation proceeded like many of the official meetings involving Nixon's national security adviser: high policy mixed with sly digs at mutual interlocutors, paranoia about leaks, and harsh denigration of critics, who in this encounter consisted of businessmen lobbying on trade issues. "Economic leaders are usually political idiots," Kissinger snapped at one point. Ushiba could at least agree on that.

Throughout, Kissinger, the diplomat, had to steer the discussion back to the White House's core message, refuting "the absurd proposition" that China would replace Japan as America's ally in Asia. "The Chinese are opponents, though maybe with our policy we can make them a little less aggressive," he explained. "But you are our friends. We will not trade our friends for opponents." It was a reassuring sentiment that seemed tailor-made for public consumption. But no sooner had Kissinger uttered it than he paused and pointedly asked, "I assume what I say is not reported by your press officer?"

For all of Kissinger's rapture about building a bridge to China, the breakthrough in Beijing was as much a moment of rupture as reconciliation. With its grand strategic recalibration that pulled "Red China" into the U.S. camp against Moscow, Washington, so the joke went, now had more Communists on its side than the Soviet Union. That such a move had been canvassed for some years in the White House, in Congress, and in the United States itself didn't lessen the shock when it happened. In one fell swoop, Nixon and Kissinger consigned a loyal Taiwan and Chiang Kai-shek's Nationalists into a diplomatic isolation in which they are still largely suspended today. Other countries that had dutifully followed

Washington's lead in shunning Beijing's Communists along cold war lines since the 1949 revolution were forced to scramble to reset their policies.

Nowhere was the upheaval greater than in Japan, which had committed itself to military, diplomatic, and economic dependence on Washington at the end of the U.S. occupation in 1951, only to find its ally had now shut it out on core issues of vital national interest. The Americans had set the terms of Japan's reentry into the region and the world after the war through the San Francisco Treaty that year and had always promised to consult closely on any change in their policy toward China. Now, with just one hour's notice of its intentions to the Japanese government, Washington had rewritten the rules. Nixon and Kissinger's deal had not only upended Tokyo's relations with Washington. The Japanese would finally have to deal with Beijing, which didn't recognize the San Francisco Treaty and the postwar regional structure forged in its wake.

The opening to China was a moment of rupture for the United States as well, one both triggered and embraced by a White House that recognized that Washington's post-1945 strategic and economic preeminence was ebbing away. Nixon inherited a draining war in Vietnam and a superpower rival, the Soviet Union, approaching strategic and military parity with the United States and encroaching on its traditional turf in Asia. On the economic front, Japan and Western Europe had emerged from the ruins of war as serious competitors. America's trade deficit was rising, and confidence in the dollar was on the decline, two themes that would strain U.S. diplomacy in Japan and then China for the next half century. Nixon had already tapped into nascent anti-Asian sentiment before winning the White House, securing the Republican nomination in 1968 in part on a promise to party power brokers in South Carolina to quell surging Japanese textile imports.

So startling was the prime-time television announcement by Nixon unveiling Kissinger's secret trip to China in July 1971 that it left its own nomenclature in its wake. A "Nixon-to-China moment" has since become a global shorthand for politicians leveraging their partisanship to cut deals with long-standing enemies. Nixon had in fact been hinting at a change of heart on China for years ahead of his stunning public about-face. In 1967, long before Kissinger became his foreign policy adviser, Nixon, then a contender to be the Republican candidate for the presidency, wrote in *Foreign Affairs* magazine about the need to bring China into "the family of nations." In the early years of his administration, according to an admiring midcareer biography about the president's national security adviser, "Kissinger was a mere passenger on the Administration's China train. The President was clearly its sole engineer."

Before long, Nixon and Kissinger were co-conspirators on China policy, as they became on diplomacy generally, drawing up in minute detail plans for the secret trip to Beijing with a small cabal in the White House. The policy's success, the pair decided, lay in its surprise. As Nixon later wrote in his memoirs, a "stomachache was scheduled for July 9–11" during Kissinger's trip to Pakistan, allowing him to feign illness and jump on a military aircraft provided by Islamabad, fly over the Himalayas, and sneak into Beijing. Nixon had been the intellectual godfather and architect of the opening to China, but the execution largely fell to Kissinger, a Harvard professor turned White House adviser steeped personally and professionally in European history.

Far from worrying about upsetting Japan with the announcement, Nixon and Kissinger saw benefits in keeping Tokyo off balance, and in check, especially with regards to Beijing. When Nixon had pressed Eisaku Satō in 1969 to control his country's textile exports to the United States, the Japanese prime minister's response contained the kind of linguistic ambiguity that has periodically bedeviled bilateral relations. In Japanese, the phrase he used meant literally "I'll do my best." "But in a Japanese cultural context, it really means—'I'll give it a shot, but don't expect too much,'" said Rust Deming, a longtime Japan specialist at the State Department. "The President of course saw that as a commitment; the Japanese did not. When Sato didn't deliver, Nixon felt he had been betrayed." Nixon didn't hide his anger. His new economic policy from that point, he said, was designed to "stick it to the Japanese."

Robert Hormats, who was on Kissinger's National Security Council staff in the early 1970s, remembers coming to Tokyo after the China opening and being asked again and again, "When are you going to dump us for China?" However strongly Kissinger might protest that the United States would never "trade friends for opponents," the Japanese had long worried that Washington would do just that, a fear that has never completely gone away. But there was another reason that Japan felt so betrayed. It had been building economic and political ties with China through the 1950s and 1960s, causing angst and anger in a Washington obsessed with the Red Menace. Tokyo had refrained for two decades from pursuing fully fledged ties with Beijing because Washington had vetoed such action. Overnight, that changed. "We leapfrogged them," said Winston Lord, then Kissinger's executive assistant.

For centuries, China and Japan had developed largely in isolation from each other. Psychologically, however, until the late nineteenth century, the pecking order had been clear—at least from the Chinese perspective. China regarded Japan as a subordinate member of a greater Sinicized region. Japan, in turn, periodically acknowledged its cultural debt to China without submitting politically to its neighbor. Japan had borrowed, and then thoroughly domesticated, the Chinese script starting in the fifth and sixth centuries. Famous cities like Nara and Kyoto and their temples were laid out and designed according to Chinese architectural and town planning principles. Confucian notions of hierarchy and meritocracy were embedded in the Japanese government, bureaucracy, and society, and within families and companies.

The traditional relationship of big brother China to little brother Japan was ruthlessly reversed when both countries were forced to open up under economic and military threat from the West in the mid-nineteenth century. A weak, internally divided China was "carved up like a melon," as its history books now bitterly put it, first by multiple Western nations and then in much larger slices by Japan. With the onset of the Meiji Restoration in 1868, by contrast, Japan was transformed from a feudal society into a modern industrial state able to compete with the West with dizzying pace and skill. Japan established control over the Ryukyu Islands, including Okinawa, in the 1870s, defeated China militarily in 1895, and a decade later inspired Asians as far away as India and the Middle East by trouncing a European power for the first time, in the form of tsarist Russia.

Chinese patriots grappling for ways to free their country from foreign domination looked on Japan with a mixture of apprehension, admiration, fear, and envy in this period. Tens of thousands of Chinese students traveled there—"the first truly large-scale migration of intellectuals in world history," in the words of one author—for an education in a country that made itself the model mediator between modern Western ideas and Asian traditions. For its part, a suddenly powerful Japan now openly condescended to China and Korea, countries it associated with squalor and backwardness. As they debated their new, elevated role, Japanese policy makers had conflicting instincts: between ruling Asia and standing apart from the region altogether in alignment with the advanced West. Japan shouldn't allow its geography to influence its policy toward a stagnant China, according to one of the most eloquent proponents of the latter view, Yukichi Fukuzawa. "We should sever all relations," he said, "with our bad Asian friends."

As bounty for its early military victories, Japan took control of Taiwan in 1895 and Korea in 1910 and then began seizing chunks of China and manipulating its internal politics in pursuit of regional domination. Its later imperialist advances were undertaken with a large dose of self-righteousness and bitterness. The West had rebuffed on racial grounds Tokyo's efforts to benefit from the post–World War I carve up of territories. The victorious white nations refused to consider "yellow" Japan their equal, another snub never forgotten in Tokyo. Japan was determined to have its colonies anyway, taking over Manchuria in northeastern China in the early 1930s and much of Southeast Asia during World War II. About fourteen million people would be killed in the war in China, many of them civilians, a conflict as brutal and transformative as any of the mighty battles in Europe.

Distant friends, wary rivals, alternatively each other's pupil and teacher, and then bitter wartime enemies, the two regional giants had never learned how to interact as equals. The triumph of Mao's Communists in 1949 and the defeat and destruction of Japan and its occupation by the United States would leave the two countries at odds again. Now they would find their relations overseen and sometimes mediated by the United States, a country that both China and Japan in different ways respected and feared, and also looked down on as an uncultured interloper in Asia.

The early years of the U.S. occupation of Japan had been idealistically front-loaded by Washington with liberal and democratic values. War criminals were locked up, business cartels dismantled, labor unions encouraged, and left-wing political parties allowed to flourish. The Americans wrote a new so-called peace constitution for their fledgling pupil, in which Japan renounced "forever" the use of military force. By the time the United States agreed to restore Japan's independence in 1951, the geopolitical landscape had changed. The Chinese Communists had forced America's ally Chiang Kai-shek and the Nationalists into exile in Taiwan. The United States and its Western partners were pitted against Kim Il Sung's Chinese- and Soviet-backed forces in the civil war on the Korean peninsula, servicing both conflicts from bases in Japan and Taiwan. The occupation's liberal pieties, a luxury in an increasingly black-and-white world, were cast aside.

Once the cold war began, U.S. policy did an about-turn, and Japan was forced to change along with it. In 1953, the young, recently elected vice president, Richard Nixon, penned a letter "to the Japanese people" in advance of the first of many visits to the country, asserting that Tokyo's constitutional disarmament had been "a mistake." "If Japan falls under communist domination," he wrote, "all of Asia falls." America now had a different game plan for Japan: as an anti-Communist bulwark in east Asia. "Yesterday's militaristic enemy was being rehabilitated as today's peace-loving ally," wrote the historian John Dower, "while at the same time [the West's] World War II ally China was demonized as part of a 'Red menace' that threatened world peace." The "mistake" to which the young Nixon referred—the U.S.-drafted constitution—would remain a logjam in Japanese politics for decades after.

The United States and Japan signed a bilateral security pact after the San Francisco conference in 1951 that set the terms of Tokyo's return as a sovereign nation. The core bargain of the treaty remains largely intact more than six decades later. Japan allowed the United States to station its military in the country and aligned itself with the West, in return for American protection from external threats. To placate regional allies, which feared the return of a militarist Japan as much as Communism, the United States signed security treaties with the Philippines, Australia, and New Zealand, which have largely survived ever since.

While Japan shared America's deep antipathy to the Soviet Union at the time of the treaty's signing, it had a very different mind-set toward Beijing. The Japanese wanted to trade with China, and many sought to make amends for the destruction they had wrought on their neighbor. Like many regional leaders from the late nineteenth century onward, Tokyo's most prominent postwar prime minister, Shigeru Yoshida, believed that Westerners did not understand Asia, let alone belong there in permanent military encampments. Long depicted as an Anglophile

because of his prewar service in London as a diplomat, an image reinforced by his predilection for British-style hats and canes, Yoshida had
worked for much longer in China and Korea and was steeped in traditional Confucian mores. He understood the need for good relations with
the powerful West but believed that Japan's security and prosperity ultimately lay with its neighbors. Mao Zedong cleverly took up the same
theme in trying to cultivate a Japanese parliamentary delegation visiting
Beijing in 1954. "Much like rare metals, colored people are as equally as
precious as white people," he told them. "Asia is our place, and our affairs
ought to be taken care of by our peoples here."

Yoshida considered China highly materialistic and individualistic,
hardly the ideal breeding ground for Communism, let alone an enduring
union with the Soviets. Japanese investment, he believed, would help
unravel their anti-Western sentiment and act as the "fifth column for
democracy" in China. Yoshida would turn out to be right on one
count—that China's ties with the Soviets weren't destined to last. But he
was wrong about the staying power of the Chinese Communist Party. In
any case, Yoshida's declaration that Japan would pursue political and
trade ties with China "whether it was red or green" did not go down well
in Washington.

John Foster Dulles, President Eisenhower's special emissary for east
Asia and later his secretary of state, traveled to Tokyo to pull Yoshida
into line. He gave Yoshida a choice: either Japan could recognize Chiang
Kai-shek's Nationalist government in Taiwan, or Yoshida might find
that the Senate would not ratify the San Francisco Treaty, restoring Japan's sovereign status. Yoshida capitulated, and as the price of regaining
independence, Japan recognized Taiwan, or the Republic of China, in a
peace treaty in 1952.

In clearing the decks for the cold war in Asia, the United States went
beyond merely remodeling Japan's foreign and domestic politics and
planting its troops on its soil. It also tried to expunge the raw, recent history of World War II in Asia and any controversy over Japan's responsibility for it. From the American perspective, according to historian
Thomas Berger, "the minimal level of contrition offered by Japan was
perfectly satisfactory," as long as Tokyo remained in the Western camp
and its prewar militarism was kept in check.

The United States had kept the emperor Hirohito in place in the immediate postwar period, effectively absolving him of any account-ability for the battles fought in his name and in the process rendering his role a taboo topic in Japan until after his death. Washington also took steps to ensure that Japan's bill for war reparations was limited. Taiwan had demanded reparations in negotiations to open diplomatic ties with Tokyo but eventually dropped its claim under U.S. pressure. Washing-ton had made its priorities clear: Japan was more important as a prosper-ous, albeit constrained, ally than as a humiliated, weakened former foe. With Japan on America's Asia team, the war was best confined to the past. "Red China," in the meantime, would be isolated in a diplomatic deep freeze.

With hindsight, the U.S. policy to sideline history proved to be a mis-take, which Washington has been unwilling and, until recently, unable to walk back from. History, of course, could not be dispensed by elite diplomatic deal making, and the issue of Japanese culpability in the war has lingered in the bloodstream of east Asian politics in a toxic fashion ever since. The United States had its own reasons for not pressing the history issue. The nation that had dropped two atomic bombs on Japan and destroyed large swaths of Tokyo in a single night's firebombing scarcely wanted a postmortem on its role in the war. For understandable reasons, the U.S. occupation kept on Emperor Hirohito after Japan's surrender, as a way to maintain stability in the unstable postwar period. But U.S. policy played into the hands of the many Japanese conservatives who either thought Tokyo had done nothing wrong or simply didn't see the benefits in a wrenching reexamination of their behavior. In the de-cades since, Japan has been haunted by its failure to address its wartime actions in the immediate aftermath of the conflict, and beyond.

Much less appreciated these days, and little discussed inside China itself, is that in the early 1950s Beijing was happy to bury the issue as well. Japan has often accused China in recent years of cynically playing the history card. After coming to power, however, mindful of China's manifold weaknesses, the CCP's top leaders deliberately left that card at the bottom of the pack. China attacked the U.S.-Japan security treaty after its signing and remained deeply suspicious of Japan's conservatives and what it regarded as their unrepentant militarism. "Japan [has been turned] completely into America's military base, and . . . is nothing but an instrument for the U.S. to enslave the Asian people and to prepare for launching another aggressive war against Asia," the official media said in 1951. Such rhetoric, however, belied the practical mood in a beleaguered Beijing, which was not in a position to dictate terms to Japan.

When Deng Xiaoping came to power in the late 1970s and China started its relentless rise, his famous dictum—that Beijing "hide its light and bide its time"—guided the country's low-key foreign policy. Such a prescription was beside the point in the 1950s. At that time, China had no light to hide. Beijing was diplomatically isolated, desperately short of investment and technology, and laid waste by decades of foreign and internecine wars. While the murderous campaigns unleashed by Mao in the years to come would weaken the country further, his government began with a more pragmatic, less ideological bent. Just as Japan worried the United States would abandon it for China, Mao and Zhou plotted how to lure Tokyo out of Washington's orbit, determined that debates over history would not stand in their way.

"You cannot be asked to apologize every day, can you?" Mao told a Japanese parliamentary delegation in 1954. "It is not good for a nation to feel constantly guilty, and we can understand this point." Zhou assured the same delegation that the painful events of the previous decades were "already in the past and we should let go the history and ensure that history is never repeated." Mao, who wielded enormous if not absolute power in the aftermath of the revolution, outlined the strategy in a document issued in the early 1950s "to drive one wedge at a time" into the U.S. alliances with countries like Japan and break the Western embargo.

In 1961, in a meeting with a Japanese Socialist Party leader, Mao went further, perversely thanking Japan for invading China, because the turmoil created by the Imperial Army had enabled the CCP to come to power. "We would still be in the mountains and not be able to watch Peking Opera in Beijing," he said. "It was exactly because the Imperial Japanese Army took up more than half of China, there was no way out for the Chinese people. So we woke up and started armed struggle, established many anti-Japanese bases, and created conditions for the War of Liberation. The Japanese monopolistic capitalists and warlords did a 'good thing' to us. If a 'thank you' is needed, I would actually like to thank the Japanese warlords."

Mao often adopted a freewheeling, sardonic style in conversation, which seemed deliberately aimed at putting his interlocutors either at ease or off balance. But his statements brushing off an apology and expressing gratitude to the Japanese for their invasion are embarrassingly discordant in today's China, and so jarring that they are sometimes airbrushed out of modern CCP-approved accounts of relations with Japan. The official explanation contends that Mao used sarcasm to underline how Japan's invasion had "awakened" the Chinese people. Chinese scholars of Japan who have tried to tread a more independent path say the truth is simpler: Mao had no interest in an apology because he genuinely believed that the CCP owed its victory in the civil war to Japan. Official policy was tailored in conformity with Mao's views for much of the next three to four decades, even as it grated with many Chinese who retained visceral memories of Japanese atrocities. As one government-connected scholar explained, "This came from Mao's mouth. There was no need for any discussion or for him to consider outside elements such as public opinion or conflicts between past and present policies. His power was absolute."

The Nanjing Massacre, in which tens and perhaps hundreds of thousands of Chinese soldiers and civilians were killed by the Imperial Army in an orgy of violence lasting several weeks in December 1937 and January 1938, is nowadays central to Beijing's narrative of Japanese brutality. Between the years of 1952 and 1959, however, the *People's Daily*, the official and at the time definitive mouthpiece of the ruling Communist Party, did not feature this now-totemic incident once. At the beginning and end of the decade, it was mentioned only a handful of times, and then only as a vehicle for the CCP's priorities—namely, attacking U.S. imperialism and the occupation's soft handling of Japanese war criminals. The moment when memories of the war were freshest in China, in effect, was also the time when the issue was least deployed as a diplomatic weapon by Beijing.

The architect of China's Japan strategy, the svelte, scheming premier and, until 1958, foreign minister, Zhou Enlai, was then in the early stages of a lengthy career, one lived largely in Mao's shadow. In time, he would emerge as the great survivor of Mao's brutal court politics and their rolling, and often deadly, purges, lasting as premier from the founding of the People's Republic in 1949 until his death in 1976. Zhou's ability to maintain his dignity throughout these upheavals won him the respect and affection of many Chinese. The iconoclastic Sinologist Simon Leys ascribed Zhou's survival to his ability to shape-shift, depending on the audience. Urbane with Western liberals, spitting fire with Third World dictators, Zhou was the "ultimate Zelig" of Chinese politics, in Leys's acerbic description, "pragmatic with pragmatists, philosophical with philosophers, and Kissingerian with Kissinger." Others saw his unstinting service to an autocrat like Mao through a darker lens. Zhou, one Chinese biographer wrote, had "a deft talent for finding some tiny crack in the wall that would allow him to appear even-keeled in his judgments."

In the 1950s, Zhou pursued a strategy to pressure Japan to break with the United States with the kinds of tactics that would become familiar to foreigners decades later, when China was opened to Western commerce. While Yoshida believed that Japanese business could encourage political liberalization in China, Zhou made the opposite wager. He calculated that Tokyo's business chieftains would quickly come over to China's side. As soon as the Japanese were enriched by the Chinese market, Zhou told his diplomats in the Foreign Ministry, they would urge their government to be more "friendly" to China.

In 1951, while the Korean War was raging, Chinese officials wrote to Japanese business leaders to suggest reopening trade. China offered raw materials like coal, salt, and soybeans to generate hard currency to buy industrial goods from Japan. The first unofficial trade agreement was struck the following year. After the signing of the Korean armistice in 1953, the Japanese dispatched a large parliamentary delegation in the expectation that the U.S.-imposed embargo would soon be eased. By 1954, Tokyo had approved expanding trade to some sanctioned goods, a development that convinced Zhou that China could press Japan to normalize diplomatic ties. A deal on fishing in disputed waters soon followed, on terms that overwhelmingly favored Japan. In 1956, Mao and Zhou personally visited a large Japanese trade exhibition in Beijing and ordered the Propaganda Department to publicize the event.

Zhou had long looked forward, as he told a delegation of Japanese union leaders, to the moment when "ministers of foreign affairs of the two governments [would] toast one another with champagne." This flurry of activity was all the more remarkable considering the intensity of American anti-Communist sentiment at the time, when McCarthyism was at its peak. U.S. policy makers were initially cautious in their response to Tokyo and Beijing's growing ties. Washington's cold war strategy rested not just on Japan as a staging point for the U.S. military; it also wanted the Japanese economy to recover and strengthen. To that end, the United States was willing to tolerate limited Japanese trade with China. That policy left a gap for the Chinese to exploit, to undermine the U.S. embargo. By the mid-1950s, Zhou very nearly got his wish of splitting the anti-Chinese alliance, only for Japan to abruptly change course. Beijing's nemesis was Nobusuke Kishi, the paterfamilias of a political tribe that would cast a shadow over Sino-Japanese relations into the twenty-first century.

If the CCP had wanted to invent a bogeyman who collectively represented everything it disliked about Japan, Kishi would have admirably fit the bill. Personally and professionally, he was deeply involved in Japan's takeover of China as a top civilian official in Manchuria, sat in the cabinet that signed off on the Pearl Harbor attack, and was responsible for the country's war mobilization as munitions minister. After Japan's surrender, he was jailed on suspicions of war crimes, although never charged. He was released in 1948 as the United States sought to boost the anti-Communist camp in Japanese politics but didn't return to public life until 1952, when the occupation's postwar purge of former senior officials ended.

Kishi took his time to shed his authoritarian instincts and support democracy as the best way forward for Japan. Initially, he was contemptuous of his American jailers. In one memorable encounter in prison, according to a biography written with his cooperation, Kishi recalled how a guard had found him late at night, writing a poem. "You are about to be hanged and you are writing a poem?" the guard asked. "I must give credit to you Japs. I couldn't write a poem even if I was in love." Kishi put away his pen and paper and asked himself, *How could Japan have ever suffered defeat at the hands of such fools?*

He would gradually develop respect for U.S. power, however, and study the ideals that underpinned its system of government. Later, prison guards were just as likely to see him reading about U.S. history and the country's Constitution at night in his cell. There were hardheaded reasons for Kishi coming around to the cause of America and democracy. His conversion won him the backing of the Americans, who were then looking for conservative Japanese leaders to solidify their anti-Communist defenses in Asia. Kishi understood that the alliance represented Japan's best option to keep the Communists at bay, at home and in the rest of Asia.

China's Communists, meanwhile, were tracking Kishi's fortunes even before they took power in October 1949. A few months ahead of the CCP victory, the *People's Daily* attacked him as one of the "Japanese invaders" whom the United States was resuscitating to bolster conservative politics. The CCP was right to be wary of him. Within a decade of his release from jail, Kishi had helped form a new conservative bloc, the Liberal Democratic Party, which would rule Japan from 1955 for most of the next half century, consigning the Left to permanent and impotent opposition. A few years later, when Kishi became prime minister, he quickly set a new course on China policy.

Kishi was more than a Chinese bogeyman; he was also the linchpin of a U.S. strategy to ensure that Japan did not become neutral in the cold war or accommodate Chinese or Soviet interests in the region. "In a literal sense, Kishi's life mirrored Japan's evolution from enemy to ally, the emergence of the Cold War in Asia, and the role played by the U.S. in forging Japan's postwar political and economic structure," said the historian Michael Schaller, who called him "America's favorite war criminal."

Kishi's resuscitation as a public figure, his role in building the conservative bloc in parliament, his efforts to undermine the Left, and his candidacies for both leadership of the LDP and later prime minister in national elections—all were supported by Washington and backed by a clutch of influential serving and former U.S. officials and private businessmen worried that Japan could slip into the Communist camp. Kishi and his supporters were also funded by the CIA, which covertly channeled money to the conservatives in Japan from the 1950s until the early 1970s. The funds were used for a second purpose, to infiltrate and undermine the Left that at various times posed a genuine threat to the conservative hold on power. The CIA might credibly claim that the covert program was one of its most successful cold war initiatives, given that the LDP managed to retain office with only a few brief interruptions until

2009. Certainly, U.S. policy makers did not regret the initiative when parts of it were exposed in the mid-1990s. "We were financing a party on our side," said U. Alexis Johnson, one of the State Department's top Japan hands who served as U.S. ambassador in the 1960s.

The details of the CIA's involvement remain murky, because the U.S. government has refused to release much documentation about the program from this period. Both sides in the arrangement were also careful to channel the funds through third parties to minimize the risk of exposure. "I had a deep relationship with the C.I.A. I went to their headquarters," said Masaharu Gotoda, a police and intelligence official in the 1950s and 1960s who later became a top LDP official. "But there was nobody in an authentic Government organization who received financial aid."

Historians point to the elevation of Kishi to the prime ministership in 1957 as the point at which the program reached liftoff. The White House feted Kishi that year with a number of high-profile events. He played a round of golf with Eisenhower at an otherwise segregated course (the newsreel headline recording the event announced, "Jap Premier Golfs with Ike") and threw out the first pitch at a New York Yankees game. Soon afterward, Eisenhower secretly approved the CIA's funding of Kishi's election campaign the following year, when he faced a strong challenge from the Socialists and other left-wing parties. The president's advisers described the decision as Eisenhower's "big bet" on Japan. As a quid pro quo to promote a strengthened alliance at home, Kishi secured a commitment from the United States that it would renegotiate the defense pact that had been imposed on Japan during the occupation on terms that gave Tokyo a more equal status.

As prime minister, Kishi inherited a country still bubbling with bipartisan enthusiasm for building ties with China. By the mid-1950s, even conservatives openly rankled at Japan's satellite status with the United States and the restrictions Washington placed on relations with Beijing. "The 'mainland' lobby" in Japan, the CIA said in a report a few years later, "runs the gamut from conservative politicians and businessmen to the most militant Marxists." The China issue, the agency noted with a nice turn of phrase, had "begun to split that basic atom of Japanese politics, the faction built up out of personal loyalties" to various party chieftains.

Kishi's instincts to side with the United States placed him in competition with another conservative political dynasty under Ichirō Hatoyama. Zhou Enlai had found a willing partner in Hatoyama, who had beaten Kishi to become the conservative prime minister in 1954. Hatoyama infuriated Washington, and thrilled Beijing, with invitations to a senior Chinese delegation to visit Japan soon after he took office. Hatoyama also resisted U.S. pressure to play a more active military role in Asia. His stance swelled Zhou's expectations that China could finally strike a deal with Japan to establish full diplomatic ties, a decision that would have arrived like a thunderclap in Washington. Dulles, by now secretary of state, who had earlier halted Tokyo's initial efforts under Yoshida to build closer ties with Beijing, feebly argued Japan didn't need China, because the mainland "was a poor area and does not have much to export."

To Washington's relief, Hatoyama faltered in office. But the issue did not disappear with him. His replacement, Tanzan Ishibashi, an economist and a journalist, had been a critic of Japan's takeover of Manchuria in the 1930s and battled General MacArthur's occupation, trying to cut the costs of keeping the United States in Japan. He also thought that Tokyo should reconcile with Beijing, rebuild its business interests in China, and avoid taking sides in the cold war, all popular positions in Japan at the time. Ishibashi, however, had a severe stroke and was forced to step aside. Kishi, an ideological and political rival, took his place, a transfer of power that, in retrospect, might have altered the course of history in east Asia.

With an eye on renegotiating the U.S. defense pact on better terms, Kishi turned his back on China and resisted pressure to further liberalize trade with Japan's giant neighbor. On a trip to Taiwan, he said he would consider it "a wonderful success if Chiang Kai-shek can retake the mainland," a statement that was a red flag to the CCP in Beijing. Kishi's refusal in 1958 to apologize after Japanese right-wingers defaced a Chinese flag at a trade fair in Nagasaki was the final straw. Soon after, China suspended trade and economic ties with Japan. Ishibashi manfully tried to defend Kishi when he traveled to Beijing the following year. "Kishi Nobusuke just has a liking for flattering people. When he is in the United States, he flatters America. When he is in Taiwan, he flatters Taiwan, and that is all," he said. "He did not say anything hostile to China in Japan." But the Chinese were having none of it. Kishi, they said, "had hurt the feelings of the Chinese people," the first recorded use of this phrase, which became a staple of China's admonishing of its adversaries.

Kishi's differences with Hatoyama over U.S. and China policy in the 1950s would be replicated with eerie echoes more than fifty years later, when Hatoyama's grandson Yukio Hatoyama angered Washington with his efforts to draw closer to China after his election as prime minister in 2009. Shinzō Abe, Kishi's grandson, who took over as prime minister in 2012, repudiated the Hatoyama policy and strengthened ties to the United States, antagonizing China. Half a century apart, the reactions in Washington and Beijing to these warring Japanese political dynasties were much the same. The United States disliked the pro-China policies pursued by both Hatoyamas and worked actively against them, to the point where Washington undermined their administrations. China, in turn, subjected Abe, like Kishi before him, to violent propaganda attacks and extended periods in the diplomatic deep freeze.

Mao had predicted in 1957 that the "East Wind was prevailing over the West Wind," his way of saying that the Communist Eastern bloc was gaining the upper hand over the West. Mao's assertion might have in fact coincided with the peak of global Communism. The Sino-Soviet split that would eventually pave the way for Kissinger's visit had already begun to harden. In China, Mao's edict a year later for rapid industrialization and rural collectivization, the so-called Great Leap Forward, sparked a mass famine and eventually led to tens of millions of deaths. At the same time, Mao was forced to watch from the sidelines as his efforts to seduce Japan failed. For a while, China was left with only one true friend, Albania.

Kishi would prove himself worth all of Washington's investment. In early 1960, Eisenhower feted him at the White House to seal the new defense pact and what the U.S. president called the two countries' "indestructible partnership." "To hell with Red China," Eisenhower told his visitor, adding that he couldn't be a friend "to a murderer or a bloody-handed assassin." The political dividend that Kishi hoped to reap at home, however, never materialized. He had expected that the revised pact putting Japan on a more equal footing with the United States would be hailed as a triumph. Instead, it split the nation down the middle and took Japan perilously close to civil conflict.

"In the summer of 1960," wrote one prominent Western historian, "Japan showed every sign of emerging as America's Hungary." The well-organized Japanese left wing, which included unions, intellectuals, and student organizations, and the many conservatives who favored a more neutral foreign policy combined to oppose the treaty. A crowd of some 330,000 protesters, the biggest demonstration in postwar history in Japan, surrounded the parliament as the vote to approve the pact neared. Kishi only managed to get the bill through by having the opposition forcibly removed from the chamber and ordering its doors locked and barricaded. A planned state visit by Eisenhower to consecrate the alliance had to be canceled. The vote would prove to be both Kishi's lasting legacy and the end to his formal political career, with the uproar over his heavy-handed tactics forcing him to resign soon after. The Americans, however, were grateful for his efforts, and conservatives like Richard Nixon never forgot them. Kishi would remain an honored guest at the White House for decades.

The *People's Daily*, which followed events in Tokyo closely, played up the role in the protests of the "Japanese masses," whom the CCP depicted as their natural allies. Kishi, by contrast, was denounced as a "fascist thug and feudal clown" and portrayed wearing an obi sash festooned with swastikas and walking in the bloody footsteps of other American lackeys into a coffin marked "U.S. imperialism." This characterization, however, was far from accurate. Despite an ignoble war record, Kishi was not the anti-China fascist the *People's Daily* portrayed him to be. Kishi was a nationalist and conservative who could not avoid being caught up in the domestic and global crosscurrents of China policy in Japan.

Stuck between the hard-line anti-Communists on the right in America and Japan and the conservatives in his own party in Japan who wanted closer ties with Beijing, Kishi had adopted a waffling "wait and see" policy to thread his way through a political maze, simultaneously supporting limited trade ties with China while opposing political relations. While he was depicted as an extremist in Beijing, in Washington he was a relative voice of moderation. "We must accept the fact," Kishi told Eisenhower, that China was industrializing and making progress. U.S. diplomats recognized the pressure Kishi was under and urged Washington to make sure it consulted Japan before it changed policy on China. It was advice that Nixon and Kissinger would ignore.

Japan never gave up its efforts to build closer ties with China. Kishi's pro-business successor, Hayato Ikeda, backed a new trade pact and, defying U.S. protests, approved government financing for the Chinese importation of a factory. "As far as China is concerned, there is no need for Japan to adopt the same attitude as the United States," said Ikeda, whose signature policy was an "income-doubling plan." "I want to encourage [economic and cultural] relations on a large scale." At one stage, John F. Kennedy felt the need to rebuke Japan for "indulging" China. In 1964, unbeknownst to the United States, Japanese diplomats conducted secret talks with their Chinese counterparts in Switzerland and Burma about normalizing relations.

At the outset of the 1970s, more than half of the members of the lower house of the Japanese parliament, including many conservatives, joined a group dedicated to securing a seat in the United Nations for Beijing. Business groups, too, began severing ties with Taiwan to curry favor in the larger Chinese market. By 1971, Japan was providing one-third of all China's imports. As late as January and February that year, only months before Kissinger's secret trip, pro-Beijing Japanese officials had been trying to make contact with the Chinese through the French, to no avail. In the meantime, the United States continued to hold Japan back. At the White House in 1969, Nixon assured Kishi what Washington had been insisting for years, that America had "no intention in the near future" of recognizing "Communist China." "Nations like the US and Japan with deep interest in China should study the consequences of recognition before they take such a big step," said Nixon, according to notes of the meeting.

But at precisely the moment the tide was turning in Washington, the government headed by Prime Minister Eisaku Satō was caught in a cul-de-sac on China. Not only had China's focus shifted resolutely toward cultivating the United States, but Beijing had also gone cold on Tokyo. For one thing, it didn't want to deal with Satō, a low-key former railway bureaucrat who was Kishi's brother and as such was considered in the same pro-U.S. and pro-Taiwan camp. (Kishi had been adopted out as the male successor to another branch of his father's family, a not unusual occurrence in Japan, and thus raised with a different surname.) Satō had decided to stick closely to Washington as he was negotiating the return of Okinawa, talks that started in 1969. He also relied on the support of the pro-Taiwan caucus in the ruling party, which he couldn't bring around on China. Beijing, in vituperative propaganda assaults designed to weaken Satō, labeled the Japanese prime minister a "new Tōjō," a reference to Japan's wartime leader.

In the White House, Nixon received a steady stream of information about Tokyo's deliberations on China in his morning intelligence briefings from the CIA. Satō won't "act hastily and believes consultation with Washington should precede any decision" on China, the CIA noted in December 1970. Thinking he was doing the right thing by Washington, Japan's foreign minister told the United States in early 1971 that Tokyo's "prime objective" in its China policy was protecting Taiwan's seat in the United Nations. A month later, Zhou Enlai pointedly announced that "leftist" Japanese businessmen, which he defined as anyone who supported cutting ties with Taipei, were welcome in China.

Koichiro Asakai, Japan's ambassador to Washington for six years beginning in 1957, had often told colleagues he lost sleep for fear that he'd wake up one morning and find that the United States had recognized China, without notifying Tokyo. "Asakai's nightmare," as it became known, was something of a running joke in the Foreign Ministry in Tokyo and the State Department in Washington. In an instant, with Kissinger's secret trip, the ambassador's nightmare came true. Whatever initiatives Japan might have had planned for China, it was now too late. Washington had leapfrogged Tokyo, in a manner that would be seared into the Japanese psyche for decades to come.

THE SEVENTIES

CHAPTER TWO

Countering Japan

I believe that we have got to frankly scare the bejeezus out of [China] on Japan. . . . They have got to become convinced that a Japan . . . without the United States is potentially more danger-ous than [a Japan] with the United States.
> —Richard Nixon to Henry Kissinger, 1971

China to us is not so simple as Cuba is to you.
> —Kakuei Tanaka to Henry Kissinger, 1972

A week before Henry Kissinger's China trip, Richard Nixon sat in the Oval Office, mulling the pair's upcoming gambit and its potential fallout. With the president was Alexander Haig, one of the few administra-tion advisers who knew about the plan. With the office's voice-activated recorder running, Nixon pondered his national security adviser's latest message, sent from South Vietnam. In private, Nixon was as crude and unsentimental about rival foreign players as he was in targeting his domes-tic enemies in his notorious Oval Office rants. Behind the profanities and machismo, though, was a seasoned geopolitical tactician plotting a path through the diplomatic obstacles ahead.

With his inner circle, Nixon had begun to rehearse arguments to de-ploy with the Chinese, to convince them of the benefits of closer ties with Washington. The president didn't have in mind the kinds of homilies that he later used publicly in favor of U.S.-China rapprochement, as a means of promoting global peace and stability. Nor, as he said elsewhere, was it a matter of "'Getting to know you'—all that bullshit." The president needed some tough talking points Kissinger could use with the Chinese, to stave off what the pair expected would be deep antagonism in Beijing to America's alliance with Japan and to the U.S. military presence in east Asia. There was more at stake in establishing relations than just cornering the Soviets, after all. Nixon and Kissinger aimed to build ties with China and simultaneously cement America's preeminence in Asia.

"[The Chinese] must be petrified of the Japanese, because the Japanese did it to them once before," Nixon told Haig, referring to the Imperial Army's subjugation of China during the 1930s and beyond. "And here sit the Japanese, needing breathing space. Who's going to keep the Japanese restrained? Who, but America?" Nixon wanted to turn the argument against the presence of "imperialist" U.S. troops in Asia on its head by getting the Chinese to imagine what might happen if the American military left the region. He had a clear strategy—to stoke China's memories of the war and with it fears of a Japanese military resurgence—to underline the benefits of keeping the United States in east Asia. The force of his own argument seemed to thrill him as he observed, "God, [China] need[s] us. If you really think straight, they need us desperately."

Nixon's argument was in fact a familiar one at that time, portraying the presence of U.S. forces in the region as the cork in the bottle of Japan's congenital militarism. Never mind that it was at odds with the constitution that the United States had written for Japan and the peaceful path the country had set itself on in the war's aftermath. Southeast Asian nations had largely bought into this argument, easing their worries about a new wave of Japanese investment into their countries from the 1960s onward. But if China had been willing for practical reasons to sideline its wartime history with Japan, Nixon and Kissinger had decided they would now deliberately play it up. It would prove to be a clever tactic.

Few politicians of his era had traveled to Asia, and Japan, as frequently as Nixon, both as vice president in the 1950s and then as a private citizen the following decade. He knew personally the country's past and serving prime ministers. Better than anyone, Nixon understood the reluctance of Japan's politicians and people to play a more assertive and high-profile military role in the region, even if it was for purely selfish reasons, to concentrate on the economy. In that sense, Nixon's warnings about a remilitarized Japan seem confected and cynical. His real criticism of Japan was not that it was militaristic but that in many respects it wasn't militaristic enough.

Like many national security hawks, Nixon had always considered Japanese security policy schizophrenic. Japan eagerly sought U.S. security protection while at the same time parading itself on moral grounds as a pacifist nation. Dean Rusk, who helped negotiate the U.S.-Japan security treaty in 1951, said Japan was like "the man who wanted to sleep with a woman one night without having to say hello to her in public the next day." In Kissinger, however, Nixon had an emissary who could make the case about Japanese militarism with conviction. Unlike Nixon, he genuinely believed that Japan was capable of rebounding as an expansionist power.

Kissinger's colleagues were never certain why he was so suspicious of the Japanese. Their style alone grated on him. He could also never find anyone whom he could deal with to address problems one-on-one. Later, in trying to illustrate the difficulties of dealing with Europe, Kissinger once quipped, "Who do I call when I want to call Europe?" With Japan, he endured the same frustration of not being able to locate the center in a system in which power was diffuse. In his memoirs, Kissinger confessed that he never grasped Japanese politics and scolded himself for not understanding the process of consensus decision making. "The truth is that neither I nor my colleagues possessed a very subtle grasp of Japanese culture and psychology," Kissinger wrote. "We therefore made many mistakes."

More viscerally, according to colleagues, Kissinger's wariness was colored by his memories of Japan as one of the wartime Axis powers, allied with the Nazi Germany that he and his family had fled in 1938. "Kissinger always thought that the Japanese were the bad guys and were the cause of all the problems," said Richard Solomon, a State Department official and longtime aide. Whatever his motivation, Kissinger was well prepared when he stepped off the plane in Beijing on July 9, 1971. He also had a stroke of luck in his interlocutor in Zhou Enlai, who had a similarly dim view of the Japanese.

From their first meeting, Kissinger was enraptured with Zhou. Critics would later contend that the Chinese premier had run rings around him on the most important item on Beijing's agenda: securing U.S. recognition of its claim to Taiwan. "Only three people really intimidated Kissinger," said Solomon. "De Gaulle, Zhou, and Mao." In negotiations over Japan with Zhou, however, Kissinger more than held his own.

The archival record of Kissinger's diplomacy, especially the opening to China, is exceptionally rich. Nixon's White House taping system is an important source of information, and Kissinger's insistence that his official meetings be transcribed verbatim, a demand that few if any cabinet-level officials have made either before or since, also provides much material. Winston Lord, whose job it was to capture the early China exchanges in official memorandums of conversations, added dramatic commentary to the transcripts, giving the encounters a theatrical flair and extra historical ballast. "The idea was to get a sense for the president of how the Chinese conduct negotiations," explained Lord. "They use protocol and stage directions, food, humor, and gestures as part of their diplomacy, to make you deal with them as a friend, as though they are doing you favors. It's the whole Middle Kingdom thing."

Lord's efforts result in the transcripts being peppered with asides that usually don't find their way into government records. At one point, "Deng spits into his spittoon." At another, "Chairman Mao toasts everyone with his tea," and "Chairman Mao and the girls laugh," and so on. Moments of puzzlement and mirth, side conversations and chatter between the Chinese interpreters, and notes on people coming and going from the meeting room are all captured for the record. Many of Kissinger's phone conservations with U.S. government officials, foreign diplomats, and journalists were also recorded and transcribed and are now accessible through public and private archives. Kissinger sometimes urged White House staff to sanitize transcripts when they were shared with the State Department bureaucracy, whom he tried to exclude from policy debates. Some records of his meetings were released over Kissinger's objections, and some papers remain under his control in the Library of Congress. The record is rich nonetheless and on Kissinger's, and Chinese, attitudes toward Japan acutely revealing.

Zhou had traveled to Japan in 1917 when he was not yet out of his teens, joining thousands of his compatriots in their efforts to learn the secrets of Japan's modernization and bring them back to China. The experience left him scarred. He struggled with the Japanese-language entrance exam for junior college and couldn't build much rapport with the locals, who he thought looked down on the Chinese. He returned home after only eighteen months. Whatever Mao's own views were on Tokyo, Zhou's early experience as a student, and then later in the war

with the invading Imperial Army, had given him sufficient familiarity
with the perils of a powerful Japan.

After decades of turbocharged growth, the Japan of the early 1970s
was vastly more formidable than the country Zhou had lived in in his
teens. It was also immensely stronger than the country he had tried, and
failed, to court in the 1950s. It didn't take long into the first meeting
with Kissinger for Zhou to demand that Tokyo have a neutral foreign
policy. "You are rearming the Japanese militarists," Zhou warned Kissinger, a theme that Zhou would return to again and again in the pair's
conversations. But Kissinger had reinforced himself with arguments to
push back against such sentiments. "If Japan builds its own military
machine, which it will do if it feels forsaken by us, and if it builds nuclear
weapons, as it could easily do, then I feel the fears you have expressed
could become real indeed," Kissinger told him. "Your interest and ours
are very similar. Neither of us wants to see Japan heavily armed." Kissinger didn't press the issue to any conclusion on this first trip. Like a
clever courtroom lawyer who makes sure to leave his arguments in
the jury's mind overnight, Kissinger let the issue lie with Zhou and in the
Chinese system.

By the time of his next, heavily publicized trip to Beijing, three months
later, Kissinger had been urged by Nixon to double down on the threat
posed by Japan. The president had been poring over the transcripts of
Kissinger's initial conversations with Zhou and was convinced that the
tactic of playing China off against Japan was working. "I believe that we
have got to frankly scare the bejeezus out of [China] on Japan," he said
in an Oval Office meeting. "They have got to become convinced that a
Japan . . . without the United States is potentially more dangerous than
[a Japan] with the United States."

At the outset of their second round of meetings in October, Zhou was
still not swayed. Didn't the Japanese want to station forces in Taiwan?
Zhou pressed Kissinger. Hadn't Kishi just been in Taipei meeting with
Taiwan's "pro-Japanese chieftains"? China sought not revenge for the
war, Zhou insisted, but rather "peace and friendship" and Japan's neutrality. Zhou wasn't certain what Tokyo was offering in return now that
it was reemerging as a world power. "[Japan] did not have to pay war
compensation and it made profits off the wars in other lands [that is, in

Korea and Vietnam]. And during the past 25 years and more, it need not spend much on its own national defense," he said. "The situation now is different. Its feathers have grown on its wings, and it is about to take off." Zhou concluded with a sharp quip about all the emollient emissaries who had been coming from Japan to China in recent years, many of whom had previously served in the militarist government during the war. "We are very clear about history," he stated.

Since the mid-nineteenth century, foreigners struggling to understand Japan's complexities have often lapsed into a kind of amateur anthropology to try to explain the country's distinctive political and social structures. In many ways, the Japanese have encouraged such ruminations with their own cottage industry of obsessing over notions of their separateness and uniqueness. The phenomenon reached its peak in efforts to grasp Japanese brutality during the Pacific War, when explanations for the apparently blind devotion of the citizens of imperial Japan to the emperor and the war effort contained a nasty racial edge.

Far from avoiding this trap, Kissinger embraced the idea of the Japanese as an odd, undifferentiated mass, a people with ingrained, almost uncontrollable, aggressive tendencies. In his conversations with Zhou and in State Department meetings, Kissinger and his advisers describe the Japanese, the United States' key Asian ally, variously as "tribal," "peculiar," "difficult," "ethnocentric," "selfish," "self-centered," "parochial," "emotional," and prone to "over react" to surprises, as if they were immature children. Whether or not he actually believed such characterizations, Kissinger appeared to strike the right note with Zhou, who responded in kind, describing Japan as a "narrow" and "strange" island mass.

Kissinger and Zhou were almost egging each other on by this stage of their second day of meetings in October. "The Japanese are capable of sudden and explosive changes," Kissinger told Zhou. "They went from feudalism to emperor worship in two to three years. They went from emperor worship to democracy in two to three months." "And now they are going to revert to emperor worship," replied Zhou. Kissinger's message to Zhou—be careful what you wish for with a neutral Japan—had begun to resonate. "I don't think you should rejoice when [the Japanese ask us to withdraw our troops]," he tells Zhou. "You will regret it, just as we today regret how we built up Japan economically." It was a masterly closing touch, warning Zhou about the chaos that would follow if the United

States quit Japan, capped with a crafty, we-don't-like-them-either note of empathy. By the end of their four-hour conversation, Zhou had dropped his objections to the United States remaining in Japan. "Japan is a wild horse without U.S. control," Zhou said, "here, there and everywhere."

Zhou would never seriously raise complaints about U.S. bases in Japan again. The Chinese official media, which just the year before had warned of the "collusion of American and Japanese reactionaries," soon commenced an about-turn: Japan was portrayed no longer as an accomplice of superpowers conspiring against China but as another victim of "Soviet hegemony." The regular incantations about vicious Japanese militarism began to diminish in the Chinese press. Before long, Zhou was telling U.S. visitors that the American bases should stay in Japan to maintain a balance of power with the Soviet menace. One of Zhou's senior advisers went even further, assuring the Japanese media that the alliance with the United States was "essential for the preservation of peace and security in the Far East."

To be sure, there was a tactical element to China's acquiescence, in service of the larger goal of building an anti-Soviet coalition with the United States and Japan. A more skeptical view holds that Zhou didn't need Kissinger to persuade him to do what he had already decided to do anyway. The rhetorical about-face was remarkable nonetheless. Kissinger had for the moment placated Beijing's concerns about Tokyo. Now the White House faced a different challenge, to make up with a Japan still bitter about being bypassed on the road to China in the first place. "The worst outcome would be if we convinced the Chinese we were getting into bed with the Japanese," Kissinger told advisers before his trip, "and if at the same time, we antagonized the Japanese."

The opening efforts did not go well.

The Japanese venting began near the end of 1971, during the first visit of a senior U.S. cabinet official—John Connally, the Treasury secretary—following the shock of the China opening. A Texas Democrat with Republican sensibilities, Connally had driven the administration's decision to abruptly quit the gold standard, the second so-called Nixon shock after Kissinger's China visit. That the Japanese were upset didn't bother Connally. "My philosophy is that all foreigners are out to screw us, and it's our job to screw them first," he told his advisers at the time. He also had little time for the Japanese in particular. "Connally said this morning that the Japanese are always our enemies," Kissinger told colleagues following a meeting of economic advisers ahead of Connally's trip. If Nixon wanted to "stick it to the Japanese," then Connally was the right man for the job.

Connally was received by Takeo Fukuda, the foreign minister, who had been especially caught short by Washington's announcement, because he had been in the hospital having an operation at the time. A diligent, deeply conservative politician who would later promote building ties with Asia, Fukuda had another reason to resent the first of the "Nixon shocks," as they were known in Japan. As the leader of the pro-Taiwan faction in the ruling Liberal Democratic Party, Fukuda had been cornered by the opening to China. Unlike his rivals for the prime ministership, he was left with no room to move in the coming competition in Japan to forge the country's own ties with China. It was no surprise, then, that Fukuda set a confrontational mood from the start with Connally. Brushing aside his visitor's misleading bromides about Kissinger's Beijing trip being solely focused on the mechanics of Nixon's planned visit to China in early 1972, Fukuda launched into a diatribe against the United States' China policy and its emissary.

Was it true, Fukuda asked, that Chinese crowds had shouted "Kissinger go home!" and "Down with American imperialism!" during the national security adviser's second trip? Did Connally realize that many Japanese thought the United States was cooperating with China to constrain Tokyo's growing power? Fukuda was correct, of course, on this second point, but Connally was having none of it. Pressed repeatedly to promise to consult Japan on China policy, Connally eventually lost his patience, insisting that it was "ridiculous on the face of it" for anyone to suggest that the United States would sell out its friends. The meeting finished sourly, with what was already becoming a regular Washington complaint about Japanese protectionism. "All the American people talk about is how unfair it is," said Connally.

By the time Kissinger visited Japan in August 1972, a little over a year had passed since the secret China trip. Weeks before he arrived in Tokyo, an offshoot of the Japanese Red Army terror group had launched an attack at Lod (now Ben Gurion) Airport in Israel with guns and grenades, killing more than two dozen people and injuring many more. The capital was on edge, with members of the terror group still feared to be at large and active in Japan. As Kissinger walked through the foyer of the Hotel Okura in Tokyo to go to his room, a man rushed at him with what looked like a projectile, sending his security detail scurrying to protect him. The lone protester, though, only sprayed Kissinger with yellow and pink confetti.

Japanese politics had still not recovered from the shock of Kissinger's secret China visit. Eisaku Satō, who had been prime minister at the time, had found out about the trip only hours before the official announcement and had been hurt, humiliated, and politically destroyed. "I did everything [the Americans] asked," Satō told the visiting Australian Labor leader, Gough Whitlam, tears welling up in his eyes. "They let me down." Like Fukuda, Satō had lost any ability to play a role in the central and obsessive debate that had taken over domestic politics: how Tokyo should build its own bridges with Beijing.

The influence of Nixon and Kissinger's China gambit on Japan's internal upheavals around this time is well known. Less understood is the way that the Chinese, who at that stage had barely any official contact with Japan, dictated events in Tokyo as well. That the Chinese were effectively wielding a veto over the choice of the next Japanese prime minister, as astounding as that seems, was no secret inside the ruling party in Tokyo.

Fukuda, the foreign minister, made this much clear when he met Kissinger. "The PRC has come back to Japan saying that the Sato government and Fukuda are unacceptable," he said. "Within the Japanese domestic political situation, the reaction is that I am the hard-nosed party." Fukuda had numerous strikes against him: he both was Satō's nominated successor and had no way to meet China's preconditions to break diplomatic relations with Taiwan and abrogate Japan's past treaties with it. In fact, Fukuda had made clear he would not accept those terms. But the Chinese objections to him ran even deeper. As a Finance Ministry official in the 1930s, Fukuda had also worked as an adviser to one of Japan's puppet governments in Nanjing, a fact the Communists had not forgotten. Beijing had made it clear it would not deal with Satō either, being wary, ironically, of Satō's closeness to the Americans after he presided over a tightening of security relations in the late 1960s. Zhou Enlai had another, more personal reason to shun Satō: as Kishi's brother, he hailed from a Japanese political clan long considered cool to China.

The man who did become prime minister, the former trade and industry minister Kakuei Tanaka, carried none of Fukuda's baggage. Fukuda represented the conservative establishment. Tanaka, by contrast, was a rough-hewn, bawdy rural politician who wore his backwoods accent and humble upbringing as a badge of honor. One former leader belittled him as a "man of the rickshaw class," but in time he would become one of Japan's most powerful prime ministers.

Like Lyndon Johnson, Tanaka fused personal charisma, boundless energy, and an inexhaustible knowledge about other politicians with a mastery of the dark arts of money and factions to make his way to the top and gain support for his signature policies. And like the former U.S. president, Tanaka had trouble distinguishing between his own personal interests and the public he was nominally serving. For years after his election to parliament, he maintained an interest in his local construction business, which profited from contracts secured by his political influence. This made him rich but also earned him a reputation for corruption. In the words of Shigeru Yoshida, the former prime minister, "Tanaka is someone who walks on the fence of the prison."

The China issue was a godsend for Tanaka. With Satō and Fukuda effectively sidelined, he campaigned as the only candidate who could get a diplomatic deal done with Beijing. "Don't miss the boat to China" became his slogan. Flaunting his lack of diplomatic experience, he had a genius in domestic politics for getting to the nub of problems and cutting deals to solve them. He took the same approach into his first meeting with Kissinger. Politics for him was about an exchange of favors, he made clear. He acknowledged that Japan owed a debt to the United States for its postwar development. "But I advise you to collect in a neat manner," he said, when discussing economic disputes between the two countries, "not like a loan shark or on a balance figure."

Kissinger went into every encounter in Tokyo battling the settled view that he was willing to cultivate China at Japan's expense. During their first meeting, Tanaka urged him to spend more time in Japan. "I know you have visited both China and Japan," he said, "but between these two countries, I think Japan is the best." Later, even Mao would upbraid Kissinger for neglecting Tokyo, advising him to spend more time there on his way back from China: "You only talked with them for one day, and that is no good for their face." But Tanaka knew Kissinger's value. In a number of conversations, both as a minister and later as prime minister, he tutored an eager Kissinger on the mysteries of Japanese political machinations. Kissinger might have come away from these tutorials more confused than enlightened. In what sounds like a parody of perennial foreign complaints about faceless, interchangeable Japanese leaders, Tanaka told Kissinger at one point, "The changes through successive prime ministers—Kishi, Sato, Ikeda and myself—is actually a change in appearance, while the actual reality stays the same."

At the time of his meeting with Kissinger, though, Tanaka had just cut a series of deals that had lifted him to the top of the pecking order of potential prime ministerial aspirants. In many respects, he owed his breakthrough to Kissinger, who had to all intents and purposes eliminated his rivals with the shock China opening. Tanaka didn't shrink from expressing his thanks. "In my heart, I am glad you did what you did," he told Kissinger. "No matter how much Prime Minister Sato wanted to go to Peking, they wouldn't open a window or a door."

By mid-1972, the new diplomatic landscape in east Asia was taking shape. In the White House, a tough realpolitik had replaced ideological hostility toward Beijing and eclipsed long-standing support for Japan, now both an ally of and a competitor to the United States. Kissinger and Nixon's raw calculation about U.S. national interest during this period was starkly laid out in a briefing the national security adviser gave to the Joint Chiefs of Staff two years later, the notes of which were obtained by the journalist Seymour Hersh. The Japanese, Kissinger was recorded as saying, "are mean and treacherous but they are not organically anti-American; they pursue their own interest. . . . It is essential for the U.S. to maintain a balance of power out there. If it shifts, Japan could be a big problem." On China, Kissinger was equally unsentimental. The Chinese, he observed, "would kill us if they got the chance and they would pick up Japan if they thought they could get away with it, but right now they are so concerned with the Russians that they'll cooperate." At the end of the day, he concluded, the U.S. objective must be to keep Japan and China worried about each other.

The opening to Beijing had pressed the reset button in Japanese domestic politics as well, offering conservatives in Tokyo the chance to form a coherent, unified China policy for the first time since the war. The long, bitter history of dealing with Beijing had made China policy "simply too dangerous for the political system itself," in the words of two scholars. In the prewar period, the struggle in Tokyo over Japan's efforts to extract concessions from China had provoked assassinations and a coup d'état and eventually a military takeover of the central government in the 1930s. Throughout the postwar era, the United States kept a heavy thumb on the scale on China policy in Tokyo, adding a sharp nationalistic edge to the issue inside Japan. The perennial opposition, the Japan Socialist Party, supported an unarmed, pacifist Japan at its foundation in the 1950s. The LDP, by and large, had backed rebuilding the country's military and maintaining a strong anti-Communist line. The conservative ruling party remained deeply divided between the pro-Taipei and the pro-Beijing camps, with neither able to gain the upper hand for long stretches of time. China, the scholars wrote, "might have been the wedge that split the government."

In that respect, support for closer ties with Beijing was perhaps the only major issue that could unify large sections of the otherwise antagonistic left- and right-wing camps. "Underlying all the pro-China arguments, from the left-wing socialists to traditional conservatives, is the desire to become more independent of the United States," wrote Sadako Ogata, the Japanese academic who later became head of the United Nations body on refugees. Thus, arguments in support of more trade with China were known as "independent trade," and pro-China diplomacy was called "independent diplomacy."

At the outset of Japan and China's rapprochement, Nixon and Kissinger seemed unperturbed about the new relationship. "They are going to want to get to China first," Nixon told Kissinger before Tanaka's trip to Beijing in September 1972, referring to the establishment of formal diplomatic ties between the two countries, which the United States had not yet managed to achieve. "That's all right. We don't mind if they do." In that respect, the two men had the same instincts as the professional diplomats at the State Department. An unsigned State Department briefing note, prepared to preview the coming Tanaka visit to China, would turn out to be eerily prophetic about long-term Sino-Japanese relations.

Whatever happens, the briefing said, Chinese views on the relationship would continue to be "heavily colored" by war memories and Japan's prewar attitudes. "Many years of contradictory evidence from a new Sino-Japanese relationship will be needed to erase the current Chinese view of the Japanese as a cunning, scheming, devious and dishonest race which alternates between abject humility (when at a disadvantage) and insensitive arrogance (when they have gained the upper hand)," the report said. "These attitudes, rather than the crude Marxian determinism in which Chinese fears of Japanese militarism are rationalized, are the fundamental cause of the depth of the Chinese suspicion and hostility towards the Japanese. They are matched, of course, by the potential Japanese resentment of China's arrogation of the role of Asia's major power."

Like the State Department, neither Nixon nor Kissinger underestimated latent Chinese hostility to Japan, however much Mao had dismissed the necessity of penitence for the war. Nor were they unaware of multiple Japanese resentments against the United States, from their defeat in the war to the shock of the surprise China trip. From the White House's perspective, the benefits to Beijing in balancing a hostile Soviet Union through closer ties with Washington were self-evident. It was also clear to Kissinger from his talks in Tokyo how much Japan still depended on the United States, not just for its security but also for the diplomacy underlying it.

Tanaka, like Fukuda, made clear to Kissinger that the most difficult diplomatic issue facing Tokyo in bridging relations with Beijing was how to handle Taiwan. "This is an extremely sensitive problem," Tanaka told him and reminded him how deep the divisions on two rival Chinas ran through the political system in Japan. "After all, we had two thousand years of interchange between Japan and China; culturally, we are heavily indebted to China," he explained. "China was our enemy in two wars, and World War II started in China." Finally, Tanaka offered a comparison that he hoped made the dilemma clearer for Kissinger. "China to us," Tanaka warned Kissinger, "is not so simple as Cuba is to you."

Tanaka went far further than Fukuda in describing the sensitivity of China and the Taiwan issue. He bluntly suggested it would be best for the United States to solve the problem on Japan's behalf: "It would be more logical and rational to have the US involved in the solution rather than to have Japan act independently. As in the case of a man and his wife having a fight, sometimes a family friend can come in and solve the problem," Tanaka continued.

"Who is the man and his wife, and who is the friend?" Kissinger replied.

"For sure, the good friend is the US. Historically speaking, the man and his wife are Japan and China, but for the past three-quarters of a century, Japan and Taiwan are the couple."

Kissinger and Tanaka quickly concurred they needed a unified approach to China and Taiwan, in private and in public. "How will our conversation be reported?" Kissinger asked. "I will have to have a press conference," replied Tanaka. "But I will never reveal what we said about Taiwan."

The White House's China initiative had wiped clean the diplomatic slate in the region in many ways, not least in partially clearing a pathway through the ideological and emotional thicket of resentment and rivalry that separated China and Japan. There was a cost to Nixon and Kissinger's penchant for clandestine diplomacy, however, because the pair had bruised ties with Japan for a generation. "The Japanese view of Americans was fundamentally altered by the fact that their closest ally had been perfidious by taking an action of vital importance to Japan without telling them beforehand," said Stapleton Roy, who served as ambassador to China in the early 1990s. Or, as U. Alexis Johnson, another senior Asia hand in the U.S. government, put it, Kissinger's "passion for secrecy, combined with his contempt for the [State] Department and disdain for the Japanese, threw a devastating wrench into our relations with Japan on the question of China."

Still, Nixon and Kissinger having come and gone, China and Japan finally had an opening to talk to each other. Tanaka, who had become prime minister in July 1972, had quickly decided on coming to office he would go to Beijing to meet Mao. Japan's crushing defeat, America's enduring victory, China's abject humiliation and now putative reemergence, and the residue of Washington's ruthless diplomacy—all of the big themes of nineteenth- and twentieth-century politics in east Asia would sit on the table in front of them.

CHAPTER THREE

Five Ragged Islands

About those G__damn islands! Where do we stand?
       —Henry Kissinger, on the Senkaku/Diaoyu Islands

Are not the wordings "repentant" and "bothersome" too light?
       —Ji Pengfei, China's foreign minister

In the manner of imperial audiences, Kakuei Tanaka was summoned without warning to see Mao Zedong. It was the third evening of Tanaka's visit to Beijing in September 1972. So suddenly did the order arrive that Tanaka didn't have time to bring a note taker with him, only his foreign minister and his chief political aide—one reason why a precise rendering of the meeting, the first ever between a Japanese and a Chinese leader in the two countries' long history, has remained elusive. A Chinese record of the conversation turned up years later in bookstores in Beijing, in a tome transcribing Mao's meetings with foreign leaders, appearing briefly on the shelves before being withdrawn, without explanation. The Japanese account was conveyed in briefings to the traveling media and published in news stories in the press in Japan in the days after the meeting.

In the Chinese telling of the event, Tanaka, a novice on the world stage and just two months into his term as prime minister, appears stiff and nervous at the outset. He had barely taken his seat before Mao tried to put his visitor off balance, needling him about the United States: "The United States . . . didn't manage to establish diplomatic relations during their visit in February this year and . . . you have run ahead of them [which leaves them] feeling a little unhappy." Tanaka retorted promptly that the Americans were still friendly to Japan.

The Japanese version of the encounter, perhaps reflecting the spin put on it for public consumption, is more understated and almost folksy, capturing the pair bantering about fiery Chinese liquor and unpredictable Japanese elections. In the Japanese press reports, there is little tension evident in their exchanges, and Mao jokes with Tanaka from the start, asking, "Well, have you finished your quarrel?" as Tanaka arrives with Zhou Enlai in the Chinese leader's study. "You should quarrel. Good friends are only made after a quarrel."

In some respects, the differences between the two accounts of the meeting mirror the internal politics of the day in both countries. The Chinese did not want to appear overly friendly toward their old enemy. The Japanese, forced to operate in a more democratic system, had an interest in conveying a sense of triumph about a sensitive diplomatic moment. It is only toward the end of the leaders' conversation that the two records converge.

Tanaka had arrived in China in the slipstream of Richard Nixon, who had consecrated his career-defining diplomatic initiative in Beijing seven months earlier. The visits of both men coincided with the tail end of one of the most dismal, nasty periods of Mao's rule. Tens of thousands of officials, teachers, and intellectuals had been persecuted by Mao's Red Guards and other thugs during the so-called Great Proletarian Cultural Revolution, which began in 1966. The ideological extremes and mass violence unleashed by Mao had left the country and its economy in a quivering, sullen mess.

Nixon had been an ingratiating guest, praising Mao as a great statesman who had transformed China. Tanaka's encounter with Mao was strikingly different. If anyone had reason to flatter Mao and seek his indulgence, it should have been Tanaka, the leader of a country that had invaded China, carved up its territory, and was responsible for the deaths of millions of its citizens. But in both the Chinese and the Japanese versions of their conversations, Tanaka was cool and businesslike at the outset, perhaps even a little nervous as well. He eschewed Nixon's fawning approach and skirted the topics of war and recent history. It was only toward the end of his encounter with Mao that their discussion took on a more intimate, familiar tone and character, and one that would have been impossible with an American visitor.

Mao had been sitting at his desk reading a book when Tanaka entered his librarylike study. The scholarly setting might have been what prompted Tanaka to switch topics late in the conversation, away from geopolitics to Buddhism and the story of a famous Japanese monk who had learned its teachings in China during the Tang dynasty. Tanaka remarked that while he had never understood the doctrine, he had copied his elders' practice of it. "My paternal grandmother chanted sutras nightly, and so I followed her example," he said. Mao took up Tanaka's theme with gusto, retailing how he had used the Confucian canon, the Five Classics and the Four Books, to needle his own father and rebel against him. "He hadn't read them. [He was] illiterate," Mao said. "Thus I bullied him. How can there be no struggle?" Tanaka found Mao's tale of teenage defiance hilarious.

Tanaka might have been a "man of the rickshaw class," but for him to discuss Chinese classics with Mao was totally in character. From a young age, Tanaka, along with other Japanese schoolchildren, was taught not only about his country's distinctive culture but also about its Chinese antecedents. Then, as now, students studied classical poetry in the original Chinese characters, which in turn formed an integral part of university entrance exams. Japan's character-based language still has everyday traces of its Chinese roots, with many words having at least one pronunciation that mimics the original Chinese.

As Tanaka stood to leave at the end of their meeting, Mao presented him with a gift, a six-volume collection of poems by Qu Yuan, a statesman-poet who lived three centuries B.C. It was no surprise that Tanaka would respond in kind, writing his own poem to express his thanks to his hosts and then sharing his work with the traveling media on the way home. The poem was published in Japanese newspapers on his return from Beijing. It was rather prosaic, akin to the kind of polite scribbled thank-you note favored by many Western politicians:

> Japan and China severed
> their relations many
>   years ago.
> But now the time has come
>   to resume these links.
> The people of China see me
>   with warmth in their
>   eyes.

Peking weather is now very
      clear and the atmosphere
       - of autumn most profound.

Tanaka had departed for Beijing with cheers ringing in his ears, and not just from his political allies. In a show of bipartisanship rare for postwar Japan, representatives of his own conservative LDP were joined by members of the Socialist, Communist, and other parties at a rousing airport send-off. The excitement about forging relations with China had forced conservative opponents of Tanaka's trip into a temporary retreat. His welcome on his arrival in Beijing several hours later might have seemed somewhat pointed by comparison, especially for someone who had last set foot in China as a member of the occupying Imperial Army in Manchuria in the late 1930s. On the tarmac, a 360-strong choir of People's Liberation Army soldiers serenaded Tanaka's landing with the old battle hymn used by the Red Army in its early struggles against the Nationalists and the invading Japanese. The song—"Three Main Rules of Discipline, and the Eight Points for Attention"—incorporated Mao's edicts for soldiers dealing with the masses, to bring them over to the Communist camp. In truth, the PLA choir's choice of material was more ritual than rebuke. The Japanese and their hosts were ready for some whirlwind diplomacy.

Tanaka had been in a hurry from the moment he had been elected leader of the LDP, and thus prime minister. Within weeks of taking office, he had dispatched a number of delegations to China to sound out its leaders about their conditions for a diplomatic deal. Encouraged by their reception, and the flailing opposition from the pro-Taiwan caucus in Tokyo, he quickly committed to go to Beijing himself. By the end of Tanaka's five-day visit, the two sides had reached agreement to terminate the state of war between them and normalize relations. All the potential stumbling blocks—war reparations, the issue of an apology, Taiwan, and an explosive territorial dispute—were swept aside to secure the bigger prize. Tanaka had been in office for all of eighty-odd days.

Tanaka had not gotten off to a good start in Beijing, crudely stirring up the ghosts of the war only hours after his arrival. Offering a toast at the state banquet held in his honor, he apologized for Japan's actions in the past but used language that might be translated loosely into English

as saying "excuse me" or "sorry to have caused you trouble." His hosts
were furious. At their meeting the following afternoon, Zhou told Tanaka
that such words were reserved for "inconsequential things" and were not
acceptable. "[This] will only buy the animosity of the Chinese people," he
said. Tanaka offered to make amends with a stronger statement, but his
comments might have been more than just an insensitive slip of the
tongue. He had not arrived in China with a mandate from Japan's conservatives to offer a full-throated apology for the war. In fact, Japanese
leaders had worried from the start that the Chinese would demand one.

The precise wordings of Japanese expressions of regret for the war had
not yet developed into the art form that they would become later, when
China began insisting on apologies and minutely parsing their content.
Indeed, even in Germany in the 1970s, apologies for the Nazis' atrocities
were only just coming into vogue. Given the rancor that came to sur-
round the issue later, it is remarkable how civilly and cooperatively the
issue of an apology, or whatever else it might be called, was discussed
when the two countries first had to broach the topic.

As Zhou Enlai's translator later recalled, Tanaka's foreign minister,
Masayoshi Ōhira, told his Chinese counterpart, Ji Pengfei, during a
drive to the Great Wall that too strong an apology would upset the pro-
Taiwan lobby in Japan. Ohira and Ji were a practical pair: one the taci-
turn son of a peasant who excelled in Japan's ruling party's factional
battles; the other a veteran Communist diplomat with acute survival
skills that helped him navigate Mao's purges. In their formal meeting,
the two men debated the meaning of the word "repentant," which Ōhira
was insistent be included in the official communiqué. "Are not the wordings 'repentant' and 'bothersome' too light?" Ji asked. The Japanese transcript of the conversation adds a note explaining that Ōhira and Ji
"exchange opinions regarding the nuances of 'repentant.'" "As the entirety of the Japanese people are repentant over the war, we hope for this
trip to express that," Ōhira explained. Ji replied by making the standard
Chinese distinction between the Japanese people and the militarists. He
then added, "China thinks rather well of Japan."

In the end, China did not insist on a formal apology, and Japan did not
offer one. The framework that Mao and Zhou had set for relations with
Japan in the early 1950s, which placed short-term strategic objectives before history and the war, did not shift. In the 1950s, China had courted

Japan as a way to break the U.S. embargo. Two decades later, with the United States and China now tactical partners, the priority was to fix Japan firmly in the anti-Soviet camp. "If you look at the normalization process, there is a clear lack of an insistence for an apology from China," said Jin Linbo, a Japan scholar in Beijing. "Why? China believed there was no need. If China had asked, I don't believe that Japan could have said no." The uproar over Tanaka's language at the banquet was all "about face," explained Jin, "not whether there should be an official apology."

China's leaders at the time had few of the public feedback mechanisms that its authoritarian leaders have access to today. There was no Internet to give angry citizens a voice and none of the consultative mechanisms that the party uses now to get ahead of public discontent, like telephone hotlines or citizens' assemblies in local congresses. But Zhou and other leaders didn't need an opinion poll to know that their policy to reconcile with Japan could provoke a dangerous backlash from intraparty rivals. "A minority had opposed the idea of diplomatic normalization," Zhou told Tanaka. "It is necessary for us to explain to the public as well." If they don't educate the public, he added, "it will be impossible to convince the masses that suffered under the 'Three Alls' policy." While that was a sharp-elbowed reference to the way China branded the Imperial Army's brutal China campaign, to "kill all, burn all, loot all," in a way it was also a bluff, because Zhou had no intention of pursuing the issue. While the Japanese leaders debated their differences openly at home, Zhou only dropped hints about the upheaval within the CCP over Beijing's diplomatic about-face. As for the public, at the time it barely figured in Chinese policy making at all.

Shortly before Tanaka's visit, the Foreign Ministry in Beijing circulated a document that established the template for any and all discussion of Japan titled "The Guidelines of Internal Propaganda Concerning Prime Minister Tanaka's Visit to China." Don't replace policy with emotion, the document warned, because "the time had changed and so did the world." The CCP propagandists acknowledged that many Chinese who had suffered at the hands of the Japanese would struggle to understand why Beijing was now diplomatically reconciling with Tokyo. But that was brushed aside with a dose of cold realism: "Currently, the greatest threat to our country is US imperialism and Soviet revisionism, especially the latter," the document said. "Tanaka's initiative to visit China and to normalize

[ties] is a beneficial move [for China] to contain US imperialism and to strike against Soviet revisionism." This was a top-down document, signaling that the leadership's decision was not up for debate. "It came from Mao's mouth," Jin said. "No need for any discussion!"

It was not so much the public that Zhou was concerned about as Mao's critics within the party, who could use Japan as a weapon against the leadership. Zhou let slip that Lin Biao, the army general who rose to be Mao's second-in-command before falling out with him, had opposed the opening to both the United States and Japan. Lin was now off the political stage. In a sensational denouement to one of the murkiest and most destabilizing episodes of elite Chinese infighting of the Mao era, Lin had fled China in a plane in September 1971 but had apparently died in a crash in Mongolia. Lin had been Mao's heir apparent, his "closest comrade in arms."

Although he didn't tell Tanaka, Zhou had been comforted by his Japanese counterpart's elevation to the prime ministership. The Chinese premier had confided to a visiting Japanese delegation that Tanaka's leadership had helped him build support within the party to negotiate with Japan. Unlike Satō, the CIA reported, quoting Zhou, "Tanaka was not controlled by the Americans."

As he had done with Kissinger, Zhou focused in their discussion on Taiwan. There were few more sensitive issues, both for the Chinese Communist Party and for Japanese conservatives. The former colony ran through Sino-Japanese relations in multiple, dangerous ways. Taiwan was more than just a living embodiment of east Asia's postwar ideological divide. Zhou and his Communist comrades knew personally many of the Nationalists like Chiang from their early joint struggles for Chinese independence. Zhou and Chiang, and many colleagues in both the Nationalist and the Communist parties, had worked together and briefly fought alongside each other against the Japanese before the two sides lapsed into civil war. Since the Communist victory and the Nationalists' flight, however, their strategic and personal enmities had only deepened. Zhou presented to Tanaka a detailed breakdown of the personalities in the Taipei government, describing their strengths and weaknesses, almost as if he were conducting a seminar. His message to Tanaka seemed to be "We know these people and we have their measure." "The Taiwanese will cause little troubles but they cannot afford large disturbances," Zhou said. "This is called trickery."

Tokyo, however, looked at Taiwan through a very different prism. Taiwan had been Japan's first colony, gained in the Treaty of Shimonoseki after its military defeat of China in 1895. Under Japanese stewardship, the Taiwanese had been less rebellious and more prosperous than the subjects of its second major colony, on the Korean peninsula, acquired in 1910. There had been periods of oppression in Taiwan, but overall the island had been governed with a lighter touch and necessitated a smaller role for the army than in Korea. The Japanese showed some respect for the Chinese culture that had taken root in Taiwan, whereas they largely disdained usage of the Korean language and script. Seoul's bitterness toward its former overseer has barely abated since the end of colonial rule, which came with Japan's surrender in 1945. Over subsequent decades, South Korea's government, often urged on by its citizens, methodically set out to destroy the administrative buildings in the country associated with Japanese rule. In Taipei, Chiang Kai-shek and his successors, by contrast, still governed from government offices built and used by the Japanese. Though he fought them bitterly, Chiang himself admired the Japanese. He didn't want Japan crippled after its defeat, a magnanimous approach that many Japanese appreciated. Chiang also employed senior Japanese officers after the war in the 1950s to train his military.

Many Taiwanese, including the elites, retained positive feelings toward Japan and shared its anti-Communist instincts. Japan, for them, was associated not just with repression and colonialism but with education and development. They regarded Chiang's Nationalists, who after all only intended using the island as a staging post to recapture the mainland, as just another group of occupiers, and incompetent ones at that compared with imperial Japan. For Japanese conservatives constantly being asked to atone for a war they considered just and forced upon them, such loyalty provoked powerful sentiments. "We have felt an emotional attachment to Taiwan," the foreign minister Ōhira told Kissinger just ahead of Tanaka's visit. The warmth toward Taiwan among a large bloc of conservatives in Japan would survive in the system in the decades to come.

Before coming to Beijing, however, Tanaka had taken the threshold decision to cut ties with Taiwan and acknowledge China's claim of sovereignty over the island. But he and his foreign minister were treading carefully. "We want to avoid a split in the LDP over this issue," Tanaka told Zhou. The matter of Taiwan divided not only conservative politicians but

Japan's Foreign Ministry as well. Its prerogatives caused the biggest blowup at the meeting between Zhou and Tanaka because of the ministry's initial insistence that it did not even have to discuss reparations with Beijing.

The Foreign Ministry argued that Chiang Kai-shek's formal decision to forgo reparations when Taiwan established diplomatic ties with Japan in 1952 meant that the issue had been definitively resolved for all of China. Zhou was dumbfounded that Japan would dare assert that Taiwan—as the Republic of China—could supplant Beijing, the People's Republic, on this matter. "This is an insult to China," Zhou said. "You cannot protect your honor using other people's belongings." It was only after Tanaka and Ōhira explained the sensitivities at home that Zhou finally relented. Beijing waived reparations without an explicit acknowledgment of its right to claim them and allowed Tokyo to announce in its own way that it was cutting ties with Taiwan.

The bilateral meetings were largely brisk and businesslike, with little of either the personal warmth that would develop between the countries' leaders in the early 1980s or the bitter histrionics over history that came later. Mao joked with Kissinger after the Sino-Japanese normalization deal that it would have been difficult to calculate how much Japan owed it anyway, observing, "No accountant would be able to do it." Chinese leaders had, in any case, made their own political calculations. They knew that prolonged negotiations over reparations would lose the CCP support in Japan and possibly scuttle any agreement as well. "Tanaka would not have been able to accept demands for a lot of cash," said a retired Japanese diplomat familiar with the talks. "There would have been objections from Japanese taxpayers." As a virtual dictator in those days, Mao was able to dismiss the need for a Japanese apology and reparations, though he was self-aware enough to recognize the anger that many Chinese still felt toward Japan. "It will be more difficult to settle relations of hostility between the Japanese and Chinese peoples," Mao told Kissinger, "than between us and you."

Among the other ghosts that seemed to be laid to rest in the talks with Tanaka was China's long-standing concern about the revival of "Japanese militarism." Zhou raised China's ritual complaints about Japan's defense policies but didn't press the point in the face of Tanaka's blandishments. Zhou could scarcely have prepared an argument to rebut Tanaka's reasoning as to why Japan would never again be a threat to

China and its Asian neighbors. "The militarists are an extreme minority," Tanaka told him, before closing on an almost comically mordant note, pointing to low Japanese birthrates and their implications for Tokyo as a great power. "The Japanese only produce two children, and at this rate, the Japanese people will disappear in 300 years," Tanaka said. "There is no reason to fear Japan."

China's willingness to forgo reparations, its lack of insistence on an apology, and Zhou's halfhearted complaints about militarism would lull Japanese conservatives into a wrongheaded belief that they had put the war and history behind them for good. Of all the understandings reached in the normalization talks, though, few would come undone as spectacularly as another issue discussed by Tanaka and Zhou: China's agreement not to pursue a dispute over the ownership of a string of scraggy rocks at the end of the Ryukyu Island chain, which trails south from Okinawa toward Taiwan. The islands are known as the Senkakus in Japan and the Diaoyus in China.

"I do not want to discuss the Senkakus at this time," Zhou told Tanaka after the Japanese leader gently raised the matter. "Because there is oil [there], it is a problem. If there was no oil, neither Taiwan nor the US would be an issue." Tanaka concurred. "Fine. We need not talk about it anymore," he said. "Let's discuss it in the future." Zhou then swiftly moved the conversation onto how the two countries should exchange diplomatic missions. In an instant, a conflict laden with all the explosive baggage that comes with sovereignty and national dignity seemed off the table. While many Japanese believed that Zhou's attitude signaled a kind of soft surrender on the territorial dispute, for China it was an expedient, temporary truce.

How did five small islands with a land mass of seven square kilometers that, as one academic put it, "you can't even find on maps," and that can be accessed only in small boats and in calm seas, become a regional flash point? The islands' only utility after the war had been as a site for target practice by the American military, which leased the islands from Japan so it could shoot at them. As the CIA said in a brief for policy makers in May 1971, "The Senkakus, uninhabited and unimportant, have emerged from obscurity to give their name to an undersea region that could conceivably cause international conflict." Zhou Enlai was right on one point: no one had even wanted to discuss the islands until a 1968 UN agency reported that the area contained potentially huge reserves of oil. "There is a high probability that the continental shelf between Taiwan and Japan may be one of the most prolific oil and gas reservoirs in the world," the report noted. But oil only partially accounted for the clash. Like the issues of reparations and apologies, the dispute over the islands was caught up in the tides of the region's history and conflicts and their winners and losers.

The impact of the UN seismic survey of the area's energy reserves in the late 1960s was electrifying. Virtually overnight, Japan, Taiwan, and China discovered a passion for the islands that had been well hidden until then. By August 1969, an aging Chiang Kai-shek began venting about the Diaoyus in his personal diary, some weeks making entries on an almost daily basis. "The Chinese government, based on 400 years' history, will never see these islands as under the sovereignty of Japan," he wrote. A few months after Taiwan staked its claim in early 1971, Beijing joined in, describing the islands as China's "sacred territory." Japan, which imported nearly all of its energy, viewed the potential energy reserves in the area as an economic game changer. With its industry expanding rapidly, Japan's annual oil needs were on track to nearly triple over the next decade to 400 million tons. According to one graphic calculation published at the time, "400 million tons was the equivalent of having a line of 100,000-ton tankers stretching at five-kilometer intervals between the Persian Gulf and Japan." By 1971, China and Taiwan had joined Japan in formally claiming the islands as their own. For Washington, the divide between Japan and Taiwan was especially problematic, because both were U.S. allies and virtual protectorates.

In the White House, Kissinger went into a near panic. In the final stages of preparing his secret trip to China, the national security adviser feared that a few islands he had never heard of could poison the China rapprochement and unravel the whole venture. In early 1971, the United States was also in the midst of finalizing negotiations to return Okinawa to Japan. Tokyo had good reason to believe it would get back the entire Ryukyu chain, which included Okinawa and the Senkakus. Since the 1950s, the Americans had given Tokyo numerous assurances that Japan retained "residual sovereignty" over the islands, which the U.S. military had effectively confirmed by paying rent to Japan when using them for target practice. But the uproar in Taiwan and China prompted the State Department officials negotiating the deal to take a fresh look at the various competing claims.

Nixon and Kissinger had agreed to start formal negotiations to return Okinawa in 1969, the price the White House believed the United States had to pay to maintain public support in Japan for the bilateral defense alliance. Without the return of Okinawa, the last major piece of territory held since the postwar occupation, Tokyo had warned Washington that support for America's military presence would crumble. If that happened, the Japanese ambassador warned Kissinger in May of that year, in a formulation calculated to capture attention in Washington, "Japan would turn to China under the leadership of the left." Japanese leaders threw in some vague assurances that Tokyo would play a more robust regional security role once Okinawa was returned, although they knew the public and politicians had no stomach for such policies. The two sides also found a formula to paper over the controversy surrounding the stationing of U.S. nuclear weapons in Okinawa.

The White House wanted two things from Tokyo in return for giving Okinawa back: a commitment to keep American bases in Japan, and a promise from the then prime minister, Satō, to limit textile exports to the United States. Kissinger would later write in his memoirs that the Okinawa negotiations "exemplified high policy," whereas textiles "proved a case of low comedy, frustration, and near fiasco." His book on this period, *White House Years*, does not mention the Senkaku/Diaoyu Islands at all. For all the momentous issues being handled by Kissinger during that period, from détente with the Soviet Union to the Vietnam War peace negotiations, it is a significant omission. The transcripts of his conversations with Nixon and other U.S. government officials in the fraught weeks before his secret Beijing trip and afterward are peppered with anxious references to internal battles over the status of the islands. Kissinger refers mockingly to Japan as "kabuki land" in his back-and-forth with his advisers on the textile issue, a reference to the elaborate, stylized Japanese theater. But Kissinger was also playacting himself throughout this period. As he fought running battles with rival officials in the U.S. government over whether the United States should return the islands to Japan, none of them, apart from Nixon, knew Kissinger was running another, clandestine agenda on China altogether.

"About those G__damn islands! Where do we stand?" Kissinger asked the State Department's Japan chief, U. Alexis Johnson, in early June 1971, only three days after Nixon had written to Zhou Enlai, accepting the Chinese premier's invitation for Kissinger to visit the following month. The State Department officials negotiating the Okinawa revision—who were unaware of Kissinger's outreach to China—had already reached their own conclusion about the status of the islands some months before. By itself, their position was hugely controversial, because it swept aside what the State Department official handling the day-to-day negotiations called the bureaucratic bible on Okinawa. The recognition of Japanese sovereignty over the now disputed islands, reaffirmed time and again during the 1950s and 1960s, said Charles Schmitz, "had been a defense against charges of U.S. neocolonialism, to deny the commies the line that we waged war in the Pacific for territorial aggrandizement." Now the old diktats on the status of the Senkaku/Diaoyu Islands were to be cast aside.

Schmitz hadn't grasped the magnitude of the territorial dispute until an oil company representative arrived at his office in Tokyo one day to tell him Taipei had granted his firm a drilling concession in the contested area. Once Schmitz started to research the competing claims to sovereignty, what he discovered did not please the Japanese. "We tried hard to find reasons why we should be more assertive about Japanese sovereignty than we were," he said in an interview during his retirement. With his colleagues, Schmitz studied trading patterns around the islands, the ocean floor, and the surrounding geological structures. If anything, he decided, Taiwan had the better claim, and that claim, in turn, was China's. Confronted with an immensely sensitive decision, Schmitz adopted a Solomon-like position: in the draft treaty returning Okinawa, the State Department recommended the United States remain neutral on competing claims of sovereignty while returning the administrative rights to the islands to Tokyo.

Kissinger was not happy with this compromise. At his request, the State Department provided him with a paper outlining the strength of Taiwan's claims. "But that is nonsense since it gives islands to Japan," Kissinger scribbled in the margins of the document. "How can we get a more neutral position?"

The low-comedy element of the interminable textile negotiations then intervened to complicate the issue even further. Japan had already fallen short of its promise to Nixon to strike a deal on restraining textile exports as part of the Okinawa reversion. David Kennedy, the U.S. envoy dispatched to Taipei to reach agreement on the parallel battle over Taiwanese textile exports to the United States, then hit upon the idea of using the islands as a bargaining chip in the negotiations. Kennedy pressed Washington to withhold returning the islands to Japanese control, and to give them to Taiwan instead. In exchange for the islands, Taiwan would agree to restrain its own textile exports to the United States. This, said Kennedy, would provide "a very badly needed shock" to the Japanese and their dawdling on the textiles trade.

"What position are we involved in?" Nixon asked when Kissinger finally took the issue to the president in the Oval Office. "Does it involve the big thing?" code for the upcoming China trip. In the end, the question of the status of the islands was so fraught that it had to be decided by Nixon himself. The president rejected the suggestion from his envoy in Taiwan, ignored pressure from Kissinger, and stuck with the State Department's proposal. To do otherwise, he said, threatened to undermine years of painstaking negotiations over the Okinawa reversion, which was finally signed in June 1971.

The decision pleased no one. At the United Nations, where China had just taken its seat at the expense of Taiwan, Beijing's envoy accused the superpowers of "running amok" and "taking the sea territories of other countries as their 'inland waters' and 'colonies.'" Taiwan was furious with the decision, and Japan, in the words of Schmitz, was "shocked, dismayed, and disappointed." For Tokyo, the failure to recognize Japanese sovereignty was another act of perfidy perpetrated by a supposed friend and ally. "This is an offense to the Japanese people," said a Japanese official after the Okinawa reversion was sealed. "Who do the Americans think they are? Why have they kept the administrative rights to these islands all these years only to throw the issue wide open when Okinawa is returned to Japan?"

Kissinger's fears, about the eruption of Chinese nationalist sentiment over the islands becoming enmeshed with his secret opening to China, proved unfounded. Weeks later, when Kissinger was in Beijing, Zhou did not raise China's claims to the Senkaku/Diaoyu Islands. Something seemed to stick in Kissinger's craw about the islands, and Japan, nonetheless. Two years later, in February 1974, Kissinger as secretary of state found himself receiving a briefing about fighting in the South China Sea. In a forerunner of China's island-building program that made headlines in 2015, the Chinese and South Vietnamese navies clashed in the Paracel Islands, with their forces occupying pieces of land. When an adviser, Arthur Hummel, one of the State Department's most experienced China hands and later U.S. ambassador in Beijing, told Kissinger that regional countries like Japan were concerned about Chinese naval actions, the secretary interjected, "Can we steer them to the Senkaku Islands?"

"Steer who?" Hummel replied.

"The PRC."

"Are you sure you want to do that, sir?"

"It would teach religion to the Japanese," Kissinger replied.

"I realize that we have to teach religion to the Japanese, but is it worth that price?" Hummel asked.

"No, no," Kissinger answered.

From the secretary of state, it was a mischievous but telling interjection. As it turned out, the Chinese didn't need any encouragement to send boats to the islands to harass the Japanese. They would do so themselves soon enough.

While Tanaka's whirlwind 1972 trip sealed Japan's diplomatic ties with China, it would take another six years before the two countries could conclude a formal peace treaty. In both nations, political upheaval delayed the completion of negotiations. Tanaka was forced from office in a corruption scandal in 1974, accused of accepting bribes on behalf of businessmen pressing local airlines to buy planes from the U.S. aerospace company Lockheed. The pro-Taiwan forces in the LDP, meanwhile, continued their spoiler campaign to slow down any rapprochement with Beijing. In China, the death throes of Mao's Cultural Revolution provoked a long-simmering showdown. On one side was the Gang of Four, the ultraradical faction from Shanghai whose members had taken senior party positions in Beijing during the Cultural Revolution under the patronage of Mao's wife, Jiang Qing; on the other were leaders like Deng Xiaoping, who wanted to chart a new, more open path.

In 1976, a series of dramatic, fin-de-siècle events unfolded in China: Zhou Enlai died in January; Deng was purged by Mao in April; Mao died in September; and finally the Gang of Four were arrested in October.

With the radicals behind bars, Deng and like-minded cadres prepared yet another comeback. The Foreign Ministry in Beijing, which had been attacked for its "rightist tendencies" in dealing with the United States and Japan, was able to start functioning again.

For the new Chinese ambassador to Tokyo, Fu Hao, who arrived in Japan in 1977, the reopening of negotiations for a formal peace treaty carried profound meaning. A former soldier in the anti-Japanese war, he, along with his wife, still harbored bitter feelings about Japan. When Fu presented his ambassadorial credentials to the emperor Hirohito, his wife, who was watching on, steamed with anger. "The thought suddenly crossed my mind," she wrote later. "Wasn't that old man who was standing right in front of me the same emperor . . . [who] bore unshirkable responsibilities for that evil war, which had brought extreme sufferings to the Chinese people[?]" When Fu paid a courtesy call on Takeo Fukuda, the now prime minister tried clumsily to display his knowledge of China. Fukuda recalled his time as an adviser to the puppet government in Nanjing in 1940. Asked what he was doing at the time, Fu snapped back, "I was in the Eighth Route Army, fighting against the Japanese aggressors!"

Fu had come to Tokyo with Deng's backing to reboot talks to conclude the Peace and Friendship Treaty with Japan. His chief interlocutor was Tokyo's new foreign minister, Sunao Sonoda, a friendly face who had longstanding contacts with China, first traveling there in the 1950s. The major sticking point in the negotiations was China's insistence that the treaty include an "anti-hegemony" clause, a barely concealed code to register Beijing's distaste for the Soviets. When Fu encountered Sonoda at a function and asked how he was, Sonoda's reply encapsulated how diplomats in the two countries were struggling to steer a middle course between rival radicals on both edges of the spectrum opposed to compromise. "I am climbing a tree and risking my life," Sonoda replied. "People come up from the left; I push them down from the left. People come up from the right; I push them down from the right." It was left to Deng, rehabilitated and refreshed, to finally broker a compromise, with a simple twist on the anti-hegemony clause. To ease Japan's concerns about singling out the Soviets, the two sides agreed to say the clause was not directed against "any third party."

That left just one remaining potential obstacle, the Senkaku/Diaoyu Islands. The Japanese were apprehensive that the Chinese would revive the issue of sovereignty, a deal breaker for Tokyo. Their fears were well based. A few months earlier, in April 1978, a swarm of about two hundred Chinese fishing boats, their occupants armed with light weapons, had suddenly appeared in the waters around the islands. More ominously, Japanese intercepts of the boats' radio communications showed that the vessels were being directed from Chinese navy–controlled ports in the coastal provinces of Shandong and Fujian. Japanese diplomats who pressed the Chinese for an explanation were told by senior leaders to ignore the armada. When the Japanese ambassador confronted a Chinese vice-premier, Geng Biao, about the boats, he was told, "The incident has nothing to do with the negotiations."

For Tokyo, the unexpected, unexplained appearance of the armed flotilla was an ominous sign, if not of a deep split in China over sealing ties with Japan, then at least of evidence of the pitfalls in Beijing of doing deals with the old enemy. "It was unthinkable that China's view toward the treaty was unified," said Nobuyuki Sugimoto, an energetic Japanese diplomat and China expert who provided the most detailed account of the affair, and Tokyo's intelligence on it. Sugimoto wrote his book in a rush in 2005, in the last months of his life, after he had been diagnosed with terminal cancer and returned home from Shanghai, where he had been Japan's consul general. "Naturally, there were people who opposed a treaty of peace and friendship with Japan, a capitalist country, which China regards as an ideological enemy."

To the immense relief of Japanese negotiators, Deng stuck with the policy on the islands first put forward by Zhou Enlai years earlier. Beijing and Tokyo should put the issue aside, Deng said, "for the next ten, twenty, or even one hundred years." Sonoda could scarcely contain his excitement, squeezing the hand of a colleague under the table on hearing Deng's words. Sonoda said later he cried in his hotel room in Beijing after the signing ceremony on August 12, 1978. Ambassador Fu was also overcome with a mass of conflicting emotions, between recalling his fellow soldiers who had died alongside him fighting the Japanese and celebrating the diplomatic victory he had just overseen. "I am a witness," he said, "to both war and peace between China and Japan."

The sense of triumph that surrounded Tanaka's diplomatic breakthrough, and the Peace and Friendship Treaty between Japan and China six years later, was not entirely illusory. The next decade would prove to be perhaps among the most productive periods ever between the two countries. In the years following Tanaka's visit, a sense of optimism reigned in official Japan. "We wanted China to become a market economy, and we believed it would help them become a democracy," said Hidehiro Konno, later a deputy-minister at the Ministry of International Trade and Industry. Tokyo launched a billion-dollar aid program, working with willing counterparts in Beijing to find areas where they could cooperate. On the Japanese side, there was also a sense of cultural affinity and respect for China's revolutionary leaders, plus a widespread (although not universal) sentiment of contrition for the war. Most Japanese held a very favorable view of the Chinese.

Unlike in Europe, however, there had still been no thorough accounting of the horrors of the war and no gestures from top leaders to cut through the diplomatic verbiage to the emotional core, like Willy Brandt's dropping to his knees while laying a wreath in the Jewish ghetto in Warsaw in 1970. Brandt had done this even though he had been part of the resistance against Hitler, and thus could credibly argue he bore no personal responsibility for the Nazi horrors. As a reporter for *Der Spiegel* wrote at the time, "He kneels, though he need not, for all those who need to but do not kneel, because they dare not, or cannot, or are unable. So he confesses a guilt that does not burden him, and he asks for a forgiveness that he himself doesn't need. Thus, he kneels for Germany."

No Japanese leaders dropped to their knees, neither literally, figuratively, nor emotionally. Sino-Japanese rapprochement was achieved without so much as a ceremony for the victims of the war. There were no joint memorials to mark the conflict, no wreaths laid, no research projects undertaken to establish a sense of shared history, and no public process to allow time for the wounds to heal. Both governments had seized the geopolitical moment to restore relations, but domestic politics in both China and Japan confined cooperation largely to a narrow commercial and strategic corridor. Like most of the bilateral relationship's sore points, the dispute over the Senkaku/Diaoyu Islands seemed to have been buried, but it had been covered over more like a land mine left just under the ground's surface than interred for good.

In Japan, Tanaka and Ōhira's main concern had been placating the pro-Taiwan wing of the ruling party and not burdening taxpayers with any extra costs for reparations. Although it only temporarily placated the naysayers, Tanaka used a tried-and-true method in Japanese politics to negotiate the contentious China rapprochement: putting in place a process that enabled his opponents to vent their disagreement, and then taking the decision he had intended to all along. Within the CCP, there was even less accountability and transparency. Zhou Enlai's talk of selling the diplomatic deal to the public was disingenuous, given the restrictions on debate in China at the time. His real audience was never the masses at large but the party elite.

In the opaque world of Chinese politics, the armed vessels that swarmed around the Senkaku/Diaoyu Islands ahead of the friendship treaty would turn out to be a signal event. The conventional explanation—that the incident was organized by remnant supporters of the recently imprisoned Gang of Four as a way to undermine Deng Xiaoping—rings true, although that explanation is contested. More important, the radicals' final choice of weapon to attack Deng underlined the enduring potency of Japan as an issue in elite Chinese politics. That the radicals might have been able to get parts of the military to do their dirty work sent much the same message about the system's sensitivities. The Gang of Four's anti-Deng putsch ultimately failed, but the incident, largely forgotten these days, was a harbinger of fights to come.

It was no surprise, then, that the issues Tanaka dispatched with relative ease would gradually find their way back rancorously into the relationship. The more nationalistic members of the respective ruling parties in both countries—the CCP in China and the LDP in Japan—soon began challenging the mainstream view that the two countries had forged a diplomatic triumph. Both believed their side had given too much away and become a supplicant in the relationship, striking at the very core of their national dignity. In Beijing, there were many who felt China should have demanded a proper recounting of the war, with an apology and reparations, if only to use as leverage over Japan. In Tokyo, a small but influential group of conservatives promoted the same sentiment in reverse, claiming that Tanaka's deal was founded on delusions of a peaceful China and a betrayal of Taiwan. Both dissenting camps believed that far from being solved, the problems of history had been negligently left to the next generation to work out.

The dissenters would turn out to be right, partly because they were so successful at promoting their views within their own respective systems. Soon, they would start to feed off each other. China and Japan enjoyed a brief, bright era in the early 1980s under a new Japanese prime minister, Yasuhiro Nakasone. But the history and territorial disputes that Tanaka and Zhou had summarily dealt with would become so fraught that the two countries would soon struggle to discuss them at all.

THE EIGHTIES

CHAPTER FOUR

The Golden Years

The historical friendly relations between Japan and China must continue onto the 21st century and then to the 22nd, 23rd, 33rd, and 43rd century.

—Deng Xiaoping

Are the officials of the Japanese Ministry of Education mentally unbalanced? Even the German fascists labeled Japanese soldiers a "group of beasts."

—*China Youth Daily*

For many Western historians, China's coming-out in the modern age was symbolized by a trip taken by Deng Xiaoping to the United States in early 1979. It was a visit made memorable for a single image, of the diminutive, Mao-suited vice-premier donning an oversize cowboy hat at a Texas rodeo, a picture that Deng ordered the Chinese media to use prominently, to signal a new era was on the horizon. For Tokyo and Beijing, though, Deng's trip to Japan months earlier was equally transformative. Deng traveled there in late 1978 when Japan was on the crest of an industrial wave that was threatening to upend the postwar global order. Japanese-branded cars, televisions, and electronics were flooding stores in the West, especially in America. The country's steel mills and auto manufacturers were putting foreign rivals out of business, leaving in their wake the beginnings of a rust belt across the midwestern United States, a process China's factories would exacerbate two decades later. For a Chinese leader on an economic pilgrimage, Japan was just as important a destination as the United States.

Deng seemed to sense that he was witnessing a new industrial revolution

as he trekked through Japan's state-of-the-art factories, whose sophistica-
tion dazzled him and his entourage. At the Nissan Zama car plant south
of Tokyo, which had just introduced robots on the production line, Deng
was told the factory produced ninety-four cars for every worker per year.
That, he said, was ninety-three more than China's then-premier car factory, the state-owned First Automotive Works in Changchun, in the
northeast. "Now," he said, "I understand what modernization is." Deng
was a hardened figure, the survivor of multiple wars, revolutionary conflict, and numerous Maoist purges. Sitting in the window seat on the
Shinkansen (bullet train) as the countryside raced by, though, he looked
like a giddy child on an adventure. "It feels really fast," he remarked.

Deng sounded like many Chinese had fifty years earlier, when thousands of young, patriotic students traveled to Japan in search of the secrets
of a successful, modern non-Western society. He openly asked for help from
Japanese political leaders and CEOs alike. Deng remembered how China's
first concerted effort to strengthen the nation in the 1920s had failed, to the
point that the country had almost fallen apart. Now he was readying the
Chinese for a renewed tilt at building a strong state and a modern economy.
"We must admit our deficiencies," he told his hosts. "We are a backward
country and we need to learn from Japan."

The Chinese valued Japan's economic model in a way many Westerners
were slow to grasp. Certainly, Chinese economists noted with admiration
how the Japanese had accumulated capital to build its heavy industries,
refined their engineering skills, and imported and copied foreign technology while building the capacity to develop their own world-class companies, products, and brands. One prominent Chinese scholar highlighted
another factor from outside the box of conventional development economics. Using Communist jargon, the scholar hailed Tokyo's clever use of
"U.S.-Soviet hegemonic contradictions" to spur economic development.
Put another way, he was giving credit to Japan for exploiting cold war tensions to save money by sheltering under the U.S. security umbrella, which
enabled the country to focus solely on economic growth. Japan, Kong
Fanjing, an economist with the State Planning Commission, wrote, "had
made foreign policy subordinate to domestic policy, and domestic policy
subordinate to economics." Deng took note. In the 1980s, following the
example of the Japanese, he restricted China's military spending to preserve resources for the broader economy.

For the Japanese, Deng's trip was a thrilling moment, and not just because he was the first Chinese leader to visit Japan in more than two thousand years of contact between the two countries. Deng showed little interest in recent history, playing down the war and the need for apologies in meetings with political leaders and with Hirohito, the emperor who had presided over the conflict. Deng flattered and charmed his hosts and brought some audiences to tears with his empathy for the two countries' shared heritage. Business leaders and students alike crammed into events to see him. In a gesture rare for a Chinese leader even today, he held a no-holds-barred press conference. A fraught hush fell over the four hundred or so journalists when he was asked about the status of the Senkaku/Diaoyu Islands. Deng brushed the question aside, putting on the record the formulation that he had used in private discussions with Japanese leaders: the issue, he said, should be left to later generations, "who would be wiser" than current leaders.

In 1984, when Yasuhiro Nakasone traveled to China on an official visit, the two countries were still basking in the afterglow of Deng's embrace. The official photograph of Deng and the Japanese prime minister at their meeting in Beijing shows both men seated in the large, overstuffed armchairs draped with antimacassars that the Chinese favor for such formal occasions. The pair, and their translators, are laughing and smiling. In the midst of one of his conversations with Chinese leaders, Nakasone couldn't resist remarking to himself on how incongruous such scenes were. "I used to be referred to by the Chinese as 'that thug Nakasone,'" he said, "but I want to make it clear that I do not have such [militarist] ideas."

It wasn't hard to see why the Chinese had always regarded Nakasone as a hawk. In a nation known for its frustratingly featureless leaders, Nakasone stood out, both in Japan and overseas. As a young politician in the 1950s, he had worn a black armband to display his belief that Japan had ceded its independence through its subservience to the United States. Once, he presumptuously presented Douglas MacArthur, then head of the occupation, with an English-language petition asserting that the U.S.-imposed constitution was crippling Japan's democratic development. MacArthur was reportedly so annoyed that he ripped the document up and tossed it away. The qualities that in theory made Nakasone unsuited to be prime minister were also the ones that made him so striking once he took office in 1982: his unabashed nationalism, nativist preoccupations, and outspoken pronouncements about Japan's role in the world, plus his relative disinterest in the factional games that were the very substance of local politics.

These were also qualities that might naturally have soured Nakasone's relations with China. The Chinese had not forgotten Nakasone's long-time agitation against the country's "peace constitution" or his steward-ship of the Self-Defense Agency in 1970, when he published Japan's first defense white paper. Nakasone had always supported efforts to bolster military spending and expand the ambit of the armed forces, the kinds of policies that set off alarm bells in China. He had also never hidden his distaste for Japan's postwar diplomacy, in which Tokyo positioned itself in the slipstream of its powerful patron, striking out on its own only in reactive, opportunistic ways.

Nakasone wanted Japan to be a forceful, distinctive player in a way commensurate with its new economic status, but he had learned not to strike out blindly. Instead of confronting China and the United States, he tried to build close ties with the leaders in both countries, to ease concern about Japan's rise. Nakasone viewed strengthening American security ties as a way to mollify mounting worries about Japan's trade policies. For the Chinese, he offered generous financial aid and lavished plaudits on China's post-Mao generation of leaders.

One upbeat encounter followed another during his weeklong 1984 visit, as Nakasone was ushered through the nation's vast leadership com-pounds and grand ceremonial halls for meetings so relaxed and friendly that they seemed like family reunions. Nakasone met with the premier, Zhao Ziyang, and the then head of the Communist Party, Hu Yaobang, both overflowing with warmth and praise for their visitor. Finally, there was an audience with Deng, by then considered China's paramount leader.

The official Japanese records of Nakasone's conversations with Chi-nese officials in 1984 have a through-the-looking-glass aspect when com-pared with the curt, combative interactions that would come later. The leaders on both sides exchange gushing compliments, stiffen each other's mutual resolve against the Soviet menace, reminisce about old political struggles, and scheme how to handle the sensitive issue of Japanese war orphans stranded in China. They even offer to carry messages back and forth for each other from the two Koreas, with Beijing to bring them from the north, while Tokyo played intermediary for the south. "Japan and China have many reasons to cooperate, and no reasons to clash," Nakasone told Zhao, who replied in kind: "I know that Prime Minister Nakasone and Cabinet Minister [Shintaro] Abe are passionate about the development of China-Japan relations."

Nakasone had come to Beijing with the backing of Kakuei Tanaka, still the LDP's kingmaker, even after having been forced out of office by scandal in the mid-1970s. Tanaka's mastery of factional and money politics enabled him to retain the power to make or break LDP prime ministers. The "shadow shogun," as he was known, didn't try to hide his clout. Tanaka sometimes drew a parallel between himself and Deng, who had also relinquished formal positions in the ruling party while retaining power behind the scenes. Tanaka also compared himself to a retired CEO who retained a 51 percent stake in a company, saying, "It is natural for big shareholders to choose the CEO." The Japanese media dubbed Nakasone's government the "Tanakasone administration" in a nod to Tanaka's enduring clout. He made it clear that Nakasone's bold diplomacy was at his discretion. "Nakasone may be a first-class political geisha dancing on the international stage," he said, "but I am the one who molds the clay of this administration."

In Hu and Zhao, China also had leaders setting out on a striking new path. Like Nakasone, they had a patron and protector—in their case, Deng, who was personally invested in the Japan relationship. Partners who would later fall out, the two men were overseeing a series of radical reforms to revitalize a country left shaken and impoverished by the Maoist era. Both had come up through the core of the CCP system, but they also recognized that the country needed economic and political liberalization to survive and prosper. In the immediate post-Mao era, Hu had taken over as head of the party's all-powerful Organization Department and overseen the rehabilitation of tens of thousands of cadres. Loyal Communists who had had their lives destroyed after being affixed with various deadly labels in Mao's mass political campaigns—Soviet revisionists, rightists, capitalist roaders, imperialist wolves, and so on—were restored to the party firmament.

The early 1980s were a heady, exhilarating, and emotional time in China. Hu and then Zhao, initially with the backing of Deng, authorized an explosion of experimentation, with the beginnings of a market economy feeding freer speech and eventually a whiff of political liberalization. In concert with Nakasone, Hu and Zhao embarked on another risky adventure—to not just bury animosity with Japan but build a genuinely close relationship with it. Zhao did not hold back his enthusiasm for the project in his meeting with Nakasone. There "was a remarkable characteristic" in Sino-Japanese relations, he told his visitor, "of increasing mutual trust and decreasing suspicion." Deng, and now Hu and Zhao, had their eyes on Japan almost as firmly as they did on the United States, and for good reason. Their neighbor had the capital, technology, and management skills China needed to drag itself out of its Maoist past, as well as providing proof, as it had a century before, that it could keep its Asian roots at the same time.

On his 1984 trip, Nakasone brought with him a nicely wrapped gift—a new tranche of billions of dollars in cheap loans. The Japanese aid program had been launched after Deng's pioneering 1978 trip and lasted for almost three decades, until 2005. The most recent frenzy of construction in China has obscured the extent to which Japan seeded the first infrastructure boom on the mainland with its financial aid in the 1980s. Totaling tens of billions of dollars, Japanese money financed airports in Beijing and Shanghai, urban subway systems across the country, and a host of transport and environmental projects. Visitors to modern China are often dazzled by the country's remarkable build-out of infrastructure since the late 1990s. In the course of just a few decades, China emulated, and then surpassed, both the U.S. highway network and the Japanese fast-train system. While the United States and Japan largely focused on one type of transport at the expense of the other—cars in the case of America and trains in Japan—China devoted resources to both.

Nakasone boasted to his hosts that he had personally intervened to force his bureaucrats to raise the value of the aid package, despite tight finances at home. "This is the result of my own instructions to increase the amount," he said, adding that it was an expression of Japan's "regret over causing great hardships during the war." Making such linkages between the war and Japanese aid would soon become frowned upon in bilateral relations. Freed from paying reparations in 1972, the Japanese had thought they were generously going an extra mile by providing financial aid to China. The Chinese viewed the issue very differently. They considered themselves the ones who had been generous by not insisting on reparations and would become angry when the aid funds were referred to as a de facto payoff for the war. Far from cementing relations between the two countries, over time the aid would paradoxically become a source of resentment.

Japanese officials often searched in vain among the finished projects they had financed for any notices commemorating their contribution. At the Beijing Capital Airport, a small plaque was tucked under a set of stairs, hidden from the day-to-day passenger traffic. China's acknowledgment of Japanese aid waxed and waned, depending on the state of elite politics in Beijing. Sometimes the announcements of projects would be front-page news in the party-controlled papers; at other times, the latest aid tranche would be buried on the orders of the party's Propaganda Department, either to signal displeasure with Tokyo or because internal ructions made any kind of favorable gesture toward Japan at that particular moment too sensitive. But the fundamental reason for China's reluctance to highlight Japan's generosity was about more than just a function of the ups and downs of politics. As with so much that divided the two countries, it could be traced back to the way that each side interpreted the 1972 deal to establish diplomatic relations. The notion that Japan was doing China a favor was, through Chinese eyes, upside down.

On Nakasone's visit, though, none of those tensions were present. Days ahead of Nakasone's arrival, Zhao had told him that he had inspected the construction site for the new China-Japan Friendship Hospital. Japan was readying finance for a telecommunications center and a meat-processing plant in the capital. During their meetings with the Chinese, Nakasone and his foreign minister, Shintaro Abe—Kishi's son-in-law and the father of Shinzō Abe—discussed numerous commercial problems afflicting Japanese companies. These were serious disputes, although not unexpected in a country just opening itself to the hurly-burly of market economies.

When Beijing suffered a shortfall in hard currency in the late 1970s, the central government had canceled a series of high-profile Japanese contracts that had already incurred large costs. Nakasone raised this issue with Chinese leaders, but in a mechanical fashion, as if he were reading from a bureaucratic brief. "We are uneasy, among other things, about China's process for cost accounting, treatment of profit and remittances," he said. Apart from that, the topics of his discussion were focused on upbeat economic opportunities—"Yen Loans," "Free Financial Aid," "Patents," "Joint Ventures," and "Technological Cooperation"—all of which reflected the central message of "little brother Japan helping get its impoverished big brother back on his feet again."

Deng, the unsentimental revolutionary, joined in the exuberance. "The historical friendly relations between Japan and China must continue onto the 21st century and then to the 22nd, 23rd, 33rd, and 43rd century," he told Nakasone. Deng candidly responded to Nakasone's questions about the highs and lows of his political career. "I believe you know what I was doing on the creation of the new China," he said. "I became an official and was thrown into the cattle houses," the term used for leaders made to do physical labor in the Cultural Revolution. For good measure, the two foreign ministers in separate meetings briefly exchanged mildly patronizing comments about the United States, by then locked in trench warfare with Japan on trade. Beset by Washington's persistent and increasingly embittered complaints about Japan's bilateral trade surplus, Abe lamented the United States "was lagging" in economic competition with Japan. His counterpart, in turn, bemoaned America's "lack of understanding" of China.

For all their naked calculation—Tokyo's desire for the vast Chinese market, and Beijing's lusting after Japanese capital and technology—these were a remarkable series of meetings. In retrospect, Nakasone's 1984 visit would come to be seen as the high tide in Sino-Japanese relations. The two countries' leaders had taken advantage of the Peace and Friendship Treaty to develop good personal relationships. Their economies were complementary. China aimed to sell its resources to fund purchases of Japanese technology and capital goods to build up its industry. Japan wanted to ensure it was the first developed country to establish a foothold in a potentially huge market. Most important of all, Japan and China, along with the United States, were aligned strategically, agreeing on the primacy of the Soviet threat. The Chinese state-controlled press remained largely mute about the danger of Japan's military buildup, even as Nakasone lifted defense spending, to cheers in the Pentagon. After all, in Chinese eyes, the Japanese military functioned as a bulwark against Soviet encroachment in Asia.

Only a year earlier, Nakasone had declared in Washington that the Japanese archipelago was America's "unsinkable aircraft carrier," sealing off east Asia from Soviet bombers. The comment landed like a bombshell, for good reason: a Japanese prime minister had rarely sounded so hawkish. Nakasone's statement had appeared in the *Washington Post* after an on-the-record breakfast at the home of the newspaper's owner, the capital's über-host, Katharine Graham. In the uproar that followed, it emerged that he had not actually used the words attributed to him: he had called Japan "a big ship," not an "unsinkable aircraft carrier." His interpreter somehow added a memorable flourish of his own in translation, perhaps dredging from memory the same phrase that General Douglas MacArthur had once used to describe the value of Taiwan to the United States.

Nakasone, however, noting how thrilled his American hosts were with his comments, deftly declined to disown them, at least in English. The following day, at successive press conferences, he told the U.S. press that he had made the statement at the same time that the Japanese press was insisting that he had not. In the event, the confusion over the translation couldn't compete with the impact of the phrase itself. Though never repeated by Japanese leaders, the idea of Japan as an "unsinkable aircraft carrier" resonated through the remainder of the cold war.

If the Chinese were upset by Nakasone's hawkishness, they showed no signs of it. As long as China was "not their target," Chinese generals told U.S. officials at the time, Beijing would not complain about Tokyo's military budget. A State Department cable bullishly reported soon after Nakasone's 1984 visit that the Chinese "privately . . . wanted a consensus on Pacific defense involving the US, China and Japan." The cable relayed, and seemingly accepted at face value, Beijing's insistence that Chinese naval forces were purely "defensive." "We believe that this amounts to a Chinese recognition and acceptance of the naval role to be played by the US and Japan in the waters further out from the Chinese shores," State reported. Not all U.S. analysts agreed that China sought an explicit entente with America and Japan. The U.S. Defense attaché added a prescient dissent to the cable. The Chinese had warmed to the U.S. Navy for two reasons, he suggested: because it provided security against the Soviets, and because it gave them potential access to the latest technology. If they weren't threatened themselves in the event of a regional conflict, the attaché concluded, the Chinese would be happy "to sit on the mountain and watch the tigers fight."

Japan and China's economic complementarity and strategic convergence proved to be only temporary phenomena. Even as bilateral ties blossomed, the roots of future discord were starting to stir. Within the CCP, resisting Japan remained a bedrock source of political capital. As early as 1982, the two countries had had a taste of future crises over what would become a bitter, running sore. In June of that year, Japanese newspapers reported that the Education Ministry in Tokyo had approved school textbooks that changed the phrase describing the Imperial Army's "invasion" of northern China in the 1930s to an "advance" into the area.

To the Chinese and other Asian nations, the substitution of this language symbolized the Japanese right wing's resistance to acknowledging the truth about the conflict and its determination to impose its revisionist views on local teachers, students, and schools. There was some truth to this. At its core, the battle over textbooks reflected a fundamental split within Japan about how to view Tokyo's invasion of China and other Asian nations and its prosecution of the war. The split was not just between Japan and China and the other Asian nations. Japan itself was deeply divided. Conservatives wanted students to be taught a more positive image of the past. In 1982, the LDP had called for the textbooks to "cultivate the Japanese spirit and foster national pride." The Left in Japan, and countries like China and South Korea, joined forces on the opposite side of the debate, to oppose anything that smacked of the glossing over of Japan's wartime record.

Overlooked in the outrage overseas were the complicated political dynamics of the textbook debate inside Japan. Far from the central government in Tokyo dictating the choice of textbooks, the Education Ministry had struggled for years to impose its will on the content of school courses. The ministry didn't have the power to prescribe textbooks for classrooms and could only approve a selection of course materials, with local school boards having the discretion to choose which they would use. In the 1980s, 1990s, and into the twenty-first century, very few schools opted to use the textbooks with the most egregious whitewashing of the war. As late as 2001, only about 0.04 percent of schools adopted the textbooks promoted by the revisionists, a fact all but ignored in Chinese coverage of the issue.

On top of the ideological issues, there were perverse commercial incentives at play as well in Japan's valuable education book market. Textbooks had often been written with a left-wing bias to curry favor with the Communist-dominated teachers' union, one of the few institutions in the country that had resisted co-option by the conservative postwar order. The unions and their members, the publishers hoped, would favor the more critical books and generate sales and profits. The Education Ministry official who ordered the change from "invasion" to "advance" offered the standard conservative lament about the Left's insistence on a "masochistic" view of the country's history. "Japan is being painted unfairly as bad and evil," the official said in an interview after he retired. "Postwar texts depict only negative aspects of Japanese history. There's too much self-flagellation."

Such intramural nuances mattered little, however, outside Japan. With China and South Korea growing richer and finding their voice, the textbook disputes were easily turned into international diplomatic incidents. Japan's Foreign Ministry was immensely sensitive about the issue, as can be seen from cables emanating from the American embassy in Seoul in 1982. When U.S. diplomats asked to see the list of the corrections that South Korea had demanded for the textbooks, the Japanese would provide only a partial accounting—thirteen of the thirty-nine alleged "errors" noted by the Koreans. "This entire issue is so sensitive that [Japanese diplomats in Seoul] cabled Tokyo for permission to respond to our request," State Department officials reported. The wounds of Japan's history of colonialism were just as raw in South Korea. In both countries, the Japanese diplomats lamented, textbooks would continue to strain relations "until the matter fades from memory."

Japan might have gotten through the textbook controversy had it not been for the machinations inside the Politburo in Beijing. The affair erupted just ahead of the once-every-five-years Communist Party congress in Beijing, the authoritarian equivalent of election season in a democracy. Just as diplomacy usually aims to minimize differences, elections, or selections, as they are within the CCP, give license to candidates to amplify them. Deng, and by extension Zhao and Hu, were already fending off criticism from conservatives in the CCP opposed to the rapid opening of the economy to market forces. The toxic mélange of issues that would blow up periodically in the 1980s alongside the liberalization of the economy, which would ultimately result in the Tiananmen Square protests in 1989, was already simmering. The theft of public assets, nepotism within the CCP, rampant inflation, and rising unemployment were all upending the grim, ideological certainties of the Maoist economic order. Japan was dragged into this tide of negativity, with the flood of Japanese consumer goods coming into China branded as a new "invasion."

Deng had to walk a delicate line between warring factions to keep his market reforms on track. For the top leadership, in such circumstances, going soft on Japan was not an option. In exchange for the support, or at least the acquiescence, of conservatives for economic reform and clearing out retired military commanders, Deng gave ground on political and ideological issues. The compromise was reflected in the communiqué issued at the close of the congress. The party conclave supported Deng's direction to open the economy, a policy with monumental global implications, but also warned of "corrosion by decadent ideas from abroad."

For an entire month after the initial Japanese press reports about the textbook changes, there was no reaction from the top in Beijing as the Politburo wrestled over how to respond. Then, as often happens with the Communist Party's propaganda system, once a decision is made, it is as though a switch had been flicked. The eerie silence on the issue was replaced by a torrent of vitriol, like a dam bursting its banks. "Are the officials of the Japanese Ministry of Education mentally unbalanced?" asked the *China Youth Daily*. "Even the German fascists labeled Japanese soldiers a 'group of beasts.'" The old tropes all came tumbling out: "Japanese militarism," "beautifying aggression," "samurai forebears," and so on. Graphic pictures of Japanese atrocities filled the newspapers.

With a prime ministerial visit already scheduled for later that year, Tokyo backed off and promised that future textbooks would take into account prevailing sentiment in other countries in the region. It was a substantial concession from the Japanese government, which had been jolted by the angry, emotional reaction in China. For the moment, with the insertion of what the Japanese called the "Asian neighbors clause," code for agreeing to bear in mind sentiment in China and South Korea, the crisis was defused.

On a trip to Tokyo in 1983, Hu Yaobang barely mentioned the history issue. Indeed, the textbook controversy spurred him to redouble his efforts to build closer ties with Japan. No one in China was more responsible for the heady turn in bilateral relations, and took greater risks, than Hu. The diminutive Communist Party secretary was given to impromptu, disarming gestures of friendship in his dealings with foreign visitors, especially the Japanese. Nobuyuki Sugimoto, later one of Japan's top China diplomats, recalled in his memoirs how Hu invited the entire staff of the Japanese embassy in Beijing to Zhongnanhai—literally, "Central South Lake"—the sprawling walled-off compound astride Tiananmen Square in central Beijing that houses China's top leaders and their families, a place rarely opened to foreigners, for a banquet. He ordered a school be set up for Japanese children in Beijing, a first for foreigners. In meetings with Japanese visitors, Chinese cabinet ministers would come to take notes, because Hu invariably made major announcements on those occasions. "We were treated by the party as if we were 'number one,'" said Sugimoto in his memoirs, "a unique friend who stood out among other foreign countries."

When he touched down in Tokyo, Hu ordered the members of his delegation to make sure they were seen waving in a friendly way from the plane. He shared cigarettes and swapped anecdotes with the Japanese media. In private meetings, he was even more open about wanting friendly relations. The Japanese public, especially young people, sensed Hu's enthusiasm. Students stood in long lines in the cold for hours for a chance to see the Communist Party chief. The trip was, of course, an attempt at mutual seduction, with Nakasone laying on the full trappings of a state visit. The United States looked on with awe and admiration at Nakasone's staging of the trip and its political impact. "The reception orchestrated for Hu was not only a masterpiece of political showmanship," the Pentagon reported from the American embassy. "It had the practical result of [building] 'real' relations to the point where they are the envy of every Western country." Hu's speeches on the trip were written by one of the Foreign Ministry's fledgling Japan experts, Wang Yi, who would go on to become foreign minister three decades later.

But then Hu went too far. With only cursory consultation with his advisers, he invited three thousand Japanese students to visit China to promote "youth friendship." It was a gesture typical of Hu: spontaneous, generous, flamboyant, and over the top. Even the Japanese were surprised at the number. "We invited about three hundred Chinese; Hu invited about three thousand Japanese," said Kunihiko Makita, then one of the Japanese Foreign Ministry's top China hands. "He overdid it." Hu's supporters defended him on many grounds, arguing that the effort would cost little and was aimed at building a long-standing stable relationship. One of Hu's protégés, Hu Jintao (no relation), who would ascend to the position of head of the CCP in 2002, later publicly defended the gesture. As a then-senior official in the China Youth League, Hu Jintao was responsible for overseeing the trip.

Within the party, though, Hu's gesture would turn out to be a grave misstep, because his critics in the leadership noticed the discrepancy in the number of invitees between the two countries. Later, they would add it to his list of sins in office and make him pay dearly for his magnanimity.

Nakasone cultivated Hu in 1983, and Hu and other Chinese leaders returned the favor in 1984. In both Japan and China, public support for closer ties was strong. The two countries seemed to be entering into a new cooperative era. The statesmanlike dealings at the top, however, masked fundamental shifts under way within both countries' political systems. In China, a backlash against Deng's economic reforms, and their enthusiastic implementation by Hu and Zhao, was gathering pace. The party had also begun to reintroduce patriotism as an ideological tool. In Japan, anti-China sentiment, or at least antagonism to Japan's rapprochement with China, had been brewing for much longer. Both movements ensured that the next time the history wars broke out, the cost of dousing their fires would be much higher.

The denizens of the Communist Party's Propaganda Department in Beijing have always been hypersensitive to any stirrings on the Japanese right. The CCP had tracked Nobusuke Kishi from the moment the war ended, years before he returned to top-level politics. They watched especially closely any developments at Yasukuni Shrine, the memorial in central Tokyo dedicated to Japan's war dead. In the early 1970s, in the afterglow of Sino-Japanese normalization, the Propaganda Department pounced on a nascent group of nationalists in Japan disgruntled with Tokyo's China rapprochement. To be fair, the Blue Storm Society, as they were called, went out of their way to be noticed. The conservative upstarts staged samurai-style oaths as part of pledge rituals, cutting their thumbs and sharing each other's blood. In one intra-party meeting, they created a ruckus by upending desks and throwing pieces of sushi at their opponents. They were thrilled when the *People's Daily* ran a series of articles attacking them as an anti-Chinese organization dedicated to reviving Japanese militarism, and they held a press conference to highlight and then refute the charges.

These "young Turks" had multiple interlocking grievances against the mainstream LDP, which all clustered on their contention that Japan had lost its national dignity in the postwar period. They railed against the nation's subservience to the United States, and now, they claimed, to China. They also feared the developing bonds between the United States and China, suspicious the two countries would conspire against Japan. Deeply anti-Communist, they were furious at the abandonment of Taiwan and suspicious of Beijing's Sinocentric view of the world. One member referred to the way Tokyo's pro-China politicians dealt with Beijing as being "just like a peasant licking the boots of a feudal lord." Tanaka's money politics, elite bureaucrats, dizzying economic growth, and dishonorable diplomatic deals were all sapping Japan's traditional spiritual sustenance. One of the most famous members of the group was the author turned politician Shintaro Ishihara, who would work hard for decades at being a thorn in China's side. For all his attention-grabbing theatrics—it was Ishihara who had come up with the idea of the "blood oath" to galvanize media attention—the former author was quick to grasp what few others had after the 1972 deal with Beijing, that there was a substantial audience in Japan for standing up to China.

The young men from the Blue Storm Society eventually grew into middle-aged politicians, accepted ministerial posts, and became thoroughly embedded in the mainstream LDP while retaining their chip-on-the-shoulder conservatism. Far from settling the controversy over Japan's past history, they understood better than most that their political elders had left the issue festering for a younger generation to solve. The views of the young Turks occupied a prominent place in the epic battlegrounds of postwar politics, no more so than in the fight to control Yasukuni Shrine.

More than any institution outside the military itself, the memorial has become a totemic symbol of Japan's never-ending postwar battles, with all its ambivalence about war guilt and resentment over demands to take responsibility for the conflict. Unencumbered by its historical baggage, the shrine, founded in 1869, is a strikingly serene and beautiful building, approached through a series of sculptured traditional gates made of thick native timbers, leading into a courtyard in front of the main temple. Even before World War II, the shrine was identified with the noxious fusion of emperor worship, state Shinto, and militarism that propelled Japan into the conflict. After the war, the occupation prohibited Japanese officials from visiting there. As with most organizations proscribed by the Americans, Yasukuni survived in a modified form to ensure it blended in with the new democratic postwar system. The shrine was placed in the hands of a nongovernment body, and political leaders visited there in a "private" capacity, so as not to breach the postwar constitutional separation between church and state.

The conservative push to make Yasukuni a legitimate and indeed, in the eyes of conservatives, an inspirational national war memorial—"just like Arlington"—had powerful supporters. Japan's leading veterans' group, which had the stature of similar organizations in the United States and European nations, had gradually become woven into the fabric of the political system. In most countries, veterans' groups' ranks naturally diminish with time as members age and die off. In Japan, though, the longer the distance from the war, the greater their power became because of a quirk in the way the group's members and their benefits grew. The Japan War-Bereaved Families Association initially consisted mainly of war widows, until its numbers were substantially enlarged with the addition of the family members of dead soldiers. With the passing of time, the association argued, "the pain of losing children and grandchildren only deepened." As Japan became richer, the funds dispersed to these individuals swelled. By the early 1970s, the veterans' association and its nationwide units had become one of the largest social organizations in the country and, along with doctors' and farmers' cooperatives, a key vote getter for the LDP. The veterans' lobby didn't just support LDP leaders paying their respects at Yasukuni; it demanded they go there for ritual veneration.

Still, Yasukuni didn't become truly radioactive until later in the decade. In 1978, the shrine's newly installed chief priest did what his predecessor had not dared to since the war's end: he enshrined the souls of the 14 Class A war criminals at Yasukuni, joining the 2.46 million dead already there. These were the men who conceived, planned, launched, and prosecuted Japan's wars with Asia and the West—men like Hideki Tōjō, the wartime prime minister; Kenji Doihara, the intelligence chief in Manchukuo; and Heitarō Kimura, the chief of the Burma army, responsible for overseeing the construction of the region's notorious railway to Thailand. Most had been executed or died in prison after their conviction in the Tokyo War Crimes Tribunal. Their enshrinement was heavy with religious and political meaning; they were both deified as gods and praised as heroic spirits.

The conservatives had no illusions about the explosive implications of what they planned to do, either in Japan or overseas. Far from bringing the Class A war criminals into Yasukuni in the open, the enshrinement was done, metaphorically, in the dead of night and kept secret. The news that the worst of the war criminals had been accepted into Yasukuni was not reported until the following year. The head priest did not discuss why and how he had ordered their enshrinement until he gave an interview in 1992. It wasn't until 2006 that the depth of the emperor's fury at the decision was revealed, through the publication of an aide's diary. Hirohito and his son and successor, Akihito, had already made their views clear by staying away from Yasukuni. (No emperor has visited the shrine since the late 1970s.) The diary described Hirohito's anger and quoted him as telling the grand chamberlain that the enshrinement would cause "serious problems" with Japan's neighbors. The head priest was unrepentant about his decision. "Overturning the verdicts of the Tokyo Tribunal is essential to achieve Japan's spiritual renaissance," said Nagayoshi Matsudaira in his 1992 interview. "Therefore, it is necessary to enshrine those who are called Class-A war criminals."

Japan's and China's diplomatic policies in the late 1970s and early 1980s were running in parallel in many respects. Both countries, for different motivations, wanted to get along with the United States. Both were suspicious of the Soviet Union, although in China's case that antagonism was starting to wane. Both, for practical reasons, worked hard to have good ties, but it was here that domestic politics intervened. The dominant political groups in both Tokyo and Beijing were intent on planting the seeds of a spiritual and patriotic revival among their respective populations, a pursuit that drew the two countries into inevitable conflict.

The United States had little interest in Yasukuni's political refurbishment, at least if the official paper trail is any guide. In the collection of documents chronicling U.S.-Japanese relations in the Digital National Security Archive in Washington covering the period 1977 until 1992, the shrine barely rates a mention. The Chinese, by contrast, never let it out of their sights. In 1974, years before the enshrinement of the Class A war criminals, the People's Daily reported extensively on left-wing opposition to conservative efforts to nationalize Yasukuni with an act of parliament. The bill, which would have allowed the government to fund the shrine, failed in the face of fierce criticism. Yasukuni, the People's Daily said, was a tool of Japan's ruling class "specifically dedicated to the imperialist aggression pursued by the militarists." If there were ever any doubts about Yasukuni's status in China, the enshrinement of the war criminals a few years later ended them.

Even in their "private" visits, Japanese leaders had generally made a point of staying away from the shrine on August 15, especially sensitive because it marked the anniversary of Japan's announcement of its surrender. Nakasone's instincts, and those of his conservative base, ran in the opposite direction. Unlike previous prime ministers, Nakasone sought, and received, legal approval to go to Yasukuni in his official capacity as prime minister without breaching the constitution. In 1985, he chose the fortieth anniversary of the surrender to pay a visit and took most of his cabinet with him. His aim, he said, was "a complete resettlement of postwar politics." China warned in the days beforehand that such a gesture would "hurt the feelings of the Chinese" people, which was code for stating that Japan would pay a political price for the visit. Afterward, as with the textbook controversy, the official reaction was initially muted. It wasn't until anti-Japanese student protests broke out at Peking University that anger over Nakasone's action blew up.

The students in Beijing hung big-character posters denouncing the Japanese and Nakasone in vitriolic tones and marched to Tiananmen Square. "The new devils are enshrining the tombs of the old ogres!" read one placard, while another reportedly proclaimed, "I used to be a Japanese imperialist decapitating 50 people in Shenyang [during the war]; but now I am selling you color television sets." Soon the protests spread to other cities, and to as many as 150 campuses, with crowds of up to thirty thousand in Beijing and Shanghai. There were calls for a boycott of Japanese goods. Chinese leaders instinctively understand the dangers of student protests, especially ones that target government weakness in dealing with foreigners. Anti-Japanese protests led by students had destabilized Chinese governments in the late nineteenth and early twentieth centuries. This latest protest was tied to CCP leaders in a particularly worrisome fashion. The only people who could afford Japanese consumer goods were corrupt senior officials. Demonstrating against Japan, therefore, was akin to protesting against the party itself.

The authorities sealed off the Peking University campus, dispatched Foreign Ministry officials to talk the students down, and then sent a vice-mayor of Beijing to do the same. With Vice President George Bush due in Beijing, the government even switched Japanese cars out of his motorcade, replacing them with Chinese vehicles. Student leaders were summoned to meet Li Peng, then a rising political star on the Central Committee, in the leadership compound in Beijing. Article after article was published in the official media explaining Beijing's position, with veiled threats against the students should they not cease their demonstrations. Still, protests continued to break out across the country.

It was only the remarkable, and abject, backdown by Nakasone that defused Chinese anger. The Japanese prime minister not only canceled his next planned visit in late 1985 to Yasukuni but announced he wouldn't go there again at all. He explained that he was influenced not so much by the substance of Chinese objections as by concern about the impact of his actions on Hu Yaobang. "If I continue to visit the shrine, student demonstrations will continue, and Hu will lose his job," Nakasone told a colleague. "It is not in Japan's national interest to see a pro-Japan government in China toppled." Japanese conservatives were furious and pressed Nakasone to visit the shrine the following year. Nakasone's hard-edged cabinet secretary, Masaharu Gotoda, who possessed a somewhat sinister reputation befitting a former head of the National Police Agency, backed his prime minister and flatly ruled out another visit. Nakasone was entitled to go, he said, but it would not be a wise thing to do. For good measure, Nakasone sacked his education minister after that official said the massacre in Nanjing by the Imperial Army was just "part of war."

The next time Hu and Nakasone met, in 1986, the Chinese leader chastised Nakasone in his own inimitable fashion. Hu suddenly jumped to his feet during the meeting and launched into a lecture about the sensitivities of history. We have only barely stopped talking about the British burning down the Summer Palace (in 1860), Hu told him, and the Eight-Country Army (foreign soldiers who put down the Boxer Rebellion in 1899 and 1900). "He was saying, it takes a long time! And if it takes more than eighty years to stop talking about the Eight-Country Army, imagine what it takes for the '30s and '40s," said Kunihiko Makita, the Japanese diplomat, who was at the meetings. Hu's impulsive speeches had their moments of levity. "He would stand up spontaneously and talk about how important Japan relations were," said Makita, "and his dentures would fall out." Nakasone, ironically, was visiting Beijing at Hu's invitation to open a Sino-Japan youth exchange center, a gift from Tokyo.

In Japan, Nakasone's onetime supporters were having none of China's complaints. The head of the veterans' association threatened to take his members out of the LDP, warning, "Neither God nor man will forgive Nakasone's submission to Chinese intervention in our affairs." Hu's meeting with Nakasone was, in fact, his last. Two months later, Hu was forced to resign by Deng at a hastily called Politburo meeting. Hu's chief sin had been moving too quickly on market reforms. But prominent on the charge sheet drawn up by his conservative foes was Japan. His "arbitrary" invitation for three thousand students and his closeness to Nakasone were cited. His opponents called him a "tool" of the Japanese—an especially incendiary term in the CCP, because it resonated with wartime charges of collaboration with the enemy. China's tone on Japan changed abruptly in the following months, with the next series of lectures coming ominously from Deng himself, who warned Japanese visitors that he would not be able to hold back the students in the future. "It will be impossible to control them," he said. "I want you to understand the position we are in."

Deng's tirades only grew more fierce as the year wore on. In mid-1987, he broke with long-standing protocol and suggested to a China-friendly Japanese politician that Tokyo make financial amends for the war. "In 1972, China did not ask for reparations. Frankly we harbor dissatisfaction on this point," he said. Japan, of all countries, "has the biggest debt to China" and should be more humble. A senior Japanese Foreign Ministry official told reporters Deng's comments could be explained by his age, suggesting in not so many words that he was senile. Deng, as he phrased it, had his head "up in the clouds." When China protested, the Japanese official was sacked.

After this outburst, the Japanese no longer looked to Deng as someone who could rise above the history wars. For their part, Chinese senior officials lost much of the faith they had invested in Nakasone. Years later, Xu Dunxin, who served as a diplomat in Tokyo in the 1980s and as ambassador in the 1990s, said that he believed that Nakasone hadn't backed off from visiting Yasukuni because of his stated reason—to protect Hu Yaobang. That was just "an excuse" for him to fend off the veterans' groups at home who were angered at his decision to no longer visit the shrine. "According to my understanding, Nakasone and his cabinet miscalculated," Xu observed. "They thought China might compromise, but there can be no compromise on an issue of principle. We had to show clearly our stance."

Mutual disillusionment was starting to settle in as the unresolved contradictions at the heart of the relationship between the two nations were laid bare. Powerful players in each country felt the other was abandoning the spirit of reconciliation. Each now had a list of issues that could be deployed to test the good faith of the other. China had made visits to Yasukuni a litmus test for every future Japanese leader; conservatives in Japan would urge prime ministers and their cabinets to go, if only to make a point about ceding sovereign decisions to China.

From that point on, China carefully calibrated each change in every Japanese history textbook to see if it reflected a "sincere" approach on the war. The Japanese responded by beginning to point to the ways in which the CCP manipulated its own history. The Chinese increasingly treated Japanese soft loans as de facto war reparations. The Japanese, in turn, resented China's ingratitude for their financial largesse. When Japanese ministers strayed from what Beijing dictated as the "correct" view on history, China would demand they be sacked. Often, they deserved to be for denying factual events like the Nanjing Massacre, but China's interference rankled anyway.

The history wars, in other words, had started playing out well before the big geopolitical shifts triggered by China's emergence as a major power. Many senior politicians in both countries, and in their foreign ministries, remained committed, professionally and emotionally, to establishing better ties and worked hard after each crisis to stabilize relations. Many Japanese still felt Tokyo's future lay with Beijing, and in Asia, not with Washington and the West. For the moment, though, the issues that bedeviled Sino-Japanese ties would be overshadowed by another conflict. It is often forgotten that in the 1980s Japan, not China, was the emerging economic superpower. When Washington looked across the Pacific to assess its rivals, it was Tokyo, not Beijing, that was at the top of its list.

CHAPTER FIVE

Japan Says No

The Japanese are truly foreign. It is much like France, only more so.

—Memo to Secretary of the Treasury Donald Regan, 1981

When the U.S. thought that Japan could be a threat to their status as a hegemon, they squeezed Japan with every means possible. That story is over. . . . Now, Japan is a kind of safeguard. But they can't clamp down on China like they did to Japan.

—Hidehiro Konno, former Japanese bureaucrat

In early March 1984, George H. W. Bush summoned a team of advisers on Asia to his office. The subject was seemingly prosaic, on the surface hardly worthy of the vice president's gathering his regional trade and national security specialists on short notice. Bush wanted a decision on a simple issue: whether negotiators from Washington should be dispatched immediately to Tokyo to discuss the latest trade dispute between the two countries, over Japan's growing dominance of the market for semiconductors. The trade team had refused to leave for Tokyo until Japan had put concessions on the table; the national security bureaucrats had insisted that the talks proceed. After a brief exchange of views, the meeting came to an abrupt finish when Gaston Sigur, the gruff, rotund assistant national security adviser, slapped the side of his chair and declared, "We must have those bases. Now that's the bottom line." Clyde Prestowitz, a longtime trade negotiator who was present at the meeting, said later that no one had raised the issue of America's military bases in Japan and that Tokyo would have panicked at any suggestion that the

United States might abandon them. But no matter: Sigur's outburst ended the discussion. The trade talks would proceed.

In a conventional account, the dispute that played out in front of the vice president pitted two deeply antagonistic camps in the U.S. government against each other. On one side were the administration's national security professionals, whose overriding interest was safeguarding the U.S. military presence in Japan, the linchpin of Pax Americana in east Asia. On the other were the trade negotiators and Commerce Department representatives, who felt constantly marginalized in turf battles over Japan. Sigur wasn't the only senior member of Ronald Reagan's administration to frame the choice in such stark terms. Mike Smith, another of the trade negotiators in Bush's office that day, recalled a similar comment, attributed to Secretary of Defense Caspar Weinberger, that had been made at a cabinet meeting. When the issue of Japan came up, Weinberger, a World War II veteran and a committed cold war warrior, declared, "It is more important for the United States to get night landing rights for our naval carrier pilots in Japan than it is for us to save the machine tool industry in the United States."

By the early 1980s, trade disputes with Tokyo had evolved into much more than just dealing with problems of market access for U.S. goods. The clashes over the tactics to be deployed against Japan had become among the most bitterly contested fights in domestic politics and a constant source of tension between Congress and the White House. For the trade camp in particular, the issue wasn't just one of the traditional divide over the economy, pitting advocates of an untrammeled free market against supporters of domestic industrial policy. Japan's rise had given U.S. economic debates an existential dimension. Many Americans had begun to worry that Japan, far from beating the United States at its own game, might now be playing on a different field altogether.

Here, seemingly, was an economy that didn't fit the model the U.S. political and business establishment propagated as indispensable for success: an undiluted mix of markets and democracy. Never mind that this ideologically skewed formula conveniently ignored crucial ingredients of the U.S. model, including publicly funded research labs and military spending. Japan's bureaucratically guided capitalism, backed by a single ruling party in power uninterrupted for decades, had willfully broken Washington's official rules for winning. Instead of falling flat on its face, the Japanese system had managed to outperform the West not just in heavy industries, like steel, where bureaucrats and bankers could easily husband resources for companies. The Japanese also quickly surpassed the United States in low-wage industries like textiles in the immediate postwar years. By the time Reagan became president in early 1981, the Japanese were also beating the West in high-end consumer markets for cars and electronics, in advanced tech sectors like semiconductors, and in the production of machine tools that equipped factories around the world. Once they had obtained the requisite technology, the Japanese seemed capable of outcompeting foreign companies in almost any field.

A December 1981 memo to the president, Reagan, from the U.S. trade representative, William Brock, laid out Japan's share of the U.S. market sector by sector: automobiles, 21 percent; motorcycles, 65 percent; radios, 46 percent; cameras, 29 percent; video recorders, 100 percent; watches, 14 percent; and machine tools, 11 percent. "No major US manufactured export enjoys more than a ten percent market share in Japan except aircraft, which the Japanese do not produce," Brock wrote. In the eyes of many Americans, this was more than just a dispute about who prevailed in a few sectors of the economy; it was a competition between fundamentally different systems, and the United States was losing.

The anger in the United States ran in parallel with rising disdain in Japan toward its former overlords. Commentators in Japan began to speak of the "American disease." In 1980, one prominent critic in the leading left-liberal daily, the *Asahi Shimbun,* wrote, "Watching the United States suddenly lose its magnificence is like watching a former lover's beauty wither away. It makes me want to avert my eyes." The Japanese depicted Americans as alternatively bullying and lazy, or inefficient and wasteful, unwilling to invest for the long term and unable to manage globally competitive businesses. The new class of Japanese titans scorned U.S. businesses primarily as the playthings of financiers obsessed with money games at the expense of manufacturing products consumers wanted to buy. "For them, the name of the game is nothing but quick profits," said Akio Morita, then chair of Sony Corporation, the company that was the Apple of its day. In Morita's pithy formulation, "America looks forward ten minutes; Japan looks forward ten years."

A few brisk decades later, the quarter-century-long trench warfare on trade between the United States and Japan has largely disappeared into a geopolitical black hole, recalled hazily even by some of its combatants. In Washington, once Japan ceased being considered a threat, much of the political (although not military) establishment paid little attention to the country at all. The stream of novels, nonfiction books, and Hollywood movies that attempted to come to grips with the Japanese system—many of them serious efforts, while others portrayed the country as an insidious, tribal colossus—had begun to dry up by the mid-1990s, as had the audience for them.

Just as Washington had prevailed over Moscow in the cold war, it seemingly went on to win the economic battle with Japan as well. For many policy makers, the conflict with Japan has become little more than a footnote to the real great game in Asia, the one between the United States and China. But this misjudges the import of America's decades-long battles with Japan. Not only did it nearly undo Pax Americana in Asia; it was, in many respects, a practical and psychological dress rehearsal for America's coming rivalry with China.

It didn't take long after the war for the United States to become ambivalent about Japan's resurgence, just as it would be later about China's success. Japan's economic revival had initially been welcomed as a vindication of Washington's postwar plan to nurture a strong ally that could serve as a force multiplier in the cold war in Asia. It was only after Japan emerged as a genuine competitor that the relationship became more contested. U.S. demands for relief from Japanese imports ran simultaneously and often at cross-purposes with Washington's other priority—its desire for Tokyo to increase military spending and play a greater role in U.S.-led defense efforts in the Asia-Pacific. The alliance managers on both sides of the ocean tried to build a firewall between the two to ensure that trade disputes never got entangled in the security relationship. But as Japan grew and its manufacturing prowess developed, the firewall started to crack.

The first pleas from U.S. presidents to Japan to lessen export sales came only a few years after the end of the occupation, and they continued for more than three decades. "The President was delighted that Japan controlled exports so that the demand of US manufacturers for high protective tariffs [for textiles and stainless steel] has been reduced," according to the notes of the meeting between Dwight Eisenhower and

Nobusuke Kishi in January 1960. Eisenhower secured the first voluntary restraints on textiles in 1957; the Kennedy administration engineered a longer-term deal of its own for textiles; the Nixon White House negotiated five-year-long caps on Japanese steel imports, as well as demanding further relief on textiles; and Presidents Ford and Carter demanded and got restraints on specialty steels and color TV sets, respectively.

When Kakuei Tanaka as prime minister met Henry Kissinger in 1972, the pair discussed in eye-watering detail how to reduce the bilateral trade deficit. "I have a list in front of me detailing the items that can be increased," said Tanaka, in deal-making mode. "Gas turbine generators, for example." Tanaka said Japan wanted to get the previous year's $3.2 billion deficit under $3 billion, although he warned it could take some years to do so. He canvassed the idea of Tokyo's buying more arms from the United States: "This is now an estimated $750 million. [Let's] make it $850 million." After U.S. demands for oranges to be imported in Japan's off-season hit a snag—"My official said no, this was not possible"— Tanaka suggests an idea for "mixed blending orange prices." How about more cattle instead? "It is now 5,000 yen a head. We could consider going up perhaps twice or three times that amount." By this stage, Kissinger, with his notorious phobia for economics, was doubtless flagging under the sector-by-sector minutiae. "We will approach it in a spirit of friendship," he concluded. Later, however, he wrote approvingly to Nixon that Tanaka had suggested Japanese purchases of "grain, enriched uranium, aircraft, military equipment and other agricultural and industrial equipment to meet our needs."

The opening years of Ronald Reagan's presidency only compounded the problem of America's rising deficits. Reagan cut taxes and lifted military spending, fueling a surge in consumer demand in the United States and a spiraling fiscal shortfall that had to be funded offshore. The value of the U.S. dollar rose as demand for the currency soared, which in turn made imports cheaper and the trade shortfall deeper. In the space of a few years in the early 1980s, the United States experienced a historic, unnerving transformation, from a near-century-long period as a global creditor to a massive borrower on world markets. As Japan moved rapidly up the value chain, the challenge to the American economy from across the Pacific created deep fractures among the new administration's policy makers.

Reagan's cabinet hadn't required much prodding on one aspect of

Japan policy: to enlist Tokyo in Washington's all-hands-on-deck global competition with the Soviets. Soon after the president was sworn in, Reagan's cabinet members were bluntly delivering a singular message to the Japanese that they needed to spend more on defense and increase their contribution to regional security. U.S. governments had been gently pushing Tokyo on this matter for years, both to remove itself from the straitjacket of its peace constitution and to contribute more to the cost of U.S. forces stationed in Japan. As Secretary of Defense Caspar Weinberger noted in a personal memo to Reagan ahead of a visit by the Japanese prime minister, Zenkō Suzuki, in early 1981, "Every US administration in the past 20 years had tried unsuccessfully to persuade Japan to increase its defense spending." Weinberger intended to finally make it happen, gently or otherwise, and told Reagan that he should ask Japan to "double its maritime and air defense capability in the Northwest Pacific within this decade."

The Japanese had become highly practiced at skirting U.S. requests for higher defense spending, taking shelter behind the public's postwar distaste for the military in all of its manifestations. Doing so suited their policy priority, a laserlike focus on economic growth. When the Japanese prime minister Eisaku Satō won the Nobel Peace Prize in 1974 for helping halt the spread of nuclear weapons, prominent Japanese conservatives joked among themselves about it. "The Americans were always asking us to do this and to do that, to take over the burden of their Far East policies," said Sunao Sonoda, the acerbic MP who served as foreign minister in the late 1970s. "But all their efforts were sabotaged by one Japanese cabinet after another. That's why Satō got the Nobel Peace Prize. He got it for his accumulated achievements in the field of sabotage. I guess he's the only prime minister to have got the Nobel Prize for sabotage."

Within Japan, senior bureaucrats gave Tokyo's single-minded pursuit of its economic interests a veneer of intellectual rigor. Naohiro Amaya, a legendary strategist at MITI (the Ministry of International Trade and Industry) when the department was at the height of its powers, urged Japan to adhere to its role as a "merchant nation" and leave security issues to "samurai nations" like the United States and the Soviet Union. "For a merchant to prosper in samurai society, it is necessary to have superb information—gathering ability, planning ability, intuition, diplomatic skill, and at times, the ability to be a sycophant." If that meant getting on one's knees to beg for oil, then so be it. "When money can help," Amaya said in the early 1980s, "it is important to have the gumption to put up large sums."

On the advice of old Japan hands, American leaders and senior officials had always couched requests for higher defense spending in discreet terms, respectful of Japanese sensitivities. Sweeping late into his first meeting with the Japanese foreign minister, Masayoshi Ito, ahead of Suzuki's visit—Weinberger had been held up giving testimony on Capitol Hill—the defense secretary dispensed with that practice and instead reeled off a series of demands. The end of détente with the Soviet Union had changed the game, Weinberger informed him, and Japan's army, navy, and air force needed to be bigger. Tokyo also had to pay more for the cost of the U.S. bases and fifty thousand or so troops stationed there. "Precisely because the times are so urgent, the area to be covered is so enormous and the US does not have all the resources necessary," Weinberger said, "Japan's help is urgently needed." The defense secretary struck an apocalyptic tone on the same issue with Prime Minister Suzuki a few months later. If Japan did not join the United States in countering the Soviet military buildup in Asia, "we could face defeat in either surrender or subjugation."

Nicknamed "tape recorder" for his ability to perfectly memorize answers to potentially embarrassing questions, Suzuki invariably stumbled without a script. When he was asked on his return from Washington why the subsequent joint communiqué described the U.S.-Japan relationship as an "alliance," Suzuki struggled to answer, first denying the word was in the document at all and then insisting that it didn't necessarily refer to military issues. His difficulties illustrated why Japanese leaders had to tread carefully where military matters were concerned. The Japanese had always used the word "treaty" to describe relations with the United States, and even as late as 1981 the word "alliance" carried the stench of Tokyo's wartime ties with Nazi Germany. Suzuki and Reagan's communiqué was the first time the term had been used in an official document to describe U.S. and Japanese cooperation. Ito, in accordance with Japanese political practice, took responsibility for the incident and resigned to save his prime minister.

In retrospect, it seems remarkable that the Japanese would flinch at the use of "alliance" to describe relations with a country that had had troops stationed in Japan for its protection for more than a quarter of a century. In some respects, the word "alliance" was something of a euphemism, because the Japanese had in fact largely contracted out their security to Washington. If the Japanese were in an alliance with the United States, they were very much the junior partner. But it is often forgotten that during this period the U.S. presence, far from being taken for granted as permanent, was considered by some influential thinkers to be in its final days. According to their analysis, the stationing of U.S. troops was a transitory phenomenon, which the Japanese would dispense with once their economy had recovered and their political system had reordered itself.

In 1972, Zbigniew Brzezinski, who would later become Jimmy Carter's national security adviser, predicted the "die would be cast" on the fate of the U.S. troops in Japan by the middle of the decade. "The Japanese expect that by 1975, most American forces will be out of Japan," he wrote. "It may also be expected that the Japanese will quietly press for the removal of most American bases by that date." Once Japan had created its own security doctrine, Brzezinski argued, it could finally confront the fundamental question: "Should it go nuclear?" Brzezinski had spent a sabbatical in Japan in the early 1970s and came away wowed by the country's prospects. But such predictions proved to be wildly unrealistic, overestimating Japan's independent bent and underestimating its reliance on the United States. Japan still had an interest in sticking with its powerful friends, especially as Soviet deployments in Asia grew.

Weinberger was not quite pushing at an open door with his demands for Japan to do more on security. Despite American insistence, the Japanese would not take on a broader regional role. But Japan's door was ajar, especially to the north. At that time, Moscow maintained about one-quarter of its military strength in Asia, which was anathema to Tokyo after the Soviet occupation of Japan's northern islands in the dying days of the Pacific War. Japan's rapid economic growth had already naturally pushed defense spending higher. Jimmy Carter's declaration that the Persian Gulf was essential to U.S. security, prompting him to shift military resources out of Asia to the Middle East, had also alarmed the Japanese.

With little public drama, Japan began taking steps to integrate its forces more tightly with those of the United States. Suzuki pledged on his Washington trip that Japan would take responsibility for the defense of its sea-lanes at one thousand nautical miles from the shores of its main islands. When he took office in 1982, Yasuhiro Nakasone went further, with a promise to defend U.S. ships in Japanese territorial waters and to export military technology to America for the first time. Needless to say, despite Suzuki's confusion, the word "alliance" was probably more accurate at that point in time than it had ever been to describe relations with Washington.

Nakasone, a lifetime hawk, had once memorably likened Japan's emerging security posture to "a rabbit with long ears, with the defenses of a porcupine." The ears were for intelligence gathering around its islands; the sharp quills were for protection when attacked. With such skills, and the additional hardware acquired during the economic boom of the 1970s, Tokyo gradually made itself indispensable to the United States in bottling up Soviet forces in the seas around Japan. Beijing could hardly object to Japan's expanding its security role. Tokyo hadn't added any firepower to enable it to threaten Beijing, and the Chinese wanted the Soviets contained in the seas along their coast as well.

Around this time, U.S. intelligence reports noted, the Chinese and the Japanese began exchanging intelligence on Soviet missiles deployed in Asia and building their own informal military ties. Beijing had by then already allowed U.S. intelligence to establish listening stations in western China to monitor Soviet compliance with arms control deals. In an episode largely forgotten in the strategic suspicion that typifies current U.S.-China relations, the CIA's top officials had traveled in secret to Beijing in 1980, negotiating for an entire week an agreement to place the surveillance equipment on Chinese soil. In the spirit of subterfuge, Stansfield Turner, the head of the CIA, even grew a mustache for the visit. Having been in an intelligence war since 1949, top leaders in both countries ushered in a remarkable period of cooperation that lasted until 1989. Japan was eager to come on board as well, and China had every practical reason to welcome its neighbor's assistance.

With the Soviets in the firing line, the United States, Japan, and China were aligned on security. Trade, however, was a different story. The Reagan administration fashioned a single, strong coordinated message to Japan on security. As the showdown in Vice President George Bush's office in 1984 illustrated, there was no similar consensus on trade. The battles began in the opening days of the administration and quickly

became bitter and personally acrimonious. The opposing camps in
Washington were known respectively as the "Chrysanthemum Club" (or
less frequently, the "Cherry Blossom Protection Association") and the
"Black Ships Society." The names were freighted with pejorative meaning. As Japan's official flower, chrysanthemums carried the implication
of blind favor to Tokyo, as did cherry blossoms. This camp opposed taking a tough line with Tokyo, constantly playing up Japan's role as a security ally rather than an economic competitor. The "black ships"
referred to the U.S. expedition that had forcibly opened Japan in the
1850s and was synonymous with gunboat diplomacy, and thus supportive of measures to pry Japanese markets open. In the early days of the
administration, as they had been for years in Washington, the "Black
Ships Society" was in the minority, pitted against not just successive
White Houses but the Pentagon and the sprawling national security establishment. The State Department was considered part of the "Chrysanthemum Club," also nicknamed the "Japanese Embassy on 23rd
Street," a reference to its Washington address.

In his retelling of these conflicts, Mike Smith of the U.S. trade representative's office made negotiations with the State Department over
Japan's restrictions on one U.S. export commodity, beef, sound like a
black comedy. In this internal U.S. government dialogue, the State Department official starts by citing Tokyo's objections to allowing American imports to compete with Japan's most expensive cut of local meat,
Kobe beef, which reputedly owed its exceptional tenderness to farmers'
massaging their cattle:

> The desk officer would ask, "How can you do this? Kobe beef
> is part of Japanese culture." We'd say, "We're not attacking
> Japanese culture. We're not attacking Kobe beef. We're after
> the other cuts [of beef]." The desk officer would say, "You'll
> upset the Japanese beef farmer." We would say, "What about
> the American farmer?" The desk officer would say, "Well, we're
> a big, rich country." I would say, "Well, we're running a $50
> billion trade deficit with Japan, and they're getting to be a rich
> country, too." The desk officer would say, "Well, we've got se-
> curity requirements." We would say, "What's a security require-
> ment got to do with beef?" The desk officer would say, "If you

upset the Japanese farmer, the LDP will lose support, and we won't be able to get Japan to defend the 1,000-mile radius [east of Tokyo] for antisubmarine warfare." I would say, "Well, then, all their ships will be sunk."

At the National Security Council, Gaston Sigur's balance sheet for the relationship with Japan was calculated on very different terms. Sigur, who began his career at the Ford Foundation in the early 1950s, a job that included funneling CIA money to various Japanese recipients, saw the alliance firmly through the prism of the cold war. He didn't tally exports and imports to calibrate its value. Along with like-minded colleagues scattered across the national security and free trade camps, he placed more weight on statements like that of Nakasone at the 1983 G7 Summit of developed nations in Williamsburg, when the Japanese prime minister declared Tokyo to be not just a U.S. ally but part of the Western alliance. The personal chemistry between Nakasone and Reagan—unusually for a Japanese leader, he asked that the U.S. president address him by his first name, thus establishing the famous "Ron-Yasu" relationship—irked the trade negotiators. They viewed this faux intimacy as a tool for the Japanese to dissuade Reagan from tough measures on trade. For the likes of Sigur, though, the "Ron-Yasu" relationship was invaluable in cementing ties and staving off the trade hard-liners. Sigur considered officials like Mike Smith narrow, unbalanced, and immature. "You know the old Confucian statement . . . : An inferior man blames others; a superior man examines himself," he said. "I think so many of our problems with the Japanese show whether we're inferior or superior people or not. So much of our difficulties have to do with ourselves . . . and have little to do with them."

From the beginning of the Reagan administration, the trade hard-liners struggled to surmount an important hurdle that was a forerunner of later disputes with China. They couldn't easily point to a raft of formal import tariffs and quotas in Japan, because most had been eliminated. That left them with the more difficult argument: convincing the White House that the United States should be targeting not just Japanese trade policies but the country's entire political and economic system. "The real import barriers are structural," Marc Leland, an adviser to Secretary of the Treasury Donald Regan, wrote in a memo in the first months of the Reagan administration, before adding some lurid cultural color to drive his point home. "Japan is still xenophobic; its industrial structure is cartel-like; anti-competitive practices are tolerated; dealing with government officials is time-consuming and difficult; the distribution system is impossible; the Japanese language is hard, and the Japanese are truly foreign. It is much like France, only more so."

Leland's complaints about difficult Asian languages and the French were not persuasive, nor was the blunt summation of his advice. Don't worry about the details, he told Regan. Tell the Japanese "to buy more US goods or else." The Treasury secretary, however, instinctively resisted what he regarded as protectionist measures, as well as pressure to lower the U.S. dollar, which he insisted would be "strong to the end of the decade." In any case, if Japan was subsidizing industry, that was good for the United States, argued one of the administration's senior economists, because "a share of the benefit of the subsidy will accrue to us." President Reagan, who would ultimately have to make the call, showed little interest in getting tough with Japan so early in his administration. In one of the first interagency meetings to discuss the trade deficit with Japan, Reagan appeared to doze off.

In Tokyo, the Japanese government experienced a split that mirrored the bureaucratic divisions in the United States. MITI generally took a hard line with the Americans, while the Foreign Ministry, which had an interest in the broader relationship, counseled restraint. So deferential did many Japanese think the Foreign Ministry had become to the United States that it was branded the "Asian Department of the U.S. State Department." Occasionally, when MITI could see trouble down the road, it took a tactical decision to accommodate America as well. Early in the Reagan administration, MITI's Amaya negotiated "voluntary restraints" on car exports after Congress threatened to impose quotas on Japanese autos. The compromise did not win him praise. The Japanese press, egged on by angry car industry executives, called Amaya the "foreigner's concubine" for his troubles.

The flexibility initially suited both the White House, which didn't have to sully its free trade credentials, and Tokyo, which avoided the threat of worse punishment without conceding on principle. But such deals proved irresistible and ultimately corrosive. The Japanese would often vehemently object to American complaints that their economy was attuned to anything other than market forces. Then, when pressure from Washington mounted, they would agree to deals to restrain exports, which had the effect of confirming their critics' claims that Japan was truly a managed economy in which powerful bureaucrats could manipulate private firms.

The Japanese were alternatively resentful, resistant, or nonplussed by U.S. complaints. Their attitude frustrated even George Shultz, secretary of state under Reagan and long considered the cabinet member with the best knowledge of, and empathy with, Asia. A U.S. diplomat recalled Shultz's presenting Minister of Foreign Affairs Shintaro Abe with a gift of chocolates at a meeting in Tokyo, a gesture that he regularly made with Japanese interlocutors to underscore the country's restrictions on imports of the sweets. "He told Mr. Abe, 'You know, right now Japan is running a huge trade surplus with the United States and this means that some day Japan is going to have to start running a deficit because we can't run a deficit forever.' And Abe gave him a look that said, 'What do you mean? A surplus is just a matter of course and Japan's due.'"

It wasn't until the complaints of U.S. industry merged with national security concerns in the battle over semiconductors that the game changed in Washington. On the surface, the dispute over the tiny silicon-etched chips had characteristics that were familiar to other bilateral trade battles and also echoes of today's fights with China. U.S. tech companies pointed to the Tokyo bureaucracy's role in overseeing the cartel-like behavior of Japanese firms; the cheap capital that helped local industry to weather business cycles; the dumping of low-cost product in the United States; and the seemingly insurmountable barriers to entry for foreigners trying to sell into Japan.

There was one crucial difference, though, in the case of semiconductors: The national security establishment in the United States had a stake in the fight as well. Among other things, the semiconductors were needed to make certain that missiles found their targets. For the trade hawks, the dispute was a godsend, because it finally enabled them to take their concerns beyond the economic ministries clustered around the White House and across the Potomac River to the most empowered agency in Washington—especially during Reagan's presidency—the Pentagon.

"The semiconductor agreement was an exception because we got the national security community on board," said Glen Fukushima, a former trade negotiator. "USTR [the Office of the U.S. Trade Representative] and the Commerce Department stressed the national security implications of the U.S. becoming completely dependent on Japan for semiconductors. We knew that unless we did so, State, the Pentagon, and the National Security Council would not support us in negotiating a results-oriented agreement with Japan."

The result was the most controversial trade agreement of the 1980s, one that the Japanese came to bitterly regret and that the Chinese have made certain never to emulate. Rather than acting on the request of an aggrieved private company, the U.S. government took the rare step of initiating a dumping action itself. The agreement subsequently negotiated included a side deal in which Tokyo appeared to agree that U.S. companies would get a 20 percent share of the Japanese semiconductor market within five years. Instead of market access, U.S. firms had been all but guaranteed market share, a heretical step toward managed trade.

Worse was to come. When the Tokyo bureaucracy's exhortations to local firms to reduce exports and buy more overseas chips failed, Reagan headed off threatened congressional action in April 1987 by imposing 100 percent tariffs on some Japanese semiconductor imports. The retaliation was, in the words of one writer, "among the most dramatic events of postwar U.S. trade policy." Japanese bureaucrats hated the semiconductor agreement for good reason. While Japan insisted the deal was a one-off, the United States would later try to use the agreement as a template for demanding similar targets for market share of American goods in other sectors.

Reagan's belated hard line on semiconductors came on the heels of another monumental agreement, also primarily designed to drive down the U.S. trade deficit with Japan. This time, the mechanism was the exchange rate. The Plaza Accord, named after the New York hotel in which it was announced in September 1985, was signed by the United States, Japan, the United Kingdom, and then West Germany and France, empowering their central banks to buy the yen and deutsche marks and sell the dollar. Although designed to benefit the United States, the agreement was in many respects imposed on a Reagan administration ideologically resistant to intervening in the exchange rate. Congress and many U.S. trading partners had become exasperated by Reagan's hands-off approach to the looming trade wars, not just with Japan but also with Europe. The threat that Congress might take the issue out of the White House's hands with veto-proof protectionist legislation brought the matter to a head. The result was a huge, and unprecedented, orderly devaluation of the U.S. dollar against its major trading partners, aimed to stimulate U.S. exports and consumer demand in Japan and Germany. Far from ending the trade disputes, however, the Plaza Accord proved to be a way station to further conflicts.

It took someone from outside Tokyo's technocratic elite to really sharpen the knives in Washington. A novelist, screenwriter, and film director in his youth, Shintaro Ishihara had made his name as a nationalistic bomb thrower with a flamboyant turn of phrase that was boastful to the point of parody. "If I had remained a movie director, I can assure you that I would have at least become a better one than Akira Kurosawa," he once said, referring to Japan's most storied filmmaker. In the same 1990 interview in *Playboy* magazine, Ishihara denied the Nanjing Massacre had taken place, an assertion he repeated throughout his career. Ishihara's statements, outlandish to foreign ears, often caused him to be dismissed as an outlier. Such assessments, however, underestimated his influence. In his half century in public life, Ishihara had an uncanny ability to whip up debates in Japan on his extreme nationalistic agenda. That foreigners were furious only helped him. Early in his political career and toward its end, he was notorious for his antagonism to China's Communist rulers. In the United States, however, Ishihara gained fame for different reasons.

By the late 1980s, after being in and out of parliament for more than two decades, Ishihara had worked his way up the ladder to become transport minister. He was quickly disillusioned by life at the top of Japanese politics, typified, in his eyes, by the conduct of cabinet meetings, where, he observed, "generally, the ministers sleep through them." In a series of speeches to constituents in his Shinagawa district, near the Sony headquarters in central Tokyo, a restless, frustrated Ishihara vented about everything from the dead hand of government to the Japanese people's growing softness and inability to do physical labor. "I feel . . . the Japanese people will evolve into something like ET, with pronounced eyes and noses and a big head, making them top-heavy, over an abnormally thin body and slender arms and legs," he said.

What angered him most was the same issue that had driven him to co-found the anti-China Blue Storm Society in the 1970s—Japan's inert foreign policy and the "mental stagnation" of its diplomats. Ishihara advocated a more aggressive posture. He said Japan should use its technology as leverage in negotiations with the United States. The next time the Americans started making demands on Japan, Ishihara stated bluntly, the government could respond by offering its advanced technology to the Soviet Union. Ishihara zeroed in on the made-in-Japan semiconductors used by the U.S. military, which gave the Pentagon's missiles a crucial targeting advantage over the Soviets'. "If Japan sold chips to the Soviet Union and stopped selling them to the U.S., this would upset the entire military balance," he said. "Now Japan is at least five years ahead of the U.S. in this area, and the gap is widening." For good measure, Ishihara offered praise for the Japanese officer who planned the sneak attack on Pearl Harbor.

In early 1989, Ishihara's speeches were transcribed and packaged into a book alongside more sober critiques by Morita, the Sony chairman, of U.S.-style capitalism and their own countrymen's inability to find a place on the world stage. It was a made-for-the-moment volume, with a title to match: *The Japan That Can Say No*. A bestseller in Japan, its popularity might have ended there in the pre-Internet age if not for one of the U.S. agencies targeted by Ishihara. The Pentagon's secretive research arm, the Defense Advanced Research Projects Agency, which considered Tokyo a competitor as much as an ally, translated the book, and soon thousands of bootlegged copies were being handed with alarm around Washington. One congressman had the text put into the *Congressional Record*. Larry Summers, then an economist at Harvard, wrote in the *New York Times* in response to Ishihara, "I suspect your America bashing may have made a stronger case for a new American policy toward Japan than any American ever could." A toned-down official translation was later published in English, with an embarrassed Morita's contributions diplomatically excised. (Sony was then in the midst of buying Columbia Pictures.)

In *The Japan That Can Say No,* Ishihara argued that Japan's rise was doubly significant because it spelled the beginning of the end of "white

Westerners" dominating the world. As such, it was a warning to the United States to shed itself of racial prejudice toward Asians. "The only reason they could use the atomic bomb on Japan," Ishihara wrote, "was because of their racial attitude." In the same way that much U.S. criticism of Japan had a racial edge, Tokyo's rise pushed to the surface the chauvinism that was part of everyday life in Japan but that attracted little attention when the country was relatively weak. When he was prime minister, Nakasone said the "level of Japanese society" surpassed that of the United States because the numerous "blacks, Mexicans and Puerto Ricans" dragged down educational standards. Michio Watanabe, the LDP's policy chief and later foreign minister, called the Chinese "cave dwellers" and claimed that black Americans happily walked away from their debts. Theories of Japan's purity of race, blood, and mystique all enjoyed a revival and even permeated trade negotiations. One trade official famously rejected European skis on the grounds they weren't suitable for Japanese snow. Another later insisted that U.S. beef was unfit for Japanese intestines.

The notion that Japan was overwhelming the United States was not an idle thought bubble confined to Washington think tanks and parts of the national security establishment. It penetrated deep into the American consciousness. According to a poll published by *Newsweek* in late 1989, Americans viewed the threat from the Japanese economy to the United States as being on par with that from the Soviet Union. Other polls recorded similar trends. After the fall of the Berlin Wall and the Soviet Union's implosion, the potential threat posed by Japan loomed even larger in American politics. "The red menace is dead; long live the yellow peril," wrote Walter Russell Mead, only half tongue in cheek.

A 1992 Pentagon document laying out a post-cold-war strategy for the United States singled out Japan and Germany as two countries in Asia and Europe, respectively, that could threaten America's status as the world's sole superpower. The document, the drafting of which was overseen by Paul Wolfowitz and Lewis Libby, who would both be instrumental in George W. Bush's decision to invade Iraq, was modified following the uproar after its leaking. Years later, Robert Hormats, who served in both Republican and Democratic administrations, looked back on the document's notion that Japan was a singular threat to the United States with a mixture of stupefaction and anger. "Remember, this was when the

U.S. had troops not just in Okinawa, but also Yokosuka [just south of Tokyo], and in a military garrison downtown near the U.S. embassy!" Within the CIA, the main Japan analyst at the time was a cerebral and ambitious young official, Mike Morell, who later gained fame as the agency's deputy and then acting director in the Bush and Obama administrations during the "war on terror" years. In the words of Joseph Nye, the Harvard professor who served in Bill Clinton's administration, Morell was "one of the hard-liners" on Japan. With the encouragement of his bosses, Morell wrote a report circulated within the bureaucracy about the dangers of Japan's techno-nationalism.

To understand the Japanese challenge in context, it is worth casting one's perspective forward for a moment, to the state of Sino-American relations three decades later. A striking number of the arguments deployed in the United States at the time against Japan (a democracy, however flawed) have eerie echoes in the current debate over China (a single-party state), albeit on a much larger scale.

The United States and Japan were connected by their security alliance and at war over trade. The United States and China, from the late 1980s onward, were in the opposite situation: they were at odds ideologically but at least initially bound by growing commerce and investment. For many years, trade with China was ensnared in domestic U.S. debates over linking human rights to economic cooperation, a problem that did not apply to Japan. The Chinese economic model, too, differed from Japan's in significant respects. Japan, along with South Korea, shunned foreign investment in industry and put up barriers to consumer imports, like cars and electronics. In catch-up mode, Chinese leaders took a different tack when they opened the economy in the early 1980s. They solicited overseas partners in sectors like automobiles and welcomed full foreign ownership in low-tech manufacturing. Until the early 1990s, China was an energy exporter and still has large reserves of coal and other resources. Japan imports nearly all of its energy and has tailored its foreign policy accordingly.

The evolving U.S. relationship, first with Japan and later with China, however, displayed many of the same pathologies. Washington portrayed both as managed economies with manipulated currencies, where the market took a backseat. Each was accused of taking—or stealing—foreign technology to modernize its economy on the cheap. Washington charged Japan and then China with pursuing mercantilist policies to promote exports while limiting imports and restricting foreign investment. Japan's powerful Ministry of International Trade and Industry "took its place beside the KGB as one of the principal Lucifers in the American pantheon of demons," according to a prominent Tokyo-based writer. Likewise, Washington viewed Beijing's economic planners as the chief obstacle to market reforms in China. The United States bemoaned the weakness of civil society in both countries and their inert courts and corralled lawyers. This last complaint was mostly worn with a badge of pride in Japan and China, where the powers that be, to different degrees, believed that the law should serve the state, rather than the other way around.

U.S. competition with China and its ruling party always had an ideological edge that distinguished it from that with Japan. But even in this realm, Japan lost much of its luster as a fellow democracy when trade tensions with the Americans reached their peak. The revisionist school of Japan watchers, who tried to overturn what they regarded as a damaging misreading of the country's political system, depicted Tokyo's outwardly familiar democratic institutions as a sham. "Labour unions organize strikes to be held during lunch breaks," wrote the Dutch journalist Karel van Wolferen in his iconoclastic classic, *The Enigma of Japanese Power,* published in 1989 at the peak of anxiety over the Japan threat. "The legislature does not in fact legislate; stockholders never demand dividends; consumer interest groups advocate protectionism; laws are enforced only if they don't conflict with the interests of the powerful; and the ruling Liberal Democratic Party is, if anything, conservative and authoritarian, is not really a party and does not in fact rule." In this interpretation, Japanese life was "like a play that has suffered a bad mix-up in its staging. The lines the actors speak do not fit the characters their costumes indicate they portray." The headline of one of the most widely read revisionist texts, by James Fallows in the *Atlantic Monthly,* summed up the threat from Tokyo in a term borrowed from the cold war: "Containing Japan."

The critique of the Chinese system was in many respects uncannily similar to that of its Asian neighbor. Like Japan, China was run ostensibly by a government but ruled in reality from behind the screen by a secretive Communist Party that oversaw the military, the security services, big business, the media, the courts, civil society, and intellectual life in universities and think tanks. China's old-fashioned interlocking directorate, to use the Leninist term, which placed all public and private power centers under party control, bore resemblances to Japan's more narrowly focused *keiretsu* system, the interwoven corporate and banking cartels that were closely tied to the bureaucracy. In China, the head of a state-owned oil company might be transferred within the party system to become a provincial governor or big-city mayor. In Japan, top government officials near retirement age were parachuted into the corporate world, a practice known as *amakudari,* or descent from heaven. The long-standing joke about Japan—that it was the world's most successful Communist country—was only funny because it rang true.

The Western fixation with grappling with the Japanese and Chinese governing systems went beyond merely trying to discern how they worked. Academics and commentators praised them for being both nimble and dynamic compared with cumbersome, sclerotic democracies. For all the mistakes that Japanese bureaucrats might make, van Wolferen observed, they had the information and agility to second-guess the market and drive business with a "shared industrial policy and trade strategy." Twenty years later, Thomas Friedman echoed these arguments on China. "One-party autocracy certainly has its drawbacks," he wrote in his influential *New York Times* column. "But when it is led by a reasonably enlightened group of people, as China is today, it can also have great advantages. That one party can just impose the politically difficult but critically important policies needed to move a society forward in the 21st century. It is not an accident that China is committed to overtaking us in electric cars, solar power, energy efficiency, batteries, nuclear power and wind power."

These formulations of enlightened if often authoritarian bureaucrats leveraging the collective wisdom embedded over centuries in Confucian Asia carried with them a racial and militaristic undertow. *Time* magazine described the surge of Japanese car imports into the United States in the early 1970s as a "business invasion" backed by "a mighty industrial economy that has been shaped by Oriental history and psychology." *Newsweek* announced Sony's purchase of Columbia Pictures in 1989 with a cover titled "Japan Invades Hollywood."

Even the conventional argument mounted by both Japan and later China to explain their persistent surpluses came with a sting in its tail. The Japanese and Chinese saved and invested; the Americans borrowed and spent. Economics 101 dictates that by definition in such circumstances the two countries would run current account surpluses with the United States. Underlying that simple, and incomplete, formula was the implication that their success was the fruit of hard work in solid industries, whereas America's failure was rooted in a slothful labor force and greedy financiers playing money games bereft of productive purpose. Needless to say, criticism of American capitalism became mainstream in the United States itself after the 2008 financial crisis and the subsequent deep recession. While Japan and China have both had their own systemic financial problems, nothing diminished the faith of both nations, and of much of the rest of Asia, in the U.S. colossus more than its addiction to using finance to drive economic growth and the seemingly regular crises this model left in its wake.

The Chinese sat on the sidelines during the battles between the United States and Japan, but they were watching the confrontation closely. In the early years of the twenty-first century, when Washington began to put pressure on Beijing to strengthen its tightly managed currency, Chinese officials responded by hectoring their U.S. counterparts about the Plaza Accord, the agreement that forced a massive revaluation of the yen. To offset the impact of a rising currency on exports in the mid-1980s, Japan's central bank flooded the economy with cheap money, which in turn rapidly bid up the price of shares and land. Japan's infamous bubble economy followed, peaking in 1989 and taking decades to deflate. The majority of Japanese policy makers didn't blame the Plaza Accord for the economic woes that came in the wake of the agreement. Rather, in retrospect, they blamed themselves for overreacting to the currency revaluation with an overly aggressive monetary easing, which fed the bubble.

The Chinese viewed the Plaza Accord through a darker lens. When David Loevinger arrived in Beijing in 2005 as the first Treasury officer to be posted to the U.S. embassy in China, carrying a brief to pressure the Chinese to revalue their currency, he found the Plaza Accord constantly being played back to him. The Chinese viewed the agreement as something that Washington had forced on Tokyo to stymie the threat to its global dominance from Asia. Japan's great stagnation, in other words, was more than just the product of American pressure. It was the result of a considered U.S. policy aimed at eliminating a competitor. "The consistent talking point on the exchange rate with China was 'We are never going to let you do to us what you did to Japan,'" Loevinger recalled. "I never stopped thinking that most Chinese leaders believed this version."

Although top leaders were less conspiratorial in their comments to their U.S. ministerial-level counterparts, Chinese officials stuck doggedly to this interpretation with officials from agencies like the World Bank and the International Monetary Fund, a sign that this was not some stray theory but official dogma. The Chinese sense of timing was astute, though, in one respect. In 2006, when the United States was pressing hard for a currency revaluation, China's share of global exports reached the same level that Japan had achieved in 1985, the year of the Plaza Accord.

One senior Japanese diplomat, and veteran of many tussles with the Americans, watched with cynical bemusement, and some admiration, China's parrying of U.S. pressure to widen access to its market. Shinichi Nishimiya was appointed Japan's ambassador to Beijing but tragically died in September 2012 before he could take up his post. He often privately observed how the Chinese made many promises to the Americans similar to the ones that the Japanese had made, pleading for time to corral intransigent domestic interests to restructure their economy, to wean it off a reliance on exports and investment, while always insisting that change was just around the corner. "The Chinese were smart," Nishimiya said during an earlier posting in Beijing in 2005. "We used to say exactly the same thing as what they are now, but it took us decades to realize that's what we had to do. The Chinese learned to say it much earlier than us."

For all the parallels between Washington's interactions with Tokyo and its later ones with Beijing, the geopolitical dimensions in the three-way relationship began to assert themselves decisively from the mid-1990s onward. Much of what remained of any idealism about China dissipated in the wake of the 1989 military crackdown on protesters in Beijing and other Chinese cities. Compared with Japan, China was a different beast—bigger, more nimble, more hostile to the West, and more formidable than any other rival the Americans had faced in the postwar period.

The United States, through a combination of idealism and arrogance, and confidence and insecurity, has often assumed that rival political systems will converge with its own democratic norms. The realization that a competitor may in fact be diverging from the U.S. model has the ability to galvanize Washington, in both positive and negative ways. The rolling crises with Japan forced U.S. industry to become more competitive but also triggered an ugly backlash from parts of the system that couldn't countenance the emergence of a rival power. Ultimately, Japan faded as an existential threat. China, by comparison, combined the economic competition of Japan with the security rivalry of the Soviet Union. It was, to use Amaya's formulation, a samurai and merchant nation all in one.

Richard Holbrooke, the longtime U.S. diplomat, said that every time during the cold war that U.S. and Japanese trade negotiations were on the verge of collapse, a deal would be justified by pointing to how Moscow benefited from disagreements. It wouldn't take long before the terms of that equation changed. Soon it was China, not the Soviet Union, that was bringing the Americans and Japanese back together. In turn, the United States quickly discovered the pressure it could bring to bear on a dependent ally like Japan couldn't be replicated with China.

"When the U.S. thought that Japan could be a threat to their status as a hegemon, they squeezed Japan with every means possible. That story is over," said a former MITI deputy-minister, Hidehiro Konno. "Japan is not a threat anymore; it is a mature economy and a status quo power. Now, Japan is a kind of safeguard.

"But they can't clamp down on China like they did to Japan."

THE NINETIES

CHAPTER SIX

Asian Values

How do we know that you won't abandon us for China? They are the new girl; we are the old mistress.

—Koichi Kato, Japanese politician

The economy is still stuck in the doldrums. They can't make any hard decisions. They've got a government that doesn't seem to be able to function at all. . . . Can anybody tell me what is wrong with Japan?

—Bill Clinton

Before he became known for his ruthless accumulation of power, Jiang Zemin stood out for his other, more eccentric qualities. No matter the setting, Jiang liked to impress interlocutors with impromptu snippets in their own language. In a celebrated interview with Mike Wallace on *60 Minutes,* Jiang recited several lines in English from the Gettysburg Address, a party trick he repeated for Bill Clinton. Jiang spoke some Russian and Romanian, from his time in those countries before the Sino-Soviet split. He snapped at pesky Hong Kong reporters in Cantonese and always dropped a few words in Shanghai's distinctive dialect on occasions when he was back in the city where he had first risen to prominence.

When he met the Japanese, Jiang did the same, trying to conjure up a few, almost childlike phrases, despite speaking little of the language. He greeted guests with a polite "suwatte kudasai" (please sit down). Once seated, according to Japanese diplomats, Jiang sometimes pointed to the ceiling and said, "Kore wa denki desu" (This is a light). The language demonstration over, Jiang would usually turn the conversation, in a less friendly tone, to history.

Jiang was initially dismissed as a transitional figure when he was made head of the Chinese Communist Party in May 1989, a creature of Deng Xiaoping and the council of elders who selected him at a moment of crisis in Beijing, weeks before PLA troops swept into the city to remove protesters. With little personal authority and hazy revolutionary credentials, Jiang initially had no choice but to stay in lockstep with his patrons. In his early years in power, he backed without apology the brutal military crackdown on demonstrators in Beijing and multiple other Chinese cities on June 4 and eventually swung behind economic liberalization at home. In time, both policies would come to be identified as his own, or at least reflecting his convictions. Around the same time, though, Jiang made another decision that, in retrospect, was out of character for someone who became known as vehemently anti-Japanese. In line with Deng's wishes, Jiang extended a hand of friendship to Tokyo, pressing Japan during a visit in 1992 to allow the emperor to visit China.

Although the origins of Jiang's animus toward the Japanese are contested, the prevailing view centers on his family's role during his upbringing near Nanjing in the war. Whatever his motivation, Jiang made no secret of his feelings. "I was never present in a conversation with Jiang in which he did not take a shot at the Japanese. It was an obsession of his," said Douglas Paal, who headed the National Security Council staff on Asia under George H. W. Bush. U.S. officials recall that during a meeting with Secretary of State Madeleine Albright in the late 1990s, Jiang delivered a lengthy diatribe about his upbringing in Yangzhou and the mistreatment of Chinese there by Japanese soldiers. On another occasion, he recounted how enemy soldiers set savage dogs onto citizens who had been half buried and left to die in the fields, a story that is a staple of Chinese accounts of Japanese ill deeds. In meetings with the Japanese, Jiang said he had been personally attacked by dogs set loose by the enemy during the war.

Beijing had invited the emperor to visit China for the first time in 1978, without receiving a positive response. After Hirohito's death early in 1989, and the showdown with pro-democracy protesters a few months later, Beijing's entreaties to Tokyo became more insistent. Isolated by economic and military sanctions imposed by the West, China turned to Japan to help drive a wedge into the coalition ranged against it. Qian

Qichen, China's most influential and effective foreign minister of the post-Mao era, didn't sugarcoat the purpose of Beijing's outreach to Tokyo after the event. The section of his memoirs describing the courting of Tokyo is titled "Divide and Demoralize the Anti-China Forces," something he never dared to say in public at the time. Japan, Qian wrote, was "the weakest link in the united front of Western sanctions against China, and therefore the best target for attacking those sanctions."

Over two millennia of Chinese influence in east Asia, a Japanese emperor had never crossed what the two countries called the "narrow waters" dividing the two states, neither during centuries of peace nor during the decades of war and rivalry from the late nineteenth century onward. There had been none of the intermarriage and throne sharing and swapping that characterized European royalty over the centuries nor the crossbreeding of their ruling classes. The emperor's visit to China, then, was a potentially momentous event in the history of the region's two most powerful nations.

More than any other developed country, Japan had pressed to end China's isolation and position its own businesses to profit from it. Between these two poles—Beijing's efforts to defeat the sanctions and Tokyo's attempt to gain an edge against American and European competitors—diplomats from both countries saw a fertile middle ground. As well as splitting the sanctions coalition, Qian admitted that China wanted to regain the support of the Japanese public, which it had lost on June 4. Tokyo was happy to be cultivated by Beijing. The pro-China crowd in Japan had not given up hope that they could draw Beijing out and encourage it to become a more open society and, in the process, stable and prosperous and less antagonistic to its neighbor. A friendlier China also had the potential to deliver another benefit to Japan: less reliance on an overbearing United States.

At this juncture, the Americans did not mind Japan getting ahead of them on China policy. The White House quietly backed Tokyo's rapprochement with Beijing, although its efforts were shrouded in secrecy for fear of a backlash in Congress. "We used Japan as a stalking horse to try to do things that we could not do because of Congress, to bring China out of the doghouse," said Paal. Jeff Bader, another NSC official, remembers Japan's prime minister Toshiki Kaifu writing a personal letter to Bush, arguing for the importance of not isolating China. "It was a good letter, encouraging Bush's best instincts," said Bader, who later returned to the NSC as Obama's Asia adviser. "We thought that it was good that we had cover from our Asian allies."

For both countries, a visit by the emperor to China exposed the multiple raw sensitivities that the bilateral relationship had always struggled to handle. For many Japanese conservatives, to even consider the emperor's role in, and responsibility for, the war impinged on the country's dignity. Months passed as Tokyo first sought assurances from Jiang and his colleagues that the emperor would not be asked to apologize for the war or, more vaguely, be forced to pay some kind of tribute to China as the center of civilization. Some right-wingers crudely demanded that Prime Minister Kiichi Miyazawa visit Yasukuni Shrine in exchange for their support. All of the acute emotional taboos that surrounded the emperor and the war unfolded in a tense, rolling debate.

In the summer of 1992, with the government in Tokyo sensing that enthusiasm for the trip was slipping away, Miyazawa dispatched one of Japan's top diplomats and China specialists, Sakutaro Tanino, to the parliament to quell rebellious conservatives. The prime minister and most of the party's power brokers supported the idea, but the cabinet was deadlocked. With far-right nationalist groups agitating against it, major business executives were too intimidated to speak up. Tanino sensed the moment he entered the room that the mood was against him.

As he started to speak, the MPs opposed to the trip began yelling over him, with wild theories about what would happen to the emperor and his wife, Michiko, should they set foot in China. "Some even argued that if the couple went to China, they would never come back. They would be arrested!" the diplomat recalled later. With no one willing to speak up in support, Tanino was left to fend for himself in front of the rowdy mob. On the way out of the meeting, Masaharu Gotoda, the LDP elder who had remained silent throughout, dryly commiserated with the furious diplomat: "That must have been tough for you."

In the final weeks of the government's deliberations, one radical nationalist occupied Miyazawa's electorate office in protest. Another sat outside the prime minister's Tokyo residence and tried to slit his stomach in ritual disembowelment. In late October, Akihito was delivering a speech at the opening ceremony for a national athletic meeting when he looked up to see an anti-China protester running toward him, a smoke bomb in hand. Tanino, a China specialist in the Ministry of Foreign

Affairs who was then on secondment to the prime minister's office, was stalked throughout by the right-wing ultranationalists and their trademark weapon of intimidation and harassment—the hulking, menacing sound trucks that still drive around Tokyo, screeching scurrilous, high-volume attacks against their enemies. "The sound trucks circled the Foreign Ministry, yelling, 'Bring out Tanino!'" he said. "To which the joke was, tell them I have already gone to the cabinet office."

In China, the controversy was better concealed but potent nonetheless. In its internal discussions, the party promoted the visit very differently, as a kind of ritual atonement for the war and a necessary precondition that Tokyo had to meet before China could send its head of state to Japan. None of this was stated publicly, because at the time Japan was strong and China relatively weak. Jiang, on a 1992 trip to Tokyo, was on his best behavior, playing the supplicant to his hosts and personally lobbying for the emperor's visit.

Decades later, however, when Xu Dunxin, one of China's top Japan diplomats who served as ambassador in Tokyo in the mid-1990s, described how Beijing viewed the trip, he had little to say about bilateral friendship and the like. Instead, he stated that the trip reflected "conventional practice," with Japan "as the defeated nation" having to send the emperor to visit China first, rather than the other way around. "We were the victorious state after [the war]," Xu observed. "Japan also knew this reality. If the emperor visited China, he must show a clear statement on this history issue." There was a large dose of sophistry in Xu's argument. Although they dared not admit it, even years later, Chinese officials at the time quietly reassured Tokyo they did not expect much in the way of an apology from the emperor. Xu's explanation was telling nonetheless, in the way that it reduced a historic visit by the emperor to just another episode in Beijing's preferred postwar narrative, of a defeated Japan being forced to make amends to a victorious China, a tale of winners and losers in a zero-sum game.

Once the visit was formally approved, the six-day trip in October 1992—taking in Beijing, the Tang dynasty capital of Xi'an, and Shanghai—went without a hitch. In a banquet speech the night of his arrival in Beijing in late October, Akihito acknowledged how Japan had "inflicted severe suffering upon the Chinese people. This is a deep sorrow to me." The emperor's carefully scripted utterances were painstakingly delivered, as always, in crackly tones interrupted by long, uncomfortable silences—as one writer put it, "filtering the emotion from a voice still ascribed supernatural qualities." Beijing, in turn, treated the emperor with a studied, friendly politeness, accepted his expression of regret for the war, and carefully screened any ordinary Chinese who came into contact with him, to ensure there would be no embarrassing protests.

The emperor and his wife were thrilled with the trip. After he returned to Tokyo, Akihito recounted in private conversations how he had overruled his security detail to command his motorcade, which had been instructed to speed through the streets of Shanghai, to slow down. It's not clear if Akihito realized where he was when he asked his driver to put the brakes on. But as he wound down the window to greet well-wishers, he would have been able to read the Chinese street signage. His motorcade was just then passing through one of Shanghai's main thoroughfares, Nanjing Road.

While the visit was hailed as a conspicuous success heralding a new era of diplomatic intimacy, the opposite proved to be the case. The two countries wouldn't enjoy as positive an exchange for at least another decade and a half. When Qian's memoirs were published years later, Japanese politicians and diplomats were furious at how the memoirs depicted Akihito as a political pawn, exploited by Beijing in a naked ploy to undercut Western sanctions.

The early 1990s marked a profound inflection point in the relationship between Japan, China, and the United States. The end of the cold war, the resounding U.S. victory over Iraq's Saddam Hussein in Kuwait, and China's emergence from isolation shifted the confidence and calculations of all three nations. Other factors weighed significantly in both recalibrating their connections and corroding strategic cooperation and goodwill. China's stunning comeback, spurred by Deng's victory on economic policy; Japan's sour decline as the country's postwar political and economic model foundered; and America's tech-driven resurgence—all combined to transform the east Asian landscape.

If China had been diplomatically agile, the symbolism of the emperor's pioneering visit might have marked a turning point of a very different kind. It was the start of another period, in the words of Kurt Campbell, who served in senior positions in the Pentagon under Bill

Clinton and in the State Department under Hillary Clinton, when Japan was "strategically available" to China. The long-standing but often dormant conviction that the country's future lay ultimately in Asia, and especially with China, began to blossom anew in Japan during these years. According to Campbell, "There was a cohort of people in the Diet and the LDP who believed their destiny lay in much closer ties with China. They talked openly about constructing a deeper relationship with Beijing." In combination with the sentiment in favor of so-called Asian values—the notion that the region had outlived the subservient, colonial-style relationship many countries felt they endured with the West—Japan could have drifted out of America's orbit altogether.

In hindsight, Washington needn't have worried about losing Japan. Jiang's invitation to the emperor was more a crafty feint than a heartfelt outreach. At the same time he was cultivating Tokyo to host the emperor in China, Jiang was laying the foundation at home for a deep and entrenched popular estrangement from its neighbor. Japan was about to become collateral damage to Beijing's most pressing priority at the time—to rebuild the vigor and legitimacy drained from the party and the military by the bloody events of 1989.

The popular uprisings in scores of Chinese cities that year, and their tragic denouement, had shaken the Communist leadership to its core. His "biggest mistake," Deng said later, was failing to prescribe a political education to anchor the disruptions of the market economy, an error he believed stoked visceral antiparty sentiment. Put another way, the masses had become ignorant of their country's history, as Deng said, "of what China was like in the old days." While continuing to maintain a role for the market in the economy, the party opened a vast new political front to ensure that such protests never got off the ground again.

The universities, which drove the upheaval, came under greater control; supervision of the courts was tightened; new riot squads to handle protests were trained, to ensure the prestige of the military was not undermined by using it to quell civilian disturbances; and tens of thousands of party members and ordinary civilians who had supported or participated in the protests were purged or jailed. Around the same time, China laid down a marker on the Diaoyu Islands, passing a new territorial sea law that included them as part of its territory.

Perhaps no initiative, though, had as deep an impact as two letters written by Jiang to the education minister and his deputy in March 1991. Jiang's two missives on the need for greater "patriotic education" didn't so much relaunch the history wars in China. After all, every policy shift in modern China, in the words of the scholar Geremie Barmé, has involved "the rehabilitation, re-evaluation, and revision of history and historical figures." Jiang's two missives' call for a new master narrative of Chinese history, which emphasized China's "bullying and humiliation" by foreigners from the mid-nineteenth century on, was transformative nonetheless. In the opening decades of party rule, Mao had always positioned China and the party itself as glorious victors over internal foes and foreign imperialists. In this account, driven by the Marxist motor of class struggle, China's primary enemies were ideological, led by the United States and the Nationalist administration under Chiang Kai-shek in Taiwan. The Japanese militarists were just one set of foes among many; the Japanese people themselves were exempted from blame altogether.

In the early 1990s, Jiang turned that story on its head, repositioning China as a victim rather than a victor, more patriotic than proletarian. In the new narrative, China's primary enemies were the West, including, and especially, Japan, which bore the most responsibility for the destruction of the country and the deaths of millions. The campaign injected patriotic history into official documents, school textbooks, university entrance exams, and popular culture. Jiang's initial letter instructed that the new history education extend "even to the children in kindergartens." By the time the campaign got its full-throttle launch in 1994, the party's ambitions had become grander and much more explicit. The party was now aimed at developing a "patriotic united front to the broadest extent possible, and directing and rallying the masses' patriotic passion to the great cause of building socialism with Chinese characteristics." Decoded, the campaign asserted that nothing less than the survival of the Communist Party, and through it modern China, was at stake. Or as Jiang later put it more succinctly, Chinese people could now be divided into two camps: patriots and scum.

Beijing's diktat cascaded down the administrative hierarchy, through provinces, cities, townships, and villages, resulting within a few years in scores of brick-and-mortar outlets for patriotic education. The Civil Affairs Ministry chose a hundred national sites to serve as "demonstration bases," the greatest number by far commemorating the anti-Japanese conflict. Beijing's actions spurred a similar selection of sacred sites by each level of government throughout the country. Just as Americans trek to the Lincoln Memorial in Washington, and the British to the War Museum in London, Chinese schoolchildren, government officials, and tour groups began traveling en masse to the museum commemorating the Nanjing Massacre, the most important of the new sacred sites.

The country's calendar was gradually modified to accommodate the party's new foundational narratives. Dates marking various wartime events that had not been previously heralded by the state began to get more attention from the authorities. These included July 7, commemorating the attack on the Marco Polo Bridge outside Beijing, considered the start of the Second Sino-Japanese War in 1937; September 2, for Japan's formal surrender in the Pacific War in 1945; and December 13, for the Nanjing Massacre. All were marked with ever weightier political pomp as the years passed.

The party's campaign resonated with Chinese citizens, for good reason. Millions of families had memories of suffering at the hands of the Japanese during the war, a trauma that the government had hitherto neglected. But the patriotic education campaign was never just about setting history right. In calibrating the party's actions, China analysts keep an eye not just on the anniversaries the party commemorates. As the Sinologist Simon Leys wrote, any analysis also had to take into account "the non-celebration of anniversaries, and the celebration of non-anniversaries" to get the true measure of political intent.

For the party, national humiliation was only one side of the ledger. At the same time that it poured massive resources into cataloging Japanese atrocities, it constructed a tightly policed, impenetrable wall around any frank examination of its own record: of the millions starved during the Great Leap Forward; of the families and institutions destroyed in the Cultural Revolution; of the deaths of civilians at the hands of the army on June 4, 1989; and so on. Patriots were given increasing space to mark the ill deeds of the Japanese. Others who wanted to look closer to home were relegated to the category of "scum."

The patriotic education campaign had far-reaching consequences for Chinese policy toward Japan. Local scholars, activists, and ordinary people now had room to vent their objections to Beijing's decades-old policy of seeking neither reparations nor a formal apology for the war.

The authorities' attitude toward the activists was ostensibly neutral: the official mantra was don't support; don't encourage. The authorities were cautious for good reason. After all, the architects of China's long-standing policy, which had forsworn reparations and apologies in favor of strategic priorities and economic cooperation, were the two titans of the revolution, Mao Zedong and Zhou Enlai.

Without license to repudiate the party's totemic figures, criticism of Mao and Zhou in the early 1990s was initially delivered in subdued, respectful terms. The two great leaders had been generous to the Japanese in forgoing reparations, the argument went, but it had hardly been their fault that the Japanese would prove to be so ungrateful. Perhaps their decision on reparations had been "too hasty," wrote one scholar, Zhu Jianrong, who also blamed the Japanese for taking advantage of Beijing's goodwill, stating, "China's relinquishing of such claims should be etched in the hearts of the Japanese people." Rather than confront the policy head-on, the critics gnawed away at it like termites until its intellectual and political foundations all but collapsed.

The criticism hardened as the decade went on. The authors of *The China That Can Say No*—somewhat ironically, a self-conscious national-ist screed like the Japanese book it took its title and inspiration from—suggested that Tokyo's historical recidivism was disrespectful to Zhou, a sly way of demanding a fresh approach to the issue. "When dealing with nations like Japan," the book said, "it would be a crime to the next gen-eration if China doesn't address the history problem." Mao and Zhou had based their policy on differentiating between Japanese militarists and the masses, a distinction that served their theories of international class struggle. By the mid-1990s, this approach was being mocked in China as "mumbo-jumbo." Such criticisms have remained prevalent in Chinese cyberspace ever since, along with attacks on the Foreign Minis-try, which manages national policy. In postings on popular Internet bul-letin boards not deleted by state censors, one netizen posted, "We were proud of repaying evil with good at the time, but reflecting upon this in hindsight, we were confused and doubtful." In another posting, Mao and Zhou were labeled simply as "traitors."

Jiang Zemin wasn't the only leader to get under Japan's skin around this time. The fall of the Berlin Wall and the Gulf War began to change

America's calculation toward Japan as well. The crumbling of the Soviet Union and America's stunning display of logistics and firepower against Iraq left little doubt in Japanese minds about which country was the world's true superpower. For the first time in more than a decade, Washington felt it had the upper hand with Tokyo.

In the weeks after Saddam Hussein invaded Kuwait in August 1990, George H. W. Bush had begun to pull together a global coalition to expel the Iraqi dictator's armies. For all the perils of such a high-risk military operation, Bush quickly secured support from a phalanx of European, Asian, and Arab countries, who provided everything from troops to engineers to medical personnel. In face-to-face meetings, in phone calls, and through emissaries, Bush gently let "his friend Toshiki" know that Washington wanted a concrete contribution from its richest ally as well. Prime Minister Toshiki Kaifu and his government had initially condemned the invasion, locked down Iraqi assets, and stood ready to apply sanctions. Then the system in Tokyo froze.

Since the end of the Pacific War, the Japanese government had never dispatched its military overseas, and local voters didn't care to press it to do so now. Washington's argument that Japan had a bigger stake than almost any other country in securing oil from the Middle East cut little ice with much of Tokyo's political and business elites. They had long cultivated their own relationships with energy-rich states in the region and assumed they could buy oil on the market whatever the circumstances. For the Japanese, the Iraqi invasion was like the classic "fire on the other side of the river," best left to people nearby to put out.

When Washington asked Japan for logistics assistance and transport aircraft to carry supplies to the Middle East, and later supply ships and tankers, the requests were either parried, denied, or refused on constitutional and legal grounds. Tokyo considered chartering private aircraft to help with logistics, but Japanese businesses were resistant to venturing near a war zone. The government raised the idea of sending a hundred medical volunteers, but only ten applied, and they refused to go into battle zones, too. In the end, Japan did dispatch a fleet of minesweepers to the gulf, but not until the spring of 1991, two months after the fighting had finished.

Even then, Kaifu shrank from aligning himself too closely with the deployment. He refused an invitation to see off the minesweepers in person, instead watching their departure on TV. After the ceremony, he had a staff member write to the defense agency, demanding to know why it was sending the ships off with "military march music." Far from being like a porcupine with rabbit's ears, prickly and alert, as Yasuhiro Nakasone described Tokyo's security policy, Japan began to be regarded by U.S. diplomats as more akin to a tortoise—making slow, steady progress in a set direction but, when frightened, withdrawing its head into its shell and remaining immobile.

The record of Bush's conversations with Kaifu display a consummate, old-style diplomat trying to coax the tortoise out of its shell. "I am so glad to hear your voice, Toshiki," Bush said, taking one call at dinner upstairs at the White House with his wife, Barbara, by his side. "Bar will be pleased," he adds when Kaifu invites the couple to Japan. On Iraq, Bush counseled coalition solidarity, reminded Japan of its great status and global obligations, and tried to ensure that any one announcement would not preclude more commitments in the future. "I think Japan's global role is being carefully watched," he told Kaifu, "and I want to ensure that nothing comes out of this that allows criticism of the US-Japan relationship."

Kaifu, an energetic but weak leader at the mercy of the LDP's warlords, tried to respond in kind, promising in a series of exchanges that Japan would stay in lockstep with the United States and its partners. "We will be sweating with you," he told Bush, just weeks ahead of the first U.S. troop deployments, as he struggled to get the parliament and ministries to lend support to the effort. Later, meeting with Vice President Dan Quayle, Kaifu sheepishly walked back this formulation, saying, "We might sweat with you," while admitting he had not yet been persuasive enough with his colleagues to ensure a concrete Japanese contribution.

Behind the scenes, Bush's cabinet members were not nearly as diplomatic as the White House. With little on offer from Japan, Bush's frustrated secretary of state, James Baker, began ratcheting up pressure to get as much money as possible out of Tokyo to pay for the war. It was a task that the Texas lawyer was well suited for. "Basically, Baker didn't like the Japanese; he didn't enjoy dealing with them," recalled one of his top advisers. Baker's official travel schedule in office sent much the same message: as America's chief diplomat, he visited Mongolia more than he went to Japan. In the words of the same adviser, "We were brutally harsh on the Japanese (and the Saudis) to force them to fund for the Gulf War.

Baker was determined to have them do it, and when Baker was determined about something, he was a tough guy to deal with."

The hostility toward Tokyo and the sense that it was moving from being an ally of the United States to being a rival were widespread in the Bush administration. For all his velvet-gloved treatment of Kaifu, Bush himself harbored sentiments similar to Baker's, and the ongoing tangles over trade with Tokyo had only hardened views in Washington. A Treasury official recalled a meeting chaired by David Mulford, then the head of the department's international affairs division. The issue at hand was the U.S. position on South Korea's joining the ranks of developed nations in the Organisation for Economic Co-operation and Development, a status that brought with it the prestige of being admitted to an exclusive club. Mulford was not thrilled about South Korea's application, because he regarded its economy as overly protectionist. Thumping the table, Mulford exclaimed, "We are not going to allow another Japan into the OECD!" (South Korea eventually joined the OECD in 1996.)

Tim Geithner, then a young Treasury attaché posted in Tokyo, was one of many U.S. officials given the task of lobbying the Finance Ministry to provide funds for the war. These efforts were known as "tin cup" missions, a self-deprecating tag that also underlined the discomfort that Americans like Geithner felt about asking for money. In his memoirs, published after he retired as Barack Obama's Treasury secretary in 2013, Geithner said he was uneasy about Washington's paternalism toward Japan during this period, observing, "There was something ridiculous about the dance of American officials pressuring Japan to restructure its economy in our image."

In the end, Tokyo contributed a massive $13 billion to underwrite the ouster of Saddam Hussein from Kuwait and earned little gratitude and a large measure of contempt for its troubles. Dick Cheney, the secretary of defense during the war, was still boasting about the deal decades later. At a conference in late 2016, he extolled the funding of the Gulf War as a model for the exercise of U.S. power. "We ended up with a $60 billion war and only paid $5 billion," he said. The process to extract a contribution was so exacting that Japan ended up with the worst of both worlds in Washington. "This is the only bureaucracy on the planet that could give you billions of dollars and still piss you off," said one of America's most experienced Japan diplomats, then stationed in Tokyo. MITI's

Naohiro Amaya's old argument, about how Japan could prosper as a "merchant nation" while leaving "samurais" like the United States to fight its wars, never looked more threadbare. Japan painfully rediscovered an old lesson: the banker never gets the respect of a soldier.

When it came to Beijing, Washington asked neither for cash nor a rousing display of support for the war. But even extracting the one thing that Washington did want—that Beijing not use its Security Council veto to block United Nations cover for the war—was difficult. Qian Qichen, China's foreign minister, was disdainful of Baker's style, which he said was not that of a diplomat. "At the negotiating table, he liked to say: 'Let's make a deal,'" recalled Qian in his memoirs. "He tended to treat everything as if it were a business transaction." In the end, China did not vote to approve military action, nor did it exercise its veto. Instead, it abstained and in return extracted a visit to the White House, the first by a senior Chinese official since 1989. As far as Qian was concerned, Baker was lucky to get even the abstention. Qian said the war the United States had waged against Korea four decades earlier under the banner of the United Nations was still "fresh in Chinese minds," not to mention the post-1989 sanctions, which were still intact. It was a telling statement of the Chinese mind-set. "Considering all this," said Qian, "it would be a great favor on China's part if it did not veto the draft."

In Washington, the rapid military victory in the Gulf War upended the popular notion of Tokyo as an emerging global force surpassing a decrepit United States. In the phrase popular at the time, Japan was an economic superpower but a political pygmy. Tokyo's critics felt vindicated in their depiction of Japan as a self-centered, mercantilist state that could not be relied upon in an emergency. The Japanese, by contrast, were left distressed and embittered. Tokyo's global partnership with the United States looked more and more like one in which the Americans dictated the terms and the Japanese paid the bill. After Japan's heady rise in previous decades, it was an abrupt, humiliating comedown.

After the Gulf War debacle, political leaders in Japan could feel the earth moving under their feet, and few would have chosen Ichirō Ozawa as the politician with the agility to shift with it. A power broker in the LDP's dominant faction, Ozawa had been tutored in the dark arts of politics by the system's master, Kakuei Tanaka. Ozawa was more than just Tanaka's protégé. "Tanaka looked after me as if he were my father, even in private matters," Ozawa said of his mentor. Worried about Ozawa's carousing ways in his early thirties, Tanaka even chose a wife for him, informing him of it without warning in his office one day and setting the wedding day three months hence. Ozawa dutifully obeyed.

By the early 1990s, Ozawa had risen to become the LDP's number one appointed official, the party's chief fund-raiser, and a factional king-maker. To pay for the party's campaign for the 1990 election, he had simply gone to the Keidanren, Japan's leading business body, and de-manded $200 million up front, saying, "Business ought to bear the costs of democracy." Gruff, dismissive, and physically resembling a "toad who had just licked something bitter," Ozawa was the apotheosis of an old-style machine politician.

Just as he was reaching the peak of his powers, though, Ozawa was becoming disillusioned with traditional politics as a game to divide up the spoils of Japan Inc. between the LDP and the long-standing opposi-tion Socialist Party. In theory, a spirited, principled alternative, the So-cialists were in fact funded under the table by LDP power brokers and remained institutionally hostile to any compromise of the kind needed to win government. Throughout the postwar era, the Socialists refused to recognize the alliance with Washington, as well as the Japanese flag and national anthem, which they regarded as imperialist relics of the occupation. They also considered the self-defense forces unconstitu-tional. Such dogmatism maintained the loyalty of their base, but it also relegated them to permanent opposition. Ozawa likened the two politi-cal parties to a couple lounging in lukewarm baths: "Somewhere along the way, . . . the bathers forgot the fundamental democratic principle that they must at least occasionally change places."

There was a more cynical explanation for Ozawa's attitude: he knew that the old postwar political system was on the verge of collapsing, along with Japan's economic model. Whatever his motivation, the fiasco of the Gulf War was the tipping point for Ozawa, who called the episode a "de-feat" for Japan. "The only function our government is expected to perform is to enable private interests to pursue their profits," he declared. In place of this inert, isolationist mind-set, Ozawa began promoting the idea of Japan as a "normal nation," one that had to claim its rightful place in the post-cold-war world. It was an anodyne description of a radical idea.

The new Japan Ozawa envisaged would no longer be a permanent one-party state of the kind that had ruled the country since the 1950s, one driven by economic nationalism and authoritarian administrators. Everything was now on the table: a more active role for the military under the auspices of the United Nations, an economy restructured in favor of consumers rather than producers, and an end to the cozy relationship between the LDP and the Socialists. Most radically of all, Japan as a "normal nation" would be less subservient to the United States and closer to Asia, and China.

In 1993, the attitude of the incoming Clinton administration accelerated the drive for change in Japan. Early in his presidency, Clinton himself had little concern for security issues in Asia. Asked whether Clinton was interested in the region, one of the administration's intelligence appointees, the eminent east Asia academic Ezra Vogel, replied, "Yes, the day before he goes there." Clinton's advisers likewise displayed no appreciation for Tokyo's bedrock role in regional security. The new administration saw Tokyo solely through the prism of trade and the anger of American union constituencies, especially in the auto-manufacturing heartland around Michigan and Ohio. Rust Deming, the State Department's Japan specialist, recalls his first bruising encounters with senior Clinton officials to discuss policy toward Tokyo. "They always said, 'You guys, the alliance managers, always kept a leash on us. Now the cold war is over. It's our turn. You get out of the way.'"

The Clinton White House was convinced that setting import targets for Japan, with prohibitive penalties if they fell short, was the only way to get results. In the words of the administration's economist Laura Tyson, "With Japan, something akin to managed trade is often required to achieve something akin to a market outcome." As it turned out, the market was already moving on by then, in all three countries. By the time Clinton came to office, Japan was more than two years into a two-decade-long slump, in contrast with America's robust resurgence and China's stellar growth. For the now-ascendant school of Japan revisionists in Washington, who were convinced that Tokyo had invented a perpetual money machine, the notion that the Japanese economy had run out of steam took time to take root. "They were really fighting the last war," said Deming. "But no one had figured that out yet."

Ozawa, for his part, was already positioning himself for the unraveling of the postwar system. In mid-1993, he left the LDP with a band of sup-porters, marking the end of the party's uninterrupted thirty-eight years of rule. From that point until 1996, the stability provided by the old sys-tem crumbled. There were three changes of government in Tokyo, five prime ministers, and eleven different parties sharing power. With eco-nomic stagnation setting in, the traditional postwar game of Japanese politics—redistributing the spoils of high growth—was gone for good.

The turmoil at the top in Tokyo and the preoccupation with settling ac-counts on trade in Washington all contributed to a palpable sense of discord in U.S.-Japan ties. The relationship was, in the words of one U.S. official later in the decade, "like a glacier breaking apart, with pieces drifting off in different directions." Mike Mansfield, a veteran of Con-gress who had served as U.S. ambassador to Japan for eleven years begin-ning in 1977 and who became a fervent advocate of good ties with Tokyo, used to say the alliance was the "most important bilateral relationship in the world, bar none." By the early 1990s, Mansfield's mantra was well and truly out of fashion. In the vacuum left by the retreating alliance was a new idea taking grip in the region, the notion that Asians could replace the West with their own unique developmental values. The inevitable result of greater Asian solidarity, to the alarm of the advocates for a stronger U.S.-Japan alliance, was a diminished role in the region for the United States.

Japan had not always been receptive to the idea that it was part of an Asian cultural bloc. In the late nineteenth century, it had agitated to be counted alongside the advanced countries of the West rather than back-ward Asia. When Japanese leaders had embraced Pan-Asianism during the Pacific War, they had done so with a nasty, and ultimately disastrous, sense of superiority. By the 1990s, the mood was changing. The latest manifestation of regional solidarity—promoted with the most gusto by Singapore's Lee Kuan Yew in an image of the successful, soft authoritar-ian city-state he founded—was built on a stronger foundation. After Japan had built a miracle economy in defiance of U.S. business nostrums and seemingly getting little other than criticism from Washington for its efforts, much of the country's intellectual elite was warming to the idea of the rise of Asia as well.

The proselytizers of "Asian values" argued that the Confucian glue that united the region was founded on hard work, thrift, filial piety, and national pride. The United States, by contrast—so the argument went— was characterized by high crime rates, decaying morals, and a lack of social discipline. Asia's rise, in that context, was portrayed as a model of peaceful coexistence in contrast with the unstable, war-prone West. Mahathir Mohamad, Malaysia's prime minister, tried to give concrete expression to this purported cultural clash of civilizations with a plan for an east Asian caucus to act as the premier regional talk shop. Mahathir, who loved to play up racial divisions with the West, deliberately excluded the United States and nations like Australia, earning it the nickname the "caucus without Caucasians." As Asia's premier power, the United States was furious at Washington's exclusion. The hard, nationalistic edge that Mahathir brought to the debate was exemplified by the book he co-authored with Shintaro Ishihara. This time, it was titled *The Asia That Can Say No.*

The "Asian values" debate overlooked a number of inconvenient truths, notably that the region's peaceful postwar coexistence, far from being somehow organic to local political cultures, had been underwritten by the U.S. military. The rise of "Asian values" was a source of great pride to Tokyo, because Japan was by far the region's most successful country, but it also played into the country's deeply conflicted impulses: to be part of the West but rid of it as well; to embrace Asia but maintain its distance; and above all, to be part of the world or simply be allowed to keep to itself. Equally, just as the presence of U.S. military in Japan grated at Tokyo's sense of independence, few leaders were willing to countenance the policies required to secure the country in the event the Americans left. Paradoxically, the popularity of Asian values was gathering momentum at the moment when the Japan model was reaching its use-by date. Rather than focusing on Japan, regional attention was now shifting to China.

Joseph Nye sensed the new mood when he traveled to Japan in 1994 as a senior Pentagon official with Secretary of Defense William Perry. Nye, one of the latter-day "wise men" of U.S. foreign policy straddling academia and government, had served the Clinton administration as chair of the National Intelligence Council before being appointed to the Pentagon. Along with other officials in Washington, both Democratic and Republican, he was as frustrated by his government's approach as many Japanese. They believed that the Japan threat was exaggerated and overlooked the more pressing issue of how to handle a rising China. "We faced a great deal of suspicion from the Clinton people," Nye said.

A circuit breaker was needed, and it arrived in the form of North Korea. By mid-1994, the White House had become so alarmed about Pyongyang's nuclear program that it had formulated plans to bomb the country's main reactor at Yongbyon to prevent the recovery of plutonium stored there to make a weapon. The administration worried, however, that a regional war could easily break out, leaving Japan directly in Pyongyang's line of fire. In an echo of the first Gulf War, Japan's almost blasé initial response to another potential crisis—"that it would do what it could within the constraints of the constitution"—infuriated Washington. A group of senators meeting the Japanese foreign minister, Tsutomu Hata, were dumbstruck by his noncommittal stance. "America sends its young off to a distant place, exposing them to danger, and Japan docs nothing," said one senator. "What do you mean by doing nothing?"

In the formal meeting with Perry and Nye, the Japanese explained they were reluctant to issue a tough public statement about North Korea, because they were worried about the reaction in China. Over a drink later in Perry's room in the Hotel Okura, the real nature of Japan's anxieties—namely, the United States' bypassing Japan for China—emerged. "They would say, Nye-san, we notice that China is getting very strong. How do we know that you won't abandon us for China? They are the new girl; we are the old mistress," Nye recalled, quoting Koichi Kato. "I told them there is no hope of abandoning you. You are a democracy and an ally." Nye's words almost precisely echoed the reassurances that had been delivered to the Japanese earlier by Henry Kissinger and other Americans. Nye says that Kissinger had often warned him in private to beware of a China-Japan alliance, a prospect Nye dismissed. But the Japanese hand-wringing over U.S. steadfastness made a strong impression. "It was clear they were very worried," Nye said. "The immediate factor was North Korea. The real background was China."

When Nye oversaw the publication of the Pentagon's security strategy for east Asia the following year, many of the ideas he and like-minded colleagues had promoted were effectively codified in policy. In the Pentagon's eyes, the refreshed post-cold-war U.S.-Japan alliance would put pressure on China "to define its interests in ways that could be compatible with ours." The idea put forth after the cold war's close—of a troop drawdown in Japan and Asia—was tossed aside. "I can remember going to the White House, where everyone was talking about the economic situation," says Nye. "I said, we have a problem in North Korea and we are going to need Japan. That switch in mood was important." After a few years of Tokyo's being left out in the cold in Washington, the new headline message was clear: Japan was restored to its central position as a security ally rather than a trade foe.

The U.S.-Japan alliance—in the words of the historian Kenneth Pyle, "a strange, anomalous joining of two nations with vastly different histories and values, thrown together after a bitter and merciless war"—was gaining an improbable new life. More important, the security pact had a coherence that was lacking in its earlier incarnations. Rather than Washington's allocating a role for Tokyo in its own global cold war strategy, the United States and Japan were now starting to focus on their shared interest in managing the great-power challenge from China on the horizon.

In Japan, it was a welcome change. Tokyo had been obsessed with "Japan bashing" during the trade wars, a term that came to be applied to any criticism of the country, reasonable or not. By the mid-1990s, commentators were talking not of "Japan bashing" but of "Japan passing" as a characterization of how the United States might ignore Japan in favor of building closer ties with China. By the end of the decade, the mournful Japanese had begun to speak melodramatically of "Japan nothing," as though Japan didn't matter at all. Such concerns were nonsense, of course. Even after years of stagnation, the Japanese economy was responsible for two-thirds of Asian output. But the self-flagellating catchphrases underlined a larger truth—that the Japanese narrative had become one about weakness and mismanagement, not strength and invincibility.

Ahead of one of Clinton's final trips to Japan as president in the summer of 1999, Rust Deming recalled being called to the White House. About a dozen of Clinton's top economic and political advisers were huddled around a table, with an agitated president sitting at its head. Clinton looked at his briefing book and started to rant, "I've been to Japan twice, and this is the fifth Japanese prime minister that I've met with. We've been talking about the same issues, with the same talking points about their economy, and nothing has changed. Why are we even going on this trip? It's a waste of time. They keep saying the same thing and nothing ever happens. The economy is still stuck in the doldrums. They can't make any hard decisions. They've got a government that doesn't seem to be able to function at all. . . . Can anybody tell me what is wrong with Japan?" When he finished, there was an embarrassed silence around the table. One adviser turned to another, before Madeleine Albright turned to Deming. "Rusty, do you want to give it a shot?"

By the time he left office, Clinton had dealt with seven Japanese prime ministers. During a break in one meeting in the White House, Madeleine Albright and Sandy Berger, Clinton's national security adviser, passed around a blank piece of paper challenging the attendees to name all seven, in order. No one, including Albright and Berger, got their names, and the order in which they served, correct. Clinton had noticed his aides chuckling on the sidelines of the meeting, and afterward he asked Berger what they had been doing. Once told, the president grabbed a pen and wrote down all seven names, correctly and in order.

From the mid-1990s onward, trade no longer threatened to trump national security in dealing with Tokyo. The "Japan threat," as a political issue, was dead. The fears concerning Japan's pivoting to Asia would return with a vengeance just over a decade later, when Ozawa again began attempting to steer Japan closer to China. In the meantime, though, Japan had other problems to contend with, problems it had hoped it had left far behind. Fifty years after Japan's surrender, the history wars were about to become more toxic than they had ever been, now intertwined with an increasingly assertive China and the sensitive issue of Taiwan. Clinton, in the meantime, having made a peace of sorts with Tokyo, now tried to do the same with Beijing.

CHAPTER SEVEN

Apologies and Their Discontents

The U.S. will lose its share of the big China market.
　　　　　　　—Li Peng, the Chinese premier, to American visitors

Supporting the Taiwan regime to keep China off-balance has been an established policy of every American administration.
　　　　　　　—Qian Qichen, Chinese foreign minister

Henry Kissinger didn't waste any time on small talk as he sat down in the Oval Office with Bill Clinton in July 1995, his first visit in the White House with the Democratic president. "As you know," Kissinger said, "we have never asked for a meeting with you before." The president had assembled his national security team and Vice President Al Gore for the gathering. Accompanying Kissinger were grandees of the U.S.-China relationship, including Hank Greenberg, of AIG, the insurance giant, and John Whitehead, an alumnus of Goldman Sachs and the State Department. Kissinger and his associates had just returned from China with a grim message about Beijing's view of the state of its relationship with the United States. They had met there with members of the Politburo and the foreign minister, as well as Deng Xiaoping's family, who carried the mantle of their ailing father. One after another, the visitors told Clinton that they had never seen bilateral relations as bad since the 1972 opening. They even countenanced the two countries going to war. Kissinger told the group that Li Peng, the hard-line premier, had brusquely asked him, "Does the United States see China as our enemy?"

In the crosshairs of the conflict was Taiwan. After years of authoritarian rule, the self-governing island had blossomed as a democracy in the early 1990s and was now agitating for greater recognition globally. Under pressure from Congress, the Clinton administration had allowed Lee Teng-hui, Taiwan's president, to visit his alma mater, Cornell University, in New York State, after Washington had earlier reassured Beijing that it would not grant him a visa. For the Chinese, the administration's reversal on Lee's visa was part of an insidious pattern of behavior aimed at undermining Communist Party rule. Washington's post-1989 sanctions against China were still in place. In 1992, toward the end of his term, George H. W. Bush had shocked the Chinese by selling Taiwan F-16 fighter jets. Bush had engineered the deal to shore up votes in Texas, where the plane was manufactured, but China saw a more sinister motive. The visa was the last straw, serving as proof to Beijing that Washington was abrogating the "one China" policy that it had adopted since Kissinger's secret trip two and a half decades earlier.

Kissinger was always seen as carrying water for China in Washington. Later, he did business in China through his consultancy, which further colored perceptions of his views. Nixon's former national security adviser exuded a proprietary sense toward his relationship with the nation as well and always felt compelled to explain the vast hinterland of history that he perceived to be behind Chinese leaders' calculations. "We have to take into account the idiosyncrasies built up over 5,000 years," he told Clinton. "I tried," Clinton replied.

But Kissinger and his group were surely not exaggerating when they warned Clinton that the relationship was deeply strained. "If it comes to a choice between good relations with the United States and Taiwan's independence, they would rather have bad relations with the U.S.," said Kissinger. In China's eyes, even if Americans weren't actively supporting Taiwanese independence, once the process started, it couldn't be controlled. A few days before the White House meeting, China had made its intentions clear, announcing it would start missile tests near Taiwan later that month.

Clinton's response to his distinguished visitors' alarming prognosis in many respects typified his approach to foreign policy during his first term. Rather than engage in a debate on Taiwan, the president complained about his domestic political woes, a fight over closing military bases in California, and the "funhouse" on Capitol Hill under the new House Speaker, Newt Gingrich, and the now-dominant Republicans. In Clinton's view, the real issue with China was not U.S. policy but Beijing's inability to appreciate the scope of his problems at home. "[China] can't seem to stop asking that this relationship be a one-way street," he said. "We're making every effort to factor in their domestic political situation. Why can't they do the same for us?" As if to underline how Beijing should be more sensitive to Washington's concerns, Clinton strangely asserted that U.S. foreign aid was buying "30 percent" of China's exports, at which point Al Gore chimed in: "They seem to be so out of touch."

Clinton didn't make a policy speech on China during his first term, and his National Security Council did not hold a meeting devoted to the subject in his first three years in office. The president's first meeting with Jiang Zemin in Seattle in 1993 at a summit of Asia-Pacific leaders went poorly. In the kind of experience that many foreigners encountering Chinese officials were familiar with, Clinton asked Jiang a softball question about the state of the economy at the outset and got a forty-five-minute monologue heavy with facts and figures from the Chinese leader in reply. The pair was left little time for a genuine exchange. For a president trying to engage with Jiang on a personal level, the meeting was a failure.

Just as Clinton had a singular focus on trade with Japan after coming to office, his administration's policy on China had been built around human rights. That policy crumbled during Secretary of State Warren Christopher's infamous trip to Beijing in 1994. Christopher traveled there with a brief to demand an improvement in human rights in exchange for better access to the U.S. market for Chinese goods. By then, China's economy had already begun to grow rapidly out of its post-1989 torpor. The Chinese always sensed demons when foreigners pressed them on political reform, even more so after the near-death experience of 1989. The hard-liners in particular, having failed to hold back market reforms, were ready to battle the United States on what was a fundamental issue for the CCP: internal political control. Viewed from that perspective, Clinton's complaint—that the relationship was a "one-way street" in Beijing's favor—was preposterous.

To underline their position, the Chinese detained a host of dissidents before and during Christopher's trip. Then, to drive their point home, Li Peng lectured Christopher with such contempt and rancor at a formal meeting in Beijing, about how human rights were none of the Americans' business, that the U.S. delegation considered walking out. Li scoffed at America's own human rights record, pointing to the 1992 Los Angeles race riots, and dared the United States to keep trade restrictions in place, warning, "The U.S. will lose its share of the big China market." Not all U.S. officials thought the blame for the clash lay entirely in Beijing. Stapleton Roy, the U.S. ambassador, said the administration had never managed to agree on what benchmarks China should reach on human rights in any case. "It was amateur hour," as he described it. Two months later, Clinton abandoned his policy altogether. It was a decisive moment. America's concern for human rights in China had always waxed and waned, but the Christopher debacle permanently shunted it aside as a critical factor in favor of developing U.S. strategic and commercial interests.

If some in Washington had underestimated the strategic import of China after it fell into isolation in the wake of the 1989 protests, Clinton was waking up to how shortsighted such a view was. Unlike during his election campaign, when Beijing seemed weak and fractured, he now faced a China with an increasingly cohesive leadership and a rapidly expanding economy hugely attractive to American business. Toward the end of his office meeting with the self-styled wise men of the bilateral relationship, Clinton finally acknowledged the challenges in rebuilding ties with Beijing. "I've been worried sick about [China] the last several days," he told his visitors, although for his final word he drifted back to domestic politics. At the same time that Gingrich had been making "outrageous statements" about China, Clinton complained, he had been asking the White House to help send the newer Republican members there. A year later, when he was concerned that China might actually be preparing to attack Taiwan, Clinton would have a lot more to worry about than Gingrich.

Few people were better placed, and more intent on bringing to life Taiwan's distinct identity, than Lee Teng-hui. Taiwan's president was born and raised under the Japanese colonial administration and proud of it. Far from shying away from his background, he listed his birthplace as "Empire of Japan." His Japanese roots went deep. Lee's father worked for the colonial police, and his brother died fighting for the Imperial Army in the Philippines. Lee was fluent in Japanese, his first language, and the local dialect, Hokkien. His thickly accented standard Chinese was his third language. As with many politicians on an island with a diverse range of accents, viewers often had to rely on subtitles to understand his Chinese during local television appearances. Lee had only spent ten days in China in his life, in Japanese-occupied Qingdao in 1944, when the boat taking him from Taiwan for training in Japan's artillery academy was diverted to avoid an Allied blockade. He never returned to China, and later studied in the United States. Not surprisingly, Lee felt no warmth or loyalty toward a country that Beijing insisted he should think of—politically, emotionally, and indeed instinctively—as the motherland. In a single, powerful individual, Lee personified all of Beijing's fears about Taiwan.

Along with North Korea, the unfolding confrontation over Taiwan filled the vacuum in Washington left by the dismantling of Clinton's China policy. The Taiwan crisis also divided policy makers in Tokyo, triggering a fundamental reassessment of the balance between engaging China and tightening security ties with the United States. At the time the United States and Japan had recognized Beijing and cut off ties with Taipei in the 1970s, they were exchanging one authoritarian regime for another. The political landscape had changed dramatically since then. Taiwan's democratization and China's reaction to it challenged many of the assumptions that had held since Washington and Tokyo had adopted a one-China policy. Now the United States and Japan were forced to recalibrate policy, to deal with a needy Taiwan and an angry, reassertive China.

Lee's heretical views were largely buried in his early career, when he was a rising star in a Nationalist Party formally committed to retaking the mainland. Ever since the Nationalists had fled to Taipei in 1949, the self-styled Republic of China in exile maintained the pretense that it ruled over all of China extending to the country's bloated, pre-Communist borders, a vast expanse that included Mongolia. In other words, the Nationalists, who controlled the government on the small island of Taiwan, carried on as if they governed one of the largest landmasses in the world.

This charade was given life in the National Assembly, which was filled with mostly elderly men still purporting to represent the provinces in China they had fled from decades earlier. In effect, the same National Assembly elected in 1947 in mainland China remained intact in Taiwan until 1991, although few of the original representatives had survived. A number had even gone to live in America while retaining their seats and the privileges of office in Taipei. Beijing was happy to go along with this farce, because it accorded with the principle of a single, indivisible China. Once Taiwan began to open up, though, the old structures started to fall apart.

Lee owed his elevation to Chiang Ching-guo, Chiang Kai-shek's son and successor, who tapped him as vice president in the mid-1980s. Chiang backed Lee not only for his technocratic abilities honed as Taipei's mayor. He promoted him as part of a deliberate policy of Taiwanization of the ruling party and the government, to make it less heavy with the mainlanders who had dominated politics since 1949. Chiang also understood that Taiwan would only survive by opening up and had gingerly begun to liberalize the island's political system. On Chiang's death in 1988, Lee took over as chairman of the Nationalist Party and, in turn, as the island's first locally born president. While Chiang hoped to reinvigorate the Nationalists with his reforms, with his choice of Lee he inadvertently planted the seeds for the party's eventual fall.

Many of Lee's mainland-born colleagues in the Nationalist Party distrusted him as a native Taiwanese with little enthusiasm for the dogma of reunification and tried to stop him from becoming president. Their fears were well founded. Lee began to dismantle the pillars of the old regime to give voice to the local demands for democracy that had been suppressed by the Nationalists. He released political prisoners and cultivated the fledgling opposition. In 1991, he ended the state of war with mainland China, which had always been used to justify authoritarian rule. The repeal of the civil war edict, which still went by the baroque official name given to it in 1949—the Temporary Provisions Effective During the Period of Communist Rebellion—cleared the way for the biggest change of all, democratic elections, first for the parliament and then, in 1996, for the presidency.

Lee encouraged the Taiwanese to think of their country as an entity distinct from the Communist mainland. Internationally, he flaunted Taiwan's democratization, talked about his "strong feelings" toward Japan, and insisted his country should be in the United Nations. Above all, he played for time, building Taiwan's domestic strength and global profile in order to avoid being "swallowed alive," as he put it, by China. In a remarkable interview with a Japanese journalist in 1994, Lee upped the ante even further. His comments, and the forum in which he chose to air them, could hardly have been more inflammatory in Beijing's eyes.

Lee called the Nationalists "an alien regime," talked about the importance of learning Taiwanese, and grandly compared his role to that of Moses, leading the exodus from Egypt to build another country elsewhere. Having thus successfully driven a wedge between China and Taiwan, he turned his attention to the United States, where he sought to divide the White House and Congress.

In the early 1990s, China embodied everything members of Congress believed the United States should stand against in the world. In the words of Robert Suettinger, then on the staff of the National Security Council, it considered China a tyrannical regime, intolerant of religion, a trade cheat, an arms proliferator, a military threat, and a "murderer of unborn children" through its one-child policy. "Whether those formulaic perceptions accorded with reality or not, they were strongly held by congressional leaders," said Suettinger. Such perceptions made Washington a soft target for Lee's campaign to overturn the White House's decision to refuse him entry to the United States to speak at Cornell University, his alma mater. With the help of a Washington lobbying firm hired at a cost of $4.5 million, Taiwan sold itself aggressively on Capitol Hill as a U.S.-friendly democracy battling an overbearing authoritarian state. If the White House had been willing to host Gerry Adams of the Irish Republican Army that year, the lobbyists argued, why not a fledgling democracy being denied diplomatic legitimacy by anti-American Communists?

As late as April 1995, Warren Christopher had assured Qian Qichen that the White House still opposed the visa while playing down the possibility that Congress might decide otherwise. Qian delivered only the first part of that message with any clarity in Beijing, which was later stunned by a House congressional vote of 360–0 in favor of allowing Lee in and Clinton's swift decision to backtrack on the visa. Qian later said the White House's reversal was "mere sophistry, meant to conceal the administration's insincerity," because the power of visa issuance remained in Clinton's hands. Clinton himself was deeply frustrated at the corner he had been painted into. "I hate our China policy!" he exploded in one White House meeting after his decision to grant China the status of a normal trading nation. "I wish I was running against our China policy. I mean, we give them [trade status] and we change our commercial policy and what has it changed?" China had never renounced the use of force to retake Taiwan, but it also hadn't militarily threatened the island since shelling its outlying isles in the late 1950s. With Lee nailing his colors to the mast, as far as Beijing was concerned, coercion was now in order.

The dramatic climax of the crisis, in March of the following year, marked a low point in Sino-U.S. relations and also provided a shaky foundation on which they could be rebuilt. China began intensive shelling of the waters around the island just before Taiwan's first-ever presidential elections in March 1996, which coincided with the arrival in Washington of a Chinese vice-minister of foreign affairs, Liu Huaqiu, for talks on the bilateral relationship. With Chinese M-9 ballistic missiles targeting the shipping lanes at the northern and southern edges of Taiwan, any notion of a strategic dialogue with Liu was canned. Instead, Liu was confronted by William Perry, the defense secretary, and other senior administration officials in a tense meeting over dinner in the Madison Room in the State Department.

In the past, when they were asked whether the United States would defend Taiwan, the standard answer of American officials had always been along the lines of "Nobody knows." Such obfuscation was deliberate. The tactic of strategic ambiguity—of suggesting without saying directly that the United States would defend the island—although resisted by some American policy makers, was designed to keep Beijing off balance. Perry threw that approach out the window. In its place, he warned Liu in icy terms of "grave consequences"—unambiguous code for military action—should the Chinese attack Taiwan. The message was reinforced in a lengthy, tense session the following day between Liu and Anthony Lake, the national security adviser, and his team, around a crackling fire at the snow-covered country estate in Virginia owned by Pamela Harriman, then ambassador to France. To add muscle to the U.S. message, Clinton approved the dispatch of two aircraft carrier groups to the edges of the Taiwan Strait. It was the largest U.S. naval deployment in Asia since the Vietnam War.

The invective directed by Beijing at Lee underscored the intensity of Taiwan in Chinese politics, and the leadership turmoil at a time when top leaders were jostling to fill a vacuum left by an ailing Deng Xiaoping. (He would die two years later.) The official Xinhua news agency called Lee a "deformed test-tube baby cultivated in the political laboratory of hostile anti-China forces." The *People's Liberation Army Daily,* under the control

of the PLA, denounced him as "the No. 1 scum in the nation." Memorably, the paper added that Lee was like a "rat running across the street with
everybody shouting 'Smack it.'"

Clinton's decision to grant the visa humiliated Jiang and Qian, who
had reported confidently to the Politburo that Lee would not get one. In
their anger, they effectively subcontracted China's response to hawkish
PLA generals, with whom Jiang was increasingly aligned. Outwardly,
China's attempt to intimidate Taiwanese voters was a disaster, because Lee
Teng-hui won an overwhelming victory to become Taiwan's—and indeed
the Chinese-speaking world's—first elected president. Internally, the episode hardened China's view about U.S. perfidy on Taiwan. "Supporting
the Taiwan regime to keep China off-balance," said Qian in his memoirs,
"has been an established policy of every American administration."

In the end, for all the hardware deployed and missiles fired, the U.S.
and Chinese militaries did not come close to confronting each other; no
blockades were broken, nor did any U.S. ships sail through the Taiwan
Strait. But the episode had far-reaching ramifications nonetheless. The
virtuosic U.S. military performance in the first Gulf War had already
sent shock waves through the Chinese leadership and the PLA establishment, and the confrontation in Taiwan only reinforced their sense of
weakness. The bluster of Chinese leaders and the state-controlled papers
in China and their proxy outlets in Hong Kong couldn't conceal the
truth: that Beijing was powerless to challenge the U.S. carriers.

So far behind was PLA technology that the Chinese military couldn't
even track the American vessels' passage a few score miles off their coast.
"[The Chinese] were blind. It drove them crazy," said Ashton Carter,
then a senior Pentagon official and later secretary of defense under
Barack Obama. "The PLA resolved that would never happen again." Chi
Haotian, then China's top military officer, as vice-chairman of the Central Military Commission, later complained to Perry that he had lost face
in the encounter. "Of course you did," Perry replied. "What did you
think would happen? You were firing missiles into the Taiwan Strait!"

One CCP-loyal paper in Hong Kong, *Ta Kung Pao,* said Perry deserved a "slap" for the way he talked about U.S. security interests in the
region. Perry, already incensed by the missile tests, did not take kindly
to such commentary. "Beijing should know, and this [carrier deploy-
ment] will remind them, that while they are a great military power, the

premier—the strongest—military power in the Western Pacific is the United States," he told members of Congress. "America has the best damned navy in the world, and no one should ever forget that."

The combination of the North Korea and the Taiwan crises accelerated a wholesale strategic shift in Chinese military strategy. A focus on advanced technology rather than raw manpower, an effort to dominate the skies with a modern air force, and the development of long-range bomber groups integrated with the rest of the armed forces were all kick-started by Washington's displays of force in the gulf and around Taiwan. So, too, was the construction of China's own aircraft carriers, the first of which didn't appear until a decade later. Perry's taunts about having the "best damned navy in the world" had stung deeply. China had begun to mend fences with the Soviet Union in the late 1980s, but it wasn't until the Taiwan Strait confrontation with the United States that the PLA broke decisively with its longtime strategy on primarily planning for a possible war with the Russians. The navy and the air force, rather than the army, would be the PLA's focus from this point onward.

There was a deeper lesson from the Taiwan crisis, one with dismal long-term implications for Beijing. Trade between China and Taiwan, and investment in the mainland by the island's businesses, had increased exponentially since Beijing and Taipei started removing barriers to cross-strait contacts in the late 1980s. But to Beijing's annoyance, the increasing wealth generated in Taiwan did not translate into any desire for reunification. As China got stronger, its ability to seduce its neighbor, as opposed to threatening and coercing it, only seemed to weaken. Deng Xiaoping had warned early that the longer reunification was delayed, the less likely the chances it would happen. He believed the two sides should come to an agreement while the old leaders of the CCP and the Nationalists were still alive. At least they knew one another and understood the hurdles they faced in any attempt at reunification. The younger generation, by contrast, wasn't in the least sentimental about the mainland and had no time for the CCP.

In mid-1995, while the Taiwan crisis was playing out, Sakutaro Tanino was called into the prime minister's office in Tokyo. Tanino, the Foreign Ministry's China specialist who had helped manage the emperor's trip to the mainland, was being handed another seemingly intractable problem to solve. Once again, it involved relations with Beijing. Tomiichi Murayama, the prime minister, was fretting anxiously about the looming fiftieth anniversary of the end of the war. Murayama had watched despondently earlier in the year as conservatives had diluted a proposed motion in the parliament recognizing the Imperial Army's wartime atrocities. The prime minister wanted Tanino to write a genuine apology to mark the anniversary, which he hoped, with the support of the cabinet, to deliver himself.

By the mid-1990s, Japan seemed to be running out of steam. Its economy was mired in a slump, and a banking crisis lay just over the horizon. Politically, a succession of weak prime ministers had been pushed in and out of office by the shifting alliances put in play by the conservative split earlier in the decade. The war anniversary presented yet another challenge for which Japan so far had proved itself ill-equipped to handle. More than ever, the Japanese faced demands from Asia, spearheaded by China and South Korea, for a formal apology for its colonial rule and wartime conduct. There was pressure within Japan as well, from politicians and officials who recognized that the nation could never aspire to regional leadership without settling the history issue. In 1993, Japan had acknowledged under duress that the Imperial Army had helped organize a system of so-called comfort women in brothels to service frontline soldiers, a controversy that would dog the Japanese government for decades.

China's growing economic strength, combined with the party's aggressive nationalism, was already undercutting positive sentiment in Japan toward its neighbor. The two countries had recently tussled over numerous issues, including the Senkaku/Diaoyu Islands, Chinese nuclear tests, and Tokyo's bid for a seat on the UN Security Council. Beijing's intimidation of Taiwan had further hardened sentiment among officials and the public against China. Beijing regularly parried Tokyo's complaints with demands that Japan "reflect on history." Put another way, Beijing considered Japan to have no right to criticize China at all, an attitude that only soured relations further.

While the United States steered clear of the history issue, its Asian allies were immensely frustrated with Japan. "If I was an international psychiatrist that advised nations instead of individuals, I would advise Japan get it over with. Get it off your chest. Tell your neighbors we did wrong and we are sorry and we won't do it again. That clears the air," said

Lee Kuan Yew, Singapore's prime minister. "But this bashfulness, this pretense that it was all a slight misunderstanding, leaves a residue of suspicion." Many Japanese leaders were willing to apologize, in some cases just to deprive China of a ready-made issue to beat them over the head with. "We can apologize as much as China wants. It's free, and very soon China will become tired of asking for apologies," the former prime minister and cunning LDP kingmaker Noboru Takeshita confided to Foreign Ministry officials. Others viewed the anniversary in August 1995 as a chance for Tokyo to break out of history's straitjacket once and for all. But conservatives wouldn't budge. When in 1993 one relatively liberal prime minister, Morihiro Hosokawa, admitted that Japan had waged a "war of aggression," he was quickly forced to retreat into the semantic obfuscation that Japan's friends and foes alike found so infuriating, explaining that Japan had waged a war "with acts of aggression," not a "war of aggression."

Murayama, a grandfatherly figure with theatrically bushy eyebrows, differed from his predecessors in a number of crucial respects. He was the leader of the Socialists, a party that had made a fetish of antimilitarism. Not only did he have no concerns about an apology but he strongly believed one should be made. Murayama had already compromised to win LDP support to become prime minister, accepting the U.S.-Japan security alliance and recognizing the national flag and anthem, which the Socialists had always refused to do, and so had given himself some running room on the issue. LDP elders, like Yasuhiro Nakasone, backed him. By chance, his two closest advisers in drafting the apology, Tanino and Kunihiko Makita, another diplomat, both came out of the Foreign Ministry's China school. Both were Chinese speakers with extensive experience dealing with Beijing and hoped an apology might help build a new foundation for bilateral relations. All they needed to do was find a formula they could thread through the political system.

After he had written a draft statement at Murayama's direction, Tanino personally took the document to each cabinet minister, treating it as if it contained state secrets. The ministers were allowed to read the draft but then had to return it without making a copy. "If it leaked, it would have died immediately," Tanino explained. The draft acknowledged Japan's aggression, invasion, and colonialism—all red lights with hard-core conservatives and all points that China and South Korea demanded be addressed.

Murayama himself had added the word "apology." Tanino then went to see the politician who the prime minister and his advisers feared could be the biggest obstacle to getting the apology through the cabinet, Ryutaro Hashimoto, the popular trade minister, who also had a reputation as a strong nationalist.

The first time that the then U.S. ambassador Michael Armacost met Hashimoto on a courtesy call in 1989, he was taken aback by what he sensed was a large chip on the minister's shoulder. "The trouble with you Americans," Hashimoto told him, "is that you cannot forget you won the war." Armacost, an imposing six-foot-seven former college basketball player who had devoted his diplomatic career to Japan and Asia, replied that because he was eight when the war ended in 1945, the conflict had hardly shaped his worldview. In truth, Hashimoto probably had this equation upside down. The problem wasn't that the Americans couldn't forget they had won the war, although their victory had shaped the world ever since. It was more that Hashimoto and his ilk couldn't forget they had lost, with all that entailed.

At the time that Hashimoto was presented with the draft apology, he was the chair of the lobby representing Japan's war veterans and their relatives. The Japan War-Bereaved Families Association had long been a major fund-raiser and vote-turnout machine for the LDP, in return for generous financial support from the state for its members. More than other groups, it benefited from the Japanese view of themselves as victims of the war. One reason the government and taxpayers had always resisted paying reparations is that they were already footing a huge bill for their own returned soldiers and their families. Needless to say, the association opposed an apology.

Two hours after he had been shown the document, Hashimoto, to the prime minister's immense relief, sent it back to Murayama's office with his approval. "Hashimoto could have made trouble," said Makita. "He could have said, 'I don't like this statement,' and Murayama would have had a problem." Hashimoto requested only one small change, which Tanino and Makita thought, if anything, toughened the statement: substituting the phrase "loss of the war" for "end of the war." The apology was approved by the entire cabinet and delivered by Murayama in parliament. For Japan, the statement was a watershed and was welcomed with praise, and relief, in much of the region and in the United States.

The reaction in Japan itself was more complex. The die-hard conservatives registered their dissent, with eight ministers visiting Yasukuni Shrine on the day of Murayama's speech. Their opposition was predictable, but the source of the sharpest critique—a distinguished diplomat who had headed the Foreign Ministry and served as ambassador to the United States—was not. Ryohei Murata was no conservative or apologist for the war. He called Japanese militarism an "unforgivable outrage." At the same time, he insisted that all postwar issues had been settled in the San Francisco Treaty. "The . . . Prime Minister might have stated [the apology] as an expression of sincerity, but the Chinese and Korean Governments had no intention to receive it as intended," he wrote in his memoirs. "They were just ready to utilize this Japanese stupidity for the benefit of achieving their future foreign policy objectives." In this analysis, the apology was worse than wrong: it was useless, and any notion that it would help strengthen ties with China was illusory.

If there were any benefits for Japan in the apology, they were soon overshadowed by the Taiwan crisis. Tokyo had always been publicly circumspect concerning Taipei since forging diplomatic ties with Beijing. Behind the scenes, however, Japanese conservative politicians had often agitated on Taipei's behalf. Until his career ended in 1993 when he was spectacularly arrested with a stash of gold bars in his house, Shin Kanemaru was one of the LDP's most powerful chieftains, typical of the machine men who were as incoherent in public as they were audacious behind the scenes. When he was defense minister, Kanemaru held informal conferences with conservatives from South Korea, Taiwan, and Japan in his home prefecture to discuss ways to keep China at bay. Documents also reveal that Kanemaru lobbied the Carter administration privately in the late 1970s to back Taiwan independence, an explosive proposition. Such a move would not be "unreasonable," he told Harold Brown, Carter's Pentagon chief, given that a large percentage of the island's population were ethnic Taiwanese. A nonplussed Brown politely declined, explaining that it was very difficult to look a hundred years into the future and "think of Taiwan as not being part of China."

In April 1996, a month after the PLA's guns fell silent across the strait, Clinton and Hashimoto, who by then had taken over as prime minister, signed an agreement that implicitly extended the U.S.-Japan security treaty's reach to Taiwan and to the Korean peninsula. The new clause was laboriously worded, referring to "situations that may emerge in the areas surrounding Japan and which will have an important influence on the peace and security of Japan [and] the Asia-Pacific region." But its intent was clear: the Taiwan crisis had crystallized a sea change in Japanese policy toward China, converting Tokyo's mainstream policy makers into "reluctant realists" about the growing threat from Beijing.

Liu Jiangyong, a Chinese Japan scholar at Tsinghua University and generally a good barometer of Beijing's prevailing line, saw the new guidelines as transforming the U.S.-Japan security alliance, and not in a good way. Once viewed as the "cork in the bottle" of Japanese militarism, the U.S.-Japan treaties were now seen by Liu as a protective "eggshell for Japan to develop its conventional high-tech military strength." Another Chinese Japan scholar more liberal in his views, Jin Linbo, interpreted the move as payback for Chinese harping on history. "The people who think China is playing the history card want to play the Taiwan card back at China," he said. "Before the '90s, the Japanese would have never tried to play the Taiwan card. Now they want to block China diplomatically in every possible way. In the bottom of their heart, they think that keeping Taiwan helps Japan and the U.S." In his eyes, the guidelines were a turning point, signaling that the pro-Taiwan camp in Japan was slowly being let off the leash.

Japan's apology diplomacy had earned it little political capital. Its territorial disputes in the East China Sea had not gone away. The conflict over Taiwan was intensifying. And then there was Jiang Zemin. By the closing years of the decade, the Chinese leader had become the biggest bilateral irritant of all.

Conflicting accounts have been put forward to explain Jiang Zemin's antagonism toward the Japanese. The first is his official biography, covering his youth in Yangzhou, in Jiangsu province near Shanghai, and then in Nanjing, where he went to university. Born in 1926, Jiang spent his formative years either in the shadow of the anti-Japanese war or, as of 1943, at Nanjing Central University, in a city under occupation. Jiang had developed an acute political consciousness by the time he was in his teens, according to his favored foreign biographer, Robert Kuhn, an American banker who was given rare access to the Chinese leader's inner circle. At school, Jiang was forced to study Japanese, but the language never thrilled him. For someone who as an adult loved to flaunt his proficiency in foreign tongues, he always said that Japanese was the one language he didn't care for. "I was not so motivated to learn Japanese," he said pointedly in one interview.

Jiang's hero when he was young was his uncle, Jiang Shangqing, who was part of the CCP underground. He died in 1939, aged twenty-eight, but not in battle with the Japanese. This was not surprising, because, contrary to the party's creation myths, few Communists were actually fighting the Japanese at that time. Rather, Jiang's uncle died at the hands of local warlords. According to the official story, Jiang's father then adopted him out to his uncle's family, to give them a son and "extend the bloodline." His uncle's status as a martyr, notwithstanding the fact that he was killed fighting his own compatriots, gave Jiang an invaluable revolutionary luster as he rose through the ranks of the party. During Mao Zedong's worst purges, such a red lineage served as a kind of armor for anyone lucky enough to be able to don it.

As Jiang was promoted within the party, he ensured his uncle's deeds were increasingly publicized. Honor was piled upon honor. The uncle's remains were moved in 1982 to a martyr's grave in Jiangsu, which Jiang visited in 1985. A book of his uncle's writing was published by the state press in 2001. In 2009, Jiang completed the circle, ushering his uncle into the official pantheon of the CCP's model heroes. On the hundredth anniversary of his uncle's birth, in 2011, Jiang published a poem in his praise in the *People's Daily*.

Jiang's less fawning biographers, notably Bruce Gilley, a U.S. academic, don't dispute that Jiang's uncle was active in the underground opposed to the Japanese. But despite later attempts to play up his prepubescent fealty to the CCP, according to Gilley, Jiang showed few signs of being politicized in his early school and university years. It wasn't until later in 1946, after Jiang left Nanjing in the wake of Japan's defeat to go to university in Shanghai, that he pledged his allegiance to the party. It was a calculated, dangerous decision in a city under the control of the Nationalists. But the difference in dates is important in terms of intraparty prestige. Anyone who joined the party to fight the Japanese is venerated as a member of the CCP's "first generation." Joining after 1945 denoted a lesser sacrifice.

The unofficial Jiang biography, circulated by his enemies in recent years, has a very different take on his family history. The offshore media aligned with the Falun Gong, the spiritual and meditation group, claim that Jiang's father was a collaborator in the Japanese puppet regime in Nanjing and used his connections as a propaganda official to get his son into a good high school and university. In other words, according to this alternative, damning narrative, Jiang's anti-Japanese rants were faux tirades aimed at concealing a biography that would have been fatal for his advancement in the CCP.

The evidence for this story, which only emerged in public in recent years, is hardly overwhelming. The Falun Gong had good reason to besmirch Jiang, because he persecuted its members mercilessly after the group shocked his government with large protests in 1999. Inside China, the alternative story about Jiang's upbringing is blocked online. It is striking, however, to gauge the reaction of mainstream Chinese academics in Beijing when the highly sensitive counter-narrative is raised with them. After many Chinese scholars were asked the question, none dismissed it out of hand as anti-CCP propaganda. Their reaction was more along the lines of a blithe "Oh yes, I heard that." The "fake father" story is also a popular explanation in Tokyo for Jiang's anti-Japanese sentiment.

By 1998, Jiang was nearing the peak of his powers, both at home and abroad. After the Taiwan crisis, he and Clinton had worked diligently to build a personal relationship. Clinton hosted Jiang at the White House in 1997, an invitation offered with no pre-trip dramas involving human rights. Jiang placed a large order for Boeing planes, which would soon become a standard ritual for Chinese leaders visiting America, and promised to control nuclear exports. Jiang returned the president's hospitality the following year, hosting Clinton on a weeklong visit to China, a trip that Beijing insisted not include a stopover in Japan. To Tokyo's dismay, the White House complied. More important, Beijing was thrilled with Clinton's public declaration of his "three no's" policy on Taiwan—no independence, no two Chinas, and no admission for Taipei to international organizations. The United States was becoming "more disciplined" on Taiwan, said Qian Qichen, the kind of backhanded compliment the Chinese offer when they notch up a win.

Jiang was scheduled to follow his American trip with one to Japan a few months later, to cap off a summer of top-level diplomacy with China's two most important interlocutors. It was a potentially landmark event,

the first-ever visit to Japan by a Chinese head of state. The initial preparatory talks, held in early 1998, had gone relatively smoothly, perhaps because they were led by professionals committed to a bilateral relationship
within the respective foreign ministries. The Chinese officials leading the
talks were Tang Jiaxuan and Wang Yi. Just as Sakutaro Tanino was part
of the Foreign Ministry's "China school" of experts in Tokyo, Tang, the
foreign minister, a dull but abrasive figure, and Wang, who would hold
the portfolio under Xi Jinping, were both career Japan specialists and
spoke Japanese.

In their planning discussions, the Japanese persuaded the Chinese to
agree on a "future-oriented" visit, a clumsy phrase that carried specific
and weighty diplomatic meaning. Rather than replaying the corrosive
history wars and the recent Taiwan crisis, the two countries would look
at areas in which they could cooperate in the future. "The joint communiqué was done, and China didn't insist on an apology," said Tanino.
"We had come up with a sentence about the past, and then we moved
into the twenty-first century." Tang agreed with this approach, say the
Japanese, but also let slip that he didn't have "full permission" from his
bosses to deliver such a commitment.

If Jiang had ever agreed to look to the future, he had changed his
mind by the time he arrived in Tokyo in November. Fatefully, Jiang's trip
to Japan had been delayed by a few months due to massive floods at
home. In the meantime, Japan had hosted another regional leader, Kim
Dae-jung, South Korea's prime minister, who had received an apology in
writing in Tokyo for Japan's harsh colonial rule. Keizō Obuchi, who had
succeeded Hashimoto as prime minister, persuaded Japan's recalcitrant
conservatives to agree on the apology in return for Kim's guarantee that
South Korea would put the history issue to rest. The reversal of the order
of the two visits, with Kim coming before Jiang, proved to be fatal. As
soon as he learned that Kim had secured a written apology, Jiang demanded one for himself. "Tang and Wang said: 'We want what he got,'"
recalled Tanino. Obuchi was nicknamed "Mr. Cold Pizza" because of his
bland public persona. But he was also stubborn. Asked for another apology, this time from Jiang, Obuchi refused.

Once again, the two sides lapsed into an angry semantic debate in
which each fought as though his country's national dignity, and that of
its leaders, were at stake. Tokyo and Seoul's delicate minuet had taken

months of painstaking negotiations. In advance of Jiang's rescheduled visit, though, Japanese and Chinese officials had just days to strike a deal. In intense meetings before Jiang's arrival, the Japanese offered to apologize verbally while expressing "deep remorse" in writing. What might appear to be hairsplitting to outsiders was in fact the subject of serious internal politicking in Japan. A weak prime minister, Obuchi had managed to squeeze his conservative base for one written apology, but it would not countenance another. Tang had to go up the chain of command again for an answer to the Japanese proposal, which fell short of what the Chinese leader had demanded. "President Jiang is from the older generation, so I don't know if it is acceptable to him," Tang told the Japanese. The Chinese reminded them ominously, as if they needed to, that Jiang had grown up under the Japanese occupation.

What had been planned as a "future-oriented" visit quickly turned into a voyage through the past darkly. Jiang accepted the compromise on the declaration but retaliated by berating his hosts at every turn, in private and, worse, in public. "In Japan, there still remain certain people in high positions who constantly distort history and try to gloss over Japan's invasion of China," Jiang declared at the leaders' summit. On live television, at a banquet hosted by the emperor, Jiang spoke vehemently about Japanese "militarism," an unforgivable breach of protocol for Tokyo. Jiang was indignant and emotional throughout, righteously so in Chinese eyes. The Japanese, by contrast, considered Jiang's behavior rude and calculated to wrest the diplomatic high ground. "Isn't this a finished problem?" asked Hiromu Nonaka, the government's chief spokesman. "There is a school of thought that Japan has already reflected on its past and apologized to China any number of times already."

The negotiations over the joint communiqué concluded with the kind of pettiness that is inevitable when relations sour. After Obuchi refused to provide the written apology and repeat Clinton's "three no's" formula on Taiwan, the Chinese negotiators deleted a sentence from the declaration that asserted Beijing's "respect" for Japan's peaceful postwar development. To have left that in, the Chinese said, would have suggested that China had set the history issues aside. Japan asked for some acknowledgment of the generous financial aid it had provided, and the Chinese said they might include this in the declaration if Japan increased the amount on offer. According to some Japanese reports, Obuchi did offer Jiang a written apology behind closed doors. But the Chinese leader still refused to do what the Koreans had offered as a quid pro quo: an assurance that the history issue was settled once and for all. This trip "was supposed to open a new age in relations," the conservative Japanese diplomat Hisahiko Okazaki remarked after Jiang departed. "If anything, the Japanese were left with a feeling close to rage."

The Chinese later complained that the Japanese had made too much of the Jiang trip. "I don't think the idea of an apology alone guides China's Japan policy," said one of China's most prominent Japan scholars. "Jiang's 1998 trip has become a stereotyped view of Chinese policy. The Japanese say look at Jiang but I say, look at the fifteen years since then. Has everyone else behaved like that?" But the visit was a turning point in one important respect: both leaders had pushed back against the advice of their specialist diplomats, who they thought had consistently erred on the side of compromise.

In his speeches in Tokyo, Jiang dispensed with Foreign Ministry talking points and used blunter phrases crafted by a speechwriter from within the party apparatus, according to some reports. Tang himself came under pressure to resign after only months as foreign minister. Like Jiang, Obuchi was angry at the counsel he had received from his diplomats and largely rejected it. China's ultimatum—apologize on our terms or else—enraged him. To his professional detriment, Tanino recommended to Obuchi that he offer Jiang a written apology of the kind he had given to Kim. "It was only natural [China] would insist on that, but I nearly got fired," he said. "I was told that Obuchi was furious with me." In one meeting, according to officials present, Obuchi stood up and shouted down Tanino's advice, saying, "You want me to bow down in front of Jiang Zemin!" That was the end of the matter.

These bitter exchanges set a pattern that would be followed from here on in both countries. The politicians, not the experts, who had hitherto considered themselves the guardians of bilateral ties, would take the lead. The space for diplomacy was diminishing.

Two years later, Zhu Rongji, Jiang's bluntly spoken economic tsar, traveled to Japan as premier on what was widely billed as a makeup mission. Zhu had never been a Japanophile, as many of China's economic policy makers in the early reform period were. He was much more interested in the American model, which he thought was better suited to a country of China's continental dimensions and natural wealth. By the time he was in office, both Japan and Germany, another model for China, were, in his words, "feeling the pinch." Instead, to modernize the Chinese economy and state companies, he looked to the United States for guidance on financial and banking practices. With Japan, though, Zhu wanted to stabilize relations, if only to make sure that Japanese companies continued to invest in China.

Before leaving for Japan, Zhu announced that he wouldn't "offend the Japanese people" by raising the history issue. Once he landed in Tokyo, Zhu ruefully remarked that his statement had prompted "hundreds of critical comments [at home] for being too soft" on Japan. Never one to shirk discussing difficult issues, Zhu appeared on live television in Tokyo for an hour answering questions from the Japanese public. Inevitably, the war came up. "The following question is from a fifty-one-year-old male from Hiroshima," said the show's host. "He feels very remorseful for what Japan has done to China during the war. However, he wonders why China has been asking for apologies from Japan for such a long time and when that will stop?"

Premier Zhu replied, "First of all, I want to remind everyone of something. In none of the official documents have the Japanese ever apologized to the Chinese people for what happened during the war. In 1995, Prime Minister Murayama gave an oral apology toward the Asian people. Thus, it is not fair to say that China has been repeatedly asking Japan for a sincere apology. Whether or not Japan would present a formal apology to China is your business. However, we do hope that Japan would ponder over this problem."

Zhu's citing of Japan's refusal to apologize in "official documents" during his televised interview was a coy reference to the fact that this was precisely what Jiang had demanded. Predictably, Zhu's response enraged Japanese conservatives. "How can they say Japan has never apologized?" thundered the *Sankei Shimbun,* the right-wing standard-bearer in the media. "As long as China regards Japan as its enemy, it is impossible for the two countries to form a true friendship."

Privately, Zhu was much less charitable about the Japanese and what he saw as their backsliding on history issues. One of his regular foreign interlocutors, who stayed in touch with the former premier in retirement, remembers discussing with him Jiang's 1998 trip to Japan and Zhu's own visit two years later. Zhu was brusquely dismissive of Japanese complaints and said that Tokyo should have done whatever it needed to do then to settle the issue once and for all. "They didn't realize that Jiang and I were the nice guys," Zhu said. "Wait until they meet some of the younger [Chinese] leaders. Turning us down will be costly for them."

THE TWENTY-FIRST CENTURY

CHAPTER EIGHT

Yasukuni Respects

This was nothing but undisguised exoneration of those internationally acknowledged war criminals.

—Tang Jiaxuan, Chinese foreign minister

The Japanese became very frustrated but they never really grasped the reality. They thought China would fail.

—Hitoshi Tanaka, Japanese diplomat

Jiang Zemin's tirades against the Japanese were always going to provoke a backlash in Tokyo. Few people, however, had predicted blowback from within one of the Communist Party's most powerful citadels in Beijing. The headquarters of the *People's Daily,* the official mouthpiece of the Communist Party since the paper's founding in 1946, sits on a sprawling compound east of Tiananmen Square, big enough to accommodate the paper's offices and the comfortable apartments that were once part of the rice-bowl-to-retirement packages for workers in key state enterprises. For decades, locals and foreign Sinophiles alike have scoured its pages for clues about who might be on the way up, or down, in the leadership. Mao's revolutionary edicts, the downfall of the Gang of Four, the threat to blast student demonstrators out of Tiananmen Square, Deng's market reforms—all were announced in or consecrated by the party in the *People's Daily.* Careers had been made, and destroyed, by a strategically placed word in its pages. To mark special occasions, such as the opening of party congresses or National Day, the paper's borders and headlines were set in a deep, rich red, the color of Communism.

By the turn of the twenty-first century, the *People's Daily* was no

longer the voice of God in Chinese politics that it had once been, with
the Internet and the commercialization of the Chinese media chipping
away at its authority. But for editorial writers like Ma Licheng, the paper
still offered a platform to influence national debates. Tall, rake thin, and
bluntly opinionated, Ma used his perch at the paper to become an enthusiastic participant in the party's intramural fights. In a book published in the mid-1990s, *Crossing Swords,* penned with a fellow *People's
Daily* writer, Ma attacked the leftist throwbacks who had opposed
Deng's market reforms. The writers' message clearly found its audience,
because the book sold two million copies. Ma's next book, *Outcry,* took
aim at the hyperemotional nationalism that had arisen alongside the
party's patriotic education campaigns.

Impatient and blustery with visitors who didn't immediately measure
up ("You have much to learn about China!"), Ma stood out as a risk taker
in a culture that largely rewarded conformity. The Japanese, always on
the lookout for possible allies in China, shrewdly marked him out as a
defender of liberal reform and levelheaded patriotism. In early 2001,
Tokyo's embassy in Beijing offered Ma an all-expenses-paid trip to Japan.

The Japan that Ma visited bore little resemblance to the country he
had been warned about ad nauseam in China. "Even before I went, I
didn't believe everything I read, but Japan was quite different from what
I had seen on the Internet in China," he recalled years later. All the inces-
sant propaganda in China about Japanese militarism seemed at odds
with the peaceful streets, polite people, and civil-minded society he witnessed firsthand. "It didn't look nearly as aggressive as China," he observed. The contrast between the Japan he experienced and the way it
was portrayed at home became starker when he returned to China, ac-
centuated by an uproar over an up-and-coming actress, Zhao Wei. After
Zhao was photographed in a fashion shoot in 2001 in New York wearing
a dress imprinted with the Japanese imperial-era flag, she was hounded in
the media and on the Internet until she offered an abject public apology.

That was not enough for her critics. While she was on the catwalk at
a fashion show in Changsha, in Hunan, a man jumped on the stage and
smeared her clothes with excrement. Ma was horrified to read interviews
with the attacker, who said he didn't believe he had done "anything inap-
propriate." The assault on Zhao served as the opening to an essay Ma
published toward the end of 2002, comparing observations from his trip

to Japan with the explosive nationalism he saw at home. "When will our countrymen overcome such irrational impulses?" Ma asked in the piece he titled "New Thinking on Japan." "We need the generosity of a great and victorious nation and do not need to be excessively harsh with Japan."

Chinese writers describing how sensitive material can get through the censorship system often use a Ping-Pong analogy. They call articles like Ma's "edge balls," unreturnable shots that luckily squeak off the table and get counted as winners. Ma's article, for a while, looked as though it might qualify for such a description. His iconoclastic plea for China to drop the history wars and the xenophobia that came with them, and look to the future with Japan, initially won support in some quarters.

Shi Yinhong, an amiable, chain-smoking professor at People's University and an informal adviser to the State Council and Foreign Ministry, praised the idea of a rethink on Japan. He came at the Japan problem from a different, geopolitical perspective. Shi believed that stirring up animosity against Japan was not just dangerous for China but counterproductive as well, because it would strengthen Washington's hand in its mission to box Beijing in in Asia, an argument that would prove to be right. Shi advocated dropping the history issue in favor of the policy that so many in Washington quietly feared: drawing Japan away from the United States into Beijing's orbit. "We cannot forget history," Shi wrote, "but we cannot stagnate in history either."

It soon became clear that far from hitting an edge ball, Ma and Shi had missed the table altogether. Either that, or powerful party henchmen had simply called off the game and taken the table away after watching a few shots go in. Ma had published his article in *Strategy & Management,* a magazine that had carved out an independent space in internal debates about how to reconstruct Communist rule after the trauma of 1989. His decision to bypass the *People's Daily* for an alternative, activist, and more obscure outlet offered him little protection in the end. Scholars and early Internet trolls alike piled on to attack Ma in particular. The core of Ma's critics' arguments was a familiar one in the history wars: that Japan had taken advantage of China's generosity with its constant backsliding on war guilt. "Japan has not returned China's beneficence," said the scholar Bai Jingfan, who professed to have been "extremely shocked" by Ma's article. On the Internet, Ma was labeled a "traitor" and a "Japan lover," which were really one and the same.

Ma and his family began receiving death threats, and a guard was placed at his home. At the *People's Daily,* the colleagues who supported him didn't dare speak up on his behalf. Eventually, the debate stirred by his essay reached the top levels of the party. Ma told co-workers that he had received messages of encouragement from Zeng Qinghong, the senior official responsible for the party's all-important Organization Department who had just been promoted into the Politburo's inner circle. Zeng acted as a kind of cardinal-at-the-elbow for Jiang Zemin, passing on advice to his patron on everything from provincial politics to foreign policy. In the wake of Jiang's disastrous 1998 trip to Tokyo, it was Zeng who had begun rebuilding a back channel with senior Japanese politicians to try to reinstate a dialogue between the CCP and the LDP. Officials in the Foreign Ministry sent messages of support to Ma as well. But Ma's backers were no match for his more powerful enemies, chief among whom was the man who in late 2002 took over the reins of the party's Propaganda Department, Li Changchun.

Even with the rise of the Internet and the fragmenting of the dominant state media, the Propaganda Department ruled supreme over the Chinese press. Li and his officials used their position to send out daily and sometimes hourly missives about how stories should be handled, down to their length, placement, and shelf life. They also dictated which issues were to be ignored altogether. The department could, and did, turn the temperature up and down on issues like Japan, depending on the Politburo's mood. Whatever his personal feelings about Japan, Li didn't like Ma's article. Nor did he like Ma himself, whom he considered dangerously liberal, according to senior executives at the *People's Daily.* Li himself was not a hardliner, and had been an outspoken critic of the CCP on a number of issues. His animus toward Ma was most likely driven by the fundamental interests of any propaganda chief in China, namely, protecting one of his department's prize assets: the power to dictate the terms of public debate on an issue fundamental to the CCP's legitimacy.

Ma had initially stood by his essay and freely given interviews defending his views, despite the abuse and threats. To defend himself, he had always adopted Zhou Enlai's line about Sino-Japanese relations—that the two countries had enjoyed two thousand years of friendship and fifty years of misfortune. Quoting the words of former top leaders had once been a reliable way to shield oneself from criticism in China, but the old line no longer offered protection. The times had moved on. "Nineteen eighty-nine was the turning point. We were moving into nationalism," Ma said. "Sino-Japanese relations have nothing to do with Japan. It is all about internal politics in China."

It was the propaganda chief's antagonism that finally tipped the balance at the top against him. "Ma Licheng is wrong," Li told the *People's Daily* bosses, who understood only too well the meaning of these signals from on high. The paper quietly allowed Ma to leave his job there for a position at Hong Kong's Phoenix TV, still mostly working out of Beijing. Founded by a former propaganda official in the People's Liberation Army, Phoenix had one foot in the more liberal former British colony and another planted in China. Like *Strategy & Management,* Phoenix had built a space for itself to participate in Chinese debates, this time as a television news station, allowing it to take risks the traditional media could not. But even with the relative sanctuary afforded by its Hong Kong headquarters, Phoenix could not protect Ma once Li's department chased him down and complained again. "Send him back!" department officials told Phoenix executives. "How dare you employ a man like Ma Licheng?"

There was one fresh factor, however, that helped explain the antagonism toward Ma's article and the party's lack of interest in modifying its official hard line against Tokyo. A new prime minister in Japan, Junichiro Koizumi, had come to office in 2001 with his own firm ideas about how to deal with history. For the five years he was prime minister, nothing—least of all China's abject fury—could change his mind.

The election of Koizumi as head of the LDP in April 2001, and along with it his elevation to the office of prime minister, put Beijing on high alert. The Chinese were already agitated about what they saw as a resurgent rightist trend in Japanese politics. In the weeks before Koizumi's election, the Education Ministry in Tokyo had approved another school textbook that Beijing viewed as wrongheaded history. Koizumi's outgoing predecessor had also approved a visa for Taiwan's Lee Teng-hui to visit Japan, ostensibly for medical treatment. Both decisions were irritants in an already fraught relationship. Koizumi's election threatened to make things much worse. The new prime minister came to office with two core promises. The first was to privatize Japan's Post Office, a vast, lumbering network whose deposit-taking powers had turned it into one of the world's largest financial institutions. His second promise was to visit Yasukuni Shrine.

A few years earlier, Makiko Tanaka, the daughter of the former LDP prime minister and kingmaker Kakuei Tanaka, had been asked for her views on the three politicians then competing to be prime minister, the last being Koizumi. She spontaneously described them as "Bonjin, Gunjin, Henjin," or "bland man, military man, strange man." Her catchy, pithy description won her a prize from the country's Advertising Council that year. The label of the "strange man" of Japanese politics stuck to Koizumi.

Koizumi's eccentricities served him well as he rose through the LDP's ranks. Both his grandfather, whose image was defined by a tattooed dragon covering his entire back, and his father had served as cabinet ministers. Before entering parliament, Koizumi was a protégé of Takeo Fukuda, the faction boss who later became prime minister and sealed a friendship treaty with China in 1978. A third-generation politician with an insider's pedigree, Koizumi nonetheless cultivated his reputation as an oddball and ran for the leadership of the LDP in 2001 on a platform to "blow up" the ruling party. Joining his campaign was the sharp-tongued Tanaka, whose gilded lineage had also not prevented her from presenting herself in parliament as an antiestablishment candidate. Once in office, Koizumi appointed Tanaka foreign minister.

The instant Koizumi became prime minister, the Politburo in Beijing went on a diplomatic war footing. At the time, little of China's frantic machinations were on display, but years later Tang Jiaxuan, China's Japanese-speaking foreign minister, provided a revealing account in his memoirs of Beijing's efforts to keep Koizumi away from Yasukuni. Every Japanese official that China counted as remotely friendly was immediately singled out for heavy lobbying. Tanaka, whose father was credited with opening ties with China, was one of Beijing's first targets, with Tang and others urging her in lengthy meetings to make the "wise decision" to stay away from Yasukuni. Yasuo Fukuda, the son of Koizumi's mentor and now Koizumi's chief spokesman, was another.

Tokyo's ambassador to Beijing, a prominent member of the Foreign Ministry's "China school," Koreshige Anami, was also considered a potential ally by Beijing. Anami's connection with history was especially acute. His father had been war minister in 1945 and had opposed Japan's surrender to the United States and its allies, even after the bombings of Hiroshima and Nagasaki. After signing the surrender order as a member

As munitions minister in Hideki Tōjō's cabinet, pictured here in 1943, Nobusuku Kishi (back row, left), Shinzō Abe's grandfather, was a member of the Japanese government that voted for war with the United States.

Kishi (left) relaxes at the house of his brother, Eisaku Satō, after being released from prison in Tokyo in December 1948. Kishi was detained but never charged with war crimes. Both Kishi and Satō, then the cabinet spokesman, went on to serve as prime minister.

Japanese prime minister Shigeru Yoshida greeted by Secretary of State John Foster Dulles in Washington in November 1954. Yoshida recognized Chiang Kai-shek's Nationalists in Taiwan as the government of China after Dulles warned him that the United States might block the return of Japanese sovereignty. Yoshida had wanted to recognize Communist China.

Mao Zedong (right) and Premier Zhou Enlai (left), with China's chief Japan hand, Liao Chengzi, welcome Fusanosuke Kuhara, a veteran Japanese politician, to Beijing in 1955. With Beijing courting Tokyo to break the U.S. embargo, Mao told his Japanese visitors there was no need for them to apologize for the war.

Zhou Enlai and Secretary of State Henry Kissinger negotiated rapprochement between the United States and China in July 1971. Kissinger was enraptured, and intimidated, by Zhou from their first meeting.

Mao Zedong greets Japan's prime minister Kakuei Tanaka in his study in the Beijing leadership compound in December 1972, the first ever meeting between Japanese and Chinese leaders. After initial jousting, the pair bonded over traditional Chinese culture,

A rare moment of levity for Henry Kissinger in Japan, playing a game with a geisha during Gerald Ford's 1974 trip to Kyoto. Kissinger didn't like dealing with the Japanese and admitted later that he had never understood the country's political system.

Akio Morita, the cofounder of Sony, the Apple of its day, took to lecturing the United States about its short-term business culture and obsession with finance. He coauthored a book with the ultranationalist Shintaro Ishihara, *The Japan That Can Say No,* but removed his name from it when it was translated into English.

Deng Xiaoping traveled to Japan at the opening of China's modernization drive in October 1978 to sign a peace and friendship treaty with Japanese prime minister Takeo Fukuda; they are seen here with their wives. Once the leader of the pro-Taiwan camp, Fukuda sired a political dynasty tied closely to China.

Chinese Communist Party head Hu Yaobang and Japanese prime minister Yasuhiro Nakasone were most responsible for what is considered the golden era of Sino-Japanese relations, in the early 1980s. Hu became so emotional when speaking about the war in their meetings that his dentures sometimes fell out.

Yasuhiro Nakasone and Ronald Reagan, who were close enough to be on a first-name basis, enjoy a tea ceremony with their wives in Japan in 1983. Reagan's trade hawks distrusted the "Ron-Yasu" relationship as a ploy to undercut demands for Tokyo to open its markets.

James Baker, Treasury secretary under Reagan, negotiated the Plaza Accord in 1985 with Noboru Takeshita, Japanese finance minister and a powerful faction leader, underwriting a massive appreciation of the yen. The Chinese saw the accord as a U.S. plot to undermine a rival Japan.

Japanese emperor Akihito's historic visit to China in 1992 was a propaganda windfall for Beijing. No Western leader would be photographed with China's premier, Li Peng, branded the "Butcher of Beijing" for his role in the 1989 crackdown. The Japanese were later bitter at how the Chinese exploited the visit.

Tomiichi Murayama, Japan's first Socialist prime minister, displays his batting skills with rising baseball star Ichiro Suzuki in December 1994. Thrown into office by the collapse of the postwar conservative order, Murayama ensured his lasting legacy by making a formal apology for the war in 1995.

Few regional leaders annoyed Beijing as much as Taiwan's Lee Teng-hui, who opposed reunification with China and was sentimental about the island's Japanese colonial roots. He was elected president of Taiwan in 1996, as Beijing shelled the waters around the island to intimidate voters.

Jiang Zemin's 1998 trip to Japan, initially seen as a chance to solidify ties, was a new low in the two nations' relations. Furious at not having received a written apology for the war, Jiang berated his hosts in the presence of the emperor (at his left), an unforgiveable breach of protocol for the Japanese.

Bill Clinton struggled with Asia policy in his first term but struck a close bond with Jiang Zemin later in his presidency. To Tokyo's consternation, Clinton agreed to a weeklong trip to China in 1998—during which, as seen here, he conducted an orchestra in Xian—without stopping in Japan.

Prime minister Junichiro Koizumi's insistence from 2001 on paying his respects once a year at Yasukuni Shrine, which honors the souls of Japan's war dead, including Class A war criminals, poisoned relations with China during his five years in office.

Ma Licheng, an editorial writer at the *People's Daily,* was repulsed by anti-Japanese attacks in China and impressed by the peace and civility he witnessed on a trip to Japan. When he published an essay in 2002 calling for China to put the past behind it, the Communist Party was furious.

Koizumi shakes hands with North Korea's Kim Jong Il in Pyongyang in September 2002, with Shinzō Abe (at rear), then chief cabinet secretary, looking on balefully. Abe detested Kim and maintained a hard line against North Korea over its kidnapping of Japanese citizens.

George W. Bush, Junichiro Koizumi, and Chinese president Hu Jintao at an Asia-Pacific summit in Chile in November 2004. Bush broached the history issue with both men and pondered admonishing Koizumi over his visits to Yasukuni.

Shintaro Ishihara, who served as a minister and Tokyo governor, was often dismissed as an ultranationalist gadfly. But he had a canny ability to stir patriotic passions and almost caused a war with China over the Senkaku/Diaoyu Islands in 2012.

Christopher Hill, George W. Bush's representative to talks on North Korea's nuclear program, with his counterpart Kenichiro Sasae, one of Japan's top diplomats handling the United States and China, in 2007. Hill, a veteran of the Balkans conflict, disliked dealing with Japan's squabbles and quipped, "Give me the Bosnian Serbs any day."

Yasuo Fukuda was the most pro-China of recent Japanese prime ministers, and Hu Jintao was well disposed toward Japan. Their goodwill, on display in Beijing in August 2008 before the Olympics, could not overcome the mutual antagonism in their political systems.

As the Chinese Foreign Ministry's preeminent Japan hand, Wang Yi was vulnerable to attacks that he was soft on Tokyo. After he became foreign minister in March 2013, the Japanese said Wang was often brutal with them to prove his bona fides. He is pictured in April 2005, after being summoned to Tokyo to receive protests about anti-Japanese demonstrations in China.

Cui Tiankai (left), Beijing's ambassador to Tokyo and later Washington, with Yukio Hatoyama, after his election as prime minister in September 2009. Hatoyama's win caused a crisis in relations with the United States, as he tried to shift Japan closer to China.

Hillary Clinton at a meeting of Asian foreign ministers in Hanoi in July 2010, where she angered China by speaking out on the South China Sea. On the left is Jeff Bader of the National Security Council, and on the right, Kurt Campbell, the head of east Asia policy in the State Department.

Yang Jiechi, China's foreign minister, shocked many Asian foreign ministers in Hanoi in July 2010 with a vituperative speech criticizing interference in the South China Sea. The meeting marked a turning point in Beijing's relations with its neighbors.

One minister not surprised by Yang's invective in Hanoi was Katsuya Okada (left). At a meeting in South Korea in May 2010, after the Japanese foreign minister criticized China's nuclear weapons program, Yang stood and shouted at him in fury.

Zhan Qixioing was detained after he rammed his fishing boat into Japanese coast guard vessels near the Senkaku/Diaoyu Islands in September 2010. Beijing successfully pressured Tokyo to release him and ensured that he got a hero's welcome on his return home.

Chongqing's charismatic party chief, Bo Xilai, at the National People's Congress in early 2012 with Xu Caihou, the vice-chairman of the Central Military Commission. Bo was dismissed the following day over what the official media said was a plot to undermine Xi Jinping. Xu was arrested years later on related charges and died in detention in 2015.

In September 2012, weeks before he was due to become leader of the Communist Party, Xi Jinping (center) disappeared in the midst of the Bo Xilai upheaval and a confrontation with Japan over the Senkaku/Diaoyu Islands. He emerged without explanation two weeks later at China Agricultural University in Beijing.

After a two-year freeze on top-level meetings, Xi Jinping agreed to meet Shinzō Abe at an Asia-Pacific leaders' summit in Beijing in November 2014, mainly because China could not snub Japan as the host. One former U.S. official said of the frosty encounter, "They looked like they were smelling each other's socks."

Barack Obama and Shinzō Abe greet a survivor of the Hiroshima atomic bomb attack in May 2016. After an uneasy, suspicious start to their relationship, China's rise pushed Obama and Abe to work together closely on security ties and settling history issues.

Shinzō Abe rushed to Trump Tower in New York before Donald Trump's inauguration and was back in February 2017 for a trip to Washington and Mar-a-Lago, Trump's Florida estate. Trump's election panicked the Japanese, as he had criticized Japan for decades for its supposed "free ride" on security and unfair trade practices.

of the cabinet, apparently only in deference to the emperor's wishes, he committed ritual suicide. Anami's father's sword and blood-spattered clothing remain on display in the arch-revisionist museum adjoining Yasukuni Shrine.

Deluged with advice to cancel his planned trip to Yasukuni—including personal letters from Jiang Zemin; public pressure from Chinese officials, led by Tang and Wang Yi, by then heading the Asia desk at China's Foreign Ministry; the accumulated wisdom of Japan's China experts, who, if they didn't oppose the Yasukuni visit, warned the prime minister gravely of the consequences of going; and finally the dynastic custodians of China policy in Tokyo, in the form of Tanaka and Fukuda—Koizumi ignored it all. As Tang remarked later, "Our advice had no effect on Koizumi whatsoever."

Koizumi's only concession was to visit the shrine on August 13, rather than two days later, which would have coincided with the anniversary of Japan's laying down of its arms. In east Asia's date-sensitive political culture, this was put forward as a conciliatory gesture by Tokyo, although the Chinese never accepted it as such. Fukuda attempted to explain Koizumi's decision with a kind of circular logic that illustrated how trapped both sides had become in their respective positions. Fukuda told Tang that because Koizumi had promised to visit the shrine during his election, he had come under severe criticism for now prevaricating over the issue. If he postponed any further, he would become the object of the ire of Japan's far-right nationalists, which in turn would harm Sino-Japanese relations even further.

The Chinese rejected this explanation but were also wary of Koizumi's popularity. Tang recognized that many Japanese, weary after the lost decade of the 1990s and the era's featureless, failed leaders, were thrilled by Koizumi's dynamism. "His fresh style dazzled the mass of voters," he recalled. In his candid account of this period, Tang described Koizumi as "lively, . . . incisive, and appealing."

Both capitals quickly regrouped after the initial shock over Koizumi's first Yasukuni visit in August 2001, in an effort to get relations back on track. Within weeks, in the shadow of the 9/11 attacks in New York, Tokyo dispatched emissaries to China with a plan to patch up ties. They announced that Koizumi would come to Beijing and lay a wreath at the Marco Polo Bridge on the outskirts of the capital, the site of a clash between Japan and Chinese troops in 1937 that marked the start of the Second Sino-Japanese War. The Politburo accepted the Japanese proposal but added its own condition: that Koizumi go straight to the museum near the bridge on his arrival at the airport in the capital. Then, Tang said, relaying the Politburo's diktat, Koizumi should "fully and clearly" set out his perceptions of history to Chinese leaders and state whether he would visit Yasukuni again.

A receptive Koizumi was more than willing to consider Beijing's demands. In Tokyo, Foreign Ministry officials offered advice of their own ahead of the trip, urging him to stick with the terms of the 1995 Murayama apology. "I am not a right-winger. I am not narrow-minded," he told his diplomatic advisers. "I have the same historical recognition [as Murayama]. I am happy to go to any place and say some things in my own words." Koizumi made good on his promise, delivering a speech at the museum that included an apology for the horrors that Japan had visited on China. On the single-day visit, he was then whisked into the heart of the city to meet with Zhu Rongji, the premier, and Jiang Zemin, who was in the final months of his decade-plus reign atop the CCP. In these meetings, Koizumi repeated his apology.

Koizumi fell short on only one measure: He made no promises about staying away from Yasukuni. A panicky Tang dispatched Wang Yi to travel in the Japanese motorcade back to the airport to demand an assurance from Koizumi on that point. Anami, the ambassador, could do little other than equivocate, saying only that Koizumi would handle the issue with "great prudence" the following year.

It was a memorable day for many reasons. In Afghanistan, around the time Koizumi was sitting down with Chinese leaders, the United States was launching its first attack on the Taliban. Koizumi had offered the most far-reaching apology from a Japanese leader ever on Chinese soil. It was also Koizumi's first meeting with Jiang. That encounter with Jiang, and subsequent ones in coming months, left an indelible impression on the Japanese leader. Far from letting Koizumi down lightly after his gesture at the Marco Polo Bridge, Jiang lectured him about history. Jiang's style alone irked Koizumi and his advisers. As he often did, Jiang physically directed his words to his own officials, swiveling around in his armchair to face them as he spoke, rather than addressing his interlocutor, Koizumi. "He sort of used to have long monologues directed at his subordinates," one of Koizumi's advisers said.

Koizumi didn't complain in public about Jiang's private dressing-down. Indeed, a few months later, in April 2002, at the inaugural meeting of the Boao Forum, China's Davos-style alternative for global movers and shakers in tropical Hainan, Koizumi spoke about how China's economic development was a great opportunity for Japan. He delivered the key line in the speech ("Some see the economic development of China as a threat. I do not") precisely as it had been written for him by his advisers. When the speech was presented to him by Foreign Ministry officials, he read it and simply nodded his head without objection. It was a rare positive affirmation of China's rise from the leader of a country increasingly obsessed with its competitive threat. Zhu, who as China's host at Boao was sitting in the audience, applauded warmly.

A few days later, on his return to Japan, without informing the Foreign Ministry, Koizumi slipped away from Tokyo early in the morning to pay his respects again at Yasukuni. Tang, then on a trip to Egypt and Turkey with Zhu, was dumbfounded. "I could still hear Koizumi's words [from Boao] ringing in my ears!" he said later. Japanese diplomats were also caught short. "He didn't tell me," the head of the Foreign Ministry's Asia bureau, Hitoshi Tanaka, protested. Tanaka was an influential and creative adviser to Koizumi, orchestrating his controversial trip to meet Kim Jong Il in Pyongyang in 2002, an initiative that earned him the enduring hatred of many conservatives. On Yasukuni, however, Tanaka was constantly at loggerheads with his prime minister. After getting over the initial shock of the news of Koizumi's Yasukuni visit, Tanaka had a sharp exchange with him about its repercussions. As well as a predictable downturn in relations with China, Tanaka warned him that Japan's ability to take any initiatives in Asia would be grievously diminished. Koizumi was unfazed. It would have made no difference, he replied. I would have gone anyway.

From Koizumi's perspective, he had made clear his remorse for the war, in Beijing in 2001. He had declared China was not a threat to Japan in his speech at Boao a few months later. By going to Yasukuni in April, Koizumi believed that he had made a concession of sorts by avoiding the more sensitive dates that coincided with the anniversaries of the end of the war. But it had no impact. In October 2002, at the Asia-Pacific regional summit in Los Cabos, Mexico, Jiang berated Koizumi over Yasukuni. "It would be better if you refrain from such visits in the future," the Chinese leader said and "went on and on about history," according to one Japanese official present. "It was a very, very uncomfortable meeting." In a session with another Japanese politician at around this time, Jiang made it clear that this was a nonnegotiable issue, stating, "I cannot tolerate his visit to the shrine at all."

Koizumi's public reason for persisting with visits to the shrine was an old-fashioned one: that he had promised to do so when he was elected and was therefore just fulfilling a campaign promise. But he always made it clear that he had another motivation: to try to stop China from playing the history card against Japan. After his lectures from Jiang, Koizumi became convinced that the Chinese leader wasn't interested in improving relations either with Japan or with him personally. That was certainly the view of one of his informal counselors, Hisahiko Okazaki, the onetime ambassador turned conservative commentator, who was considered more influential with the prime minister than his official advisers. Okazaki had committed himself to right-wing causes after retiring from the Foreign Ministry and regularly railed against China and groups that he saw as Beijing's fellow travelers in Japan, like the Communist teachers' union. The notion of any deal whereby China would drop the history issue if Japanese leaders pledged to stop going to Yasukuni made him furious. "No, No! Listen, China, China, China picked that issue," Okazaki told one interviewer. "That is a real mistake on the Chinese side. China should climb down. That is the only solution."

The old adage that politics stops at the water's edge has never applied in Japan, which has a long history of rival factions going behind one another's backs to deal with foreigners to secure advantage at home. When Koizumi was readying a third trip to Yasukuni, in January 2003, the Chinese ambassador in Tokyo rang Fukuda and demanded he call off the visit. Fukuda, who was still Koizumi's chief spokesman and effectively ranked just behind him in the government, brusquely told the ambassador he had done his best and that the Chinese should understand his position, which was his way of saying he opposed the Yasukuni visit but was powerless to stop it. Fukuda's views were shared by most of Japan's opposition parties, and many in the LDP as well. Like Fukuda, they didn't hide their disagreement with Koizumi, either in public or with the Chinese.

The divisions that Koizumi left in his wake cut both ways in Japan. Some anger was naturally directed at Beijing and the CCP. For all the Japanese who opposed Koizumi, though, Beijing's repeated ultimatums on Yasukuni caused many conservatives to direct their ire internally, at Tokyo's traditional China experts, the politicians and bureaucrats whose advice had long dominated the government's policy toward Beijing.

Within the Foreign Ministry in Tokyo, the members of the "China school," or the "China gang," as they were known in Beijing, were the bureaucratic gatekeepers of the diplomatic relationship, giving them a lock on most important policy decisions. China school members, trained in Chinese and schooled in the relationship's founding traditions of past remorse and future friendship, invariably maintained key positions, such as ambassador to Beijing and head of the ministry's China desk. "The early China school people who studied in the mainland clearly reflected the early atmosphere of opening up; most of them had a very fond feeling toward China," said Hitoshi Tanaka, who headed Asia policy under Koizumi. "They believed they were the real experts." Within Japan's balkanized bureaucracy, the China school members guarded their privileges jealously. Kunihiko Miyake, a diplomat, who was close to Shinzō Abe and his family, remembers taking part in a review of security policy in the ministry's North America division in the late 1990s. When he called the China desk to coordinate efforts, his counterpart simply refused to discuss the issue, demanding, "Why is North America interfering with our China policy?"

The emerging rift in Japan over China policy had a whiff of Washington in the early 1950s in the wake of Mao Zedong's defeat of America's preferred leader, Chiang Kai-shek, in the Chinese civil war. The "who-lost-China debate" in Washington spurred witch hunts targeting U.S. diplomats who had displayed even a modicum of understanding as to why the Communists had prevailed. In McCarthyist America, China expertise became a dangerous liability in fashioning China policy. Nothing as horrific as the McCarthyist purges occurred in Japan, but faith in the China experts in Tokyo was souring. Their critics began referring disparagingly to them as the "China lovers" and "pandas" in the Foreign Ministry. The worst of the attacks, as was the case in the McCarthy era, cast aspersions on their patriotism.

"The China school are turncoats," Hideaki Kase, one prominent right-winger, charged. Kase's mantelpiece at his home in central Tokyo features pictures of his father, a former diplomat, who was on the decks of the battleship U.S.S. *Missouri* for Japan's surrender in Tokyo Bay in 1945. On prominent display as well is a portrait of Radhabinod Pal, the Indian judge who remains a hero on the Japanese right for his dissenting not-guilty verdicts for convicted war criminals before the Tokyo Tribunal. Fluent in English, Kase cultivated high-level contacts in the United States and in the 1990s offered himself to Washington as a back channel to carry messages between the two governments. Kase recalled being visited by one prominent China school official to lobby him to support the emperor's 1992 trip to China. "He literally begged me not to oppose the visit," said Kase, who was then on a government advisory committee. "This person swore he had dedicated his life to improving Sino-Japanese ties; I told him his personal wish had nothing to do with the national interest." Kase would hiss at any mention of Koichi Kato, a senior LDP figure who for decades was a go-between with Beijing. "To us, Kato is a traitor." The emperor, he privately complained, was a "pacifist," a word that for him carried a derogatory meaning.

The China school's authority eroded gradually through successive clashes over China policy from the early 1990s onward. The emperor's visit in 1992 and Jiang's behavior during his Japan trip in 1998 enraged the right wing. In the wake of the latter, Okazaki, the conservative diplomat who had advised Koizumi, complained that the China school's dominance in both the bureaucracy and the media would effectively stifle discussion about Jiang's actions. "The people entrusted with writing up the event are specialists in Sinology," he said. "None will be capable of setting their hands to the task." The China school had long enjoyed a tacit alliance with sections of the LDP that dominated relations with Beijing. The gradual unraveling of the longtime ruling party in the wake of the end of the cold war, though, left a vacuum on China policy, which younger politicians began to fill.

There was no longer any kingmaker, like Kakuei Tanaka and his factional successors, who were invested in a successful bilateral relationship. The billion-dollar aid flows to China, which offered valuable opportunities for kickbacks for the politicians overseeing bilateral ties, were drying up. Up-and-coming Diet members, like Shinzō Abe, had begun complaining that Japan was not tough enough with Beijing. "The younger generation were sick and tired of the way the older generation were handling China policy; it was a kind of appeasement policy in a way," said Miyake, a confidant of Abe's. "China was flexing its muscles and building up its defense. By the beginning of the twenty-first century, we were convinced they were departing from the old policy of Sino-Japanese friendship."

If there was one event that sealed the fate of the China school, it was an incident at the Japanese consulate in Shenyang, the sprawling industrial metropolis in China's northeastern rustbelt, in May 2003. When five North Koreans, including one child, entered the consulate seeking asylum, the Chinese guards chased them in and then dragged them back out. Japan strongly protested the guards' actions as a breach of sovereignty under the international convention protecting diplomatic properties. In what one writer called a "diplomatic version of *Rashomon*," China's recounting of the incident turned the tale on its head.

The Chinese media claimed the guards, far from barging in, had been invited to enter the consulate by the Japanese. In what sounded like a parody of ritual Japanese politeness, the Chinese said the consulate's staff had repeatedly bowed and thanked the guards for their help in removing the North Koreans. Japan, they insisted, should be grateful the guards had protected the consulate. After a two-week standoff, a face-saving deal was struck, and the North Koreans were allowed to leave China to travel to Seoul. The incident left a bitter aftertaste for many Japanese, who had seen video of the North Koreans being ejected from the consulate. "They really damaged their image in Japan," said Miyake, then stationed in the embassy in Beijing. "They lied and they lied and they lied. People like me were pissed."

Beijing's actions could easily be explained on one level as a means to remove any incentive for North Koreans who might be thinking of escaping the dictatorship through China. But Japan's ire wasn't directed exclusively at Beijing. Again, it soon turned inward, this time at Koreshige Anami, the ambassador in Beijing. At a staff meeting he presided over during the incident, Anami instructed his diplomats to be ready to turn away asylum seekers at the country's embassy and consulates. Whatever the humanitarian issues, he explained, "it was better not to be involved in trouble."

Once leaked, Anami's directive created an uproar and was cited as an abject example of the China school's habitual preemptive capitulation in the face of conflict with Beijing. Conservatives in the LDP were infuriated, as were many Foreign Ministry officials who believed the old ways of formulating China policy needed to change. In 2006, for the first time in more than three decades, the Foreign Ministry appointed a non-China specialist to head the ministry's China division. Although it involved only a minor reshuffle of bureaucratic bodies, it was nonetheless an unmistakable signal of a break with the past. From around this time, according to Sakutaro Tanino, another former Japanese ambassador to Beijing, there was a new rule in Tokyo: "China policy should not be in the hands of the China school."

By early 2003, a new Chinese leader, Hu Jintao, had taken over from Jiang as both head of the CCP and president, and Wen Jiabao replaced Zhu Rongji as premier. The handover was more than just a changing of the guard, although that was important in itself. It was the first time in living memory in China that power had been handed over peacefully, according to an agreed set of conventions and rules. As such, the orderly transition was a huge boost for the CCP's confidence in its governing ability and a powerful reminder for skeptical foreigners, especially in the United States and Japan, that China's rise might be built on firm political foundations after all.

The new leadership also represented a fresh stream in Chinese politics, with potentially profound implications for policy and the careers of thousands of officials dependent on patronage networks. Jiang and Zhu were part of the "Shanghai Gang," hailing from a city that was China's shiny bastion of state capitalism. Hu and Wen were protégés of, or at least owed their late career promotions to, Deng Xiaoping and Hu Yaobang, both identified in different degrees with adventurous market reforms. Hu Jintao also came out of the China Youth League, which tied him directly (though the pair weren't related) to Hu Yaobang, the faction's most influential onetime player.

The factional labels attached respectively to the Jiang-Zhu and then the Hu-Wen leaderships—the Shanghai Gang and the China Youth League—turned out to be an unreliable guide for their policies in office. Jiang and Zhu were ambitious economic reformers who had the guts and confidence to embrace a rising domestic private sector, economically and politically. Hu and Wen, despite the risk-taking roots of their patrons, operated more like housekeepers, bedding down the reforms their predecessors had unleashed and living off the export and investment boom triggered by China's entry into the World Trade Organization in 2001.

The conventional view of Hu and Wen's decade in power, that they wasted ten good years, is not entirely fair, as such political obituaries rarely are. Hu dragged Taiwan policy back from the edge of a precipice, where Jiang had left it hanging in the wake of the 1996 crisis, with China threatening war unless Taipei toed the line. Wen, refreshingly, if quixotically, talked expansively about political reform toward the end of his second term and worked hard to build a social safety net. By and large, though, the watchword for Hu and Wen was caution, which enabled many ambitious, calculating underlings to build sprawling, wealthy power bases in the party, the military, and state-owned companies, especially the energy sector, who weren't confronted until Xi Jinping came to power years later.

The one area where the monochromatic Hu distinguished himself from Jiang, and took risks as well, was Japan. As a senior official in the China Youth League in the early 1980s, Hu Jintao joined delegations to Japan initiated by Hu Yaobang. Hu Jintao also hosted the three thousand Japanese students who came to China at the leadership's invitation. Hu Jintao had witnessed firsthand the dangers in internal CCP politics of embracing Japan when his mentor's generous invitation to the students was instrumental in his downfall in 1987. Still, Hu Jintao had been impressed by the Japan he visited in the 1980s, then light-years ahead of China in development, and he carried none of the Jiang family's baggage on history.

So when Japanese diplomats put out feelers early in his first term to try to revive bilateral relations by arranging a meeting with Koizumi, then still in the diplomatic doghouse, Hu agreed. In May 2003, the pair met in St. Petersburg, where they were both attending the city's three-hundredth-anniversary celebrations. A notoriously scripted leader, Hu hewed closely to his talking points about history, while Koizumi (at least according to the Chinese version) flattered the CCP leader and talked expansively about the relationship. Hu's solemn warning to stay away from Yasukuni had no effect, though. Just as bilateral relations were finally gaining momentum, Koizumi visited the shrine again, on New Year's Day 2004. Talking to reporters, Koizumi brushed off complaints about the Class A war criminals interred there, protesting that "lashing the dead" was not part of Japanese culture. Tang Jiaxuan responded angrily: "This was nothing but undisguised exoneration of those internationally acknowledged war criminals."

By now, a kind of Yasukuni derangement syndrome was setting in in China. In his memoirs, Tang devotes an entire chapter to Japan. This was a period during which the two countries' economic ties were thriving, enmeshing their fates in a way that had no precedent in their centuries of intermittent contact. China's successful entry into the global trade system was finally allaying the fears that many big Japanese companies had about the risks of going all out on China. Even Koizumi's support for Washington in post-9/11 conflicts in Afghanistan and Iraq drew little comment. Such an expansive view of Japan's security posture would once have set Chinese nerves on edge. Yet for more than eighty pages in the chapter on Japan in his memoirs, Tang barely mentions the United States. He touches little on economic cooperation. Tokyo's ties with Taiwan come in for a few complaints, but only in passing.

Tang's memoirs about Japan, a country to which he had devoted his career, focus almost entirely on Koizumi's perfidy over Yasukuni. His past admiration for Koizumi's political style was now replaced by an array of pejoratives, describing him as "brazen," "obstinate," "obdurate," "stubborn," "shameless," and "biased." With the numeric precision characteristic of east Asian politics, he carefully describes Koizumi's first, second, and third trips, and so on, to the shrine and then details the lead-ups, the exact timing of each visit, and their aftermath. Koizumi, Tang remarks acidly at one point, had once told parliament that "when in difficulty, he modeled himself on the kamikaze suicide pilots."

The year 2005, the sixtieth anniversary of the end of the war, would prove to be a watershed. When Japan began pressing its claims to become a permanent member of an enlarged UN Security Council, the reaction in China was violent. Internet portals, usually scrubbed clean of political content, posted petitions opposing Japanese membership in the body, rapidly attracting tens of millions of electronic signatures. Over three weekends in April, growing crowds of protesters marched in major cities across the country, in many places smashing restaurants and storefronts selling Japanese food and products and attacking Tokyo's Beijing embassy and consulates. A number of bystanders were also beaten. For an entire generation of young Chinese, not old enough to have taken to the streets in 1989, or even in 1999, when the government sanctioned protests against the United States over the bombing of the Chinese embassy in Belgrade, this was their first, heady experience of marching for a cause.

Now it was Japan's turn to ask for an apology. Japan's foreign minister, Nobutaka Machimura, was sent on an urgent protest mission to Beijing to insist that China explain the attacks on Japanese property. The minister's demand was delivered live on television, causing his Chinese counterpart, Li Zhaoxing, to momentarily freeze. To apologize to Japan in front of such a large audience would be career suicide, and Li didn't dare to express even the slightest remorse for the weeks of violence. "The Chinese government has never done anything that wronged the Japanese people," he replied, in an artful seat-of-the-pants restatement of Beijing's longtime distinction between Japanese nationalists and the masses.

Beijing was equally indignant about another of Tokyo's complaints—that young protesters had been filled with hatred for Japan by the patriotic education they had received in primary and high school. "I can tell you that China has no 'anti-Japan' education at all," thundered Tang. A long lecture on history followed, and Machimura was dispatched back to Tokyo. "His visit did not get Japan the result it expected," Tang cattily noted in his memoirs, "but rather a lesson from us."

By this point, halfway into the first decade of the new century, too many ambitious political players in both countries saw value in playing up their differences to let the issue lie. Among them in Tokyo was Tarō Asō, who took over as foreign minister in 2005 and was jostling to succeed Koizumi as prime minister in late 2006. To his friends, Asō was a charming rogue, and to his critics, a slightly sinister loose cannon. His background alone might have caused anyone in his position to exercise restraint when talking about Japan's neighbors. His family's mining company had used forced labor, both Koreans and Allied POWs, to dig up coal during the war, something he acknowledged only reluctantly when he was briefly prime minister a few years later. The official history of the

Asō family and its business interests asserted that the United States had tricked Japan into war by purposely allowing the attack on Pearl Harbor.

Rather than trying to calm relations with China, however, Asō readied for Koizumi's departure with a series of headline-grabbing statements. He called China's military a "threat," praised Japan's colonization of Taiwan, and suggested that the emperor visit Yasukuni. U.S. diplomats based in Tokyo, worried about the impact of Asō's rhetoric, pressed their contacts in Japanese politics as to whether there was any rationale behind the statements. The response they received was instructive: The diplomats were told to discount his comments as nothing more than humdrum domestic politics. Asō needed publicity to lift his profile before the LDP's election of a new leader, and bashing China was now as good a way to achieve this as any. As Koichi Kato remarked, "The majority of LDP voters are anti-China."

Like Asō, the Chinese were positioning themselves for Koizumi's departure. China's new diplomatic point person was Dai Bingguo, who had taken over from Tang Jiaxuan as Hu Jintao's chief foreign policy adviser. Dai was a genuine CCP success story, or at least that is how he saw himself. Born in 1941 in a remote village of the poor province of Guizhou in one of China's officially designated ethnic minorities, Dai was one of six children. Four died relatively young from diseases that might have been treated had they grown up in more prosperous surrounds. The family could only afford to send a few of the children to school. In his memoirs, Dai recounts how he got up early each morning to work the fields with his father, who sold a pig to pay for his education. Dai was the first member of his family since the Ming dynasty, he said, to pass the imperial-era-style exams to enter the bureaucracy.

As a child, before the Sino-Soviet split, Dai viewed Stalin as a kind of god and observed a day of silence in his village when the dictator died. "What image did I have of America back then?" he wrote in his memoirs. "Soldiers with guns wearing big boots, and pot-bellied Wall Street bosses in pinstripe suits." A Russian major in university, he served as China's ambassador to Hungary between 1989 and 1991, when the Berlin Wall came down and the Soviet bloc fell apart. Dai witnessed firsthand the lessons that would be drummed into all cadres in the years to come: weakness and chaos would overwhelm China if the party fell from power.

Near the end of the Koizumi era, the two countries' top diplomats, Dai on the Chinese side and Shotaro Yachi, the leading bureaucrat in the Japanese Foreign Ministry, started meeting again in early 2006. The Japanese trusted Dai as someone who spoke for his boss, Hu Jintao. Yachi, by contrast, did not have the ear of Koizumi nor control over China policy making. But he did represent a powerful stream in Japan, in the bureaucracy and beyond, in favor of stabilizing bilateral ties and finding a mechanism to move away from the perennial history wars. China's investment in Yachi was worthwhile in any case, because he would later become Shinzō Abe's most important foreign policy adviser.

The talks began in Tokyo and then moved off-site, to a traditional Japanese inn with hot spring baths in the mountains of Niigata, the prefecture straddling the Sea of Japan in the northwest of the country's main island. The Chinese delegation was seemingly seduced by the idyllic, refined surroundings of the sort immortalized in Japanese art, soaking in steaming, outdoor communal pools in the falling snow. It is a practice traditionally best enjoyed nude, although accounts of the meeting make no mention of this. A joint karaoke session between the two parties followed. "Although Dai did not avail himself of the bath" (he said he was working too hard), he loved the picturesque setting and "proclaimed that he did not want to leave," Japanese diplomats reported.

Once again, the two sides remained in a deadlock on Yasukuni. Some Japanese officials believed China was looking for ways to wall off the issue of shrine visits so they would not poison the broader relationship. China stood to lose investment and jobs and access to the technology and management skills its firms still lacked, or so the Japanese argument went. But that was a misjudgment. As Yachi acknowledged, Dai was insistent about Yasukuni. It didn't matter how Koizumi, or any other Japanese leader, might attempt to finesse the visits, whether he went on a sensitive anniversary or slipped in a day or two beforehand. "For Beijing the issue is whether the Prime Minister goes or not, period," Yachi said. No justification would do.

A few months later, Tom Schieffer, the U.S. ambassador, was having lunch with Yachi. Their semi-regular get-together was dominated again by history and Japan's interactions with China and South Korea. Yachi briefed Schieffer on the efforts to steady relations with China after Koizumi's departure. The Chinese had joked that Shinzō Abe and Tarō Asō, both contending to replace Koizumi, should watch "their tongue and their legs," which was Beijing's way of saying they should shut up about the war and stay away from Yasukuni. But Beijing, and Seoul, had made a concession of sorts: They wouldn't demand a public commitment that the next Japanese leader not go to Yasukuni. They just wanted to make sure that whoever took over didn't. But for now, Yachi and Schieffer still had to see out the Koizumi era. Would Koizumi be going to the shrine this one last time, on August 15? Schieffer asked. Yachi replied sheepishly, "I'm afraid so."

Koizumi dispensed with numeric subtleties on his final visit and went to the shrine on the anniversary of the end of the war. For good measure, he disparaged his neighbors afterward. "No matter what day I choose to go, China and the Republic of Korea will protest, so why not go on the date of the anniversary?" he asked. Koizumi was the first Japanese prime minister since Nakasone twenty-one years earlier to visit the shrine on that date. With Koizumi's time in office coming to an end, the Chinese reaction was relatively muted, and authorities allowed only a small demonstration outside the Japanese embassy. Chinese scholars joked later about the size of the protest. It would have been awkward for Beijing, they said, if there had been no protest at all.

Koizumi might have been right in saying that Tokyo could apologize endlessly for the war and it would make little difference. Certainly, Tang didn't try to hide China's view that Japan should fester in geopolitical purgatory, forever wearing a crown of thorns that its neighbor had prepared for it. Tokyo, he said, was trying to "shrug off the historical constraints a defeated country must bear, and become an ordinary country."

But however sound Koizumi's reasoning was, his tactics were abysmal. He never tried to use Yasukuni strategically to gain leverage with Beijing. He stubbornly visited the shrine, no matter the consequences. In attempting to put an end to the history issue, he had effectively displayed it on a wide screen in a way that made it an impossible problem to solve, let alone manage. It is hardly a surprise that Yasukuni dominated Tang's memoirs to the exclusion of other issues. Koizumi's approach meant that every subsequent bilateral encounter between the Japanese and their Chinese and South Korean interlocutors had to commence with each side's ritualistic laying down of markers on history, if the meetings took place at all.

In Japan, the school of diplomats sympathetic to China had become sidelined. In China, scholars and officials who had tried to push the debate about Japan in a more positive direction had been shut down as well. Both sides had stored up large reserves of anger and bitterness, which could be drawn upon whenever the political season required. In Beijing, when invited to informal dinners to discuss affairs of the day, Shinichi Nishimiya, a Japanese diplomat who would later be appointed ambassador to Beijing, would always ask if any Chinese officials would be attending. If they were among the guests, he said, it was pointless inviting him, because he would always have to sit through a lengthy lecture on history first.

Tokyo's emissaries who were dispatched to Beijing to prepare for the post-Koizumi era used a version of the argument that the Chinese academic Shi Yinhong had used years earlier in favor of putting history aside. They argued that Beijing's refusal to allow Tokyo to have a more independent foreign policy, such as by joining the UN Security Council, inevitably meant Japan would draw closer to the United States. But they failed to find a compromise that could satisfy both sides. As Yachi, Tokyo's senior diplomat, lamented, "There is no solution."

When Japan and China had first dealt with these issues in the 1950s and 1960s, Beijing was weak and diplomatically needy. Now it was powerful and assertive. "The Japanese became very frustrated but they never really grasped the reality," said Hitoshi Tanaka, Koizumi's former Asia adviser. "They thought China would fail."

Over time, the Chinese had exploited the history issue. The Japanese had mishandled it. The Americans, until then, had largely ignored it. The U.S. ambassador Schieffer's polite queries over lunch about the state of Tokyo's relations with Beijing, and Seoul, were one thing. George Bush would soon be asking questions about history as well.

CHAPTER NINE

History's Cauldron

Hu Jintao made me do it.
—Junichiro Koizumi, on visiting Yasukuni Shrine

You know, China should have a Holocaust Museum of its own.
—Xiong Guangkai, Chinese military intelligence chief

George W. Bush wandered down the back of Air Force One, still sweating from a workout on his exercise bike. It was November 2005, and the president and his entourage were flying home from east Asia, a trip that included a summit of regional leaders in South Korea. Everything had been packed away after the meeting in Pusan, from the usual pieties about regional cooperation to the souvenirs of the annual get-together's most familiar tradition, the group photograph in which each leader is dressed in a traditional outfit of the host nation. Bush sat down in his gym gear with two of his key aides handling Asia: Michael Green, who headed Asia policy at the National Security Council, and Christopher Hill, a veteran career diplomat who earlier that year had taken over U.S. efforts in negotiations aimed at ending North Korea's nuclear program. At the end of the four-nation trip, Bush had his mind on history and wanted some advice.

Bush's image, at home and abroad, has been shaped by his administration's invasion of Iraq and the serial disasters that piled up in its aftermath. When it came to Asia, the Korean peninsula aside, however, Bush displayed few of the shoot-from-the-hip qualities that were on display in the wake of the 9/11 attacks. He had spent time in China as a young man, visiting his father when George H. W. Bush represented U.S. interests in Beijing in the 1970s before the establishment of diplomatic ties. Bush's instincts also reflected sentiment in Washington more broadly, where Asia policy has generally been crafted with respect for expertise, in contrast with that for the Middle East, long a free-fire zone in domestic politics. Throughout his presidency, Bush was preoccupied with the latter, which might have tempered any hawkish instincts he harbored in Asia. Whatever the reason, Bush was mostly a measured interlocutor with America's allies there and China alike. When he was forceful, it was usually in private. Bush was mindful of the region's success as well, something he now wondered might be unraveling amid China and Japan's bitter squabbling.

Bush had established a kind of equilibrium in relations with Beijing early in his second term, but only after a fraught start. In April 2001, in the first diplomatic crisis of his administration, a Chinese fighter jet had collided with a U.S. surveillance plane and crashed, forcing the American aircraft to land on Hainan island. For days, U.S. officials couldn't get in touch with the plane's crew members and struggled to get clear answers about them from Beijing. Jiang Zemin, then traveling in South America, refused to return Bush's calls. "Clinton had to call me six times before I called him back after the Belgrade bombing [of the Chinese embassy in 1999]," Jiang told one South American leader, who then called Bush to recount the conversation. "I am not going to call this guy back after just two phone calls." After protracted negotiations over Chinese demands that Washington apologize for the death of the Chinese pilot—in the end, the U.S. ambassador expressed "sincere regret"—the crew was released.

Bush drew clear lines on Taiwan but again only after a difficult beginning and rousing disquiet on his right flank at home. Early in his presidency, Bush said unambiguously that the United States would defend Taiwan with "whatever it took" if the Chinese attacked the island. Noticing the surprised looks among his aides in the White House where the interview was being conducted, the president asked Stephen Hadley, one of his national security advisers, "Did I say something wrong?" "Well," Hadley replied, "you have just blown away twenty years of strategic ambiguity."

Bush never walked back his statement but gradually shifted his position in response to the erratic behavior of Taiwan's then president, Chen

Shui-bian. The policy enunciated in 2003—that the United States opposed any unilateral action that disturbed the status quo—was squarely
directed at Chen, the first president in Taiwan to come from the longtime
opposition, the Democratic Progressive Party. Beijing believed, not without justification, that Chen was pushing independence for the island,
something that Bush wanted to make clear that he opposed as well. One
right-wing commentator, appalled that Bush wouldn't support a fellow
democracy, called his actions "immoral and dangerous." The Chinese, as
was their wont, praised the president but demanded that he reiterate the
new policy at every encounter. Bush became irritated with the habit of
Beijing's interlocutors of opening meetings by raising the topic of Taiwan.
"I'll repeat my position for you," he once said, cutting off one Chinese
visitor just as he was launching into Beijing's ritual catechism about "one
China." "Here's my position. Write it down. Put it in your notes."

Bush felt no such stress with Junichiro Koizumi. From the start, he
liked the prime minister and his direct style, something that U.S. leaders
had craved in their Japanese counterparts. Bush was grateful, too, for
Japan's rapid commitment of support for America's post-9/11 wars, which
avoided the embarrassment of the two countries' interactions in the first
Gulf War. Any foreign leader who offered support on Iraq went immediately into the White House's good books. "I value you as a close friend,"
Bush told Koizumi at their joint press conference after a meeting in
Kyoto, the first stop of the 2005 trip that took in, in order, Japan, South
Korea, China, and Mongolia. "I appreciate our candid discussion, just
like we had today."

What neither Bush nor his advisers said at the time was that those
"candid discussions" included one about the region's history wars. Concerned about Japan's deteriorating relations with its neighbors, Bush had
asked Koizumi directly why he persisted in paying annual visits to Yasukuni Shrine. Bush posed the question without censure or rebuke, according to officials at the meeting. Instead, he couched his query in terms of
the two countries' mutual economic and security interests in stabilizing
ties among China, Japan, and South Korea, the latter two U.S. allies in
a developing rivalry with Beijing.

Koizumi was characteristically blunt in his reply. "Hu Jintao made me
do it," he told Bush, explaining that the Chinese leader had indicated that
Beijing would resume summit meetings with Tokyo only if he stayed

away from Yasukuni. Koizumi could just as easily have said, "Jiang Zemin made me do it," because his interactions with Jiang over Yasukuni had been much nastier and more personal. But the point was the same: no matter who was in charge in Beijing, as long as the Chinese publicly demanded Koizumi stay away from the shrine, he had no option but to go.

Soon after this conversation, Bush met with Hu in Beijing and asked him in turn about China's relations with Japan. For all the depth of the two countries' economic interdependency and the multiple issues he could have discussed, Hu framed his answer almost entirely around Yasukuni as well. The Chinese leader complained that he had offered Koizumi what he considered a good deal to improve ties: if Koizumi didn't go to the shrine, the pair could enjoy a fully fledged summit meeting. Hu effectively confirmed what Koizumi had told Bush: Japanese prime ministers could go to Yasukuni or enjoy good relations with China, but they couldn't do both. Bush did not proffer a view of his own about the controversy but instead counseled both leaders to dial down the rhetoric, and he did the same with South Korea's Roh Moo-hyun, the host of the regional summit and another sharp critic of Japan.

Now, with his advisers on Air Force One, Bush asked them how the United States should respond, if at all. Hill was forceful in advocating that they issue a statement condemning the Yasukuni visits and, by implication, Japan's handling of history issues generally. As reasonable as such an argument might sound, it was in fact quite radical advice. In effect, Hill was suggesting that Washington take Beijing's, and Seoul's, side against its most important ally in the region on a hypersensitive issue that America had traditionally stayed out of.

Green, a Japan expert, was just as forceful in counseling against this course of action. He warned that a high-profile public condemnation of Japan could backfire on a number of counts. The Left in Japan would be thrilled, because it would buttress their decades-old complaints about Yasukuni and other conservative symbols of the war; the pro-American Right would be furious and feel betrayed. Worse, China, a U.S. rival, would benefit at Japan's expense. Instead, Green proposed that Bush convey any reservations about Koizumi's conduct in private, perhaps though a personal emissary, and work with mutual allies, like John Howard, the Australian prime minister, to drive the point home. More ominously, Green cautioned the president that the United States had skeletons of its own in the closet of postwar Japan that could easily be exhumed—police records of rapes by American service personnel that had never been prosecuted.

Bush took Green's advice and later dispatched him to Japan. Bush wanted him to explain that the White House trusted Japan and that the administration did not want to make the disputes over history a domestic issue in the United States. He was instructed to stress that the conflict was relevant to America because it affected its core security interests in the region. Put another way, the United States considered it not a moral or legal issue but a strategic one and thought that Japan should approach the matter with this in mind. For the moment, Bush had papered over a split that would run throughout the second term of his administration over how to respond to an at times aggravating ally in Japan. More important, though, Bush had done what no American president had attempted for nearly half a century: He had dipped his toes into the region's history wars. In the coming years, the United States would have to wade right in.

In 1958, Harry Truman was asked by the legendary journalist Edward R. Murrow whether he had any regrets about ordering the dropping of the atomic bombs on Hiroshima and Nagasaki. "Any regrets?" the former president replied. "Not the slightest. Not the slightest in the world." George H. W. Bush, who served in the war as a navy aviator, had much the same response when he was questioned years later about whether the United States should apologize for the bombings ahead of the fiftieth anniversary of the attack on Pearl Harbor. "No apology is required, and it will not be asked of this President, I can guarantee you," he responded. Such requests, Bush added, were "rank revisionism."

In 1995, during the lead-up to the fiftieth anniversary of the end of the war, Walter Mondale had become the first U.S. ambassador to Japan to attend a ceremony in Tokyo marking the 1945 firebombing of the city, which killed 100,000 people, mainly citizens, in a single night. Mondale later wondered if that had been an unwise decision, remarking to embassy colleagues that he had been stung by critical letters from U.S. veterans. Soon afterward, the U.S. embassy in Tokyo debated whether Bill Clinton should visit Hiroshima on a trip to Japan later that year. Clinton did visit Japan in 1996—the trip was delayed over one of Washington's perennial budget fights—but did not visit the city and its atomic bomb memorial.

Other presidents might have phrased their comments more delicately than Truman and George H. W. Bush, but none, before or since, have veered far from their message either. In 2016, when he became the first U.S. president to visit Hiroshima while in office, Barack Obama neither apologized in his speech for the bombings nor dared delve into the debates surrounding the weapon's deployment. American leaders have remained convinced that the bombs saved American, and Japanese, lives by forcing Tokyo to surrender ahead of a bloody invasion. Or, like Mondale and Obama, they have been wary of a backlash from American veterans should they show too much sympathy to critics of how the war was waged on Japan.

Japan, after all, had become a U.S. success story, a bulwark of democracy in east Asia and a solid, if occasionally backsliding, security partner for decades in the region's great strategic games, first as balance to the Soviet Union and later against China. There was little upside in disturbing this narrative, so the argument went, especially because the notion that the A-bombs had saved lives was also widespread among the American public. U.S. officials had always avoided being dragged into historical disputes in Asia for another reason, fearing they would be blamed whatever position they took. "Even if a dispute was formally resolved, significant domestic elements in one country or the other, or both, might feel that their side had been short-changed," said David Straub, a former State Department officer who served in both South Korea and Japan. "They would likely seek to reopen the issue, while blaming the US for an 'unfair' agreement."

American officials had first become aware of the Chinese needling them about Japan and history around the time that Clinton was mulling a Hiroshima visit. The mid-1990s was a period when the CCP was emerging out of its post-Tiananmen crouch, all the stronger for having survived. The Chinese economy was growing strongly, and renewed nationalism was pulsating through the system. Having once given the U.S.-Japan alliance a pass while concentrating on building its own economy and military, Beijing was now looking askance at the strengthening ties between the two countries.

On a visit to the United States in 1996, Chi Haotian, China's defense minister, brought with him a gift as a pointed goodwill gesture—a piece of a U.S. B-24 plane brought down over Guangxi in southern China while supplying anti-Japanese forces during the war. Meeting with his counterpart, the Pentagon chief, William Perry, Chi spoke of the scars left by the Japanese invasion on the Chinese people and the "50 million" who were killed. "World War II bound China and the United States together in an earnest cooperation against their common enemy," he said in a speech to the National Defense University. "I hope China-U.S. relations today can still reflect the spirit of that sound and positive cooperation." Chi didn't mention Japan by name, but he didn't have to. The remembrance of the Americans and Chinese fighting side by side against the Japanese soon became a theme for visiting Chinese.

On the same trip, the Americans offered to take Xiong Guangkai, the head of military intelligence, to the Korean War Memorial in Washington. Xiong refused the invitation, no doubt mindful of the perils of being photographed at a place commemorating a battle that pitted U.S. and Chinese troops against each other. Xiong was keener on an alternative: to visit the nearby Holocaust Museum. Stopping before each panel and the horrific stories it imparted, Xiong kept saying words to the effect of "Terrible! But there is no comparison to how cruel the Japanese soldiers were." On his way out, according to his escorts, Xiong added, "You know, China should have a Holocaust Museum of its own."

A decade later, after Koizumi's multiple visits to Yasukuni, the history wars were intensifying. Not only were the Chinese still pressing the Americans to intervene on their side but Beijing was also increasingly trying to use the issue to gain leverage over Japan in bilateral talks. Few played the history card more crudely than Bo Xilai, China's commerce minister and then one of the rising stars of Chinese politics. Elevated initially by his father's revolutionary credentials, Bo had become a dashing, charismatic leader in his own right, cultivating a high profile in the domestic media. His talent for self-promotion was a rare and risky skill in elite Chinese politics, one that would help bring his career crashing down a few years later, when he was ousted on corruption charges. As the point person dealing with foreigners on China's multiplying trade disputes, Bo had many opportunities to burnish his image as someone fighting in China's corner. With such a platform, Japan was an irresistible target.

In early 2006, Bo met his Japanese counterpart, Toshihiro Nikai, in Beijing to discuss contentious trade issues. As each was raised, Bo interspersed his demands with long lectures about Japan's debt to China. Bo wanted to leverage history to pressure Japan to grant China what was called market economy status, which would make it harder for foreigners to take legal action against Chinese exporters for dumping below-cost goods in their countries. He also sought to force Nikai to drop demands that China cut tariffs for imported auto parts. According to the Japanese embassy's chief economics officer, Shinichi Nishimiya, Bo said the dispute over auto tariffs was "a scheme developed by the United States and the European Union to compete with super-competitive Japanese automobile companies." With history in mind, Bo warned that Japan should not play this "game."

Bo might have targeted Nikai deliberately, because he was well known as being in the pro-China camp in Japan and potentially more pliable. Displaying the kind of independence, or perhaps arrogance, that Japanese bureaucrats customarily exhibit in dealing with their nominal political masters, Nishimiya was disdainful of Nikai's inability to handle Bo's onslaught. As a Foreign Ministry official, Nishimiya probably also felt freer in running down a minister fronting a rival Tokyo bureaucracy. In any case, in briefing the Americans about the meeting, Nishimiya made clear that he thought Bo had bested his trade minister. According to the State Department cable reporting the Japanese diplomat's account, "Nishimiya lamented that Bo had grabbed all that Nikai's delegation offered, declined all that the delegation wanted, blasted Japan on history, but Nikai had left Beijing happy."

A few months later, Tom Schieffer, the U.S. ambassador, had lunch in Tokyo with Wang Yi. Still rising through the ranks of the Chinese Foreign Ministry, Wang was now Beijing's ambassador to Japan. Apart from a short chat at the end of the meal about Iran, the pair's conversation focused almost entirely on how to manage the Yasukuni controversy. Wang said China wanted to orchestrate a "soft landing" on the issue so Tokyo could save face. Displaying a solicitude for Japan he didn't dare show in public, Wang added that with their recalcitrant views on the war its outspoken right-wingers were hurting Tokyo's international image: "If these views are heard overseas, it will put Japan in a very awkward position." Wang suggested that Schieffer, a former Texas business partner of Bush's, send a personal message to the president to put pressure on the Japanese. The United States needed to "pay more attention" to history, he said. Unbeknownst to Wang, Bush had already taken the issue up, but without taking sides. Schieffer was noncommittal. Both Japan and China had painted themselves into a corner, he said, and seemed to have no idea how to get out.

The Japanese had their own message for the United States in the diplomatic back-and-forth. It was the same position they had always adopted when the history issue had come up, and that was for the Americans to stay out of it. Quietly, various Japanese parliamentarians and academics delivered a message similar to the advice that Green had given Bush: any interference from the United States would revive latent anti-American sentiment in Japan, to the benefit of China. As one senior LDP official pointed out, many Japanese critics of China were also anti-American, and it would be in both Tokyo's and Washington's interest to keep the "ultranationalists" at bay. An unyielding Koizumi himself made the same point more bluntly after his final visit to the shrine later in 2006. In an exchange with reporters, he testily observed that he didn't think Bush would be so silly as to ask him not to go: "President Bush wouldn't say anything so immature."

Although Green's advice to Bush prevailed, it wasn't without debate within the administration. In meetings convened by the National Security Council, the Pentagon typically viewed the controversy through the prism of the security alliance. Even then, one prominent Pentagon official lamented that Bush had raised history issues with Koizumi "too gently." A number of officials in the NSC and the State Department complained Koizumi was using up precious U.S. political capital with China. "You couldn't put the China relationship ahead of the alliance, but a lot of people were very angry with Koizumi and thought it was unfair to America," said an official then serving on the NSC. "To some extent, Koizumi's embrace of Yasukuni was also anti-American." The shrine, after all, honored convicted war criminals who had led the attack on Pearl Harbor and the subsequent conflict with America.

Not only was Tokyo battling Beijing and segments of the U.S. government, but it was also facing an increasingly agitated South Korea. In early 2006, around the time of Bo's meeting with Nikai, the Japanese embassy in Seoul obtained what it called "sensitive" information, presumably through intelligence sources, that China's ambassador to Seoul had been pressing South Korea to coordinate history policy on Japan, effectively ganging up against it. Shotaro Yachi, atop the Foreign Affairs

Ministry in Tokyo, was livid, reacting as if Seoul had crossed a red line. He called in his South Korean counterpart and told him, "Such collusion on this difficult issue was unacceptable."

Seoul was fertile territory for China's entreaties, and not just because of the antipathy many South Koreans still harbored toward Japan's colonial rule. In that respect, South Korea was very different from Taiwan. When Taiwan was emerging as a democracy in the late 1980s, its newly empowered citizens focused their ire not at their former colonial master, Japan. Their attempt to build a country that stood proudly on its own feet meant separating themselves from the island's more recent overseers, the Chinese—in the form of first Chiang Kai-shek's Nationalists and later the much bigger threat of the Communist Party in China. When South Korea democratized around the same time, the citizenry's focus, and that of the social activists who wanted to rewrite and regain control over their country's history, was always Japan.

There was an extra edge, however, for South Korea. Seoul's most powerful and prominent postwar leader, Park Chung-hee, had served with distinction during the colonial period as a senior officer in the Japanese army in Manchuria. As the historian Alexis Dudden points out, had there been anything like the Tokyo Tribunal in Korea, Park "would have likely been in jail or hanged before the Korean War began." Park would later rationalize his service in Manchuria by arguing he had been preparing for Korea's ultimate liberation from plans by the three big regional powers—Japan, Russia, and China—"to swallow" his country altogether.

In the mid-1960s, as the Vietnam War escalated, Washington urged Japan and South Korea to settle their differences in an effort to anchor the U.S. strategic position in the region. The Americans promised to sweeten any deal between its allies to establish formal diplomatic ties, offering loans to South Korea, plus cash in return for Seoul's committing troops to fight in Vietnam. For its part in the bilateral agreement, Japan agreed to pay South Korea $800 million in various ways as a form of economic cooperation. In so doing, Japan demanded, and Park agreed, that the two countries would close the books on reparations claims. Tokyo wanted Park to use some of the money to compensate individuals, or their families, who had been forced into military service or forced labor by the Japanese. At that point, the comfort women were barely discussed, let alone acknowledged as potential claimants.

From then onward, as far as Tokyo was concerned, any claims that arose from the colonial period were Seoul's to handle. As an authoritarian leader who had declared martial law soon before the deal was struck, Park could, and did, do what he liked with the money his government got from Japan. Apart from some small payments made in the mid-1970s, Park earmarked the Japanese funds to build a new, national steel industry instead of distributing it to aggrieved groups. Two to three decades later, Koreans living in a democracy were able to demand much more, both from their own government and from Japan.

Forced laborers transported to Sakhalin, comfort women, Korean atomic bomb victims, and a large number of other once-marginalized groups given voice and energy in the country's new democracy now lined up to file lawsuits. Beginning in the late 1980s and gathering momentum in the 1990s, they demanded recognition and compensation. The fact that as controversial and complex a figure as Park, who was first a collaborator with the Japanese and later a Korean nationalist, oversaw the original deal only made it a more attractive target. The lid that Tokyo had thought it had put on South Korean claims for reparations for the colonial period was slowly being pried off.

As had been the case with China, Tokyo screamed betrayal when the old recriminations began to resurface more than half a century after the war's end. Japan thought it had secured a political fix over the past with South Korea, first with the 1965 treaty and then again with a written apology in 1998 (which Jiang Zemin sought but didn't get). South Korea's then prime minister, Kim Dae-jung, had agreed as part of that deal that the two countries should look to the future. Few leaders carried the moral authority of Kim, a longtime political prisoner who had had once been kidnapped by his own country's security services in Tokyo and spirited by boat out of the country, surviving only after Washington intervened. The South Koreans believed that Koizumi had promised Kim as part of the 1998 deal that Japan would establish a national cemetery separate from Yasukuni, one that excluded Class A war criminals. When this plan didn't go forward, and Koizumi's Yasukuni visits persisted, Kim's successor all but declared the bilateral deal null and void.

The anger against South Korea in Tokyo extended deep into Japan's foreign policy establishment. The diplomat who negotiated the agreement, Kenichiro Sasae, would go on to head the Foreign Ministry and serve as ambassador to Washington. Sasae, an impish, witty character who was given to strategic temper tantrums during difficult negotiations, told colleagues he felt personally "outraged" by Seoul's decision to "break the deal" under which both sides had agreed to "put historical issues in a box."

As with China, Korean-Japanese economic ties were blossoming in the early years of the new century, and bilateral trade was at record levels. Flights between Seoul and Tokyo's downtown airport at Haneda had doubled to eight jumbo jets a day. Korean soap operas and pop music had become hugely popular in Japan. South Korea's industrial advances had impressed the Japanese, and even worried them a little. But while South Korea was economically and culturally hot, it was politically cold, in the popular phrase used at the time. To America's annoyance, and Beijing's delight, the mutual antagonism between Tokyo and Seoul would only grow.

Koizumi's departure from office in 2006 offered Japan and China the chance for a fresh start, although the conditions hardly favored one. The Japanese public had been deeply alienated by the waves of protests in China, and its press reflected, and played on, these fears. A review of five hundred articles in the local media between 2001 and 2003 by a Japanese scholar found a handful of themes dominated coverage, especially that of a dangerous, militarily aggressive China that was also hollowing out the Japanese economy. It was certainly true that the Japanese media saw value in reporting aggressively on its neighbor. As one of Japan's top diplomats, Takeo Akiba, remarked, "The public loves to see China bashed in the press." The sentiment was equally glum in Beijing. From its perspective, Koizumi's Yasukuni visits had confirmed Chinese instincts that Japan was "fundamentally incapable of behaving as a responsible power and achieving genuine reconciliation with its neighbors."

Such events might have been mere "byplay," in the words of the Japan scholar Richard Samuels, when considered alongside hard measures like Chinese power and military capabilities. But even here, there were concrete signs of a more hostile posture. The most notorious occurred in late 2004 with the brazen intrusion into Japanese waters of a Chinese nuclear-powered submarine near Okinawa. The Chinese Foreign Ministry later

offered a mea culpa of sorts, and within China many officials and scholars privately expressed anger at what they saw as the navy's provocative
action. The noisy vessel was easily spotted and tracked by both the Japanese and the Americans, which might have been the intention all along.
Whatever the motivation, China's military modernization within the
past decade had vastly expanded its capabilities on the sea and in the air.
The array of missiles that China had deployed to target Taiwan, many in
Tokyo noted, could just as easily be aimed at the U.S. bases in Japan.

In Beijing, the military buildup took on an entirely different com-
plexion when it was viewed in the context of strengthening U.S.-Japan
security ties over the previous decade. The updated alliance's agreement
to cover the area around Taiwan, the joint deployment of a missile defense system, and the gradual paring back of the constitutional constraints on Japan's military were all of a piece. The United States had
become a "propellant" rather than a "cap" on the Japanese military, in
the words of a prominent mainstream Chinese scholar. Far from constraining Japan's rearmament, the Americans were now driving it. "At
least as far as China is concerned," wrote Wu Xinbo, a prominent Shanghai-
based academic who held hard-edged views on the United States, in
2005, "the bright side of the U.S.-Japanese alliance seems to be gone."

Into this cauldron stepped Shinzō Abe, elected LDP leader and thus
prime minister in September 2006. At fifty-two, he was Japan's youngest
postwar leader. The fact that he was the grandson of Nobusuke Kishi, the
former administrator of Manchuria and the wartime munitions minister,
would have been enough on its own to make Beijing's hair stand on end.
On his record alone, Abe was firmly identified with resurgent nationalistic
sentiment in the ruling party, making him the sort of individual that the
Chinese instinctively disliked, whatever his lineage. Ahead of his election,
his critics predicted diplomatic disaster for Japan. "The United States will
not be happy; China will not be happy; South Korea will not be happy,"
said Koichi Kato, one of the few remaining pro-China conservatives.
"Some say we will find ourselves left behind, alone." Kato's comments were
not welcomed on the far right. Hours after his press conference, a house
he owned, and in which his mother lived, was set alight.

In *Toward a Beautiful Country*, his political manifesto published just
before he became prime minister, Abe pressed all the buttons that had
traditionally riled Japan's neighbors. He defended Yasukuni, railed

against the pacifist constitution written by the U.S. occupation, and expressed pride in Japanese history. In Abe's mind, his critics had their priorities upside down. He argued passionately that postwar Japan had never been given sufficient credit by its neighbors for being a peaceful, democratic state. "Have any Japanese prime ministers given instructions to invade neighboring countries?" he asked. "[Have they] tried to possess long-range missiles to attack foreign countries? To arm the country with nuclear weapons? Oppress human rights? Limit freedom? Destroy democracy? The answer to all of these questions is no. Today's Japan is a democratic state that has nothing to do with militarism in any aspect."

In private, Abe was hardheaded, even cynical, about China and the pressure its leaders put on Japan. For him Beijing's Japan bashing was a calculated diversion. "They are using anti-Japanese sentiment to divert anti-party feeling," he told Admiral William Fallon, when the U.S. Pacific commander was visiting Tokyo a few weeks before Abe became prime minister. Whatever he did about Yasukuni, Abe said, the "structural contradiction" that dictated Beijing's behavior wouldn't change. In his eyes, China needed to court Japan for investment and technology while at the same time to stir up animosity against it to maintain political control. Abe insisted that bilateral relations had "not worsened that much" under Koizumi, which, on the face of it, was a remarkably sanguine statement. But, as he pointed out to Fallon, while political relations had been all but frozen for the previous five years, two-way trade had doubled.

Abe's analysis of China's interest in courting Japan proved prescient. Within weeks of taking office, the new Japanese prime minister was welcomed in Beijing and then in Seoul. The negotiations to bring Abe and Hu Jintao together—the first formal summit between leaders of the two countries in five years—were a close-run affair. Leading the talks again were Dai Bingguo and Shotaro Yachi, whose last extended dialogue had been in the hot springs of Niigata. The reporting by U.S. diplomats in Tokyo of the negotiations overflows with acid comments from their Japanese interlocutors about Abe's deep distrust of the Foreign Ministry, Yachi aside, and his efforts to bypass it using personal emissaries.

When Dai set off for Tokyo for the talks, Japan's ambassador in Beijing joked that he would erect a statue of him if the two sides could bridge their differences. Dai didn't regard the jest as a good omen. Dai and Yachi and their teams negotiated for days, often until six in the morning, haggling for hours over single words. The stress of the talks nearly overwhelmed Dai, who contracted a painful bout of shingles but soldiered on regardless. The discussions broke down at one point amid yelling and mutual recriminations on both sides, and Dai returned to Beijing, only to fly back the next day after Tokyo put forward a new proposal.

Ahead of his arrival, Wang Yi, the Chinese ambassador, called Yachi's colleague Kenichiro Sasae, getting him out of bed at about 3:00 a.m. What's wrong with you guys ringing so early? a tired Sasae snapped. It's not as if we are going to war. By 4:00 a.m., Wang was at Yachi's Tokyo home pinning down the final details. Dai said he wore sunglasses for the first time in his life when he arrived back in Tokyo to avoid the Chinese press. As he strode off the plane, his staff joked that he looked like a globe-trotting business executive.

With memories of mass demonstrations the year before still raw, the Chinese leadership took no chances with Abe's visit. Hu, generally dismissed as a timid leader, was taking a substantial risk in inviting Abe for a summit meeting. His overtures to Koizumi had all been misfires, and Abe's track record made him an even riskier bet, especially because the Japanese made no promises to stay away from Yasukuni. Security was beefed up outside the Japanese embassies and consulates. Internet chat rooms were scrubbed of overtly anti-Japanese posts. The party's Propaganda Department ordered the Chinese media to run only official reports about the leaders' meeting. The Chinese state made sure to use all of its immense powers, both by controlling the message its citizenry heard and by rounding up any naysayers who ignored it.

Only days before flying to Beijing, Abe had been batting back questions about the war in parliament. Abe had said that although Japan's wartime leaders had been convicted by the Tokyo Tribunal, "they were not war criminals under domestic law." He added, referring to his grandfather Kishi, "That was also the case for my relative." Although Abe had expressed similar sentiments in his book, to repeat such statements only days before painstakingly negotiated, fence-mending visits to Beijing and Seoul was, if nothing else, ill-timed. Abe's harping on one of his pet themes—the illegitimacy of the "victor's justice" meted out by the Allies after the war—would come back to haunt him. In the meantime, Abe moderated his comments the following day, and Chinese leaders held their collective tongues on his arrival in Beijing.

During Abe's visit, the two countries agreed to appoint a panel of historians to try to find common ground on the past. Their diplomats set up a schedule of regular official-level meetings on the economy and energy, a bureaucratic tactic to stabilize the relationship. For the first time, Hu publicly stated that Japan had stuck to a path of peaceful development since the war. On the face of it, this was the most anodyne of statements. From Tokyo's perspective, however, it was a critical acknowledgment from Beijing of Japan's postwar record that undercut China's persistent propaganda about resurgent Japanese militarism. This new understanding would keep relations on an even keel until 2009 and through three Japanese prime ministers.

That Abe might have problems with China on history was predictable. Few foresaw that his biggest problem with such issues in his first term as prime minister would be with the United States.

In early 2007, a number of American congressmen launched a motion demanding that Japan apologize for the Imperial Army's role in setting up frontline brothels with the so-called comfort women. Although he was due in Washington in a few months, Abe could not hold his tongue when questioned by reporters. "There is no evidence to prove there was coercion, as initially suggested," he insisted. As on history generally, Abe's views on this topic were not a secret. He was a founding member of a large group of parliamentarians who in 1997 urged Japan to revise its history pedagogy and get rid of what they called the Left's masochistic view of the past. But his airing such views on the eve of a visit to the White House was a mistake.

In the uproar that followed, Abe quickly found himself in a vise. He was stuck between his American friends, who told him that debating the technicalities of whether the comfort women were forced into prostitution was a no-win proposition, and fellow revisionists at home, who were lobbying to overturn a 1993 Japanese government statement acknowledging the military's role in the wartime sex trade. The Kono Statement, named after the then chief cabinet secretary, Yohei Kono, acknowledged that the military had been involved "directly and indirectly" in the recruitment, transfer, and management of the comfort women.

One of Abe's closest confidants on history issues in parliament, Nariaki Nakayama, became enraged at a heated meeting on the subject at the prime minister's office. A zealot on history issues, he demanded that the government press ahead with an inquiry to reexamine the Kono Statement, despite Abe's imminent Washington visit. Nakayama knew the outcome he wanted. He had likened the recruitment of the comfort women to the process by which a school subcontracts the running of its cafeteria. "Some say it is useful to compare the brothels to college cafeterias run by private companies, who recruit their own staff, procure foodstuffs, and set prices," he said. "Where there's demand, businesses crop up."

For Washington, the controversy was a classic Japanese own goal—nitpicking over an unambiguously horrific part of history with a massive strategic downside. If Abe reopened the issue, the State Department reported, it would be a "disturbing indication he is willing to isolate Japan in furtherance of a conservative, nationalist agenda." In turn, Japanese diplomats privately warned the Americans that it might be hard to get Abe and his cohorts to climb down. They were "true believers," the head of the ministry's Asia division told them, and then went on to suggest that Abe was obsessed with the topic. "The prime minister knows too much [about the subject]. He literally knows more about the issue than any other Diet member, having studied it for the past ten years."

America's allies weighed in with the same message. John Howard, the Australian prime minister, was a dyed-in-the-wool conservative whose priority with Japan was building closer security ties. For him, Japan's stirring up of issues like the comfort women damaged the bigger agenda, something Howard made clear on a visit to Tokyo around this time. In the midst of an otherwise upbeat meeting, Howard abruptly told Abe he could not accept his position on comfort women. "Abe's body language changed completely," diplomats in the meeting reported, "and he dropped back in his chair and gave a flat, unenthusiastic statement reaffirming" his support for the 1993 statement.

Privately, Abe explained to American friends that he had been personally offended by the congressional motion. He thought it made the Japanese appear like the Serbs in the previous decade's conflicts in the Balkans, using the cover of war to brutally rape women at will. Ultimately, though, the advice that he keep quiet about the controversial matter had been "reluctantly received and helpful." In the days ahead of his White House visit in April, Abe called Bush and explained his remorse over the comfort women and their suffering. Their two staffs, in the meantime, worked out a formula to deal with the issue diplomatically. At a press conference after their White House talks, Bush said he "accepted" Abe's apology on the comfort women, although it was not clear that Abe had actually offered one or why Bush should accept it, because he was scarcely the wronged party. For the moment, though, the strategy worked. Both sides were relieved to put history to one side again.

The comfort women episode damaged Abe's image in Washington, but it would not be the most substantive difference he had with the United States. The most serious split, which reached deep into George W. Bush's administration, concerned something else—the entanglement of regional diplomacy regarding Pyongyang's nuclear program with the emotional issue of North Korea's kidnapping of Japanese citizens.

Decades later, the accounts of Kim Jong Il's abduction program still have an unreal *X-Files* aura about them. On Kim's orders, Pyongyang deployed agents in the 1970s and 1980s to snatch over a dozen, and maybe more, Japanese and spirit them back to North Korea. The country's agents plucked a thirteen-year-old girl from the streets of a coastal town in western Japan, a mother and daughter on their way home from a shopping trip, and a romantic teenage couple off a beach in the dark of the evening. The agents lured other Japanese they befriended traveling in Europe to come to North Korea and then never let them leave. It wasn't just the Japanese whom Kim targeted, although they were especially valued because their identities were ideal for fake passports. Kim's grotesque project snared all sorts—famous South Korean filmmakers and actors, Lebanese from Beirut, Thais living in Macau. In the decades after the 1953 truce in the Korean civil war, thousands of fishermen from the south were kidnapped and taken to the north as well.

When Kim's kidnappings began to come to light in the late 1990s and the early years of the century, many Japanese politicians and bureaucrats shied away from confronting the issue. The Korean peninsula is a minefield in Japanese politics, replete with sensitivities about the colonial past and the contested status of ethnic Koreans still living in Japan, some loyal to the south, others to the north, and many of them at odds with their host nation.

Koizumi, with Abe in tow, had made a daring attempt to find diplomatic and political closure on the abductees controversy on a visit to Pyongyang in late 2002, the first ever by a Japanese leader to North Korea. When Tokyo is accused of not apologizing for the war and the brutal colonialism that preceded it, it is often forgotten that Koizumi apologized even to North Korea, one of the world's most enduringly brutal regimes. The Koizumi visit was dubbed the "double apology" trip: when the Japanese apologized for the colonial period, Kim did the same for abducting Japanese citizens. The trip was initially hailed as a historic breakthrough in Tokyo's relations with Pyongyang. Certainly, the furious reaction of Japanese ultra-rightists to Koizumi reaching out to a long-standing enemy was a measure of the visit's risks. After Koizumi's second, and final, trip to Pyongyang, in 2003, a bomb was planted at the home of the architect of the policy, Hitoshi Tanaka, who had been promoted to deputy minister at the Foreign Ministry. A note was attached to the ticking bomb, addressed to: "Hitoshi Tanaka, traitor." Shintaro Ishihara, by now Tokyo's governor, was unconcerned by the threat. Tanaka "deserved it," he said, for being at Pyongyang's "beck and call."

In photographs from the 2002 trip, Abe can be seen in the background, balefully glaring at Kim as he shakes Koizumi's hand. Kim's admission that supposedly rogue intelligence units in Pyongyang had kidnapped thirteen Japanese but that only five were still alive, far from settling the controversy, only inflamed it in Japan. Abe's anger at North Korea never abated, and the issue became his political meal ticket, giving him a profile and stature he had previously lacked. Abe later wrote that many Japanese MPs wouldn't take on the abductees' cases for fear of being labeled "right-wing reactionaries." By contrast, Abe portrayed his own pursuit of justice for their families as akin to Winston Churchill's lonely crusade against German rearmament in the 1930s. "When I see politicians, I put them into two categories," he wrote. "One is 'a politician who fights'; the other is 'a politician who doesn't fight.'" Abe placed himself firmly in the former group.

Once the abductees controversy got entangled in the dialogue to rein in Pyongyang's nuclear ambitions—the so-called six-party talks—the issue became vastly more complicated. In retrospect, the six-party talks

were just a way station along a meandering, stop-start, and thus far fruit-
less campaign to kill North Korea's nuclear program. The talks were
convened in 2003 by China, in what was widely depicted as a diplomatic
coming-of-age for Beijing, and brought together the two Koreas, Japan,
Russia, and the United States for five rounds of negotiations, which
lasted until 2007. From the moment international inspectors detected
gaps in North Korea's declaration of its nuclear program in 1992, the
United States and its allies, sometimes working in tandem with China,
tried multiple ways to bring the program to a verifiable halt. Using a
mixture of lies, bluster, and the occasional strung-out discussion, Pyongyang gave ground at times but never to the point of abandoning its evolving nuclear bomb-making and bomb-delivery capacity.

For a while, though, the U.S. diplomat Christopher Hill and his boss,
Secretary of State Condoleezza Rice, had grand ambitions for the six-
party forum. They hoped they could use the talks to persuade North
Korea to give up its weapons in return for a peace treaty to finally end
the Korean civil war. Hill and Rice, both steeped in European postwar
security institutions, also contemplated the six-party conclave being
turned into a permanent organization for east Asian nations to sort out
security disputes among themselves. One U.S. government official remembers Rice being briefed at length on the region when she became
secretary of state in 2005. At the end of the session, she thanked her
briefer and simply asked, "Why can't Asia be more like Europe?" before
walking out.

Before he led Washington's team in the Korean nuclear talks, Hill
had worked on settling the bloody conflict triggered by the breakup of
the former Yugoslavia. For all that experience taught him, Hill says nothing prepared him for the histrionics of working alongside Japan and
South Korea. He tried at first to caucus with Tokyo and Seoul to define
a unified three-way position for the broader negotiations. Although the
United States and its two allies had held trilateral consultations for years
to coordinate policy, Hill scornfully says in his memoirs that the arrangement was foisted on him by the "East Asia security club" in Washington and "charter members" like Michael Green, his colleague in the
George W. Bush administration. Once he took charge of the U.S. negotiating team for the talks, he quickly lost patience with Tokyo and
Seoul's squabbling and ended the three-way discussions. Hill didn't hide

his dim view of his east Asian allies. "Give me the Bosnian Serbs any day!" he said.

Behind the antagonism between Tokyo and Seoul that so annoyed Hill were familiar quarrels over territorial disputes and history. But the unrelenting pressure from Japanese conservatives, led by Abe, to insert the abductions issue into the six-party talks was another wedge driving them apart. As popular as this issue was at home, within the six-party talks, Japan's stand was seen as an obstacle to a greater strategic prize. "Do you have any idea how many hundreds, perhaps thousands, of our citizens have been abducted by the North Koreans?" snapped Song Min-soon, Seoul's representative at the talks, when Hill pressed the abductions during negotiations.

Over time, Hill would come to have a deeply negative view of the Japanese and became notorious for bad-mouthing them, causing a bitter rift with policy makers in Washington more sympathetic to Tokyo. "His view was that policy was screwed up because 'the Asianists' were in charge," said a Bush administration official. A State Department colleague who suggested tweaking a proposal to take account of Japan's views in the six-party talks was stunned when Hill shot back at him, "That's such complete Asia-hand, inside baseball bullshit." On one occasion, Hill traveled to Tokyo for meetings and planned to go straight on from there to North Korea without telling his Japanese hosts, a serious breach of trust in the eyes of the Asia hands. Like Henry Kissinger, Hill had become convinced that the Japanese system couldn't keep secrets. In Tokyo, he complained, everything leaked.

In the eyes of both Hill and Rice, the Japanese "lost their way" when Koizumi left office and Abe took over. "We needed a confident Japan as a partner in a changing Asia," Rice wrote in her memoirs, "and with the end of Junichiro Koizumi's term in office in 2006, those days had seemed to disappear." In that book, Rice is scathing about Japanese leadership. "Depressing," "stagnant," "aging," "hypersensitive," "impenetrable," "obscure," "insecure," and "hamstrung by old animosities" are all words Rice uses in the space of a few pages to describe America's closest Asian ally. Although she expressed frustration with Beijing and Hu Jintao, Rice's sharpest barbs after she left office were reserved for Tokyo.

Just as he was in the State Department, Hill was a divisive figure within the White House, where he was nicknamed the "assistant secretary for North Korea." Some officials admired his take-no-prisoners commitment to getting an agreement with North Korea. "If Chris could not get the North Korea deal done, then no one could have," said one administration official. They described him as a good negotiator and a poor diplomat. Others, including Vice President Dick Cheney and many of the Asia experts that Hill had sidelined, opposed the deal he and Rice eventually persuaded Bush to support. So, too, did Abe, who clashed heatedly with Rice leading up to the final pact.

In mid-2008, the United States announced that it would take North Korea off its list of state sponsors of terrorism in return for Pyongyang's declaring its nuclear program, in theory the first in a series of cascading steps that would see the program dismantled altogether. Bush knew he was taking a risk, according to his advisers, but accepted that the deal was worth trying. "There was no high-fiving in the White House the day this was announced," said one administration official. Hill had little patience for Japanese criticism, which he knew was inevitable. "If you feel so strongly about it, why don't you get your own state-sponsored terror list?" Hill told one of Japan's top diplomats when he complained. "Why rely on us?"

After the decision was announced, Abe attacked the agreement, but by then, he was shouting from the sidelines, having resigned as prime minister after only a year in office. In the end, an ailing Kim Jong Il, who had suffered a stroke, rejected the deal, as Pyongyang had done so often in the past. The U.S. intelligence community believed that once he fell ill, Kim lost any interest in a grand bargain over the nuclear program and poured all his political resources into ensuring that his son Kim Jong Un succeeded him, maintaining the family's despotic dynasty.

Like the six-party talks, Abe's prime ministership had ended in a whimper. Unhealthy and seemingly beaten down by the burdens of office, Abe had been a disappointment, at home and abroad, after starting with high expectations. At the time, few saw him making a comeback. Ironically, one of Abe's legacies was stronger ties with China. But as Bush sensed near the end of his presidency, the history wars had by then settled into east Asian domestic politics like a deeply resistant virus. Once just about the past, they were now very much alive as a security issue.

CHAPTER TEN

The Ampo Mafia

Trust me.
—Yukio Hatoyama, to Barack Obama, on Okinawa

Large-scale deep-water rigs are our mobile national territory and a strategic weapon.
—Wang Yilin, Chinese state oil executive

Whenever he led delegations to see Hu Jintao, Yuji Miyamoto made a practice of standing last in line when saying farewell. It was a small diplomatic ruse that Tokyo's ambassador in Beijing used to get Hu's attention and grab a few precious words with the Chinese leader. In early 2008, waiting until his delegation trailed out ahead of him, Miyamoto found Hu seemingly almost as anxious to talk to him as he was to the president. Hu was scheduled to travel to Japan a few months later, in May. "Hu grabbed my arm," Miyamoto recalled, "and told me he was really concerned about his visit and wanted to convey his wishes to Fukuda."

Hu was the most pro-Japan of Chinese leaders, and Yasuo Fukuda, now prime minister, the most pro-China of Japanese leaders. The pair had a potentially transformative deal on their agenda. Instead of fighting over the East China Sea, Tokyo and Beijing were negotiating a deal to develop its underwater resources together. Yet Hu was worried that he might have to cancel his visit, which had been minutely choreographed for months in advance, because of political controversy in Japan. This particular clash didn't involve the usual suspects that had traditionally upended bilateral ties, such as the history wars or territorial disputes or Chinese military maneuvers. As if to underline how fragile the relationship had become, the two leaders, and their respective diplomats, were flailing over poisoned dumplings.

It had taken years for Japan to persuade China to enter into talks on how they should divide up the oil and gas reserves both believed lay beneath the ocean. Their fishing fleets had shared the waters for more than a century. In the 1950s, when the two nations didn't have diplomatic ties, they still met to negotiate fishing rights and how to handle boats and their crews confiscated for straying into each other's territory. It wasn't until the late 1960s, when the United Nations surveyed the seas for resources around the Senkaku/Diaoyu Islands, that their competition extended to include oil and gas. For both resource-poor Japan and a China that had become an oil importer in the early 1990s, the prospect of hydrocarbons on their doorstep was a potential game changer. So, too, was a possible deal between the two countries to share it. A deal over oil could also mean a truce over their territorial disputes in the East China Sea.

The diplomats from both nations began talks in 2004 with powerful interests at home applying pressure on their delegations. It wasn't just politicians with a strong nationalistic bent who were shadowing the talks; their respective militaries were watching closely as well. They also had to deal with the local energy companies, which were eager to obtain as big a share of the potential wealth as they could. Should China start production before the two sides had a deal, the Foreign Ministry's Kenichiro Sasae warned, the Japanese who believed they had equal rights to the areas would be furious. "Japanese companies," he said, "would no longer feel constrained about development, which could lead to severe tensions." In one meeting with his Chinese counterpart, a Japanese minister picked up a cup and a straw and held it up, to illustrate how Chinese drilling in a field at the edge of the median line in the East China Sea could suck out resources from the Japanese side.

Whatever the views of corporate Japan, Chinese companies like the offshore oil enterprise CNOOC were always going to be intimately involved in the negotiations. CNOOC is a large, central-government-owned company whose top executives serve at the pleasure of the party. Its CEO is accorded a place on the party's Central Committee, giving it formidable political clout in its own right. State industry executives in China invariably parrot political and nationalistic rhetoric, because they know it can be dangerous to their careers not to. Nonetheless, the ties among the Chinese oil industry, the party, and the military run far deeper than just their assigned roles in the sprawling political networks that run the nation.

After a Chinese minister pronounced in 2002 that the East China Sea was to become one of the country's most important sites for gas exploration, he expanded on his statement in an interview with a military magazine. Chinese military writings, in turn, described the area in starkly sovereign terms as China's "second national territory." Beijing's defense white papers single out the navy's role in protecting China's "maritime rights and interests." While CNOOC has long been considered the most international of Chinese oil majors, the main onshore producer, CNPC, better known by the name of its listed arm, PetroChina, had the longest-standing and deepest ties to the military. Nonetheless, in 2012, after a CNOOC-operated rig was readied for waters in the South China Sea, the company's chairman didn't try to sugarcoat his enterprise's broader mission. Speaking in Beijing, Wang Yilin called large, deepwater rigs "our mobile national territory and a strategic weapon."

The initial talks starting in 2004 did not go well. Beijing claimed that Tokyo was late to the party, arguing that the Chinese had been developing fields in the East China Sea since the 1990s. Why should they accommodate Tokyo's "sudden" interest in the issue? Chinese diplomats said Beijing would "never accept" the inclusion of long-established fields in any agreement anyway. Bluster aside, the negotiations were complicated by the two sides' contradictory interpretations of the UN treaty governing the law of the sea. The treaty allows each nation to claim an exclusive economic zone of 200 nautical miles from its coastline. Given that the sea separating Japan and China was only 360 nautical miles, some compromise had to be found. The Japanese proposed drawing a line down the middle, as it were, and then jointly developing fields that crossed over the area in which both sides had a legal claim. Citing another clause of the law, Beijing said it was entitled to everything above the continental shelf extending out from its coastline, which took its claim all the way to the waters off Okinawa.

As if the negotiations over oil and gas weren't fraught enough, another bilateral battle broke out, over a staple of Chinese cuisine that was also popular in Japan—dumplings. On one level, it was not hard to understand how mere foodstuffs could provoke a huge controversy in Japan. Scores of Japanese had fallen ill after eating the dumplings, which had been found to contain pesticide and were traced back to a company in Hebei, the province adjoining Beijing. In the immediate wake of the scandal, China's quarantine body gave the Hebei plant the all clear after a brief, perfunctory inspection and then promptly announced that the pesticide must have been added to the dumplings in Japan. In a highly regulated country that was fastidious about food and food safety, China's explanation was never credible.

It would be two years before a culprit was found and five before he was put on trial. A thirty-nine-year-old factory worker in Hebei admitted to using a syringe to inject a toxic chemical into frozen dumplings. It was not because he hated Japan, as had first been rumored. His reasons were much more prosaic and redolent of widespread complaints of China's working poor: he was angry about his low wages and poor conditions and the fact that his wife, also employed at the factory, did not get a bonus when she went on maternity leave. The worker was sentenced to life in prison, but the verdict came far too late. The outbreak of illness, and China's handling of the matter, had already alienated large sections of the Japanese public, who continued to view the affair as a case of its neighbor's indifference to the dangers of exporting its substandard health regulations offshore.

In Tokyo, Fukuda's supporters were worried that the prime minister's already tenuous popularity would not survive a visit from Hu in the midst of such controversy. In Beijing, Chinese diplomats saw two years of painstaking diplomatic repair being undone by a strategically irrelevant issue. To underline the absurdity of the situation—of a dispute over food nearly derailing the relationship between two of the biggest economies in the world—try to imagine something similar happening elsewhere. Germany, France, and the U.K. have fought wars and sniped at one another for centuries, but it is hard to think of their relationships being subsumed by, say, the mislabeling of French wine exported across the Channel or rancid German sausages being found on neighboring countries' shores.

For some Chinese strategists, Japan's open political system and its media's freedom to report on the scandals only made the situation worse. "In China, once Hu Jintao and others decided to improve relations with Japan, all the media organs had to run pro-Japan stories," Liang Yunxiang, a Japan expert at Peking University, told U.S. diplomats. "Meanwhile,

Japan's free press was able to run stories about Chinese-manufactured tainted gyoza/dumplings poisoning [the] Japanese and the 'rise of China' to sell papers and increase suspicion in Japan."

To make sure that Hu appreciated the depth of anger in Japan, the Foreign Ministry in Beijing took the unusual step of bypassing the usual protocols for sending advice up through the system to top leaders. Instead, it dispatched a report directly to Hu's office about the calamitous impact of the dumplings dispute. Furious at the damage to a relationship he had tried so hard to stabilize, Hu summoned the ministers for quarantine and public security to his office in the central leadership compound for a rare personal dressing-down. He was especially angry at their preemptive public announcement blaming the Japanese for adding pesticide to the dumplings, asking them, "Did you think about international public opinion?"

Chinese leaders had another reason to tread lightly in this period. In the lead-up to the Beijing Olympics in 2008, Beijing had tried to moderate its diplomatic voice and avoid confrontation with its rivals, lest it spoil the games. Even given this self-imposed restraint, the efforts of Hu and Wen Jiabao, his premier, to rebuild ties with Japan were striking. Wen traveled to Japan in April 2007 and became the first Chinese leader to address the Japanese parliament, an event televised live in both countries. In his speech, Wen used a text similar to that used by Jiang Zemin in his ill-fated 1998 trip. The address began with an appreciation of China's relationship with Japan and then went on to discuss the war, though Wen spared the Japanese another lecture on history. Later that year, Fukuda, who had taken over from Abe as prime minister in September, visited China. It was the first time in the two nations' lengthy history that both leaders had visited each other's country in the same year. Despite the food-poisoning controversy, Hu stuck to the May timetable for his trip to Japan, the first by a Chinese president to Japan in a decade.

Behind the scenes, however, the whispers persisted. Miyamoto, the Japanese ambassador, reported that Hu had traveled to Japan over the opposition of many party and government officials. Following the trip, the hawks in Beijing had then assailed him for not making enough of the history issue, he said. Mindful of his vulnerability, Hu's aides took countermeasures, ordering the state-controlled media to run articles comparing his approach to Japan to that of Deng Xiaoping. In Tokyo, Fukuda struggled with similar backbiting. Only a month after Hu's visit, which both sides had considered a hard-won triumph, Japanese conservatives were openly deriding Fukuda's China policy as weak. Tarō Asō, the former foreign affairs minister, told a visiting U.S. senator that "liberals" like Fukuda were out of touch with "mainstream" public opinion, which was antagonistic toward China. "Now we are in the center," Asō said, referring to conservatives in the ruling party. Asō had ulterior motives for criticizing his weak prime minister, because he was eyeing Fukuda's job.

Hu's trip, and his relationship with Fukuda, initially laid the groundwork for an agreement over the East China Sea, though neither side felt confident about announcing it immediately. Partly that was because on May 12 the Sichuan earthquake intervened, a devastating event that killed approximately seventy thousand people. Both sides were also nervous about the inevitable political blowback once the details of the accord were released. Under the deal, Japanese companies were to be invited to participate in an existing Chinese project, the Chunxiao/Shirakaba gas field. The real prize, however, was the development of a new field to the north that both countries believed had significant deposits. In the meantime, they temporarily set aside their differences over sovereignty and agreed to make the area a "Sea of Peace, Cooperation and Friendship."

With the announcement of the agreement, Fukuda came under fire from conservatives, with the inevitable complaints that he had given up too much. A bigger problem, ironically, was the widespread elation elsewhere in the system in Tokyo at having finally struck a deal with Beijing on a highly sensitive issue. "We thought we had a fair deal, but there was too much excitement in Japan about it," said one of Tokyo's negotiators. Privately, the Japanese insisted that Beijing had agreed to divide the fields covered by the agreement based on a median line, although neither side would ever say so in public. The Chinese were equally vehement in private in insisting they had not and that they would never have accepted such an arrangement.

Beijing's diplomats were defensive for good reason. They had come under fire at home because many officials in the government, the military, and the oil majors believed that the deal was based on exactly that provision—splitting the East China Sea in half—which made it ripe for criticism, because it suggested that Beijing had compromised on sovereignty. Asked if the Chinese public was pleased with the agreement, the Chinese diplomat briefing the Americans was about as pointed as he could be. With a population of 1.3 billion citizens, he replied, it was difficult to know how each individual felt. The killer blow came when the Japanese media reported that the two sides had agreed to "jointly develop" the fields. The use of the word "jointly" was toxic in Beijing, because it implied shared sovereignty. "That was a deal breaker," said a Chinese diplomat handling Japan.

On the Chinese side, the final negotiations had been led by Wang Yi, the ministry's top Japan expert, who had just finished his term as ambassador to Tokyo a few months earlier. Wang had been a rising star in the ministry from the moment he joined in the early 1980s. His connections didn't hurt, having married the daughter of Zhou Enlai's former political secretary. His close relationship with Japan over many years, however, made him immensely vulnerable within China. Wang was, in effect, the head of the "Japan school" in China, a position that had to be handled with care.

As the Chinese ambassador in the hothouse of Tokyo, Wang had a high profile, something that was beyond his control, as was his portrayal by the local popular press as a sometimes debonair diplomat with the dramatic features of a Kabuki actor. Wang was always careful not to flaunt his excellent Japanese in public, because the clips of him speaking could find their way onto nationalistic Internet sites in China and leave him open to attack. "People like him have to be more Catholic than the pope on Japan," said one of the State Department's top Asia hands.

Many Japanese officials came to dislike Wang intensely because of the tough, bullying posture he began to take with them. It was an approach they believed he had adopted as a show for the leadership and his colleagues, to demonstrate how hard he was on Japan. But in the negotiations over resources in the East China Sea, his Tokyo counterparts praised Wang's efforts to reach an agreement. "The Chinese negotiators were under pressure from the companies and conservatives who were very angry," said one Japanese negotiator. "They could not deliver, although they tried. Wang Yi worked hard, but he failed."

Wang's career didn't suffer, however, and he was soon appointed to head the Taiwan Affairs Office, a crucial position overseeing Beijing's relationship with Taipei. The Taiwan post also allowed him to distance himself from Japan, something he was keen to do to maintain his rise through the diplomatic bureaucracy. In 2013, he was promoted again, this time to the job he had always wanted, foreign minister. The East

China Sea deal, however, didn't survive. In 2009, Chinese oil companies resumed drilling in a contested area. For Tokyo, Beijing's willingness to abide by the terms of the agreement was a crucial benchmark for whether the relationship could work. The deal's unraveling would prove to be a bellwether of crises to come, but not before Tokyo manufactured a crisis of its own at home, this time with the United States.

In November 2009, Yukio Hatoyama welcomed Barack Obama to Tokyo. It was the second meeting between the two leaders, who on paper had much in common. Both headed left-of-center parties, and both were elected with the promise of bringing once-in-a-generation changes to their respective political systems. As the scion of a Kennedy-like dynasty, Hatoyama was a fourth-generation politician in what he liked to joke was the "family business." His great-grandfather had been the speaker of the parliament, his grandfather prime minister in the 1950s, and his father the foreign minister. Even with this pedigree, Hatoyama's sweeping victory in elections in August of that year was in some ways just as momentous as Obama's win in the U.S. presidential elections nine months earlier.

Hatoyama's Democratic Party of Japan didn't just beat the conservative Liberal Democratic Party, which had ruled for virtually all of the previous half century. It swept the floor, winning more than 300 of the parliament's 480 seats. It was not only a triumph for Hatoyama but a victory, and a comeback, for the onetime "shadow shogun" of conservative politics, Ichirō Ozawa, the man who had triggered Japan's political revolution by walking out of the ruling LDP in the early 1990s. Backed by a popular mandate and formidable political firepower in Ozawa, the DPJ's agenda was, by Washington's standards, radical as well. Hatoyama wanted to build an autonomous east Asian community of nations, as the "US-led era of globalization," in his words, was coming to an end.

After the 2009 elections, the LDP, the pro-U.S. bastion of postwar Japanese politics, looked threadbare. Following Koizumi's departure in 2006, three LDP prime ministers—Shinzō Abe, Yasuo Fukuda, and Tarō Asō—had come and gone in quick succession, marked down as weak leaders of an underperforming nation. Their sole notable legacy had been to improve relations with Beijing, but they had hardly done so from a position of strength. In the cases of Abe and Asō, the rapprochement with Beijing was often made through gritted teeth. Hatoyama, by contrast, promised to denounce Japan's wartime behavior and keep his distance from Yasukuni Shrine. Without this baggage, he promised to build a relationship of genuine trust with China. In Washington, Hatoyama shaped up as America's worst nightmare—a popular politician who believed he had a mandate to shift Japan away from the United States toward China.

Yet when Hatoyama greeted Obama in Tokyo, it was not as a confident politician who had just enjoyed a landslide victory. From the moment he had taken office two months earlier, the new prime minister struggled on multiple fronts. He had come to office promising to wrest influence back from the all-powerful civil servants and develop a more pro-China foreign policy. In an instant, he made a set of powerful enemies, both at home in the bureaucracy and overseas in Washington. The tight group of bureaucrats in Tokyo who had managed the American alliance for decades had been accustomed to sorting out problems quietly with their U.S. counterparts. Collectively, the "Ampo mafia," as they were known—"Ampo" being Japanese shorthand for the security treaty— quickly pushed back against the new government. In their eyes, Hatoyama and his ministers were amateurs.

If the tilt toward China wasn't bad enough, Hatoyama was threatening to tear up an agreement regarding U.S. marines stationed in Okinawa. A broken chain of reefs and volcanic islets stretching seven hundred miles to near Taiwan, Okinawa had been strategically vital and politically toxic since the last days of the Pacific War. After the deaths of tens of thousands of citizens on the island in one of its final pitched battles, Okinawa became, in the words of one historian, "an immense, neglected military dump." The United States didn't return sovereignty of the island chain to Japan until 1972, and then only in exchange for keeping its bases there. The festering local resentment about the presence of the main U.S. encampment, which had eventually come to be surrounded on all four sides by a busy city, exploded after the horrific rape of a twelve-year-old girl by three U.S. servicemen in the mid-1990s. Desperate to quell the public backlash, the Americans and Japanese rapidly negotiated the first deal to move the marines off the Futenma air base. Some were to be relocated elsewhere on the island; others were to go to Guam.

More than a decade later, the implementation of the agreement was still stalled. In the meantime, local anger at the marines' presence lingered. Chip Gregson, a top marine commander in both Japan and at

Central Command in the United States, didn't blame anti-U.S. sentiment solely on the island's legion of agitators who had long been ideologically opposed to the American military presence. "Many of the problems in Okinawa were our fault," acknowledged Gregson, who also served as the head of Asia policy in the Pentagon in the Obama administration. He cited "an old colonial mentality," which meant the military conducted exercises like firing artillery across civilian roads that it would never have done in America.

During their November meeting in Tokyo, Hatoyama sought to reassure Obama that he could deliver on a new site for the marines in Japan, leaning over toward him and saying, "Trust me." His intimate gesture momentarily took the air out of the room. "My reaction was: That's a fairly dramatic way for a head of state to articulate his position," said Jeff Bader, who headed Asia policy on the National Security Council during Obama's first term. "He personalized it, and by doing that he gave it added weight. It was Hatoyama telling Obama that you are going to see lots of back-and-forth over this, but we will get this ship into port." In the short term, Obama had no choice but to take the Japanese prime minister at his word. In the end, his promise was hollow and would contribute mightily to his fall.

Hatoyama's nickname was "the alien," a reference to his otherworldly style, his bulging, slightly startled eyes, and his high, arching forehead. (The cute dolls that Japanese souvenir stalls sell of prime ministers depicted him as an extraterrestrial.) Hatoyama's signature policies, though controversial, had hardly arrived in Japan in a proverbial spaceship. His antagonism to Japan's rule by powerful bureaucrats was reflected across the political spectrum, in both his party and the LDP. In his case, his distrust of the bureaucrats had been reinforced by his personal experiences with the big ministries. Hatoyama had served as a senior official in a short-lived coalition government in the early 1990s. On taking office, he had never forgotten how the new prime minister had summoned one of the nation's top bureaucrats for a briefing. The bureaucrat sent a message that he was too busy and would try to come by the next day.

Hatoyama's desire for Japan to become more self-reliant in defense and foreign policy, and less dependent on the United States, likewise had deep roots in postwar politics. As prime minister in the 1950s, his grandfather had wanted to establish diplomatic ties with China, over American opposition. Every few years there was a fresh initiative of some kind aimed at binding Japan closer to Asia. At one stage, it was the creation of a "yen zone." In the late 1970s, Japanese and Australian academics promoted a plan for regional economic integration, which years later would become APEC, the Asia-Pacific Economic Cooperation forum. In the late 1990s, during the Asia financial crisis, Tokyo floated a proposal for a regional monetary fund. The United States crushed that and also came down hard on the Japanese Trade Ministry's idea early in the new century for a regional economic grouping. The annual East Asia Summit started in 2005, initially without the United States.

The 1997 U.S. campaign against a Japanese-led regional monetary fund rankled for years in Tokyo. In Washington's eyes, Tokyo had breached the unwritten protocols of the U.S.-Japan alliance by not consulting America about the idea in advance. The Americans feared the Japanese plan would undermine the role of the International Monetary Fund in managing financial crises by handing out money with no strings attached. Once the Singaporeans leaked the secret Japanese draft for the new body to the United States, Larry Summers and Tim Geithner at the U.S. Treasury soon discovered many Asian countries were against it as well, especially China. "China was opposed to it from the beginning, and much of the region was ambivalent, because it was Japan," said a senior Treasury official of that time.

The Americans disliked the Japanese initiative for another reason, one that Washington didn't like to discuss in public. In a memo to brief his colleagues in preparation for a dinner in 1997 with Japanese Finance Ministry officials, Geithner listed all the reasons the United States opposed the fund. The final one, which he requested his colleagues in the Treasury keep confidential, gave the game away: "The probability [is that] we could not participate given budgetary and Congressional considerations." This point was the most salient for the Japanese. Whatever the setting, the protocol, or the level of attendees, the Japanese believed that the Americans would never approve of the creation of any new institution in the Asia-Pacific that they weren't running themselves.

Soon after his election in 2009, Hatoyama had flown to New York for the annual gathering of world leaders at the UN General Assembly. He met Hu Jintao on September 22 and, the following day, for the first time, Barack Obama. "He was entirely reassuring, and everyone felt reassured," said one official who attended the meeting. That mood changed once the Americans began to get reports of what Hatoyama had said to the Chinese the day before. U.S. officials briefed on the contents of the meeting said that Hatoyama had told Hu he wanted to downgrade the affiliation with the United States. "He basically trashed the U.S. and said he wanted to develop a new kind of relationship with China," said one senior U.S. official.

How the Americans obtained a detailed account of Hatoyama and Hu's conversation is not clear. They either had the meeting room at the Waldorf Astoria bugged or had the contents passed on by one of the Japanese bureaucrats who was there. Certainly, the United States had lots of experience securing the Waldorf for top-level meetings. U.S. presidents had stayed at the hotel for decades when visiting New York, a custom Obama maintained until a Chinese insurer purchased the hotel in 2014. The next year, when he was in New York, Obama switched his lodgings because of security concerns.

In late 2009, Obama was presiding over a frail U.S. economy that was still shedding jobs. His signature health-care bill was battling its way through Congress, draining political capital. With the Pentagon and his national security team, he was struggling to implement a strategy for the war in Afghanistan, which had taken months of tortuous internal debate to finalize. With partners around the world, the United States had just accused Iran of building a secret nuclear facility. In the midst of all this, Japan, a reliable ally and bulwark of U.S. power in east Asia, looked as if it were reconfiguring its postwar foreign and defense policy in a matter of a few weeks. Just as the White House was preparing its pivot to Asia, Japan seemed to be heading in the other direction, with its own pivot to Beijing.

It wasn't just Tokyo's new approach to China and the Okinawa issue that were roiling Washington. Hatoyama's government had a laundry list of demands. It wanted the United States to reveal its secret agreements with past conservative governments regarding bringing nuclear weapons into Japan. It proposed ending the Japanese navy's mission refueling U.S. ships in the gulf as part of the war on terror. "They overloaded the system, and we went into a tilt," said one Pentagon official. "We knew that if you unhinge Japan, you unhinge the entire region." Wendy Cutler, a veteran of many difficult trade negotiations with Japan, was taken aback when told by one of the new government's interlocutors that the two countries were like a couple stuck in a bad marriage. "In the U.S., before we get a divorce, we usually go through marriage counseling," she replied.

The task of dealing with Japan largely fell to Kurt Campbell, who was Hillary Clinton's east Asia chief in the State Department. Like his boss, he hailed from the hawkish wing of the Democratic Party, or at least that part that had shed its phobias about seeing U.S. foreign policy through the prism of the disasters of the Vietnam War. Campbell wasn't new to Japan. As a senior official in the Pentagon under Bill Clinton, in the mid-1990s he had negotiated the original deal with Tokyo to shift the U.S. bases to a new location in Okinawa. Alternatively genial and gruff, diplomatic and blunt, Campbell plunged himself into a kind of shuttle diplomacy within weeks of Hatoyama's taking office to triage the wounded alliance.

What quickly became clear as Campbell and other U.S. officials began to do their rounds was that few in the Japanese system actually knew what was going on. The politicians had one interpretation of Hatoyama's intentions; the bureaucrats, cut out of the policy-making loop by the new government, had another. Multiple people turned up in Washington claiming to be acting as personal emissaries for Hatoyama, all carrying different messages, sowing further confusion. Hatoyama himself provided little clarity. On some occasions, he spoke of the need for new regional institutions without the involvement of the United States. On others, he was at pains to stress that the United States remained at the heart of Japanese foreign policy. The bilateral conversations, laid out in detail in WikiLeaks cables, had a fraught tone from the start. "No more surprises," Campbell told the new foreign minister, Katsuya Okada, soon after landing in Tokyo in mid-September. The United States expects to be treated with the respect due to an ally, he added, and not be backed into a corner.

During that trip, Campbell had barely sat down with Akitaka Saiki, then head of the Asian and Oceanian division of the Foreign Ministry, before the complaints about the Japanese government started pouring out. The first thing Saiki told him was that Hatoyama's threat to tame the bureaucracy "would end in failure." Saiki had not yet scaled the heights of his career; he would later rise to head the ministry, traditionally an enormously powerful position in Japan. Still, he spoke to Campbell with overweening authority in any case. Saiki praised the intellect of Okada, his minister, but then added that he didn't understand what the new government meant in wanting an "equal relationship" with the United States. If they were simply trying to display their power to usher in a bold new foreign policy, Saiki observed, such thinking was "stupid." "They will learn," he added.

After only a few weeks in office, the new Hatoyama government found itself squeezed by Washington and its own bureaucrats, on one side, and by anti-U.S. sentiment on the other. In Okinawa, the many people who hoped that the U.S. bases would be removed from the island had had their expectations raised. Robert Gates, the defense secretary, put an end to any changes in the Okinawa base plans in a series of meetings in Tokyo on October 20. He warned his Japanese hosts to honor the terms of the original deal or there would be no return of any land in Okinawa at all. "Gates was very, very blunt with Hatoyama, because they were touching on real U.S. equities," said one U.S. official in the meeting.

At the same time that Washington was digesting possible changes to the policy on the Okinawa bases, Hatoyama continued to push his plan for a new Asian community, excluding the United States. Hatoyama's proposal had some logic from a Japanese perspective, because it balanced the U.S. alliance with the need to bind China more tightly into regional forums. In some respects, Hatoyama was building upon the efforts of his LDP predecessors, who had tried to repair relations with China after Koizumi. Like other Japanese, Hatoyama worried whether the United States would remain a reliable partner in any case. "The U.S. was doing a rebalance; we were rebalancing as well," observed Okada, the foreign minister, who said later he was perplexed at American criticism of Hatoyama's initiatives.

But Hatoyama and some of his ministers seemed oblivious to the sensitivities of his American allies regarding the bigger issues in play. In Beijing for a trilateral summit with South Korea and China in early October, Hatoyama justified his plan for a new regional forum by declaring that Tokyo's foreign policy had been excessively focused on the United States. Obama was shocked, and a week later Campbell was back in Tokyo. If you have something to say to China related to the U.S.-Japan alliance, Campbell told Japanese officials, consult with us first. "Imagine the Japanese response if the U.S. Government were to say publicly that it wished to devote more attention to China than Japan," he added.

Campbell's counterparts in the Foreign Ministry and the parliament in Tokyo seemed as dismayed as Washington about their prime minister's comments. The insults flowed freely in bilateral meetings. Hatoyama's plan was "unthinkable," Japanese officials said; he was "weak" when dealing with strong-willed individuals and had "personality" shortcomings. Hatoyama, undeterred, was out and about only two weeks later stumping for his plan—this time in Thailand, at the annual meeting of ASEAN, the ten-member Southeast Asian group, at which the Chinese and South Koreans were also in attendance. On the final day, other regional leaders, including Kevin Rudd, Australia's then prime minister, joined them.

Rudd was best known internationally as a Sinologist, which initially caused some to think he would be a captive of Beijing. In Washington, however, he was considered a strong supporter of the U.S. alliance and an occasional informal provider of advice on China to Obama. After hearing Hatoyama's proposal for a new Asian architecture without Washington, Rudd was so alarmed that he phoned Jeff Bader at the National Security Council in the White House. As Bader recalled the conversation, Rudd said Hatoyama's enunciation of his plan in Thailand had been a "mindblower." Vietnamese leaders, Rudd told Bader, had approached him after the speech and urged him to do something about Japan. Communist Vietnam had long since dropped its hostility to the United States after prevailing in the two countries' lengthy war and was focused on reining in China, its neighbor and traditional rival. Still, the irony of Vietnam's imploring the Americans to take action regarding Japan, Washington's closest ally in Asia, was not lost on Bader.

Hatoyama, facing pressure on all fronts, tried another tack to get around the impasse on the Okinawa bases. In his telling, he unwisely fell back on the advice of his bureaucrats and agreed to a deadline of the following May 2010 to find a new location for the main U.S. base. It was a promise he could never keep. It was impossible in a few short months to secure a site in Japan to which to move the huge bases, a problem that had defeated every Japanese leader for more than a decade. Nowhere else in the country that might have been suitable wanted to host the American military. After leaving office, Hatoyama said setting the new deadline was the worst decision he ever made and claimed that it had been foisted on him by the bureaucracy. "The message they were sending to the Americans was: 'Don't listen to what Hatoyama is saying.'" The Okinawans also felt betrayed, because they had been promised that Tokyo would end what many of the island's residents regarded as a de facto occupation, only to be let down again.

By this time, the United States was winding back its public pressure on Hatoyama because a number of senior American officials worried Washington had gone overboard in criticizing his government. "We had to consider whether we were prepared to ruin the relationship," one observed. From there on, the Obama administration tried to ensure there would be no more ultimatums of the likes that Gates had delivered to Hatoyama. But the United States had little new to offer on how to solve the impasse in Okinawa, either. With neither party offering a viable plan, one by one Japanese cabinet ministers started to fall into line with the existing U.S. agreement to shift the bases elsewhere on the island. The backdown drained Hatoyama of the little credibility he had left, and in June 2010 he resigned as prime minister. After being elected in a momentous landslide, he had lasted all of nine months in office.

The rough treatment meted out by the United States to Hatoyama—Obama barely acknowledged him at a nuclear summit in Washington in the midst of the crisis—left a bitter narrative in its wake. The Ampo mafia had destroyed Hatoyama by portraying him as the "incompetent head of an anti-American government," in one account of his demise. The Tokyo-based writer Tag Murphy said the Hatoyama administration had been "deliberately sabotaged by a de facto alliance of Pentagon functionaries, the establishment press in Japan, and Japanese spokesmen in the United States committing what amounted to treason against their own government." Some Americans later privately regretted taking such a tough line against Hatoyama in his early months in office. "We miscalculated," said one Pentagon official. "Maybe we underestimated how dirty the Foreign Ministry and the LDP in Tokyo were going to be in bringing him down."

But Washington's hardball tactics and U.S. officials' ties with the pro-U.S. bureaucracy in Japan are only one part of the story. It wasn't just the Ampo mafia who lost patience with Hatoyama. Many in his own party also despaired at his handling of the United States. The DPJ

itself was a classic big-tent political party whose members held conflicting views on the alliance and China. Many of Hatoyama's colleagues had
never been convinced of the wisdom of building ties with China if they
came at the expense of the United States. They were even less impressed
with Hatoyama's conduct of the issue. "A lot of people were shocked" at
the prime minister's statements in Beijing, said Akihisa Nagashima, a
vice-minister for defense who had close ties to Washington. "It was
pretty naive and not thought through."

All the controversies raised by Hatoyama—the Okinawa bases, moving the marines to Guam, and setting up new Asia political structures—
had one issue in common: how Japan should respond to the rise of China.
In that respect, building closer political and security ties with Beijing, and
institutions to buttress them with, had a compelling logic. Hatoyama's
execution of his plan, by contrast, was chaotic, almost casually alienating
Washington, Japan's security guarantor for the previous half century, in
the process. At the same time that Hatoyama was calling for a more independent foreign policy, he barely discussed the profound ramifications
of going down that path. If Japan was to free itself from the United States,
it would have to dramatically loosen the constitutional shackles on its
own armed forces so that it could credibly defend itself. Hatoyama, however, never dared to broach such a monumental subject in public.

But there was another, bigger mystery in the melodrama surrounding
Hatoyama's brief, ill-starred administration. It wasn't how Japan should
respond to the rise of China, but how China should take advantage of
the availability of Japan. Put another way, when Hatoyama and his senior advisers offered a hand of friendship in late 2009, why didn't Beijing
grasp it? After all, Beijing, in the form of Hu Jintao and Wen Jiabao, had
the most Japan-friendly administration in more than two decades.

Did Beijing's hubris overwhelm its judgment? Did China pass up a
historic opportunity to deliver a fatal blow to Washington's preeminence
in east Asia? It is not an exaggeration to say that the fate of an entire region, as well as America's global standing, turned on such questions. East
Asia, more than it had ever been since the United States became the leading power in the region after 1945, was for a brief interval up for grabs.

The answers to those questions lie more in China's calculation of its
own strength than in Japan's weakness. In the first decade of the twenty-

first century, Beijing began to perceive that it was finally returning to the ranks of the world's great powers. At first, it had contemplated its new, elevated role in the world with a touch of humility. Over the course of the decade, however, it became less and less willing to look to the outside world for validation. After more than a century of humiliation, Beijing's leaders were finally in a position, they thought, to demand their due.

CHAPTER ELEVEN

The Rise and Retreat of Great Powers

If you make any nice words about Japan, then you will get an angry reaction from students. As a scholar of America, I never worry about public opinion. People might not agree with me, but they never call you a traitor.

—Chu Shulong, Chinese academic

Vietnam, Japan, and the Philippines are America's three "running dogs" in Asia. We only need to kill one and it will immediately bring the others to heel.

—Dai Xu, PLA colonel

The summons came unexpectedly, as they always did from the Politburo to anyone outside its rarefied orbit. Qian Chengdan and Qi Shiyong, both professors of international relations, received phone calls from the Education Ministry in early 2003, asking them to address the party's twenty-five-odd top leaders on a topic they had studied, the rise of great powers in history. The Politburo study sessions, as they were called, recruited experts from academia and think tanks to keep leaders abreast of the big economic, social, and diplomatic trends buffeting China and the world. The office of the then party leader, Hu Jintao, screened the topics and the lecturers, and each speaker went through dress rehearsals beforehand. Qi was so annoyed at how his presentation was rewritten that he later refused to allow it to be published. Once under way, however, the sessions could be relatively freewheeling, at least compared with the debates permitted in the media. Certainly, they were taken seriously, and Politburo members were expected to attend if they were in town.

On the day of Qi's and Qian's presentations, the ninth session since Hu had taken over as the party chief late the previous year, the formal theme was "A Historical Investigation of the Development of the World's Main Powers Since the Fifteenth Century." The leaders listened politely through an hour of speeches and then asked questions. They displayed none of the vengeful bravado that characterized later public discussion of foreign policy in China, insisting on the need to banish the stain of past humiliations, take back lost territories, and oust the United States from the region, according to people with knowledge of the meeting. They didn't discuss how China itself would become a great power, which was the implicit subject of the talks. Instead, the leaders asked mostly straightforward questions about economic development and how growth would make China stronger.

While the leaders' reactions were never made public, at least one person who learned of the session was thrilled by the topic. A Beijing television producer heard of the speeches on his car radio while caught in traffic on one of the capital's clogged ring roads. The excitement that Ren Xuean felt on listening to the news—"nine great powers over more than a century!"—led to his producing a pathbreaking documentary, *The Rise of Great Powers,* which aired in 2006. The program was distinguished not just by the scale of its production. CCTV, China's state broadcaster, produced a twelve-part series, with an eight-volume set of books published to accompany it. The span of time from when Ren got the idea for the series to the year in which it was broadcast marked a critical period in the evolving political climate in China.

In the early years of the new century, China was still making its way up the global rankings of power and wealth. Its economy had grown to become the eighth or ninth largest in the world. China had only just entered into the World Trade Organization, which in the eyes of some Western pundits spelled doom, because they figured global companies would kill off China's inefficient state industries and its economy as a whole. The CCP had never abandoned its bedrock ambition to maximize its collective economic, military, and political power so it could match the United States in Asia and eventually supplant it as the region's dominant nation. But Deng Xiaoping's old dictum for China's global posture—to "hide its light and bide its time"—still largely prevailed. The CCTV series about the secrets of great powers reflected a simple fact:

China at this juncture was, outwardly at least, a much humbler nation than it would become just a few years later.

Instead of the Marxist staples explaining the rise of the West, with a focus on colonialism, violence, and theft of resources, the series looked at the institutional, technical, and political drivers of great-power status. "The documentary does not point out the 'right way,'" said Qian. "Instead, it asks audiences to think." Even the famously acerbic dissident Liu Xiaobo, who was later jailed for his political views and then awarded the Nobel Prize in 2010, praised the series for "avoiding the propaganda colorations of the past." There were limits, of course. One Chinese scholar counted how often the word "democracy" was mentioned—a dozen times in twelve broadcasts. "Most of them occur as parts of proper names," he pointed out. "There is no serious discussion of the meaning of democracy." Overall, however, the series exhibited one of China's greatest strengths of the first three decades of the reform era—not just a willingness to learn from the successes of the West but a capacity to as well.

With the kind of ideological running room rarely allowed to the state broadcaster, the series offered, by Chinese standards, a liberal take on the rise of the West. Using interviews with local and domestic experts and shot on location around the world, the programs tried to explain the secrets of successful countries and the empires that sometimes arose from them. They examined how the Netherlands, Spain, Portugal, Great Britain, Germany, France, Japan, Russia, and the United States all rose and, where appropriate, the reasons for their fall. They also lauded Britain's Magna Carta, the French Enlightenment, Germany's university system, and America's political and scientific creativity.

In retrospect, one of the most striking segments was that concerning Japan. The familiar plaudits, for its fusion of traditional values with Western technology in the early years of modernization in the late nineteenth century, were highlighted, as was the disaster of the militarist takeover of the 1930s and the country's subsequent ignominious defeat. This was all familiar as far as it went. But throughout, the program resisted demonizing Japan. "Many issues in Japan's century as a world power have yet to be resolved," the neutral-sounding narrator said. "But whatever the conclusion, one thing is certain, the worth of any country's rise to power lies in whether it brings its own people happiness and well-being, and whether it brings the world peace and security." In Qian's own words, he said he wanted "to let people know that Japan modernized and became stronger only because they opened their door and learned from the West," before they took "the wrong road."

By the time the series was broadcast in 2006, China's mood had already begun to shift. Its economy was going from strength to strength, upending the pessimistic predictions of what would happen when it was exposed to the full force of competition from global trade. The narrative had switched from one of a creaky public sector's collapsing to one of an effervescent private sector thriving. In neighboring Japan, Koizumi's recalcitrant Yasukuni Shrine habit had damaged bilateral ties, despite the thaw that followed his departure, and bolstered those in China who wanted to take a hard line against Tokyo. Perhaps most important of all, the curiosity on display in the Politburo and in the CCTV series, the kind of willingness to learn from the outside world that had been so characteristic of China since the reform period, was beginning to slip away. So, too, was the humility of some of the audience.

While Chinese liberals might have liked *The Rise of Great Powers*, the so-called New Left, a vocal contingent that hankered for the Maoist Eden of the command economy and a foreign policy of out-and-out hostility to capitalist countries, hated it. They complained that it overly praised the United States and would "stimulate America and other enemy forces to mount a new high tide in their efforts to hold China back." One of its members claimed that "*The Rise of the Great Powers* wants regime change." As the dissident Liu Xiaobo pointed out, criticizing the show in those terms was akin to suggesting the producers be jailed for subversion. When it came to Japan, in particular, the resurgent Left had become especially aggressive, drawing up a target list of those who did not toe the party line.

Chinese fury at Japan had done more than just spill into street protests by this time. Anti-Japanese sentiment had settled deeply into the sediment of national debate. In cyberspace, hostility toward Tokyo had become a fixture in the form of a permanent page on the Internet that listed China's "Top Ten Traitors," most of whose alleged sins related to Japan. The names on the list, which would periodically change, included pillars of academia in Beijing and Shanghai, as well as authors of Chinese school textbooks. The traitors' list of sins was long and varied. Fan Shuzhi, of

Fudan University in Shanghai, was tagged for defending the so-called Japanese "pirates" in the Ming dynasty, who he argued were only responding to China's ban on maritime trade; Jiao Guobiao, of Peking University, had dared to suggest that Japanese colonialism hadn't been all bad ("After Japan took over Shanghai, it changed the practice of Chinese people driving rickshaws for white people, and forced white people to drive for the yellow people"); Liang Yunxiang, also of Peking University, had erred by stating that it was an "unstoppable trend" for Japan to become a permanent member of the UN Security Council; and Wu Jinan, the director of the Japan Institute at a Shanghai think tank, erred by suggesting that Japan couldn't carry the title of "defeated nation" indefinitely.

At the top of the list throughout was Ma Licheng, the *People's Daily* editorial writer forced into professional exile to escape the fallout from his article of a few years earlier pressing for a reassessment of Japan. Shi Yinhong, the Beijing academic who had also supported a rethinking of Japan policy, albeit on different grounds, was number two. Another scholar who was on and off the list was Zhou Yongsheng, of the China Foreign Affairs University in Beijing. His transgression had been suggesting that China accept Japan's proposed compromise to end the two countries' territorial standoff in the East China Sea by drawing a line down the middle of the ocean, which he described as "the relatively fair, practical, and reasonable way to resolve territorial disputes" there.

Zhou had been careful, only airing his thoughts in full in a book published in Japan, in Japanese, but that offered no protection from the patriotic zealots. All of the familiar tactics used by the ultranationalists, both within the system and outside it, were marshaled against him. Zhou's address was published on the Internet, and his family threatened. Instead of defending him, the university pressured him to be more careful about what he said on the topic in the future. Like colleagues caught in a similar predicament, Zhou decided to protect himself by writing his newspaper columns in China under a pseudonym.

The impact on debate in China on an issue of vital national interest like Japan was chilling. If any of the scholars had required reminding, the traitors' list reinforced for them the need to watch their words on anything to do with Tokyo. Chu Shulong, a prominent international relations professor at Tsinghua University in Beijing, one of China's top schools, said Taiwan and Japan were the two issues that the leadership had to be most resolute on, and thus that commentators had to be most careful about touching. "You can see from the Internet and the news media and street demonstrations. These are not mobilized by the government," he observed. "For teachers, if you make any nice words about Japan, then you will get an angry reaction from students. As a scholar of America, I never worry about public opinion. People might not agree with me, but they never call you a traitor." As one of the professors on the infamous anti-Japan list explained, "These critics cannot distinguish between what is real patriotism and what is real betrayal."

A similar pattern of outreach followed by retreat was also on display in one of the defining debates on foreign policy in the early years of the new century. The nasty doctrinal dispute revolved around two innocuous-sounding words used to describe China's global emergence as a "peaceful rise." Zheng Bijian, a CCP veteran who had worked for years within the system as an intra-party theorist, coined the term in 2003. The theorists acted as the party's intellectual butlers, formulating terms to package sensitive policy changes and then guiding them through the CCP system. The theorists' skill lay in dressing policy flip-flops in suitably socialist garb, enabling the government to push controversial reforms without cannibalizing the Communist canon that was the foundation for the entire apparatus. They issued phrases that have often baffled outsiders but that made perfect sense internally, such as describing a nominally Communist state as having a "socialist market economy," or "capitalism with Chinese characteristics."

Zheng had a long track record in reframing the canon to keep it abreast of the times. He had edited one edition of Mao Zedong's collected works, helped draft language that allowed the CCP to disown the Cultural Revolution without dumping Mao himself, and worked as a secretary to Hu Yaobang. He had also written speeches for Deng Xiaoping's 1992 "southern tour," which beat back the leftist drive against China's market reforms. In the early years of the twenty-first century, Zheng detected the need for a new campaign to combat what he regarded as a profound and dangerous misunderstanding overseas of how China would behave in its new role on the world stage. He wanted to respond to what the Chinese propaganda organs labeled the "China threat theory"—the fear that Beijing would aggressively upend the existing regional and perhaps even international order as its power grew.

The "China threat theory" was a wholly pejorative concept in China, one that embodied the dark, underhand tactics foreigners were using to further their centuries-old mission to contain Beijing and keep it down. As many Chinese acknowledged privately, though, the idea of a "China threat" was hardly just an invention of insidious foreigners. The shelling of the waters off Taiwan and other incidents in the region had galvanized preexisting misgivings in Washington, Tokyo, and elsewhere about Beijing's worldview and its intention to enforce it.

In place of the "China threat," Zheng came up with the alternative terminology of China's "peaceful rise," designed to reassure the West and neighbors like Japan. Those words, in Zheng's telling, were a neat way of stressing a larger point—that the United States should not treat China as a rival and enemy, as it had the Soviet Union. "The Chinese Communist party is not like the Communist party of the Soviet Union," Zheng said in an interview at the time. "China will never use violence to disturb the current economic order of the world. So you should have a different strategy for dealing with China."

The "peaceful rise" phrase then followed what two U.S. scholars called "a curious and atypical path for party slogans." After Zheng used the words in a speech in 2003, Wen Jiabao took up the theme. Soon after, in early 2004, Hu Jintao expanded on it at the Politburo's tenth study session, immediately following the lecture on the rise of great powers. Consecrated from on high, the phrase seemed on the way to becoming part of the official CCP lexicon. But almost as quickly as it had taken on the status of de facto national strategy, a host of critics emerged from within think tanks, academia, and party bodies to shout it down. Within months, "peaceful rise" was excised from leaders' writings and speeches. In its place came the more anodyne "peaceful development."

The "peaceful rise" died a quick death for numerous and contradictory reasons. The People's Liberation Army didn't like it, because it threatened its expensive plans for military modernization. Some officials worried that even acknowledging China's "rise" could disturb its neighbors. China's hawks disliked it most of all, worried that it could send the wrong signal about Beijing's determination to respond to any provocations from Taiwan and Japan. "One does not restrain one's options," Shen Dingli, a prominent diplomatic specialist at Fudan University in Shanghai, said in one of a series of interviews on the topic. "China's growth is not like quick growth in Cambodia or some African country," said Yan Xuetong, a hawkish academic at Beijing's Tsinghua University. "It will change the world dramatically and I think the world should prepare for that." Yan joked sardonically that he "frequently uses the word 'rise'" but seldom placed "peaceful" in front of it. It was a remarkable episode in retrospect. An effort to disarm China's critics with a bland, reassuring slogan that was briefly adopted at the very top of the country's leadership was rapidly shot down in public with alacrity and intellectual force.

The short life and quick death of China's "peaceful rise" carried with it an important lesson. The cast of characters jostling for a say in China's foreign policy had by now expanded. The PLA, a more professional service, and thus in some respects more independent, had become increasingly outspoken about what it defined as China's national interest. Scholars could exercise influence, if the time and topic were right, as they had shown by helping derail the "peaceful rise" theory. Large state enterprises, which had been freed and at times directed by the government to invest offshore, had begun to meddle in policy, especially toward oil-rich foreign states where they had investments, like Sudan. Chinese citizens, empowered by the Internet and a more commercial media, had at their fingertips more outlets than ever through which they could express their viewpoints, which always seemed to be in favor of being tougher with foreigners, especially the Japanese.

A Chinese academic pithily described the new foreign policy actors as *jumin* (military), *gumin* (shareholders), and *wangmin* (netizens). The Foreign Ministry's lack of formal standing within the party system— none of the country's chief diplomatic representatives had served on the Politburo since the 1990s—had always limited its influence. The burden of dealing with foreigners on behalf of a party that had built its legitimacy on standing up to them hardly helped the ministry gain traction. Chinese diplomats recounted how they often received anonymous letters at the Foreign Ministry in Beijing stuffed with easily crushed chalk, a none-too-subtle message that they needed to add more calcium to stiffen their spines in dealing with the outside world. The influence of Foreign Ministry officials was sometimes underestimated, as their expertise alone often made them an influential source of advice when crucial decisions

were made. But in China, as in many countries in the modern era, there
was a broader lesson—that foreign policy was no longer the preserve of
an elite.

After more than a decade of annual double-digit budget increases,
PLA commanders had not only a stronger voice in policy debates but,
increasingly, the means to back their statements with timely displays of
military firepower. When the Taiwanese president, Chen Shui-bian, was
stirring up pro-independence sentiment in 2004, the PLA carried out
amphibious training exercises on nearby islands. Just ahead of negotiations with Japan on a disputed gas field the following year, China sent
advanced destroyers to patrol the seas there for the first time. A few years
later, to demonstrate its ability to break through the island chain extending from northern Japan to south of Taiwan, China dispatched its largest
flotilla of ships and submarines ever steaming through the Miyako Strait
into the western Pacific. To drive home the point, the two submarines
surfaced and hoisted the Chinese flag.

Compared with its crude shelling of the waters off Taiwan in the mid-
1990s, the PLA, with the support of top leaders, now had the ability to
engage in vastly more sophisticated ways of signaling China's strength
and resolve. Over the decade, the Chinese navy had increased the "frequency, duration, complexity, and distance from the mainland of its
operations," building and refining its capability. It had taken years of
methodical weapons acquisitions, and a costly investment in military
manufacturing and training, but by the start of the twenty-first century,
for the first time in the country's modern history, China finally had the
strength to contest the control of disputed territories far from its immediate coastal waters.

In Beijing's eyes, the key to unlocking China's status as a great power
was overcoming the curving, interlocked perimeter of islands and sea-
lanes that blocked free passage to the Pacific Ocean. The "first island
chain," as the Chinese called it, was anchored by Japan. Dai Xu, an air
force colonel, talked about the "C-shaped encirclement" that he believed
had been built by the United States and its allies in the cold war as a
barrier to keep China hemmed in. Some Chinese strategic writings went
further, depicting this barrier as extending beyond the arc stretching
from northern Japan to south of Taiwan, all the way around Southeast
Asia to Afghanistan. The "first island chain" became part of China's

strategic lexicon, as shorthand for a host of weaknesses that had to be overcome. Such frailties made the country vulnerable to naval blockades, restricted access to resources off the coast, and put Chinese coastal cities in range of precision-guided missiles positioned along the archipelago. "Because of the nature of geography," wrote two PLA navy colonels, "China can be easily blockaded and cut off from the sea."

Along with China's arms buildup came the accoutrements of a home-grown military-industrial complex. Long sheltered in the secretive military and the opaque party-connected companies that competed for defense contracts, serving and retired officers began issuing populist, hawkish commentaries in the mainstream media. Dai Xu, whose book *Sea Totem: China's Carrier* equated the country's new naval vessel with national rejuvenation, was one of the most prominent. He denounced Vietnam, Japan, and the Philippines as America's "three running dogs" in Asia, adding, "We only need to kill one and it will immediately bring the others to heel."

Another of the militant military men, the retired army major general Luo Yuan, invariably donned his full uniform for television interviews. The officer's objective in making such public appearances seemed to be to hold the rest of the system's feet to the fire should anyone contemplate backsliding in competition with the United States and Japan, especially over Taiwan. In the case of the Senkaku/Diaoyu Islands, Luo offered a sardonic formula for ways in which China and Taiwan could join forces to take them back. "Chinese aircraft can bomb the islands on Monday, Wednesday, and Friday," he said, "while the Taiwanese can launch attacks on Tuesday, Thursday, and Saturday." All soldiers had a duty to be "hawks," he explained in one interview with the foreign media. "It's crucial to express your standpoint and bottom line so others will know that China is committed to the use of diplomatic measures to resolve the dispute, but China is also not afraid of conflict."

Power and confidence, in diplomacy as in life, can breed magnanimity and generosity in those who possess such qualities, or alternatively, contempt and condescension. Certainly China's confidence had grown immensely by the time of Yukio Hatoyama's becoming Japanese prime minister in late 2009. The election took place at a moment that at the time seemed to mark a changing of the guard in the postwar world. The

United States remained mired in a recession after the financial crisis, trying to crawl out of a pit as much psychological as economic. The aftermath of the crash had sapped many sturdy, built-to-last private companies and public institutions of the confidence that had been an American trademark. Instead of the country pulling together, the Obama administration had to chart a course forward amid deeply partisan acrimony. Japan's economy had been struggling for more than a decade, so the blow to its confidence from the financial crisis was less dramatic. In the United States, though, this felt like more than just a downturn. It was a systemic crisis that called into question the core tenets of the free-market system.

As Washington, and Tokyo, looked to Beijing, the contrast couldn't have been greater. With China on the verge of a calamitous recession like much of the rest of the world, the central government announced in late 2008 a massive financial package to support growth. It was comparable in amount to the U.S. fiscal stimulus, although China's economy was only about one-third the size of the United States'. Once the Politburo, and then the State Council, had made their decision, there was no dissent, or at least none that outsiders could see. With a discipline other governments envied, China's state-owned banks began doling out large loans. The 2008 Beijing Olympics and the celebration of the CCP's sixtieth year in power the following year added to the bubbly zeitgeist. By mid-2009, as Western leaders waited for the crisis to bottom out, economists were already revising upward their estimates for Chinese growth. China was rising, peacefully or otherwise.

Chinese leaders took one lesson from the financial crisis to heart after they had engineered a way around it: compared with that of the shell-shocked West and a stagnant Japan, the Chinese system worked. One of the most powerful Chinese politicians of his generation, Wang Qishan, underscored this sentiment with Hank Paulson, then Treasury secretary. "You were my teacher," Wang told Paulson on the sidelines of the U.S.-China conclave in 2008. "[But] I look at your system, Hank. We aren't sure we should be learning from you anymore." It was, Paulson said, one of the "most humbling moments" for him of the financial crisis. In his book on China, Paulson paints the conversation as a brief exchange. Others at the meeting said Wang berated Paulson at length about America's shortcomings, and that afterward, Paulson seethed at the lecture.

With Japan, China was marking an additional and weightier land-mark. In 2010, the Chinese economy surpassed that of Japan in size, making it the second largest in the world. The reaction in Japan was muted. Some right-wing papers in Tokyo sneered at the reliability of Chinese statistics. The walking pace of an aging old nation could not be compared with that of a growing country, noted one academic. In any case, China remained far behind in per capita income and would strug-gle to catch up on that index. In truth, Japan had gotten over "GDPism" as a measure of national vitality decades earlier. A series of articles about the China-Japan reversal published by the *Nikkei,* the country's leading financial daily, however, had a sharper edge. "To the Japanese, China is an alien country under a different political system," the articles' authors said. "But the reality is that Japan is no longer recognized without refer-ring to its superpower neighbor. How will Japan deal with that?"

At the direction of the Propaganda Department, the Chinese official media eschewed any triumphalism. But for mainstream Chinese schol-ars, the significance of surpassing Japan went beyond economics. Yuan Peng, a senior figure in a major Beijing think tank, called the moment the "most significant landmark in Asia's history since Japan's defeat of China in the First Sino-Japanese War [in 1894–95]." In finally climbing back to the top in Asia, he said, China had corrected a "major contradic-tion" in the regional order. In short, China was back where it belonged. "The power pattern of an Asia-Pacific led by Japan or by America and Japan," he said, "is about to change." Like many Chinese leaders and scholars, from that point on Yuan only had eyes for the true great game of global politics: pitting Beijing against its sole peer, Washington. "If in the past thirty years from 1979 to 2009, the major problem in Asia-Pacific [was] the power struggle between China and Japan," he wrote, "the ten to twenty years from 2010 will be between China and America." More to the point, in the eyes of some Chinese decision makers, after decades of serial missteps, Japan had ceased to matter at all.

A swaggering China overlooked Japan's many remaining strengths—its advanced technology, its world-class companies, the soft power of both its traditional and its modern culture, and a social cohesion that had survived decades of low growth. Instead, China emphasized the country's manifest weaknesses—a repeated failure to retool its economy, high debt, a dispiriting inability to lift incomes, and a moribund political system with revolving-door prime ministers. Worst of all, Japan was heading off a demographic cliff, projected to lose a third of its 128 million population by 2060. As Chinese scholars debated how to manage relations with the United States around this time, Tokyo usually barely figured in their calculations.

China's confidence was all too evident when Ichirō Ozawa landed in Beijing in December 2009. The former shadow shogun who pulled the strings of conservative administrations, Ozawa had left the LDP in the early 1990s and exacted his revenge over a decade later by engineering the election of Yukio Hatoyama. At home and abroad, Ozawa was considered in effect the prime minister. He had been a regular visitor to China for decades, but there had never been a trip like the one he made soon after Hatoyama's victory.

Ozawa brought with him a delegation of more than six hundred DPJ parliamentarians and their supporters, giving the trip a whiff of the old-style tributary relationships that China expected of its smaller neighbors in imperial times. If there were any doubts that Beijing would roll out the red carpet for Ozawa in return, they were swept away when Hu welcomed him in the Great Hall of the People, the vast ceremonial edifice astride Tiananmen Square. Hu shook hands individually with hundreds of the Japanese visitors and showered praise on Ozawa as "an old friend of the Chinese people." In addition to a reception that would have flattered a head of state, Hu threw in a touch that Chinese leaders at the top of the Communist apex rarely extended to any visiting foreigner. Rather than simply meeting him in his role as China's president, Hu welcomed Ozawa as head of the Chinese Communist Party. In China, the title of president was largely a formality that made Hu head of state for the purposes of receiving foreigners. His real power, though, derived from his position as party chief. As such, Hu was able to meet Ozawa in his own role as secretary-general of the Democratic Party of Japan, as if the pair were peers. Hu also wanted to strengthen the party-to-party dialogue with the DPJ, to establish the kind of informal links that over the course of decades had provided an important back channel to the LDP. Within the Chinese system, Hu's actions bestowed enormous prestige on Ozawa and, by extension, the new Japanese government.

A few months later, in early February 2010, the Japanese power broker was in Washington, meeting with Kurt Campbell, the State Department's Asia policy head. Campbell was still performing triage on the bilateral relationship after Washington's tense, rolling clashes with Tokyo in late 2009. With the China trip in mind, Campbell suggested to Ozawa that he might like to bring a delegation of DPJ members of parliament to America, just as he had done a few months earlier to China. Ozawa had a withering rejoinder. Hu Jintao had had his photograph taken with every one of the 140-plus parliamentarians in his delegation in Beijing. Ozawa asked pointedly whether they could receive the same treatment at the White House if he brought a group to Washington, a courtesy he knew would never be extended. He would be lucky to get in the front door of the White House on his own, let alone bring a delegation with him. In fact, the White House hadn't been certain that Campbell should even meet Ozawa on his trip to the United States.

Ozawa's animus toward Washington was due in part to his conviction that the United States had dropped him during his wilderness years. After helping solve thorny trade issues with Washington in the early 1990s, he felt ignored by the United States while he was out of power. That was clearly a misjudgment on Washington's part, for as much as many in the U.S. capital disliked him, Ozawa remained a key player in Japanese politics, scheming throughout to build a new opposition to the LDP. China, by contrast, had invited Ozawa to visit Beijing in 2006 and 2007 and received him at high levels. His latest trip in 2009 with the large business delegation provoked a snide reaction in Washington. Richard Armitage, the former senior Pentagon and State Department official, called it "the specter of the Japanese liberation army descending on Beijing."

Washington came to view Ozawa as pro-China and anti-American, although this was a caricature of his views. In fact, Ozawa wasn't so much anti-American as anti-LDP. Ozawa gave his critics plenty of ammunition on both counts, though, deriding past LDP governments as "foolish" for following in lockstep with George W. Bush's foreign policy. Ozawa's rivals within the chaotic DPJ administration only encouraged negative views of him among Americans. Days before Campbell's meeting with Ozawa, another minister, Seiji Maehara, the minister of state for Okinawa, was also in Washington and told Campbell not to trust

Ozawa. He'll tell you he supports the alliance, Maehara cautioned, because he tailored his views depending on whom he was speaking to.

In the end, for all his barbs, Ozawa didn't pander in his meeting with Campbell. He talked up his contacts with the leadership in Beijing but also warned of the growing influence of the Chinese military in domestic politics and the need to deal with them from a position of strength. From the record of their conversation, though, Ozawa seemed to be viewing Washington through a dim rearview mirror. Ozawa sensed, he said, that distrust of Japan from the years of the trade wars still lingered in Washington. He told Campbell that whenever he met Americans, he felt they assumed the Japanese were all "liars" who never keep their word. He would keep his word, he assured Campbell, but he made it clear that Japan had its own agenda these days and "could no longer . . . accept everything the United States said."

A few days after Ozawa's trip to Beijing to meet Hu Jintao in December 2009, China sent its own high-level visitor to Tokyo, Xi Jinping. Xi had been marked out as Hu's heir apparent at the quinquennial party congress in 2007. In preparation to take over as head of the CCP, Xi had been traveling the world, almost like a tourist ticking countries off a bucket list. In Japan, he had requested to see the emperor, only to be rebuffed by the Imperial Household Agency. Sealed off behind the moat at the Imperial Palace in central Tokyo, the agency had long been a prickly power unto itself, with its own permanent bureaucracy and studied rituals. The agency's rules dictated that any meetings with the emperor be requested at least one month beforehand. Xi's request had come in just a few weeks earlier, so following its protocols, the agency said no.

Ozawa and other senior members of the DPJ quickly got to work to overturn the decision. So, too, did Cui Tiankai, the Chinese ambassador in Tokyo, who would later go on to represent Beijing in Washington. Cui was not a Japan specialist, a fact that, he privately admitted, paradoxically helped him in his job. Unlike his predecessors, Cui didn't always have to act the tough guy in Tokyo as a way to beat back suspicion at home that as a Japan hand he had fallen under the spell of his host country. Cui by all accounts liked Japan immensely. A courtly, urbane character, Cui had a personality that dovetailed nicely with the exquisite formality and mindful politeness that Japan brought to bear in receiving important guests.

In this instance, Cui was also effective. He lobbied Ozawa, Hatoyama's office, and other like-minded politicians and bureaucrats. They in turn pressured the palace to grant an audience to Xi until its officials relented. The Imperial Household Agency agreed to the meeting only through clenched teeth. "If you are asking for the emperor to play a role to deal with a pending issue between countries," an official of the agency said, "that's not the emperor's expected role under the current constitution." Ozawa was dismissive of his complaints and told the head of the agency that if he was unhappy about the visit, he could resign. On the day of Xi's audience with the emperor Akihito, right-wingers protested noisily outside the palace.

The stars, then, appeared aligned for a blossoming of Sino-Japanese ties. Japan had a left-of-center government that had expressed remorse for the war and promised to stay away from Yasukuni without asking Beijing for anything in return. China's geopolitical status, meanwhile, had been growing rapidly. The CCP system seemed more resilient than ever, delivering economic growth that was the envy of developed and developing countries alike. If Japan wanted to keep "moving with the powerful," as one analyst had described its foreign policy, the time was ripe to tilt in Beijing's favor.

Some ideas that would have seemed inconceivable only a year earlier were now being canvassed. One proposed scenario had Hatoyama visiting Nanjing to pay his respects over the massacre, while Hu Jintao would reciprocate by going to Hiroshima. The election of the DPJ was a "golden opportunity" for China, said Kunihiko Miyake, the senior diplomat formerly stationed in Beijing. Some senior officials in Washington, meanwhile, took note of this diplomatic thaw with a sense of foreboding. "China believed they had secured Asia without a shot," said one of the Obama administration's top Asia advisers.

As it turned out, China hadn't secured Asia and certainly didn't manage to pull Japan away from the United States. There are many explanations for why Beijing failed to do so. After their early welcome of Hatoyama and Ozawa in Beijing, the Chinese saw little return in embracing too tightly an administration that they judged to be on a downward slide.

They were proved correct in this respect, because Hatoyama's government, in the end, lasted less than a year, with the prime minister resigning in June 2010. Ozawa stepped down from his party post in the same month after a lengthy investigation into allegedly corrupt fund-raising. One Chinese official said that Beijing worried whether Tokyo's new government would be able to deliver on policy change, whatever it promised. "We offered to have talks about the East China Sea, but then Ozawa was forced to step down," he said. "In the Asian way of human relations, you exchange gifts. You give one; you naturally expect one from the other side. We sort of wasted our effort."

In both countries, though, many officials and scholars were bewildered that Beijing hadn't reached out more enthusiastically to an overtly friendly government in Tokyo. "I have never understood why China didn't use a more effective wedge between Japan and the U.S.," said Kazuhiko Togo, a retired Japanese diplomat. One Chinese scholar who informally advised the government believed Beijing misjudged the situation. "Maybe the bureaucracy was too slow. Maybe they were too cold and too objective, and worried Hatoyama's word would not count for anything," he said. "But I think China missed a precious opportunity to reach out to Japan and isolate the U.S." The existence of the "traitors list" and the like drained the courage of some officials and scholars who might otherwise have pressed for bolder action. Another scholar said he had written numerous newspaper columns urging Beijing to embrace Hatoyama, though he allowed them to be published only under a nom de plume, blunting their impact.

Then there was the leadership itself. Hu Jintao had been able to quickly reestablish a top-level dialogue with Japan once its leaders stopped visiting Yasukuni Shrine. But carrying off a more dramatic shift in policy, with a full-fledged embrace of Tokyo, was a more difficult endeavor. Hu was probably too weak a leader to manage that, even had he wanted to. Hu not only lacked the revolutionary status of a leader like Deng Xiaoping but also faced a military uncompromising on sovereignty, as well as a population easily driven into the streets to demonstrate against Japan.

Hu was still vulnerable as well to sniping from the sidelines from Jiang Zemin, his predecessor, who in retirement had never stopped meddling in top-level politics. Jiang and his supporters were blamed for stirring up rumors about Hu's weakness in the face of Tokyo's alleged "betrayal" of Beijing on Taiwan, by allowing the island's former leaders to visit Japan. Hu therefore didn't just have to persuade his immediate colleagues to change course on Japan but had to bring along the *jumin,* the *gumin,* and the *wangmin* as well. Not only that, but many officials in China had simply discounted Japan's value. "The real reason that China was cautious," said an Obama administration official handling Asia, "is that they did not think they needed Japan."

The sentiment that Japan was permanently on the decline in relation to China was shared at top levels in Tokyo as well. Before Hatoyama's election, one of the Foreign Ministry's top officials, Takeo Akiba, was asked by the U.S. ambassador about Japan's position relative to China. Akiba was deeply pessimistic. China has a bigger population and more land and would soon have a larger GDP, he said, while Japan's population was shrinking. On top of that was the pressure from China's growing military might and its mid-range missiles, which had Japan in their range.

Akiba had headed the ministry's China division since the final days of Koizumi's prime ministership and the rapprochement that followed. The slight uptick in relations had done little to cheer him up. The headline on the WikiLeaks cable reporting his comments was "No Joy in Arranging Hu Visit to Japan." Two years into the position, he requested a transfer. After a series of difficult negotiations, Akiba confided that he was exhausted.

CHAPTER TWELVE

China Lays Down the Law

China is a big country, and other countries are small countries, and that's just a fact.

—Yang Jiechi, Chinese foreign minister

The Chinese thought Tokyo was weak. They thought we can bully Japan, maybe for the first time since the Meiji revolution.

—Shinzō Abe adviser

It was after the third speaker that Yang Jiechi, red-faced and angry, got up and walked out of the cavernous hall in the national convention center in Hanoi. Watching China's foreign minister's departure were his counterparts from the ten Southeast Asian nations that made up the regional ASEAN group. Seated around the table with them was an array of ministers of countries that attended the annual security forum as guests of ASEAN, including the United States and Japan. No one was in any doubt as to the reason for Yang's dark mood at the meeting in July 2010. One by one the ASEAN foreign ministers were taking turns to express their concerns about Beijing's actions in the South China Sea. Hillary Clinton had put her name down on the list to speak, as had the foreign minister seated next to Yang, Japan's Katsuya Okada.

Whether Yang left the room to seek instructions from Beijing on what he should say when he took his own turn at the microphone, as some around the table suspected, is still not clear years after the event. When he returned, however, the speech he delivered would go down in the history books, and not just for its vitriol. The Hanoi meeting marked an inflection point for the Asia-Pacific, a moment when regional nations finally mustered the courage to complain collectively about Beijing. To China's fury, the United States not only had encouraged their outspokenness; with the cooperation of Tokyo, Washington had also helped build the platform for Asian nations to vent as well.

The disputes about who held sway over the South China Sea and the seemingly barren islands and atolls dotted through its oceans were not new, nor were the passions they aroused. The vast seas in the area in question cover 1.4 million square miles, while the tiny islands, atolls, rocks, and shoals at that time together added up to only about 6 square miles. Yet they were ferociously contested, occasionally in short, sharp battles, as each side tried to stake its claim to them. Richard Armitage, who served in the Pentagon and the State Department, vividly recalled the aftermath of one of the biggest battles, which took place in 1974 between the navies of South Vietnam and China over a section of the Paracel Islands. Then a young military officer stationed with the United States in Vietnam, Armitage remembered the thousands of citizens gathering on the docks to welcome their local soldiers home after the battles in which the Chinese had forced the Vietnamese off a number of islets. The episode made a deep impression on him. "These islands might be pieces of dirt to us," he said, "but they matter to them."

Among the overlapping claims, Beijing's were by far the most expansive, first laid out in a map produced by the Nationalist government of Chiang Kai-shek in 1947. Although Mao Zedong's Communists drove Chiang and the Nationalists into exile in Taiwan two years later, they maintained their enemies' prerogatives in the South China Sea. The claim was marked out by a series of short, unconnected lines that looked as if someone had walked on top of a map of the seas binding China to Southeast Asia and left his footprints behind. The original map produced by the Nationalists featured an eleven-dash line, snaking all the way down from China, past the Philippines, before doing a U-turn off the coasts of Brunei, Indonesia, and Malaysia, and then heading north past Vietnam back toward the mainland. During an era of fraternity with the anti-imperialist forces of North Vietnam in the 1970s, Zhou Enlai ordered that two of the eleven dashes be removed, leaving the nine that remain today.

China had another skirmish with regional rivals following the 1974 battle, in 1988, and there were occasional clashes among fishermen from different countries. Southeast Asian nations also began to stake their own claims to a number of small island outposts. None of the rival claimants, though, had an immediate interest in pressing the issue. In newsrooms in the region in the 1980s and early 1990s, stories about the contested islands were mostly jokingly dismissed as filler on slow news days. In the early years of the new century, that started to change. On one level, China allowed for a degree of fuzziness, never clarifying whether it claimed all the waters within the now nine-dash line. Beijing, however, made clear that it had "indisputable sovereignty" over all the island groups in the vast, teardrop-shaped area. Under the UN Convention on the Law of the Sea, especially in the manner that Beijing interpreted it, China had effectively granted itself maritime rights over most of one of the world's most strategic waterways.

The PLA navy, now equipped with a bigger, more capable fleet, began conducting regular patrols in the South China Sea. Using its paramilitary coast guard fleets and fisheries administration, Beijing also pushed forward on a range of other fronts, unilaterally enforcing fishing bans and increasing scientific research and energy exploration in disputed areas. To underline its sovereignty claims, the various arms of the Chinese state planted flags on exposed rocks and reefs to mark out Beijing's territory. In the meantime, the 2002 agreement between China and ASEAN to negotiate a code of conduct for the South China Sea, which was meant to prevent confrontation and reduce tensions, lay fallow.

Chinese diplomats began to add their muscle to the effort as well. In 2009, Fu Ying, the ambassador to the United Kingdom, visited BP's London headquarters and warned the company to cease work on an offshore project negotiated with Vietnam in waters also claimed by China. A disarmingly charming figure when on her best behavior, Fu seemed to her many foreign interlocutors to become increasingly hostile toward the West as she rose in the Chinese Foreign Ministry. With BP, she was brutally direct. If BP didn't comply with China's demands on the project off Vietnam, Fu said, Beijing would reconsider all contracts the company had been awarded in China, where it was a major investor. She also raised the threat of out-of-control patriotic mobs massing on the doorsteps of BP's numerous projects in China, saying Beijing would no longer be able to guarantee the safety of the thousands of its employees in the country. Asked why she had demanded that BP withdraw its claim, Fu told the journalist Bill Hayton, "I love BP and I didn't want to see them get hurt." The message was not lost on BP, which pulled out of the block near Vietnam. Nor did it go unnoticed by Southeast Asian nations. Fu would later assert that the South China Sea issue had been "under control" before 2009, placing the blame on Washington for inserting itself into the disputes and upsetting the regional balance. Such arguments, however, belied Beijing's and other Asian nations' actions on a multitude of fronts during this period.

Faced with a deadline set by international treaties, Vietnam and Malaysia lodged claims in 2009 based on the far reaches of their continental shelves. Although modest compared with China's, those claims took them deep into the areas of the South China Sea that Beijing insisted were its own. The Philippines parliament also codified its baseline claims around the same time. For a host of reasons, ranging from China's growing strength to the refusal of Southeast Asian nations to concede, and a desire to grab new fishing grounds and potential oil and gas reserves, disputes that had remained largely under the surface for decades began emerging into the clear light of day. China's so-called smile diplomacy, which had been a feature of Beijing's regional outreach in the 1990s, was becoming a distant memory. Many regional nations were suddenly confronted with claims that once existed largely in theory now being enforced in their own backyards. For Southeast Asia, the peaceful rise that had been touted earlier in the decade was disappearing, just as China's hawks had promised it would.

There was little mystery about China's more assertive approach. Gaining control of the South China Sea was a long-standing national objective for China. The difference was that Beijing was now finally accumulating the military firepower to do something about it. The same applied in the East China Sea, where Beijing was butting heads with Tokyo, and in foreign policy in general, where it was asserting itself in its dealings with Washington on several fronts. At the annual Shangri-La Dialogue of regional defense ministers held in Singapore in 2010, Robert Gates, the Pentagon chief, wondered out loud from the podium why Beijing had responded harshly to the latest U.S. arms sales to Taiwan, when, he said, the Chinese had known since normalization of relations in 1979 that

Washington was committed to pursuing this policy. Gates's query was disingenuous in many respects. While the United States had passed a law committing it to Taiwan's defense, China had never accepted it. A retired PLA general took the bait in any case, to explain why Beijing had suspended military-to-military ties over the latest sales. His answer succinctly summed up what many of Beijing's interlocutors believed was driving recent Chinese assertiveness. "Because we were weak [then]," the PLA officer said. "But now we are strong."

It is hard to underestimate the psychological impact on the region and its leaders of China's willingness to herald its arrival as a great power. The Japanese had already become disillusioned with China and doubted its interest in forging a trusting bilateral relationship. In Southeast Asia, by contrast, Beijing's 1990s charm offensive, anchored by blossoming trade ties, had been unencumbered by the baggage that weighed down regional relations with Japan. In such circumstances, China was initially often welcomed as a benign, benevolent presence, finally coming home to Asia.

In Singapore, Simon Tay, one of the city-state's most articulate scholars, extolled the gradual displacement of Western democratic values in Asia by Chinese-style good governance dispensed by a meritocratic elite. At the moment when American influence was ebbing, he said in his 2010 book, *Asia Alone,* China had embarked on a sustained and multidimensional campaign to enhance friendships and gain influence, especially in Asia. What's more, he argued, the program was working: "This effort has largely succeeded in ending enmity and suspicion." Tay even suggested that ASEAN had begun to socialize a rising China to the region's "norms of cooperation and peace." Although he delivered that assessment with caveats, Tay was hardly alone in his optimism about the prospects for a kind of Pax Sinica to fill the vacuum left by a weakened Washington.

Prominent regional statesmen like Lee Kuan Yew, however, were starting to view China's rise through a darker prism. Few Western politicians traveled to Asia without trying to secure an audience with the Singaporean founder and patriarch. For decades after rising to power on an anti-Communist platform in the 1960s and building Singapore into an independent, prosperous state, Lee enjoyed his status as the preeminent wise man of Asian politics, always at hand to interpret the region for Western walk-ins. Lee had long combined lectures to his visitors about the West's decadence with his theories about Pan-Asian values and the benefits of soft authoritarian rule.

As late as the 1990s, Lee was still warning about the perils of resurgent Japanese militarism. Famously, he once said allowing Japanese troops to contribute to peacekeeping forces in Cambodia was like "giving a chocolate filled with whiskey to an alcoholic." Lee had once had views similar to Tay's, foreseeing a new era in which Asia, including China, could look after itself without American support. Lee's views—or at least the emphasis he gave to different strands of them—though, began to shift in line with the region's own evolving power balance. By the turn of the century, he rarely bothered cautioning about the dangers of Japan. Many of his own diplomats had told him to keep quiet on the subject and that his views about so-called Japanese militarism were out of date. Instead, Lee started to urge the Japanese to strengthen their ties with the United States, in anticipation of the rise of China.

Lee soon began ditching his old rhetoric of Asia-for-the-Asians with Washington as well. "A world leader must hold its ground in the Pacific," Lee told the interviewer Charlie Rose in 2009. Two years later, he spoke in starker terms of his concern about China, which he painted as potentially the chief menace to regional stability. "China tells us that countries big or small are equal, that it is not a hegemon," he told an American political delegation. "But when we do something they do not like, they say, you have made 1.3 billion people unhappy. So please know your place."

The South China Sea disputes played into this emerging narrative of a China reverting to the habits of treating its smaller neighbors as tributary states and bullying them in the bargain. As Lee remarked, "Will an industrialized and strong China be as benign to Southeast Asia as the United States has been since 1945? Singapore is not sure. Neither are Brunei, Indonesia, Malaysia, the Philippines, Thailand, and Vietnam." The worries were especially pronounced at the time in Vietnam and the Philippines, where the clashes with Beijing over territorial claims, energy exploration, and fishing rights were most pronounced. Tay's notion that Chinese charm and largesse were about to take the place of American arrogance and demands seemed more and more off the mark.

Certainly, Vietnam was not cheering China's rise. As the host nation for the 2010 ASEAN meeting, Hanoi spotted an opportunity to use the event to elevate its concerns about Beijing's behavior and gather backing in the region in the process. Vietnam had long tried to find ways to hedge against its overbearing neighbor, reestablishing diplomatic ties with its old foe, the United States, in 1995. Hanoi wanted to draw Washington closer, not just back into the region but onto its side in its territorial disputes. Vietnam's timing could scarcely have been better, because the Hanoi meeting coincided with a sharp rethink in Washington about Beijing as well.

Since being confirmed by the Senate as the chief Asia policy maker in the State Department in mid-2009, Kurt Campbell had been working on re-refurbishing America's Asia policy. Campbell had always been suspicious of the Washington policy makers whom he described as the "China first" crowd, who had little time or respect for Washington's allies in Asia. Campbell's own policy was more like "Asia first," which he began putting into action as soon as he arrived at State, convening regular collective lunches in Washington with the ambassadors of all ten ASEAN members.

U.S. officials were never under any illusion that the proceedings of these lunches would be kept secret. Nations like Laos and Cambodia were by then drifting into Beijing's camp. "We knew it was all getting back to the Chinese," said one administration official. Though of no great moment of themselves, the lunches were symbolic of the early stirrings within the Obama administration of what would become known as the pivot, or rebalance, to Asia. The formal branding of the administration's Asia policy as "the pivot" in late 2011 was in fact a lagging acknowledgment of a plan that had effectively been in place since Barack Obama was elected.

Obama's first foreign visitor to the White House was Tarō Asō, Japan's then prime minister. The first formal state visit to the White House was bestowed by the administration on South Korea's Lee Myung-bak. Hillary Clinton's first trip as secretary of state was to Asia, setting a pattern of regular visits to the region and attendance at its multilateral forums. In Thailand in July 2009, Clinton committed the United States to a regional treaty of amity and cooperation, another important symbolic pledge to the Asia-Pacific. Japan, as anxious as ever, lobbied hard to attract the attention of the incoming administration. "The Japanese ambassador was coming into my office every other day: You have to visit Japan before China. You have to call Asō before you call Hu," said Jeff Bader, Obama's chief Asia adviser at the National Security Council. Tokyo would have its own problems with the Obama administration soon enough. By the end of the president's first year in office, however, it was China's hubris in the wake of the financial crisis that was over-shadowing any efforts to build good relations between Beijing and Washington.

Bader had been determined to prevent Obama from making what he judged to be the same mistakes Ronald Reagan and Bill Clinton had made in their presidential election campaigns: to adopt positions on China they inevitably had to reverse on taking office. Reagan had to drop plans to have "official government relations" with Taiwan, while Clinton backed down on linking human rights to trade. Both presidents depleted their political capital with Beijing in the process and lost lever-age in the relationship, or so the critics argued.

Eager to avoid similar pitfalls, Bader postponed the visit of the Dalai Lama to the White House scheduled for October 2009, a month ahead of Obama's first trip to China as president. Bader argued that meeting the Dalai Lama just ahead of traveling to Beijing was more trouble than it was worth. The Chinese, however, saw the tight timing of the two visits as an opportunity to drive a wedge between the White House and the Tibetan spiritual leader. At the end of the key preparatory meeting for that summit, as the pair were leaving the room, Yang Jiechi had pulled Bader aside to deliver just one message: don't meet the Dalai Lama.

Washington's conciliatory gestures, however, went unreciprocated. Once Obama was in China, Beijing pulled many of the now-familiar stunts of a ruling party unabashed in its conviction that it alone had the right to dictate what its citizens saw and heard. The Chinese censored an interview with Obama, refused to allow questions at a press conference, and restricted access to a town hall event in Shanghai. The rescheduling of the meeting with the Dalai Lama, once leaked, had already set the tone for the media's perception of the China trip. As the November visit unfolded, the administration's outreach to Beijing was mercilessly rein-terpreted as weakness. The prominence given to Obama's insular domes-tic political team in the entourage over the administration's regional experts only reinforced that perception. "We were about 40 vans down in the motorcade and got barely any time with the president," said one senior official. "It was like the Obama campaign was visiting China."

A combative, intense figure, Bader bristled at the way the visit was portrayed, complaining later that the U.S. press always described interactions with China as akin to a "gunfight at the OK Corral," with only two possible outcomes. "You either have a bigger gun or a smaller gun," he said later. "You either whip them, or you appease [them], and are weak." In early 2010, the United States announced arms sales to Taiwan and welcomed the Dalai Lama to the White House. Far from being a toughening of policy, those decisions had always been in the pipeline. But the damage had already been done with the initial delay in meeting the Dalai Lama and the transparent efforts to soothe China.

Evan Medeiros, Bader's then deputy who went on to head Asia policy at the NSC, said after leaving office that the administration had "sent inconsistent signals" to the Chinese early, with the Dalai Lama decision and other issues. Bader himself conceded that other factors were in play that magnified the claim that the United States was weak. "There was a belief in some quarters in Beijing that the U.S. was a declining power," he said, "and that China was on the rise." Others in the government were less charitable about the effectiveness of the administration's early China policy, especially after Beijing's indifferent response to North Korea's role in sinking a South Korean naval ship in March 2010. "It became clear to many of us that this was not working," said one senior official. "They were taking advantage of us."

China's ambitions seemed to be expanding rapidly at this time, especially in the South China Sea. After Bader and James Steinberg, the State Department deputy secretary, returned from a trip to Beijing in March 2010, the *New York Times* reported that Chinese officials had told Washington that the United States should respect its claims in the region. The South China Sea, the Chinese officials were quoted as saying, was part of China's "core interest" of sovereignty. Beijing's labeling of an issue as a "core interest" was not a matter of mere semantics. The use of the phrase carried with it an ominous warning from Beijing. In a Chinese context, the term elevated the South China Sea to the stature of issues like Taiwan and Tibet—territorial red lines that, if crossed, Beijing would go to war to protect.

The characterization of the South China Sea as a "core interest" was buried deep in the *New York Times* story, which largely focused on tracking China's growing naval power. In the region, however, the report raised alarm. Steinberg and Bader's protestations that no Chinese official had ever said this to them had little impact, because many regional players, and some of the Americans' own colleagues back in Washington, were inclined to believe it was true. "We had had lots of discussions, including about the South China Sea, but the Chinese had not gone that far," Steinberg said.

Beijing was initially loath to deny the report, a position not as perverse as it might have seemed. To have done so would have been perilous for an individual official or military officer within the CCP, because it could have been interpreted as a step back from Beijing's sovereignty claims. Instead, Beijing's rhetoric backing its rights over the island and land features within the nine-dash line strengthened. A few weeks after the Hanoi meeting, the PLA issued a statement claiming "indisputable sovereignty" over the South China Sea.

Some Chinese claimed the United States had intentionally leaked the "core interest" phrase as a way of publicizing the issue and rallying rival Southeast Asian claimant states against Beijing. Three years later, the Chinese state press was still running indignant articles claiming that "false rumors" had been spread in the United States, Japan, and Southeast Asian nations that Beijing laid claim to the entirety of the South China Sea. "No internal or public Chinese document or declaration at the time made that claim," said an article in the *Beijing Review*. Adding to the confusion, Hillary Clinton said that Dai Bingguo, Hu Jintao's chief diplomatic adviser, had told her personally in May 2010 that the South China Sea was a "core interest." "I immediately said we don't agree with that," she replied bluntly. "So they were on notice."

With the Hanoi ASEAN meeting only weeks away, Clinton was now primed to take the South China Sea issue to another level. Thanks to the Asia team at the State Department, the groundwork had already been laid.

U.S. officials visiting Campbell on the sixth floor of the State Department at Foggy Bottom sometimes spied a whiteboard in his office. Campbell and his team were using it to track the positions of the ten

ASEAN members on China's handling of the regional territorial disputes. More precisely, they wanted to determine which countries would agree to speak up against Beijing's behavior in the South China Sea in a meeting at which China's representatives would be present. Beijing's position had always been to negotiate one-on-one with rival claimants, creating contests that smaller Asian nations felt they could never win. As Robert Gates put it, "They are easier to intimidate that way." Campbell was offering the ASEAN members a chance to stand together. The U.S. message was akin to what old-style trade unions had always told potential members: in solidarity lies strength. Most Southeast Asian nations were eager to hop on board.

Vietnam's foreign minister was the first to speak when the Hanoi meeting got under way. The Philippines, Malaysia, and Singapore followed, all of them critical, either directly or indirectly, of Chinese diplomacy in the South China Sea. Clinton delivered perhaps the sharpest blow of all toward the end, declaring that the United States considered the stability of the seas to be in American "national interest," seemingly mirroring what the Chinese had (or hadn't) said months before. By the end of the meeting, nearly all of the ten ASEAN foreign ministers had spoken up in an unprecedented show of defiance.

When Yang finally got to his feet, his response was explosive. "He reacted volcanically, with an intimidating, bullying speech," recalled Bader later. For much of the time he talked, he glared at Clinton. Speaking for about half an hour without notes, Yang took aim at a number of targets in the room. He chastised his hosts, the Vietnamese, on the grounds that they had somehow violated an unspoken Communist canon. You are a fraternal socialist country, he said. I just met the secretary-general of your Communist Party. You should not be fooled by the spokesmen of countries that are not Communist or socialist like us. Turning to Singapore's George Yeo, Yang said, "China is a big country, and other countries are small countries, and that's just a fact." About ten minutes into Yang's tirade, Campbell handed Bader a note on which he had written a single word: "Wow."

The one foreign minister who was not shocked at Yang's outburst was Japan's Okada. The earnest scion of a wealthy retailing family whose best-known hobby was collecting frog figurines, Okada had had his own baptism of fire a few months before the Hanoi event. In Seoul, Okada had raised questions about China's nuclear forces, once in a bilateral meeting with Yang and again shortly after, in a three-way session with South Korea. Yang was so furious that he rose to his feet, stood back from the table, and began screaming loudly while pointing at Okada. In a large room, one of Yang's staff leaned over to turn on the microphone, which he had forgotten to do, to make sure his minister could be heard by the Japanese sitting across the table. Yang's attitude was a familiar one: How dare a representative of Japan criticize China? Yang added that his relatives had been killed by the Japanese during the war.

At the end of Yang's speech in Hanoi, Okada raised his hand. The Japanese foreign minister had been surprised that so many Asian countries had spoken up against China, but not at Yang's intemperate response, because "I had seen it before," as he said later. Okada didn't think the meeting should end on such a sour note and recalled, "I tried to speak calmly. I did not want to stimulate [Yang] any further." He offered "very levelheaded comments" about how the South China Sea was an issue of national interest to Japan. After the meeting concluded, Clinton approached Okada to congratulate him on his decision to speak last, telling him, "That was very courageous."

Yang could be as blunt as any Chinese interlocutor, but he was not the obvious candidate to deliver a bellicose screed at an all-but-public meeting of his peers. He was one of China's first barbarian handlers of the modern era, escorting George H. W. Bush on a visit to Tibet in the late 1970s. After the 1989 Beijing military crackdown, he had been dispatched to Washington to try to reestablish an equilibrium in relations. The Bushes gave him the nickname "Tiger Yang" and pronounced him a friend of the family. As meaningless as such professions of friendship are in top-level diplomacy, the Bushes' bestowal of a nickname was at least an acknowledgment of personal familiarity. Faced with an organized effort to challenge China in Hanoi, however, Yang as Beijing's representative had little choice but to lash back at his assembled critics.

Bader, among others in the administration, was convinced that something deeper was afoot with Yang's tirade, reflective of a fierce struggle within China. Bader's own sense of the divisions in Beijing had been buttressed by U.S. intelligence about a dispute in the Politburo over the course China should set for foreign policy. Put crudely, the debate set the hawks, who wanted a more aggressive approach, especially in Asia, against the traditionalists, who favored a conciliatory stance, along the lines of Deng Xiaoping's old dictum counseling a low profile for the Chinese.

Yang's reaction at the Hanoi meeting gave the issue an extra edge. Around this time, he was battling to win favor from the leadership to succeed Dai Bingguo, a decision that was due to be made at the party congress in late 2012 and then formally announced early the following year. As foreign minister, Yang ranked below Dai, who was the state councillor for diplomatic affairs, and being assertive with foreigners could only help his ambitions. In time, the personnel issue would be resolved with Yang's taking over from Dai in an orderly succession. In the short term, as far as many in Washington were concerned, though, Dai prevailed in the ideological contest over the direction of diplomacy in favor of a modest diplomatic posture.

Dai's policy ascendancy was announced in a typically Chinese manner, which is to say it wasn't really announced at all. There was no major set-piece speech to frame it, nor the kind of blood-and-guts debate in the media that would have taken place in Western countries before a resolution on such a major issue could be reached. Instead, Dai published a lengthy article in the official media about Beijing's steadfast adherence to the path of "peaceful development." The article was austere, repetitive, and riddled with the dense codes beloved by CCP theorists ("What is the relationship between the path of peaceful development and the building of a harmonious world?"). Along the way, however, Dai pushed many familiar buttons that by themselves sent a reassuring signal about the direction of policy.

China would never seek hegemony, Dai wrote, nor did it seek to impose a Monroe-style doctrine on the region. There would be none of the war and plunder perpetrated by Western countries when they were rising as global powers. Beijing's core interests were loosely defined, with three main pillars: preserving the CCP-led political system, economic development, and the country's territorial integrity.

At the White House, Tom Donilon, Obama's national security adviser, held up the article for reporters visiting his office, describing it as a rebuke to Beijing's behavior in the South China Sea and to Yang's rant in Hanoi. Bader felt much the same, observing after leaving office that the article was Dai's way of reassuring the traditionalists within the system and academia that they could now speak their minds. Hitherto, they had complained to Bader, they were branded as "traitors" if they criticized the hawks. "There was an internal debate, and Dai prevailed," Bader said. "He won the day."

Dai's word had particular credibility because he was considered by Bader, others in the administration, and Japan and Europe to speak with the authority of Hu Jintao. A few months later, Dai repeated his reassuring encomium in an op-ed article for the *Wall Street Journal,* published shortly before the annual U.S.-China ministerial dialogue. The only thing Beijing wants, he wrote, after the country had endured so much hardship over so many years, is to "lift the Chinese people out of poverty." Later, at a luncheon meeting with scholars in Washington, when he was struggling to find words to send a similar message about China's peaceful intent, Dai reached for a rich French fruit tart that had been placed in front of him for dessert. "We want this," he said, and nothing more, picking up the tart and displaying it to the room.

In Washington, Dai's statement was read as a definitive course correction. In retrospect, it was merely a momentary resolution of endemic tensions within the system. A few years on, only a foolhardy U.S. official would assert that Dai had "won the day" in Beijing. Deng's dictum about China "hiding its light and biding its time" did not describe pursuing a path of peaceful development in perpetuity. Read properly, the statement advocated tactical caution until China had the capability to project power itself.

Dai, for his part, always contested this interpretation. Writing in his retirement, he blamed Westerners for speculating "that China's claim to take a path of peaceful development was a conspiracy carried out when the country was not powerful enough." Few in Washington would believe such an assertion today. In retrospect, Yang's outburst in Hanoi was the more accurate reflection of Beijing's long view. As far as the Japanese were concerned, any illusions about a tentative rapprochement in bilateral relations from 2007 onward had well and truly been stripped away by the end of the decade.

On September 9, 2010, a few months after the Hanoi meeting, the Japanese coast guard intercepted a Chinese fishing vessel near one of the Senkaku/Diaoyu islands. It wasn't the first time that Japanese patrols had come upon Chinese fishermen in the seas that both countries claimed but that were under Tokyo's administration. In the past, such incidents had been contained. The Chinese vessels would be ordered to leave the area, and generally they complied. If not, the Japanese favored a brief detention followed by a rapid repatriation, with the less said by either side the better.

This time was different. The Chinese boat captain, the Japanese said later, was drunk. His small, rusty blue trawler looked as if it might break apart at any moment, but he deployed it like a weapon, repeatedly ramming the Japanese vessels in an effort to escape. He ignored Japanese commands, delivered over a bullhorn, to stop. As one Japanese parliamentarian who viewed tapes of the incident later said, the captain made "a universally recognized hand gesture" to let the Japanese know what he thought of them.

After they boarded the boat and took the captain into custody, the Japanese did not send him home. He had strayed into Japan's territorial waters at a politically fraught moment, just as the ruling Democratic Party of Japan was readying for an internal leadership ballot. The contest pitted Ichirō Ozawa against Naoto Kan, who had taken over as prime minister after the resignation of the hapless Yukio Hatoyama in June. Although the contest wasn't a proxy fight over China policy, Ozawa was being touted as the candidate who favored closer ties with Beijing. Supporting Kan was Seiji Maehara, the transport minister, who had immediate responsibility for crafting Tokyo's response to the fishing vessel incident.

For a politician who represented Kyoto in Japan's parliament, Maehara had chosen an unusual theme for his office decorations. Instead of displaying the treasures of the country's ancient capital, Maehara's wall was covered with large, blown-up photographs he had personally taken of his life's passion outside politics, steam locomotive trains. In politics, however, Maehara was anything but a train spotter. Beijing had never forgotten a speech he had delivered at a think tank in Washington in 2005, in which he said China's rapidly expanding military budget made the country a "realistic threat" to Japan. From that point on, Maehara was a marked man in Beijing, which kept a steely eye out for any unfriendly statements from Japan. When he went to China soon after that speech, he was snubbed. "I was targeted by China for years," he complained. Within the Democratic Party of Japan, his hawkishness had initially put him on the outside with the dovish Hatoyama. But with Hatoyama gone, Maehara's views on China had moved closer to the mainstream.

Once the Chinese captain had been detained, Maehara, who believed Japan had to respond firmly to incursions into its territory, ordered his formal arrest. "We will take strict measures based on our domestic law," he said. "It's as simple as that." The attention of the government nonetheless largely remained on the leadership ballot, just days away. Distracted or not as it was by internal party ructions, the arrest of the captain would prove to be a serious misjudgment on Tokyo's part. On September 12, two days before the party vote, Dai Bingguo summoned Tokyo's ambassador in Beijing to the Foreign Ministry. The episode was the start of a steep learning curve in diplomacy for Uichiro Niwa, a businessman whom the DPJ had appointed ambassador as part of its efforts to break the bureaucracy's grip on foreign policy.

The timing of the summons alone conveyed a message. The ambassador was pulled out of bed and dragged into the ministry before dawn for a dressing-down. (In China's diplomatic armory, the 3:00 a.m. phone call was used regularly as a tool to put pressure on its interlocutors.) Dai issued a single unambiguous demand to Niwa: Tokyo must release the captain, his crew, and their boat immediately, with no preconditions. What one journalist described as a "minor fender bender on Asian seas" had escalated within days to become a full-scale diplomatic battle between two powerful states. Tokyo responded by freeing the trawler's crew members and their boat but holding the captain. After Kan won the leadership ballot, he named a new cabinet, this time with Maehara as foreign minister, in effect keeping a China hawk in charge of an increasingly volatile situation. On September 19, ten days after the captain had been taken into custody, Tokyo announced that his detention would be extended, a signal that he would be put on trial.

From Beijing's perspective, Tokyo had crossed the line. Trying the captain in a local Japanese court was an unambiguous assertion of Tokyo's sovereignty over disputed territory, overturning a decades-long understanding not to highlight such claims. The situation had begun to spin out of control. The battles over the islands had formerly been confined to ragtag groups of nationalists in both countries who could easily be rounded up and pulled back in line. Now the central governments were facing off against each other, with the United States as a treaty ally on Japan's side.

Beijing's response to the extended detention of the captain was not subtle. A day after Tokyo announced its decision, four Japanese construction company employees, sent to China by Tokyo to remove chemical weapons left over from the war, were arrested. All ministerial-level contacts were cut. The Chinese media raised the threat of nationalist opinion being fired up and let loose unless Japan relented. In Xiamen, a coastal city in Fujian province near the disputed islands, boatloads of patriotic protesters readied to set sail. The backlash did have its comic moments. After a panda on loan to the Kobe zoo died, China solemnly dispatched a forensic team to examine its body. The panda had expired on the operating table after being sedated to extract semen for an artificial insemination. On the Chinese Internet, angry youth suggested Xing Xing had been deliberately killed to humiliate China.

Maehara described Beijing's reaction as "hysterical," but by now Japan was all bluff. Four days later, on September 24, the local district prosecutor's office released the trawler captain. From Tokyo's perspective, it was a humiliating backdown. Having insisted that the captain's fate was in the hands of an independent legal system, Tokyo abruptly intervened to set him free. Kan had panicked under pressure, worried about the affair's impact on Japan's hosting of the annual summit of Asia-Pacific leaders in a few months in Yokohama. "Did we back down?" Maehara said. "That's how people looked at it. There was an inconsistency in the government's attitude. It was not handled in an understandable fashion."

Chinese officials were pleased that their hardball tactics had brought Tokyo to heel but were also astounded at what they regarded as Japan's incompetent handling of the standoff. One Chinese official gave a pointedly bureaucratic account of how Beijing had tried to give Tokyo room to yield, only escalating its response when the Japanese refused. The first statements were delivered at a low level, by the Foreign Ministry spokesman, then by the assistant minister, then the vice-minister, then the minister, and finally by Dai Bingguo himself, with the 3:00 a.m. phone call. "In these encounters, both sides made mistakes," the official said, "but the Japanese side made more mistakes."

One sanction that Beijing ordered against Tokyo—an embargo on the export of rare earths—would reverberate for years. China had a near monopoly on the supply of these elements, which were used in high-tech products and were relied on by Japanese manufacturers. The suspension of these exports was as dramatic as any of the diplomatic sanctions, because it marked Beijing's apparent willingness to use crude economic measures as political leverage. In that respect, the cutoff of such vital essential resources broke a pragmatic template that for decades had dictated that trade and economic ties could remain intact even as political relations went into periodic deep freezes. Beijing always publicly denied that the supplies to Japan had been halted, and independent analyses conducted later suggested that Beijing was correct and that the Chinese had in fact reduced exports months earlier in an effort to gain control of a chaotic local market. At the time, however, Chinese officials privately told their U.S. counterparts that the reports were true and that the exports had been suspended to punish Japan. Whatever the truth, the damage to perceptions that China wouldn't mix politics with trade was immense.

When the Chinese trawler captain, Zhan Qixiong, flew home in a jet chartered for him by the government, he emerged from the plane in Fuzhou like a returning head of state, flashing two "V for victory" signs with both hands. Senior officials waited on the tarmac with his wife and son to greet him. A small child presented him with a bouquet as the media crowded around seeking comment. Zhan was ready for his close-up, offering his appreciation in a form that perfectly matched the cascading hierarchy of power in China. "To be able to safely return, I really thank the Party, the government, and the people of my country for their concern for me," he said. A month later, the Chinese government was still holding one of the Japanese construction company employees. Beijing made no effort to try to "hide its light" in this showdown with Tokyo but rather was intent on displaying its power and resolve for all to see.

Within Japan, the mismanagement of the crisis and its humiliating denouement were etched in the minds of many in the government. One senior diplomat who later became an adviser to Shinzō Abe as prime minister remembered the next meeting between the two countries' leaders in 2010. Wen Jiabao and Naoto Kan huddled for less than half an hour in a corridor of a Brussels conference center after a dinner of leaders at the annual Asia-Europe summit. They both stuck to their talking points about the need to restore relations, even as they held to their positions over the disputed islands. Japanese diplomats say Kan was visibly shaking as he read his prepared comments in front of Wen from a piece of paper. "The Chinese thought Tokyo was weak," said one of the diplomats who watched what was for him a galling sight. "They thought we can bully Japan, maybe for the first time since the Meiji revolution."

With both sides hardening their positions, the next confrontation over the islands would have much greater consequences.

CHAPTER THIRTEEN

Nationalization

No one would doubt the pulses of patriotic fervor when the motherland is bullied.

—*People's Daily*

The TV says in simple language that Japan is a thief who stole Chinese territory. Even elementary-school children can connect the flag, theft and my photo.

—Uichiro Niwa, Tokyo's ambassador to Beijing

In a small room at a sprawling conference center in Vladivostok, in the Russian far east, the leaders of nearly two dozen countries had gathered for what was, by their standards, a small meeting. The size of the annual APEC summit of twenty-one Asia-Pacific leaders often precluded any meaningful dialogue between the heads of state, making impossible the intimacy that can nurture progress on contentious issues. At the September 2012 meeting, the Russian hosts tried to get around this problem by staging what was billed, in the jargon of global summits, as a "principals-plus-one" session. Normally surrounded by a large court of advisers, leaders were allowed just one staffer, and perhaps an interpreter, by their side in the room.

Hillary Clinton was in attendance in place of Barack Obama, who had begged off attending because he was in the midst of his reelection campaign. Accompanying Clinton was one of her senior State Department aides, Robert Hormats, who found himself chatting with Felipe Calderón, the president of Mexico, over a coffee during a break in the proceedings. As they spoke, Hormats's attention was caught by movement a few feet away, where Hu Jintao, China's president, was seated. Hormats watched as Japan's prime minister, Yoshihiko Noda, walked over and stood directly in front of the Chinese leader, demanding to talk.

In the revolving door of elite Japanese politics, Noda had taken over from Naoto Kan, who in turn had replaced Yukio Hatoyama. Since Koizumi's retirement in 2006, Japan had had six prime ministers in less than six years, three from the Liberal Democratic Party, the traditional party of government, and now three from the interlopers, the Democratic Party of Japan. Even by Japanese standards, it was an embarrassment and spoke volumes about the country's chronic political weaknesses.

The contrast with Hu's government was palpable. The Chinese leader was coming to the end of ten years, or two five-year terms, in office as the head of both the Communist Party and the state. Widely criticized as a lackluster leader, Hu, along with his premier, Wen Jiabao, had nonetheless presided over a near decade of double-digit annual growth rates in the economy. As he faced Noda, Hu could rightly take credit for being in charge of a country on a stunning upswing. Noda, in comparison, headed a state that seemed stuck on a permanent downward glide. Hu had pointedly not agreed to a meeting with Noda in Vladivostok, forcing the Japanese leader to take his chances in an impromptu conversation. The problem at hand was all too familiar—the disputed Senkaku/Diaoyu Islands, which had led to Beijing's yet again freezing top-level contacts between the two countries.

Japan's central government had announced it would buy a number of the islands from their private owners, a last-ditch attempt to head off a purchase of them by Shintaro Ishihara, the perennial nationalist warhorse who had deployed his considerable political skills to become Tokyo governor. Elected in 1999, he was now in his final year in the job. All of the central government's private and public efforts to explain to Beijing that it was only stepping in to buy the islands to prevent a manifestly worse option—that of a professional China baiter like Ishihara's gaining control of them—had come to naught. Beijing regarded the acquisition as effectively nationalizing the islands, something that put the issue of sovereignty up in bright, flashing lights and demanded a strong response.

Hormats and Calderón watched as Hu stood to face Noda. What unfolded was one of the most astounding meetings ever between a Chinese and a Japanese leader. Hu only had an English interpreter, so the conversation proceeded from Chinese to English and then into Japanese, with the same process in reverse when Noda was speaking. The trilingual dialogue allowed the tiny group of bystanders, few of whom spoke both Chinese and Japanese, or either language, to listen in. Noda started politely, offering his condolences for a recent natural disaster in China. In the same spirit, Hu thanked him. The niceties concluded, Noda complained to Hu that Japan had repeatedly asked for a formal meeting on the islands but had been refused. Nothing we are doing, he insisted, would affect the status quo. Hu dismissed that argument and warned that if the current status of the islands changed, there would be serious consequences. Japan, he said, had better "fully recognize the gravity of the situation."

Noda then took one step closer to Hu. By now, the pair were only a few inches apart, while others in the room watched transfixed. Noda pressed his point. Our diplomats should be talking about this, he said, motioning to the one aide he had with him in the room, Shinichi Nishimiya, who was slated to be Tokyo's next ambassador to Beijing. Hu, a stiff figure at the best of times, was visibly shaking with anger by this point. He scowled and fired back, Our diplomats can talk about it if you like, but don't dare do anything that affects the islands. Hu repeated himself: There will be severe consequences.

With the two having made their points, they stepped away from each other, and the conversation ended. Hormats and Nishimiya, close friends who had worked together in planning the summit, immediately huddled to compare notes to make certain they had the exchange, as conveyed by the interpreters, accurately recorded. Hormats then made his way over to Clinton, who was standing at the side of the room. She, along with other leaders in the group, had been gripped by the spectacle. In the coming hours, members of the Chinese delegation would approach both Hormats and Nishimiya to be briefed on the diplomatic drama that had taken place.

The latest, and most serious, standoff over the Senkaku/Diaoyu Islands had begun far away in Washington five months earlier, with a speech delivered by Ishihara to the Heritage Foundation. Scholars at the heavyweight conservative think tank had no idea what Ishihara planned to say when he was invited. When one watches the speech, it's not hard to believe them. The formal subject of the speech was U.S.-Japan relations. In fact, Ishihara barely touched on the topic. His first words at the podium—"I don't like Communism"—might have seemed as if he were pandering to his audience. But that was merely a jumping-off point for an eccentric, bewildering, devil-may-care forty-minute *tour d'horizon* of Ishihara's worldview.

Ishihara talked about Mao Zedong's "theory of contradictions" before moving on to the physicist Stephen Hawking, outer space, climate change and the melting Arctic ice, the clash of civilizations between Islam and Christianity, the Vietnam War, the historian and philosopher Arnold Toynbee, and Japan's backward accounting practices. After shifting onto more familiar ground, bashing the United States for unfairly "crushing" Japan's fledgling aircraft-manufacturing industry, and stressing the need for Tokyo to have its own independent nuclear deterrent, Ishihara eventually got to his longtime bête noire, the threat from China.

What Ishihara said next would have an explosive impact, although at the time it seemed as if he had merely tacked it onto the end of a rambling speech. He announced that Japan had to consolidate its control of the Senkaku/Diaoyu Islands to keep China's "radical movements" at bay and protect important fishing grounds. The Foreign Ministry was "too scared" to buy the privately owned islands, while the central government itself wasn't "courageous enough." If Japan didn't secure the properties, he said, the country "would lose respect." So, in the absence of the central government taking action, the Tokyo municipal government would buy the islands instead and take control of them. "The U.S. will not oppose us, will you?" he asked in conclusion, a remark that was met with great applause. Throughout the speech, Ishihara referred to China as "Shina," a pejorative word associated with Japan's wartime occupation of the country, somewhat akin to an American politician calling the Chinese "Chinks." The Heritage Foundation's chief Asia scholar thanked Ishihara, with a touch of bemused understatement, for "his wide-ranging and provocative" remarks.

Ishihara's address triggered a chain reaction of desperate political maneuvering and bitter political infighting in Japan; of brinkmanship in Beijing, where Xi Jinping was only months away from taking over as head of the CCP; and of extreme anxiety in Washington, which worried about diplomatic tensions spilling over into armed conflict. For Xi, who was put in charge of the internal party committee calibrating China's day-to-day handling of the controversy, it was his first real leadership test and a dangerous one at that, fatal to his prospects should it be fumbled. Washington looked on nervously, initially from the sidelines, assured by Tokyo that everything was in hand but never quite believing that it was.

As canny as ever, Ishihara was fast out of the blocks after his speech, with the central government struggling to keep pace. The Tokyo governor had been quietly cultivating the reclusive family that held the title to the islands for years. He was also close to the shadowy right-wing groups in Japan whose meat and drink was stirring up controversy on hot-button nationalistic issues like the Senkaku/Diaoyu Islands. With his backing, one patriotic group had built a lighthouse on one of the islands a decade earlier. Ishihara now tapped into these nationalist networks by launching a public appeal to raise funds to buy the islands. Very quickly, millions of dollars started to pour in.

Ishihara's antics sent Beijing's blood pressure soaring. Again, China targeted select Japanese officials to warn of the dire consequences should the islands' status be changed. They had some success with Tokyo's ambassador to Beijing, Uichiro Niwa. In an interview with the *Financial Times,* Niwa warned that Ishihara's plan would cause a "grave crisis" in bilateral relations. If this was meant to be a wake-up call for Tokyo, the Japanese government seemed to sleep through it. The businessman-diplomat's intervention was not welcomed in Tokyo, and when Ishihara complained angrily, Niwa was removed from his post soon after. Kenichiro Sasae, by then heading the Foreign Ministry, tried to calm his Chinese counterparts, advising them that the more they denounced Ishihara, the more money he would raise. By then, though, it was too late: the nationalist genie was well and truly out of the bottle in both countries.

In Tokyo, Noda secretly convened a small group of senior advisers and bureaucrats and instructed them to prepare a plan for the central government to buy the islands instead. As Noda and his advisers saw it, that alternative was much like Churchill's view of democracy: the worst option, except for all the others. Quietly, the Japanese set out to explain their position to the Chinese, to persuade them that the central government's buying the islands was the only way to head off the patriotic zealots, led by Ishihara. Changing the islands' ownership, they insisted, was just a formality, a piece of paper that wouldn't affect the status quo. They studiously avoided suggesting that the purchase would in any way "nationalize" the islands. A number of senior Japanese politicians and bureaucrats began to believe that the Chinese were signaling that Beijing could live with that compromise. Tokyo briefed Washington that everything was in hand. "Are you sure you know what you are doing?" one senior U.S. diplomat handling the issue said he asked the Japanese. "They told us everything will be fine."

But everything wasn't fine. Noda's government was well aware that Ishihara had backed it into a corner. "Ishihara raised the bar on patriotism. We had to match him," said Akihisa Nagashima, the senior DPJ figure appointed by Noda to liaise with Ishihara. "It was public sentiment. The DPJ felt pressure to do something." A former vice-minister for defense, Nagashima knew Ishihara well and had good contacts in the United States, where he had studied and worked in a Washington think tank. The Japanese government, he admitted later, had been swept along in a wave of emotional patriotism that Ishihara had assiduously worked at pumping up. From Beijing's perspective, this only underscored the farcical nature of the purchase. Far from keeping the Japanese rightists at bay, the weak Noda government seemed to be making concession after concession to them. In that respect, Beijing argued, tacit approval for the purchase would simply embolden the right wing even more.

By July 7, the central government had formally committed to buy the islands, for ¥2.05 billion ($25 million). It hoped to keep its decision secret, to give itself time to work out a deal with Beijing, or at least a diplomatic process in which both sides could save face. That plan foundered the following day, when the left-leaning mass daily, the *Asahi Shimbun,* announced the decision on its front page with a single, huge word: "Nationalization!" The headline alone was devastating for any chances for a quiet diplomatic settlement. "The *Asahi* ran with the big 'Nationalization' headline," said Nagashima. "That destroyed everything."

Japan could hardly have thrown a more toxic issue into the party's lap, and at a more sensitive moment. Just how sensitive came into clear view only years later, when the full extent of China's own political crisis at the time was detailed. Beijing was then in the midst of the closest thing the country has to election season in a democracy, the selection of the CCP's next leader at the once-every-five-years CCP party congress, to be held at the end of the year. Xi Jinping had been singled out as the heir apparent in 2007 but still had to formally claim the position. Under the party's evolving institutional rules and conventions, China would be choosing its leadership for the next ten years, giving Xi at least two five-year terms until 2022, unless he bucked convention by remaining in office longer. With the Senkaku/Diaoyu controversy, Xi was handed an issue that combined two of the CCP's most contentious points in a single noxious brew: Japan and sovereignty. If that wasn't enough, the CCP itself was locked in the deepest internal schism since the leadership split over the pro-democracy protesters in 1989.

In early 2012, a few months before the islands returned to the headlines, elite Chinese politics had experienced a veritable earthquake with the toppling of Bo Xilai. The Chongqing party chief's fall was straight from the pages of an Agatha Christie murder mystery, mixing family psychodramas with transnational corruption and homicide by poison. The lurid plot had its denouement in a room in the dingy, three-star Lucky Holiday Hotel on a hilltop in the city, where Bo's wife fed cyanide to a British consultant and family fixer whom she had once employed to help spirit illicit funds off-shore. The uncovering of the murder, and the subsequent flight of Bo's police chief to seek refuge in the U.S. consulate in the nearby Sichuan provincial capital of Chengdu, were unforgiveable transgressions in the CCP. Bo and his wife would ultimately be detained by the party and later separately tried and jailed on charges of corruption and murder.

It is hard, though, to resist the conclusion that Bo's real sins were political. Bo was genuine CCP royalty, the son of Bo Yibo, one of the so-called Eight Immortals of the revolution who were accorded immense lifelong prestige from having taken part in the founding of Communist China. After surviving being purged under Mao, Bo Yibo returned as part of an informal group of party elders who were pivotal in guiding the CCP through the upheavals of the reform period. He had helped oust Hu Yaobang in 1987, backed Deng Xiaoping's decision to call in the military in 1989 and then the economic reforms that eventually followed in the crackdown's wake, and worked to keep Jiang Zemin in power when he was under challenge in the late 1990s. Until his death at the age of ninety-eight in 2007, the elder Bo assiduously promoted his son's career in the party as well. With such revolutionary currency, if anyone should have understood the CCP's unwritten rules, it was Bo Xilai.

In the years leading up to the party conclave at the end of 2012, though, Bo became reckless. As commerce minister, he had cultivated publicity by hoisting himself on a patriotic platform, attacking the United States, Japan, Europe, and other foreigners on trade and economic issues whenever he saw a chance. Such targets were at least tolerable in China, if not his methods. In Chongqing, however, a city-province with twenty-eight million people in an area the size of Austria, Bo upped the ante. He engineered a violent crackdown on the local mafia and its lawyers and held large public rallies extolling Maoism. He also brazenly cultivated a higher public profile in an effort to force his way into the inner circle of the CCP leadership, the Politburo Standing Committee, when its membership turned over at the 2012 congress. Bo's antics drew sharp criticism from within the CCP, which abhors senior leaders openly campaigning for promotion to high office. In this respect, the CCP is much like the deep national security state in the United States, which much prefers wary cooperation to open infighting.

Tracking Chinese politics is sometimes akin to the work of an archaeologist who must painstakingly piece together ancient artifacts, gathering a shard of information here and there over an extended period of time until the murky outlines of a past event gradually come into view. In Bo's case, new information would emerge over the next two years tying him to a wider plot. The details dribbled out, first through the Beijing rumor mill and samizdat Chinese Web sites overseas before eventually appearing in a more cast-iron form starting in 2015, in the official media.

As if corruption and murder weren't enough, Bo's ambitions went far beyond just securing his own promotion. He was accused of conspiring with Zhou Yongkang, the country's police chief, and senior officials in state security and the military to form their own political "clique," a term that is CCP-speak for establishing a virtual rival administration. At worst, the reports suggested that Bo and Zhou had been attempting to prevent Xi from taking over as party chief altogether. Given the delicacy of transition politics in the CCP, there is almost no graver charge. Years later, Xi was still furious about the plot. In his New Year's address in 2017, he said that Bo, Zhou, and other top military officers and government officials had been "not only greedy financially and corrupt in their lifestyles, but . . . also politically ambitious, often agreeing in public but opposing in secret, and forming cliques for personal interests and engaging in conspiracy activities."

Within the CCP, Zhou was head of the party's Political-Legal Committee, an enormously powerful post. Roughly translated into American terms, he sat de facto at the top of the court system, parts of the FBI and the CIA, and the national police and the Justice Department. As Treasury secretary under George W. Bush, Hank Paulson had tried to leverage his relationship with Zhou to persuade him to intervene with Hu Jintao to establish a new top-level dialogue between the two countries. Over time, America's relationship with Zhou inevitably deteriorated in clashes over what Washington alleged was Beijing's aggressive cyber theft of U.S. commercial secrets.

Admiral Dennis Blair, who served as the first director of national intelligence in the Obama administration, had a heated meeting with Zhou in late 2009 over cyber spying. At the end of a difficult conversation, Zhou said to Blair, "You know, Director, keeping peace with 1.3 billion people is a very difficult thing." Blair said later that "for a millisecond I almost felt sorry for him." That sentiment passed quickly. "If you didn't rely so much on internal repression," Blair told Zhou, "you wouldn't have such a hard time of it." After Bo fell, Zhou would go down as well, bringing with him multiple officials from the networks he controlled in Sichuan province and within the petroleum mafia, the name given to the powerful cabal of officials-cum-executives in the oil industry. The wheels of justice and retribution in the party turn slowly, and the formal investigation into Zhou was not announced until mid-2014. He would be the most senior leader jailed for corruption since the 1949 revolution.

With hindsight, then, it is possible to get a clearer picture of the political adrenaline running through Beijing in 2012. Xi was simultaneously fighting off a serious challenge to his authority within the CCP and marshaling a response to Tokyo's purchase of the Senkaku/Diaoyu Islands. The dual crises ran in tandem. Ishihara's speech in Washington in April came just weeks after Bo's removal as Chongqing party chief in March 2012. In June, as Noda huddled with his advisers in Tokyo trying to game out Beijing's response to the islands' purchase, the new party chief in Chongqing was publicly laying out Bo's crimes. In July, after Japan formally decided to buy the islands, Chinese prosecutors announced that Bo's wife would be charged with murder. In September, when Bo was formally expelled from the party, the CCP's way of publicly announcing his guilt, Noda and Hu were facing off in Vlad-ivostok, and Xi was taking charge internally of Beijing's response to the dispute.

The notion that some Japanese were propagating—that Beijing was ready to allow the purchase of the islands to go through with a wink and a nod—seems, in retrospect, nonsensical and even rash. Displaying weakness of any kind in such a supercharged environment as then ex-isted in China was not an option. Japanese diplomats nevertheless flooded the Chinese system, looking for signs of assent. They met and spoke with Dai Bingguo and other top Chinese diplomats on numerous occasions, and the response was always the same. "China never said yes; Dai never said yes," recalled one of the top Japanese diplomats advising Noda. "Some politicians were trying to tell people they had, but they made a big mistake." Nagashima, the go-between in Japan linking Ishi-hara with the government, agreed. "China's response was basically con-sistent throughout. We sensed they would be furious, but hoped they would tacitly understand why we had to do it."

At the same time as Japanese diplomats were desperately seeking Bei-jing's assent, Tokyo assured Washington they were close to attaining it. "[Kenichiro] Sasae [of the Foreign Ministry] believes that China actually understands the necessity of these actions and will accept them," Kurt Campbell wrote in an e-mail to Clinton and his colleagues in early Sep-tember but added parenthetically, "I'm not so sure." In Vladivostok, in a meeting with Noda and Clinton, Daniel Russel, then at the National Security Council, asked the Japanese whether Tokyo had a plan to soften the purchase of the islands, perhaps by immediately designating them as a nature reserve. Noda said no. Skeptical from the outset at Tokyo's handling of the dispute, Washington was angry when the purchase plan failed to defuse the situation. In the words of a senior U.S. diplomat dealing with Tokyo at the time, someone who generally sympathized with America's ally, "Japan had totally miscalculated."

Far from clearing the air, the showdown in September between Noda and Hu in Vladivostok, if anything, made the situation worse. Immediately after the contretemps with Hu, Noda and his advisers gathered in a room at the Vladivostok APEC center and discussed delaying the final approval for the purchase of the islands for a week or a month. But Noda had decided to go ahead, telling them, "My mind is not shaky." His advisers concurred. "Finally, we decided even if you delay the date, you won't change anything," said Nagashima. The next day, Japan announced its decision to proceed with the purchase. From Beijing's perspective, it amounted to a grievous loss of face for Hu. "We never imagined that Japan would nationalize the Senkakus right after Hu and Noda met in the sidelines of the APEC summit," said Tang Jiaxuan, the Japan expert who had served as Hu's first chief foreign policy chief.

For weeks, and indeed months, afterward, the mere mention of Japan or Noda would produce physical paroxysms of fury from Chinese officials. One White House aide recalls being in an otherwise workmanlike lunch with Yang Jiechi. When the topic of Japan came up, the Americans were stunned at Yang's venom. "It was like pushing a button," the official recalled. His face reddening, as if someone had injected puce dye into his neck, Yang began a lengthy rant against the Japanese, citing everything from their historical revisionism to the double-crossing of China over the Senkaku/Diaoyu Islands.

Beijing was angry, but it was also ready to respond. U.S. officials observed that they had never seen China move its diplomatic armory out as effectively as it did after Japan formalized the islands' purchase. Unlike in 2010, the statements demanding that Japan reverse its "illegal and invalid purchase" now came from the top. Chinese maritime surveillance ships swarmed into the waters surrounding the islands, ignoring Japanese protests. As with most public displays of patriotism in China, the mobilization was both spontaneous and heartfelt, and also monitored, manipulated, and guided by the party through its security organs and the United Front Department, which manages relations with groups not formally aligned with the party. The biggest protest came in the form of anti-Japanese street demonstrations that gradually built up and spread throughout the country in the early weeks of September.

The mass demonstrations had all of the baroque, staged qualities that made so many foreigners cynical about the Chinese protests. The demonstrators were given placards and lunch boxes and told when to arrive and when to leave. By way of text messages delivered at the directions of state security with eerie, geographic precision to mobile phones in the protest zones, the demonstrators were thanked for their patriotism, which was the authorities' way of telling them they had made their point and could go home. "Can I shout 'punish corruption'?" one protester asked as he arrived at the marshaling point out near the Japanese embassy in Beijing, according to an account in a prominent Chinese magazine. No! the police replied. "Only slogans concerned with the Diaoyu Islands are allowed."

The nationalistic sentiment among so many young Chinese might have been tapped and channeled and then packed up and sent home by the CCP, which by now had rich experience in dealing with anti-Japanese marches. The upcoming party congress, less than two months away, required extra vigilance to ensure the demonstrations didn't morph into anger at grievances closer to home. But there was no mistaking the powerful signal that Beijing was able to transmit with the protests. With people marching in upward of two hundred cities, the anti-Japanese rallies were among the most widespread demonstrations in modern Chinese history. China had allowed anti-U.S. protests in the early 1950s during the Korean War. There were anti-Soviet demonstrations in the 1960s in the wake of the Sino-Soviet split. In 1989, Chinese students, intellectuals, and some workers turned on the party itself, with disastrous results for both sides, especially the protesters. But there had rarely been anything on the national scale of 2012. In the *People's Daily,* a signed editorial drove the point home: "No one would doubt the pulses of patriotic fervor when the motherland is bullied."

Then, as happens so often, Beijing overreached. The Chinese government had already dispatched a flotilla of coast guard boats to sail around the islands. Now it went a step further, setting off alarm bells in both Tokyo and the White House by sending military aircraft to fly over the disputed zone. Foreign diplomats grappling with the resolute opacity of the Chinese political system typically either rely on their Chinese counterparts to tell them what is going on or divine the flow of events from the tea leaves scattered through the official media. Intelligence gathering is vital as well, but U.S. officials say that apart from what one described as the occasional "soda straw" sucking information out of the Politburo, the apex of the party is well defended against U.S. spies. In the crisis of 2012, however, the Chinese leadership offered no reassurances to the United States about how far it might go. The media provided little guide beyond the bombast, and intelligence didn't fill in the gaps. After the military flights, Washington realized it was in the dark. "We were deeply worried," said one official guiding the U.S. response.

Then, during the first two weeks of September, at precisely the moment the islands crisis was escalating, Xi Jinping disappeared from public view. The episode was almost a parody of old-style Communism, when the official media would airbrush top leaders out of the day-to-day news narrative without explanation. Hillary Clinton visited Beijing in early September and met with Yang Jiechi and Dai Bingguo but not with Xi. When she asked to speak to Xi by phone, her request was refused. In the absence of official comment, rumors proliferated: Xi had back trouble; he had suffered a stroke; his car had been attacked by supporters of the deposed Bo Xilai; he was being operated on for liver cancer; there was an assassination attempt; he was playing a game of brinkmanship with enemies trying to stop his elevation to head the CCP a few weeks later; and so on.

In the information vacuum, the most florid theories gained traction. A number of Western newspapers credulously reported that Xi had been hit and injured by a chair thrown after a fight broke out during a heated meeting of Beijing's princeling families. Then, just as abruptly as he had vanished from public view, Xi reappeared, with the state media announcing on a Saturday that he had spent that morning at China Agricultural University in Beijing, marking National Science Popularization Day.

With the inviolable *omertà* surrounding the leadership, Xi's disappearance was never explained. His role in heading up the party group coordinating the response to the Senkaku/Diaoyu had by then not been publicized. This entire episode, however, had been deeply unsettling for the White House. "The opacity was very dangerous," said one senior U.S. official handling the crisis. After all, a Chinese attack on the Senkaku/Diaoyu Islands would trigger the U.S.-Japan security treaty, obligating the United States to join the defense of the islands. For over a decade, successive administrations had gradually hardened the U.S. commitment to defend the islands alongside Japan should they come under attack. In other words, a Chinese miscalculation might mean the United States could find itself at war.

The White House decided to make its concerns official, directing senior diplomats in Beijing to deliver a message directly to the Chinese. "Given our clear commitments under the treaty, we had to clarify for them what was at stake," explained one senior official. "We had to tell them—we take our treaty commitments very seriously." On October 2,

Kurt Campbell e-mailed Clinton with an initiative to reinforce the message: "We assess that the Chinese and Japanese positions are hardening due to a variety of factors despite a shared understanding that prolonged friction would be harmful to regional stability and the global economic recovery." Campbell's plan was to send a bipartisan group of former senior U.S. officials to both countries to cool tensions. He stressed that "speed is of the essence." Clinton replied barely five minutes later: "We should go ahead."

The quartet assembled for the mission—two veterans of Republican administrations, Richard Armitage and Stephen Hadley, and two Democrats, Joseph Nye and James Steinberg—were all schooled in Washington's national security establishment and in east Asian affairs. They set off in mid-October, just a fortnight ahead of the U.S. presidential election. The quartet distilled its message into a few simple points. First, the U.S.-Japan security treaty applied to the islands, but, they said, it should be irrelevant, because the United States didn't want to have to resort to that. Second, the two sides had to step back from the crisis and establish protocols that would extend through the entire chain of command about how to handle disputes and accidents. Finally, China and Japan had to find a way to take the issue of sovereignty off the table. "You have to avoid a situation," Hadley told the Chinese and Japanese, "where a couple of hot-dogging pilots or drunken sea captains get you into a dust-up that neither country can back down from."

As they shuttled between Tokyo and Beijing and back to Tokyo in late October, they were given deeply conflicting accounts of which side was to blame for the confrontation. Noda insisted the Japanese government had done what it had to do to head off Ishihara. There was no deal with him, the prime minister told them; this was not Kabuki. In Beijing, Yang Jiechi said the opposite, insisting that Ishihara and the Japanese government were in league. "They have changed the status quo at a very difficult time," Yang told them. "Since they have changed the status quo, we have to change the status quo." Steinberg recalled that the Chinese tried to enlist the Americans to constrain any drift in Japan toward militarism and nationalism: "Their main pitch was, open your eyes. This is a danger to you as well as much as to us, and you are not as attentive to this problem as you ought to be."

For Armitage, one thing that Yang said stood out. Yang insisted that

China wanted good relations with Japan, but attached a proviso: "If this thing got out of control, we will not be able to stop it," adding that if Japan "puts people on those islands, there will be tumultuous response." As the group traveled back to Tokyo, they marveled at how Yang had worded his warning. His formulation was both vague and full of foreboding, giving the Chinese maximum flexibility to act if they wished. "'People' could be soldiers, businessmen, or fishermen. They could define it however they wanted to," Armitage recalled. "Then there was 'tumultuous.' We had a hell of a time explaining its meaning to Japan."

The Chinese made it clear from the outset that they didn't regard the American contingent to be good-faith mediators. How could Washington arbitrate a dispute involving Chinese sovereign territory? The *Global Times,* the populist, party-backed tabloid that positioned itself at the sharp end of nationalistic sentiment, depicted the United States as congenitally biased. "While the US is scurrying to prevent military clashes between the two Asian giants so that its own interest would not be harmed, it is also trying its best to encourage Japan to boost its defense to contain China," said the Japan analyst Wang Pin.

In a sense, the Chinese were right: The quartet were all, one way or another, supporters of a tighter relationship with Tokyo, although in their eyes that didn't automatically make them antagonistic to China. Armitage himself had worked for decades to build closer defense ties between the United States and Japan, both in government and as a private consultant. Speaking after the trip, he said the Chinese had told the delegation, "'We appreciate your neutrality,' and we [would respond], 'We're not neutral. We just haven't declared [on sovereignty] one way or the other.'" As Armitage made clear, though, Washington could hardly sit on the fence given its obligations to Japan. "We're not neutral," he said, "when our ally is a victim of coercion or aggression or intimidation."

The crisis and its aftermath—a permanent, militarized standoff around the islands—made for a depressing coda to the final days of the DPJ government. Only a few years earlier, Yukio Hatoyama had been elected with his promise to build with China a "sea of fraternity" in the region. "The DPJ started out very friendly to China," said Nagashima, "and three years later ended with furious demonstrations against it." For Uichiro Niwa, the ambassador, it was painful to even turn on the television as he prepared to return to Japan. "Now, Chinese TV programs

constantly show the Japanese flag and a photo of my face," he said. "And
the TV says in simple language that Japan is a thief who stole Chinese
territory. Even elementary-school children can connect the flag, theft
and my photo. In China, I am feeling like I'm the ringleader."

In coming months, Beijing began setting its template for dealing with
the issue that it has used ever since, one that has the dual aim of harass-
ing Japan in the vicinity of the islands and asserting its claim over them.
Sets of Chinese vessels would stalk the islands in concentric circles, with
fishing boats nearest to their shores, coast guard vessels circling the next
outer perimeter, and finally the gray-hulled navy patrolling at a distance.
In the early 1970s, when Tokyo and Beijing first forged diplomatic ties,
the two capitals had adopted the "three no's" policy—no landing, no
construction, and no residences—with respect to the islands to keep the
matter off the agenda. More than forty years later, such diplomatic understandings were a distant memory. The new "three no's" were entirely
antagonistic in nature: no recognition, no shelving, and no dialogue. In
the words of one of Japan's top diplomats, "The Chinese hope that they
can keep the new normal for ten to twenty years. Then we will be forced
to negotiate."

In the early months of 2013, after he had left government, Campbell
visited Japan and China, now as a private citizen. Freed from diplomatic
protocol, he was occasionally received at higher levels of government
than when he had been in the State Department. In conversations with
leading figures in both countries, he was struck by the mirror imaging
in the two capitals after the crisis of the previous year. "Both sides are
saying we have clearly the right position, and we have got these guys on
the run, and a little bit more pressure and they're going to fold," he told
a conference in California, adding, "And neither side is going to fold."

Why did China take such a hard line over the islands with Japan? The
iron rule of the party's internal politics, to stand rigid on sovereignty, is
the most obvious explanation, especially at a time of leadership transition. Tokyo's behavior, easily seen from Beijing's perspective as a provocation, provides another justification. China's own rising military
strength and self-confidence, which were reinforced by the Western
banking crisis in 2008, were factors as well. In other words, the Chinese
were more assertive because they had the means to be. The Chinese were

also preparing for Shinzō Abe's return to office, with national elections due in Japan later that year.

But there were other factors motivating Chinese behavior. The Obama administration's policy of pivoting, or rebalancing, toward the Asia-Pacific was one, as were the lessons that Beijing had drawn from one of the key tests of the pivot, the face-off between China and the United States over the Scarborough Shoal, in the Philippines, in mid-2012.

The history of the Obama administration's turn to an Asia pivot has been entangled in intramural fights over who gets credit for the policy and how it should be branded. Though its direction had been set from the opening days of the administration, the pivot wasn't announced until Hillary Clinton attached her name to an article in *Foreign Policy* magazine in October 2011, well into the second half of Obama's first term. The United States, Clinton wrote, had reached a "pivot point" and needed to lock in substantially increased investment, "diplomatic, economic, strategic, and otherwise," in the region. The administration's policy to shift resources to Asia ran in tandem with a desire—indeed, desperation—to escape the draining Iraq and Afghanistan wars launched by George W. Bush in response to the 9/11 attacks.

Washington's allies and partners in Europe and the Middle East hated the term "pivot," because it implied that the Americans were turning away from them. Within the White House, the term was disliked for similar reasons by senior officials, including Tom Donilon, who became national security adviser in late 2010. Donilon not only preferred the term "rebalance" but also resented the plaudits that flowed to Clinton, and Campbell, for launching and driving a policy he thought the White House should get credit for as well. Donilon sardonically asked visitors to his office in early 2013 if Campbell was really writing a book called *The Pivot*. (Campbell, who stepped down from the State Department after Obama's first term, published his book *The Pivot* in June 2016.) Campbell, a policy entrepreneur, and Donilon, more of a bureaucratic gatekeeper, always had an up-and-down relationship. Such rivalries aside, the pivot prospered initially because it had strong support across the administration, most notably at the top, from Obama himself. Born in Hawaii and raised partly in Indonesia, Obama proudly called himself America's "first Pacific president."

The internal splits over the policy went beyond mere branding. Campbell and his supporters were critical of policies that emphasized relations with Beijing above all, which they argued came at the expense of ties with regional allies like Japan and Southeast Asia. By contrast, Jim Steinberg, deputy secretary in the State Department, whose focus, like Donilon's, was primarily on China, worried that Washington would find itself in an unintentional conflict with Beijing. He came up with a new formulation for China, one of "strategic reassurance," designed to find ways to build trust and transparency with a geopolitical rival to prevent relations from running off the rails. The phrase, however, was soon killed off. "That [phrase] caused a lot of anger and angst elsewhere in the administration about mixed messages, as it sounded too conciliatory," said one White House official.

The pivot needed time to make its way through the bureaucracy to be translated into actual decisions. It took a formal moot within the White House ahead of a Clinton trip to Asia in 2011 before the administration agreed to take part in the East Asia Summit. Southeast Asian nations, which launched the annual meetings of top leaders in 2005, had said the United States could join only if it committed to send the president as its representative. Advocates of the pivot had to overcome opposition from Treasury and economic officials, who worried that participation in the East Asia Summit would dilute other regional forums. The president's domestic advisers didn't like the idea either, because it meant Obama would have to make at least two trips to Asia a year, a large chunk of time they didn't want to give up. In the end, Obama backed Clinton, and the Asia team, and agreed to attend the forum.

The vast machinery of the Pentagon took longer to wind up. Officials put pressure on the military to offer specifics on how the new policy would play out. "They did not want it to be seen as a big nothing," said a senior Pentagon official responsible for putting flesh on the bones of the policy. The overselling of the plan, and the Pentagon's own tightening budgets, fueled perceptions that little of substance was being done. The Pentagon's capability, posture, and base arrangements in the region all had to be examined. Some exercises with the Indian military were embarrassingly canceled when the money couldn't be found to fund them. The air force struggled to get long-range bombers reassigned to the area. The first major announcement of the pivot, which included the stationing of marines in Darwin in tropical northern Australia, had little to do with the policy's core focus, the new threat arc extending out from China, past Japan and Taiwan. Even then, the details of the agreement with Australia took five arduous years to negotiate.

Privately, there was never any doubt about the pivot's purpose. "It was a shorthand code for China, even though we said it wasn't," a Pentagon official acknowledged. For all its shortcomings, the policy did galvanize the U.S. government and military to focus on the challenge from China in Asia. Beijing had been able to chip away at the region without consequences, in the belief that an ambivalent, distracted America could not sustain its stewardship of the region. The Bush presidency, preoccupied with the Middle East, might have believed it was "managing" the rise of China, but from the perspective of the incoming Obama administration the opposite was true: China was managing the decline of the United States. As Campbell put it in his book, "Rarely in history has a rising power made such prominent gains in the international system without any response from the established powers." Certainly, Beijing recognized the gravity of the pivot, if not how its own behavior had provoked it.

Japan was at the core of Washington's new strategy, with the two militaries' long-standing ties naturally placing Tokyo at the forefront of plans to push back against Beijing. But there was a flip side to a more intense intimacy. Under Shinzō Abe, who returned as prime minister in 2012, Tokyo aimed to make a weightier contribution to the alliance. Japan had accepted by then that it was on the front line of the China challenge, and its leaders wanted to adopt a more aggressive posture accordingly; they urged Washington to do more as well. "I always encourage the U.S. to show their guts," one of Japan's top diplomats said, in part in frustration at Obama's unflashy, undemonstrative approach to diplomacy. "Perception matters, because at the end of the day, China has made a judgment that the smaller countries won't be able to push back."

This new dynamic—of Asian countries not only imploring the United States to return in force to Asia but also attempting to enlist it in their running battles with Beijing—proved to be a double-edged sword if a balance was not properly maintained. In early 2012, with Japan looking on, the United States received a lesson in what could go wrong when the scales were inadvertently, or incompetently, tipped too far in one direction, when Beijing and Manila faced off in the South China Sea. The

Philippines stumbled into the crisis and then dragged the United States along into it.

That April, North Korea's young dictator, Kim Jong Un, had ordered the launch of a rocket to put a satellite into orbit, only to see it break up and fall into the ocean. One of the Philippines' few naval vessels, a decommissioned U.S. Coast Guard cutter, had been dispatched to search for the debris and was returning to home port when at the last minute Manila diverted it on another mission. A Philippine surveillance plane had spotted Chinese fishing boats in the Scarborough Shoal, a tiny outcrop of islands and rocks around two hundred kilometers west of Subic Bay. Manila would have ordinarily sent its own coast guard vessels to detain the trespassing Chinese fishermen and their boats, to ensure routine checks didn't become military confrontations. On this occasion, though, the naval frigate was dispatched because it was conveniently nearby. For the Chinese, who also had maritime-surveillance boats in the area, it proved to be a heaven-sent opportunity to assert their claim over the contested reef.

The Chinese quickly sealed the lagoon off with an ever-growing armada of Chinese patrol and fishing boats, trapping the Philippine vessels inside. For ten weeks, the two parties were locked in a standoff. The Philippine boats, with hundreds of sailors on board, began to run out of food and water. The one large gun on the frigate's deck was jammed. The Chinese ruthlessly prosecuted their position. Beijing raised pressure on Manila by cutting tourist flights to the Philippines and quarantining valuable fruit imports from the country, leaving them to rot in storage. At the same time as the official press in China railed against "nationalist warmongers" in the Philippines, Chinese generals called for an attack on the country to teach it a lesson. With typhoon season fast approaching, a panicking Manila called in the Americans.

The negotiations over the Scarborough Shoal between the United States and China were an impromptu affair, taking place in early June in a four-star Marriott hotel in Virginia, about an hour from Washington. Fu Ying, China's vice foreign minister for Asia, was attending the annual conference of the Bilderberg Group, the high-level political and business networking event long a favored target of conspiracy theorists for overseeing a de facto world government. Accompanied by Chinese officials, Fu slipped away from the conference to meet at the nearby Marriott with the Americans, led by Kurt Campbell and Evan Medeiros, by now the Asia chief at the National Security Council. Fu knew the Philippines well, having served as ambassador to Manila in 1999, when the Chinese had first planted a military installation on another reef in dispute.

Beijing cleverly manipulated the framework of the negotiations from the start, consenting to talk to the United States even as it castigated it for emboldening Manila. The Chinese also sensed that the American negotiators were in a weak position. With a U.S. presidential election on the horizon, the White House had little interest in a symbolic show of military force in the Philippines. The administration regarded the Philippines as feckless and unreliable, a view that was largely mirrored across the government, in the Pentagon and the State Department. "No one wanted to send a destroyer from our side," said a senior U.S. diplomat familiar with the talks.

Nonetheless, perched on the edges of beds with Fu and other Chinese officials in a hastily booked hotel room for a few hours, the Americans believed they had negotiated a successful compromise, with both sides agreeing to a carefully phased withdrawal from the area. The Philippine vessels sailed out, followed by a number of Chinese boats; other Chinese vessels, however, remained and over time were replenished. Fu later denied there was any agreement for mutual withdrawal. "All China is doing is to keep an eye on the island for fear that the Philippines would do it again," she said. As one Philippine official remarked tartly of Fu, "If there's anyone who knows how to steal islands, it's she."

For Beijing, the episode was a victory in more ways than one. Aside from securing control over the territory and easily intimidating a militarily weak Philippines, it had managed to get through American efforts at mediation without cost. By engaging Washington, Beijing turned a dispute over a small group of otherwise insignificant islands into an issue that could have damaged a vastly more complex bilateral relationship with the United States. In the negotiations, Chinese officials constantly invoked bellicose, nationalistic voices at home, as Yang Jiechi had done with the Japanese, to keep Washington and Manila on the defensive.

Manila was outgunned and overwhelmed. Washington was outmaneuvered in what was for the United States a clarifying moment. In the words of Ely Ratner, later deputy national security adviser to Vice President Joe Biden, the crisis "demonstrated that U.S. efforts to deter Chinese assertiveness were not working." Soon, he said, "Chinese officials and pundits began speaking of a 'Scarborough Model' for exerting regional influence and annexing disputed territories."

Japan is not the Philippines. Tokyo has a modern military, and American troops are stationed in the country. But Tokyo does have one critical concern in common with Manila: the fear that it will lose U.S. support. The Japanese hated, for example, Steinberg's notion of "strategic reassurance," which they thought provided a platform for the United States to make concessions to China without properly taking into account its allies in the region. They watched the events at the Scarborough Shoal and wondered whether the same fate awaited them in the dispute over the Senkaku/Diaoyu Islands.

From the Chinese perspective, Japan and the Philippines had something in common as well. Both countries had leaders—Abe in Japan and Benigno Aquino in the Philippines—whom Beijing regarded as adversaries. A 2014 report issued by a think tank attached to Tsinghua University in Beijing, one of the country's most prestigious colleges, considered how "regime change" in both countries could be in China's interest. The report's authors did not have in mind an Iraq-style invasion, but pointedly recommended Beijing make sure that citizens of the two countries understood there was a cost to opposing China. "The purpose of isolating the Abe and Aquino regimes is not to isolate Japan and the Philippines; it is to urge the people of the two countries to realize that a strategy of antagonizing China will do them more harm than good," the report stated. "This will help their new governments quickly improve relations with China after the change of these regimes."

Aquino, restricted to a single five-year term by the Philippines' constitution, stepped down in mid-2016 and was replaced, to China's initial delight, with a viscerally anti-American president, Rodrigo Duterte. Abe, though, had staying power in his second term. For China, he not only was a much more formidable foe but also carried historical baggage. That made him more than just a passing adversary, especially for a leader like Xi Jinping.

CHAPTER FOURTEEN

Creation Myths

*It is not my intention at all to hurt the feelings of the Chinese and
Korean people.*

—Shinzō Abe, after visiting Yasukuni Shrine

*There are two Xi Jinpings. One has the enlightened genes of Xi
Zhongxun in his blood. The other is heir to the red nation of the
Communist Party.*

—Gao Wenqian, CCP historian

Barack Obama crossed his arms, as he sometimes did when he was
tired. The president was in Brisbane, Australia, the semitropical capital of Queensland. He had taken the best part of a week to go to China,
and then Myanmar, to attend different regional summits in late 2014.
The jet lag was setting in as he sat down for a trilateral meeting with
Shinzō Abe and the host nation's prime minister, Tony Abbott.

Abe struck a jaunty tone at the meeting's opening, regaling Obama
with an anecdote from the summit of east Asian leaders in Myanmar a few
days beforehand, which all three had attended. In one of the informal sessions, Li Keqiang, China's premier, had been lecturing Abe about history
when Abbott joined the conversation. With the sultan of Brunei at his side,
Abbott felt the need to step in to lower the temperature of an increasingly
tense exchange. "Yes, Premier Li, history is a good teacher," Abbott said,
interrupting their talk, "but a bad master." The Australian leader's intervention had stopped Li in his tracks, Abe told Obama with approval.

Abe and Abbott had formed a strong bond in office. Both were outspoken national security conservatives, deeply suspicious of China, who

wanted their countries to forge closer defense ties. That day, their conversation was less friendly. Once the meeting between the three leaders
was under way, however, Obama and Abbott both complained to Abe
about what they regarded as Tokyo's tepid condemnations of Moscow's
carving up of Ukraine and its occupation of Crimea. Abe, with an eye
to improving relations with Russia, had offered only muted criticism of
Vladimir Putin's actions. Abbott then departed for another meeting, as
scheduled, leaving Obama with Abe and their advisers on their own.

As with the Bush administration, the Obama White House and its
diplomatic advisers had debated how to talk to Japan, and Abe in particular, about history. Obama had long since passed the threshold that
George W. Bush had grappled with crossing—namely, of whether to
raise the issue at all. The history wars had simply become too damaging
to Washington's interests in east Asia, and too beneficial to Beijing, to
ignore. The White House's primary focus was repairing relations between Japan and South Korea, whose leaders were barely talking. "We
just could not have a situation where our two closest allies in the region
could not speak to each other," said Ben Rhodes, Obama's deputy national security adviser. "There was an imperative to address history as a
strategic issue."

Abe and South Korea's Park Geun-hye had been elected within a few
months of each other, in late 2012 and early 2013, respectively. The countries were neighbors and key U.S. allies, but the two leaders had met only
once, in March 2014, on the sidelines of an international gathering in
The Hague. They agreed to be in the same room only after Obama's
advisers had cajoled them to come together with the promise that the
U.S. president would be in attendance, as chaperone. In the meantime,
while snubbing Abe, Park had met multiple times with Xi Jinping, who
saw South Korea as the soft underbelly of Western alliances in Asia.

The Americans had another reason to bring Abe and Park together.
They were worried that the blowback from the history wars in the region
might affect Japan's constitutional reforms at home as well. Abe was laying the groundwork to unwind the country's postwar pacifist constitution and the restrictions it placed on Tokyo's military. Washington
backed his plan as a means to strengthen the military alliance against an
expanding, assertive China. It was crucial, in Washington's eyes, that the
rest of Asia be on board with Abe's reforms as well.

The White House did not underestimate the prickliness of the South Koreans nor the cynicism of the Chinese. Japan remained a toxic issue in the internal politics of both neighboring countries and was easily used as a weapon against anyone trying to bridge the divide with Tokyo. But like the Bush administration, the Obama White House looked askance at Abe and his supporters' statements downplaying imperial Japan's role in the comfort women issue and other wartime controversies. For Rhodes, whose views were invariably aligned with Obama's, it was clear where much of the blame lay. "Abe's approach was particularly challenging at a time when the region's territorial disputes were percolating," he said. "His comments on the comfort women especially were unnecessary; it forced the Koreans to elevate the issue. I don't think Park would have had to develop so much attitude on the comfort women if Abe hadn't raised it."

By the time of the meeting in Australia with Abe and Abbott, midway through Obama's second term, both the administration and Japan had a target in mind by which to try to get the history issue settled, or at least politically neutralized: August or September 2015, marking the seventieth anniversary of the end of the war in Asia. For its part, Beijing was planning its own massive commemoration, which was sure to target Tokyo. Abe was preparing to make a major statement on the war around that time to decisively draw a line under the conflict. The United States attempted many different ways to engage Abe on history issues in the two years before the anniversary. Few were as straightforward as Obama.

Once Abbott left the room in Brisbane, an exhausted Obama turned to Abe. What followed was perhaps the bluntest exchange ever between an American leader and a Japanese leader on the festering history wars. He told the prime minister that there was only one country that was benefiting from the never-ending controversies, and that was China. Obama acknowledged that the problem was not all Japan's fault, and that the issue was complicated, but stressed that it had to be fixed. Obama was unsentimental and abrupt. "He laid right into him," said one person with firsthand knowledge of the conversation. Abe said little in reply, and the prime minister's staff would later play down the exchange. If nothing else, Obama's intervention illustrated the sea change in U.S. policy.

After years of trying to stay out of the trenches of east Asia's history wars, Washington was finally, reluctantly, digging itself in. The White House was already concerned about an assertive China pressuring Japan in the East China Sea, a recipe for conflict that could potentially destabilize the entire region. Sino-Japanese relations were still raw in the wake of the 2012 clash over the Senkaku/Diaoyu Islands, which only amplified the traditional tensions. Tokyo and Seoul's mini cold war, meanwhile, made it harder than ever to coordinate policy on North Korea.

Before heading to Brisbane, Obama had discussed Japan with Xi Jinping at the summit in Beijing the previous week. Xi told Obama that a lot of anger and negative sentiment had built up regarding Japan and it would take a long time to work through it. "He said Japan's behavior created pressure on him domestically, with the Chinese public's view of history," recalled Rhodes. "When Abe says these things, he said it raised the temperature and limited his ability to be cooperative." It's nothing personal, Xi assured the U.S. president. But in many ways, it was.

The complex interactions of two powerful countries like China and Japan cannot be reduced to the biographies of their two leaders and their families. The life stories of Xi and Abe, nonetheless, embodied the ominous trends in bilateral relations in striking ways that were little appreciated outside the region. Both men, who came to office at about the same time—in Abe's case, for a second term—were products of their respective countries' ruling political elites. Their families and their political patrimony were both tied indelibly to their countries' past conflicts with each other. Both their immediate families—his father in the case of Xi, and his grandfather in the case of Abe—launched their careers in the Sino-Japanese war on opposing sides. The two political dynasties suffered tremendous setbacks at different times in the decades after the war and then prospered, to take over the leadership of their countries. With the honor of their families and nations in mind, each had an interest in discrediting the other's version of the past. In that respect, the pair were more than just resolute guardians of the national interest. Whatever Xi might say, their divisions were deeply personal as well.

When Xi Jinping met the son of Hu Yaobang, the party head forced out of office in 1987, he left no doubt what he considered binding their two clans together. Both families had their roots in Yan'an, the Communist Party's revolutionary base in the 1930s from which Mao Zedong and his ragtag band of guerrilla fighters would emerge to take over the entire country. "Our families have been united since our mothers joined the anti-Japanese struggle together," Xi told Hu Deping, Hu Yaobang's eldest son, who was himself born in Yan'an in 1942, when they met at the Zhongnan-hai leadership compound in July 2012.

Yan'an and its near-mythical status confer instant prestige on families that can trace their lineage to its dusty caves and deadly battles, both against the Nationalists in the civil war and within the Communist Party itself. Xi's father, Xi Zhongxun, was stationed there as a Communist guerrilla fighter in the mid-1930s. Hu Yaobang, one of the youngest veterans of the Long March, escaped to Yan'an after being held as a prisoner by allies of Chiang Kai-shek. Both Xi and Hu met their wives in the small town in Shaanxi province where they attended the makeshift Resist-Japan Military and Political University.

Xi's father never fired a shot against the Japanese, at least according to the CCP-approved biography of him, published in two thick volumes in 2008 and 2013. That is not as surprising as it might sound. Though victory over the Japanese is the leitmotif of the party's claim to legitimacy, Mao's forces did little of the actual fighting against them, leaving the war largely to the Nationalist armies. Nonetheless, that moment in Yan'an would define Xi and his family's politics for the rest of their lives.

Like those of many of his peers who graduated from Yan'an into top party positions in the 1950s, the elder Xi's life of power and privilege was periodically devastated by Mao's political campaigns. Xi's own family was broken up in the Cultural Revolution, and Xi Jinping himself dispatched to work in the countryside. Many of his father's peers and their families didn't survive the purges, some dying in captivity or committing suicide. When he was fully rehabilitated after Mao's death, the elder Xi, not surprisingly, returned as a strong supporter of Deng Xiaoping's economic liberalization. Alone among Politburo elders in 1987, he refused to vote for the ousting of Hu Yaobang as party secretary.

When Xi Jinping came to power, far from repudiating Mao, though, he embraced his legacy, in tandem with Deng's. Xi always understood that abandoning Mao would be akin to repudiating the party, which could bring the whole edifice crashing down. Hence, Xi's instruction that no party members negate the "two thirty-years": the first three-decade period under Mao and the second under Deng, despite the vast gulf in these eras' governing philosophies. What may look like a contradiction to outsiders is, in Xi's view, more of a continuum across different periods of party rule. "There are two Xi Jinpings," said Gao Wenqian, a U.S.-based scholar and party historian. "One has the enlightened genes of Xi Zhongxun in his blood. The other is heir to the red nation of the Communist Party."

Xi's outwardly curious allegiance to Mao is best understood as an extension of his absolute belief in the Communist Party and the right of its hereditary aristocrats, like him, to rule China. Hence, his father's official biography emphasizes not how Mao nearly destroyed the elder Xi but how he once saved his life in the 1930s. Equally, his fall from grace in the early 1960s is blamed on Mao's notorious secret police chief rather than on the chairman himself. As one China analyst put it more pithily, Xi "talks like Mao and acts like Deng."

Pulling the political levers at his disposal as party chief, Xi was able to usher in a once-in-a-generation overhaul of the military, establish a new national security council, and aggressively prosecute Beijing's expansive territorial claims in the East and South China Seas. Xi's decisive and—compared with those of his predecessors—risk-taking political personality had an outsize impact, for good reason. When Hu Jintao took power, China was the eighth- or ninth-largest economy in the world, with a low-tech military and little capability to project power beyond its shores. By 2012, when Xi became the leader, China had the second-largest economy in the world and had its most formidable military in centuries.

In ways that were mostly out of sight for foreigners, the party also amplified the elder Xi's biography to add luster to his son's handling of high office. When Xi visited the large anti-Japanese war museum near the Marco Polo Bridge on Beijing's outskirts in 2014, he was taken to see a new panel recording his father's "extraordinary contribution in creating the [Yan'an] base." The following year, the museum's curator gave an interview to the *Beijing News* about how Xi Zhongxun had personally approved the building of the museum. In the state media's burnishing of the Xi family story, filial piety merged seamlessly with China's historic triumphs.

The span of Abe's life story, and time in office, has uncanny echoes of Xi's own. Like Xi, Abe imbibed his politics from his earliest years—in his case, literally on his grandfather's lap. In his memoirs, Abe recounts his vivid memory as a five-year-old in 1960 of bouncing on Nobusuke

Kishi as protesters surrounded his grandfather's Tokyo home denouncing the upgrading of the U.S.-Japan security treaty. For Abe, the lessons learned in that episode stayed with him for life. Kishi had not been prepared for the size and the ferocity of the protests against it and was forced to resign soon after the treaty's passage. Abe vowed he would not make the same mistake.

Hanging over Kishi in perpetuity, and Abe after him, were the war and the judgment rendered on Japan in the wake of an abject defeat. Kishi acknowledged after the conflict that he was ashamed of the atrocities carried out by the Imperial Army, but he didn't believe that Japan alone should be condemned. "By no means can the terrible crimes committed by many Japanese soldiers be justified," he said, "but do you feel that the atomic bombings were morally more proper than some of the Japanese atrocities?" Like Kishi, Abe could never understand why Japan was singled out as uniquely culpable. Japan had, after all, only followed the example of the colonizing West in conquering and subjugating foreign lands. Just as Kishi had tried to regain Japan's independence with the 1960 security treaty with the United States, Abe wanted his country to be able to stand on its own feet again, without being bound to a constitution dictated to it by an occupying power.

Like Xi, Abe launched a headline-grabbing plan for economic revival once he returned as prime minister, but he, too, displayed little appetite or feel for the difficult decisions needed to put it in place. Instead, like Xi, Abe made his mark in foreign policy and domestic political consolidation.

Xi centralized power in his office, emasculated his cabinet, and took firm control of the military, and Abe did much the same. Japanese bureaucracies had traditionally retained far more autonomy than their nominal equivalent institutions in China, where the party retains overarching control. But under Abe, Japan mimicked after a fashion some of the practices of the CCP personnel system, consolidating the power to choose the top bureaucrats in the prime minister's office rather than in the ministries themselves. Abe adopted a similar approach toward the powerful cabinet office that oversaw all legislation, making sure that any constitutional changes would be managed by a handpicked official and not one independent of his control. With the signature policy of his second term, easing the postwar shackles on the Japanese military, Abe left nothing to chance.

Abe was trying to finish a mission that his grandfather had started, although not in the way that China, or at least its propaganda organs, liked to portray. Clouded by the demands of the Propaganda Department that Abe be depicted in the worst possible light, any nuances in Japanese defense policy were lost in China. As long as the two countries were in conflict, the party refused to allow an open debate about Abe and Japan, with predictable results.

For a dependable guide to official opinion of Shinzō Abe, and Japan, in China, there are few sources better than Liu Jiangyong. A Japan expert at the prestigious Tsinghua University, he is steeped in the country, its language, its history, and, most important, its sins against China and Asia writ large. Minutes into a meeting in his office in 2015, unprompted, Liu recited off the top of his head in Japanese all the different ways Tokyo had apologized for the war over the years. As if he were performing a party trick, he listed the series of expressions used by various Japanese leaders, which ranged from "personal sorrow" to "sincere regret," and to "deep remorse" and "heartfelt apology" for the "unfortunate experiences" of the past, and so on. Liu's political performance art was his way of illustrating how Japan's apologies had always been framed according to who was delivering them and the political exigencies of the moment.

Once the conversation turned to Abe, Liu's mood darkened further. He saw the Japanese prime minister as more than just the product of his family, let alone his country. Liu painted Abe as a native son of one particular region in Japan, Yamaguchi Prefecture, where the southwest tip of the main island curls around like a boot to face the Korean peninsula. Liu had available at the flick of a synaptic switch a different kind of list on Yamaguchi, one altogether more sinister than his recitation of the ways Japan had said sorry. One by one, he reeled off the Japanese prime ministers from the region, many of whom hailed from Chōshū, the domain that led the fight to overturn the Tokugawa shogunate and usher in Japan's nineteenth-century modernization. Chōshū was to the Meiji Restoration what Virginia was to the American Revolution and the early American Republic, both the incubator of the uprising and the main source of its leaders.

Hirobumi Itō, Japan's first modern prime minister, who hailed from Yamaguchi, led the country during the First Sino-Japanese War. This prime minister took Taiwan, Liu said. That one colonized Korea, and another grabbed the Senkaku/Diaoyu Islands. One bribed Chinese warlords to win port concession in Shandong, while another sent troops to China and undermined Manchuria's status on the mainland.

In modern times, Japanese prime ministers from Yamaguchi have included Kishi; his brother, Eisaku Satō; and Abe himself. All three built closer security ties with Washington, were regarded in Beijing as hostile to China, and cultivated relations with Taipei. "This prefecture is the source of war criminals, going back to the Ming dynasty," said Liu. "When you meet ordinary Japanese people, they are very welcoming. But the nation as a whole is like a snake. The skin is not poisonous but the head and the teeth are, and the body follows the head."

Liu, like many Chinese, held strictly to the line that Abe represented a return to Japan's rightist, militarist traditions. Even the mention of Abe's name could stir a deep animosity in China. One senior U.S. political figure recalled meeting Cui Tiankai, who served as Beijing's ambassador to Tokyo and Washington, soon after one of Japan's periodic clashes with China. Cui, who was no Japan basher in ordinary times, visibly quivered with anger when discussing Abe.

Privately, reactions in China to the Japanese prime minister were more sophisticated and nuanced. Many Chinese admired Abe's initial efforts to shake up the economy. Even if they were angered by his revisionism over the war, they understood why he wanted to make his country stronger after decades of relative stagnation. They also understood that Japan's changing security policies were introduced specifically in response to China, and North Korea, not as the expression of some congenital militarist impulse within the Japanese system. Unencumbered by politics, the two countries' finance ministries and central banks had usually had good relations, and their officials would often go out drinking after bilateral meetings. "We always showed each other our hearts," said one of Xi's economic advisers.

In the current hostile political climate, however, few Chinese officials and scholars dared to express such views in public. Consorting with the Japanese could be dangerous. One prominent Japan expert in China, Jin Xide, was arrested in 2009 on charges of selling state secrets to Japan and South Korea. In 2013, a Chinese academic based in Japan, Zhu Jianrong, was detained for months without trial during a trip home to China and held for questioning about his research. He later told friends that the authorities had quickly realized he had done nothing wrong but held him to save face. In 2017, the Chinese charged the man, who for three decades had headed a China-Japan friendship association with spying. In the darkest days of bilateral conflict, Chinese scholars who had met with Japanese reporters in Beijing were sometimes called in by state security to have tapes of their conversations played back to them.

Many Chinese scholars who knew Japan well felt straitjacketed by the routine denunciations of their neighbor in the state media. In this narrative, Tokyo was always plotting to revive plans to dominate Asia by force, a view distilled in the short phrase, a hardy perennial of Chinese propaganda, about the threat from "Japanese militarism." For anyone who knows modern Japan, the phrase is jarringly inaccurate. Not only has defense spending rarely risen far above 1 percent of GDP in the past seventy years, but the military itself has long been relegated to a lowly status, socially and politically.

As late as the 1990s, Japanese prime ministers would try to avoid being photographed with uniformed officers. Japanese military officers were acutely aware of the taboo. They nicknamed Toshiki Kaifu, the prime minister who served for two years beginning in 1989, "Sunday Toshiki," because he would only meet them on weekends, and not at his office, to minimize attention. Uniformed officers almost never met political leaders without civilian officials alongside them. The chief of the navy choked up when he was invited by the then prime minister, Ryutaro Hashimoto, to his office for a farewell drink in 1997. In a career lasting three decades, the navy chief had never been in the prime minister's office before, with or without civilians. Unlike in the United States, where the military is highly visible and invariably venerated, it is still rare to see Japanese officers in uniform in public. Chip Gregson, who was the marine commander in Japan for four years beginning in 2001 and head of Asia policy in the Pentagon in the Obama administration, recalled being in a restaurant in Japan when one of his colleagues pointed out, "Look at that. There's someone in a uniform outside, walking in the street."

In China, the obsessive repetition of the threat of revived "Japanese militarism" trapped debate about Japan in a caricatured cul-de-sac from which officials and scholars struggled to escape. "We do not really think that militarism is being revived," said one adviser to the Beijing government. "But it doesn't mean there is nothing going on with Japan's defense policy. It just means that we cannot discuss it properly." A senior Chinese Foreign Ministry official handling Japan didn't deny in a meeting in 2016 that Japan had changed tremendously in the postwar period. He acknowledged the warm hospitality he had received traveling throughout Japan. But in grasping for an explanation for Japan's refusal to get along with China, he fell back on old tropes about an island culture that naturally tended to extremes. "When the external environment changes, Japan changes rapidly," he said. "If we look back, the fundamental features have not changed; their ambitions could be rekindled."

Japan's security policy had in fact changed substantially since the mid-1990s, albeit often at a snail's pace, due to the ossified defense bureaucracy. Naval forces and an F-15 squadron had been deployed to the south of the country, to face China rather than Russia. Japan developed a rapid-response amphibious force to be deployed near the Senkaku/Diaoyu Islands to defend them from the Chinese. The United States and Japan had begun sharing more bases and increased their efforts to blend their forces operationally. These reforms, largely undertaken in response to actions by China and North Korea, were inevitably filed under the single, heavy-handed classification of "Japanese militarism."

There were practical reasons for Beijing to fall back on its reliable memes. The Chinese media didn't want to acknowledge that Japan's defense reforms were a reaction to Beijing's own military buildup, as well as to Pyongyang belligerence. More important for the CCP was the maintenance of a consistent propaganda stance. "We have not learned any new language to describe Japan," lamented one of China's most eminent Japan experts. "We can only describe them through the lens of history."

China wasn't the only country that couldn't rise above past history when it came to Japan. After Shinzō Abe's return to power on Boxing Day in 2012, the Obama administration struggled to manage the issue as well. In the early days of Obama's second term in early 2013, Daniel Russel, who had taken over from Kurt Campbell as the head of east Asia policy in the State Department, gathered a group of former officials and think tank experts for an off-the-record briefing. Such private sessions are common in Washington as a way to keep the sprawling national security state informed and inside the tent. When one of the participants asked Russel about how the United States might work with Abe, then just starting his second term in office as well, the longtime Japan specialist had a sharp rejoinder: "You would need a microscope to find one iota of an upside in the return of Shinzō Abe."

Many of the specialists in the room were shocked by the statement, but Russel was not alone in his views. At around the same time, John Kerry, the new secretary of state, convened a smaller group of Asia experts in Washington. "The biggest problem in Asia . . ." Kerry began, before a pregnant pause. The participants at the meeting leaned forward, expecting him to express concerns about China or North Korea, but instead were surprised that he nominated Japan, a staunch American ally, as Washington's most serious challenge in Asia.

Obama and Abe, and their advisers, had eyed each other warily from the start. The White House, along with much of the State Department, disapproved of Abe and his supporters' stirring of the history pot because of the potential damage to Western alliances in Asia and coalition-building efforts to constrain China. Many U.S. officials were simply offended by the reopening of the comfort women issue, a move they regarded as politically tone-deaf and morally beyond the pale. One senior State Department member often referred to the "right-wing nut jobs" among Abe's core supporters—the sort of comment that didn't please the prime minister when it got back to him in Tokyo. Abe complained about China's viewing him only through its distorted lens of history, but his American critics thought the Japanese prime minister was constantly magnifying the focus himself.

Abe made no secret of his disdain for what he and his supporters called the "masochistic" version of history foisted on Japan as the war's loser. In 2013, Abe again criticized the postwar Tokyo Tribunal, Asia's version of the Nuremberg trials, stating that the guilty verdicts "presented the judgment of the victors, not the Japanese people." Rather than repudiating the Japanese government's 1993 apology on the comfort women, he set up a committee to investigate the historical material on which the statement was based. In so doing, he could plausibly argue that the official statement hadn't been withdrawn while standing by as its credibility was called into question. In Beijing, the "spectacle of a Japanese government caught up in a contorted process of un-apologising," as one historian put it, only provided grist to the Chinese propaganda mill. In Washington, however, the renewed revisionism had more serious ramifications, because challenging the verdicts of the Tokyo Tribunal had the potential to undermine the basis of the entire postwar settlement.

Senior American officials believed that Abe had also blundered when he suggested that one reason he got on well with Park Geun-hye, South Korea's prime minister, was that his grandfather and her father had been friends. (Park Chung-hee, a dictatorial leader of South Korea for eighteen years, was an officer in the Japanese military in Manchuria. In the mid-1960s, he worked closely with Kishi in negotiations to normalize bilateral ties.) In the words of one U.S. official, "It was sort of like 'Her father worked for my grandfather.' It went right to her great vulnerability, [being] the daughter of a dictator who collaborated with a fascist regime."

There was also a partisan edge to the divide between the Obama White House and Abe's government. Democrats had long been annoyed by the perception that it was only Republicans who valued relations with Tokyo, a view they believed conservatives encouraged. Democrats were branded as protectionist on trade and weak on defense. "The Japanese told us, 'We have you Americans figured out. The Republicans are businesspeople. Their priority is to make money,'" said Glen Fukushima, a former U.S. trade negotiator and a Democrat. "Many Republicans tell the Japanese, 'You should prefer us to the Democrats, because they are captured by the unions. And Democrats love China and they will take China over Japan any day.'" By the time Obama came to power, this divide was a caricature, because many centrist Democrats were just as supportive of the U.S.-Japan security alliance as their Republican counterparts. But such perceptions lingered in Washington anyway.

In Tokyo, the new Abe administration nurtured its own grievances against what it regarded as an unwelcoming White House. "Their image at the start was Abe as a right-winger with a militarist past. They were quite cold," observed an Abe adviser. Just as the White House was annoyed by Abe's renewed excursions into history, the prime minister resented being told to keep his counsel on the issue. "On history, the message is if you just want Japan to shut up and take China's version, then we aren't going to do it," the adviser said. "Japanese nationalism is coming up, and we have to control it."

From Tokyo's perspective, there was a partisan edge to the history issue as well. Abe's advisers regarded Obama and others in the administration as overly liberal on the subject, effectively interjecting themselves into an internal Japanese debate on the side of the Left. According to Mike Green, who served in the National Security Council under George W. Bush and who is close to Abe, "Abe believes that the lectures delivered in the U.S. enable the Left in Japan to campaign on the same issues, and that is the same left wing which has campaigned against his family for three generations." As another Abe confidant put it, "Look at the right side of the face in America, you see [the pro-Japan] Rich Armitage. Look at the left side, and you see the Japan Socialist Party."

When Abe came to Washington in September 2013, the White House icily noted he attended the conservative Hudson Institute to receive an award, handed to him by Lewis Libby, a former adviser to Dick Cheney. Libby was a longtime supporter of closer ties to Japan. Abe jokingly played up to his stereotype in his Hudson speech while discussing Chinese criticism of a mild increase in Japan's military budget, the first in eleven years. Without mentioning China by name, he told the audience that Japan had an "immediate neighbor" whose military spending was twice that of Japan and who had lifted its outlays on defense by 10 percent for two decades since 1989. "And then, my government has increased its defense budget only by zero point eight per cent," he said. "So call me, if you want, a right-wing militarist!"

In 2013, U.S. officials debated among themselves at length the best way to calm tempers on the history controversy. One proposal, for a special envoy on history, had been shot down in the bureaucracy. Eventually, they decided to dispatch Joe Biden to Japan and South Korea to deliver a delicate message to Abe—an appeal that he not inflame the issue and stay away from Yasukuni Shrine—and to Park that she build bridges with Japan as well. Biden, according to his colleagues, had a unique diplomatic style. "It's unlike any diplomacy I have seen," Campbell wrote in an e-mail to Hillary Clinton while on an earlier trip with the vice president to China in 2011. "Any possible topic or reference or poet or Irish lymric [sic] or historical reference or 60s pop culture data point can appear with little or no warning. Entertaining but unpredictable." With Abe, Biden played the same "good old uncle Joe" routine in warning the Japanese prime minister that the history wars were damaging U.S. interests in the region. But, according to officials in the meeting, he overdid his pitch, annoying his hosts. The Japanese pushed back, saying they had tried everything with the South Koreans, not to say the Chinese, but that whatever they did, it was never enough. From the Japanese perspective, what was the point of doing more? With his message delivered, Biden traveled on to South Korea, where he discussed the history issue with Park.

On his return to Washington, Biden phoned Abe, this time pressing him harder not to go to Yasukuni. In an interview in the final months of his vice presidency, Biden claimed credit for bringing Abe and Park together. "I go to see Abe and he says to me, 'Will you help me with Park?'" Biden recalled. "And I call her and say, 'Will you do this?' And I don't negotiate the agreement, but the end result was, because I had a personal relationship with both of them and they trusted me, I could be an interlocutor, [though] that was more like a divorce counselor, putting a marriage back together."

In the first instance, however, Biden didn't put anything back together. Abe made no promises in his meeting with Biden. On December 25, without informing his cabinet, Abe made an early morning visit to Yasukuni, the first Japanese prime minister to go there since 2006. "It is not my intention at all to hurt the feelings of the Chinese and Korean people," Abe said, a statement that did little to alleviate anger in Beijing, Seoul, and Washington.

For Abe, the shrine visit was as much about local politics as about national pride, a gesture to his core supporters who had stood by him in exile and supported his return to office. In his first term, Abe had confounded his base, and Beijing, by reaching out to China in the wake of Junichiro Koizumi's departure. He traveled to Beijing within days of taking office to open a dialogue with Chinese leaders while retaining a studiously ambiguous posture regarding visiting the shrine. In his second term, he inherited a relationship with China that was worse than it had been in 2006. After the confrontations over the Senkaku/Diaoyu Islands in 2010 and 2012, Abe was no longer in a frame of mind to accommodate Beijing. He was more hawkish in public and said openly that he regretted staying away from Yasukuni in his previous term as prime minister. Abe's uncompromising attitude, according to his supporters, was all China's doing. "If there were no assertive kind of behavior by China," said Kunihiko Miyake, the former diplomat, "then there would have been no Prime Minister Abe a second time as well."

In 2013, Abe believed he had little to lose with Beijing by going to Yasukuni, because the Chinese were refusing to talk to him anyway in the wake of the islands dispute. He was tired of the constant lectures from South Korea. He spurned his critics by appointing a crude right-wing businessman to head NHK, the national broadcaster, the equivalent in Japan of the BBC, and stood by as his supporters denounced any media critical of him, especially the left-leaning *Asahi Shimbun*. Abe was also increasingly annoyed at the American meddling in the history issue, along the lines of the Biden visit. "That was one reason he went to Yasukuni at Christmas," said Mike Green. "That was about us." The White House didn't attempt to hide its anger. For the first time, the U.S. government issued an official statement condemning a visit to Yasukuni by a Japanese prime minister, saying it would exacerbate "tensions" with Tokyo's neighbors.

By that stage, it wasn't just China, South Korea, and left-leaning Democrats in the United States complaining about Abe and history. Prominent Republicans who were pillars of the Japanese alliance were also aghast at the geopolitical fallout. One of Japan's most prominent conservative supporters in Washington was vehement about Tokyo's handling of the issue. "I have said to Abe privately, 'I don't give a shit if you go to Yasukuni,'" he said. "But I told him, I take issue with him helping out Wang Yi [the Chinese foreign minister] and doing his bidding for him. This is propaganda for China." The speaker, who has served in senior positions in Republican administrations, complained about the nitpicking debates in Japan aimed at minimizing wartime atrocities. "They want to get all legalistic, arguing whether it is 200,000 or 50,000 and 20,000 who were killed in Nanjing. One killed is too many. Abe's statement—'that it all depends on the meaning of aggression'—as to whether Japan waged an aggressive war, well, I think if you were in China in 1931, it would look like aggression to you."

The Japanese were stung by the administration's critical statement issued after the Yasukuni visit, if only because they thought it empowered their enemies in China and South Korea. "Don't you dare do that to us again," Japanese officials snapped at visiting American politicians and officials. Whatever the fractures among the United States and Japan and South Korea, however, the Chinese soon gave them a chance to mend.

On November 23, 2013, just days before Joe Biden departed on his east Asian tour, Beijing surprised the region with an unexpected announcement: It declared a vast part of the airspace in the East China Sea to be under its control. In effect, it was stating that any foreign aircraft coming into the new air zone, which extended far beyond its sovereign territory, had to declare themselves for the purposes of national defense.

Beijing might have had good reason to declare an air defense identification zone, as it is known. Japan had its own expansive air defense zone, which it had inherited from the United States in 1969 on the reversion of Okinawa. As the Chinese liked to point out, no one had ever consulted Beijing about that. South Korea, Vietnam, and the Philippines had likewise all declared air defense zones in the past, although usually in consultation with the countries around them. China, pushing back against the American-made world in east Asia, had decided that it would have its own zone, without telling anyone beforehand. When Beijing's Asian neighbors objected, China's state media had the victim card ready to hand. Xinhua, the official news agency, evoked an old Chinese saying: "The magistrates are free to burn down houses while the common people are forbidden even to light lamps."

The hawks in the People's Liberation Army had been planning to declare an air defense zone covering the East China Sea more than a year beforehand. Officers had taken the plan to Hu Jintao and his chief diplomat, Dai Bingguo, on multiple occasions, according to U.S. intelligence sources, only to be rejected. Since Tokyo's nationalization of the Senkaku/Diaoyu Islands in 2012, Japanese and Chinese vessels had been bumping up against one another with alarming frequency. In one week during October 2013, Japanese fighter jets had been scrambled three times after Chinese planes approached their airspace. Later in the same month, the Japanese media reported that Tokyo was threatening to shoot down any Chinese drones that were caught flying over the islands.

That was the trigger that China's hawks needed. The PLA went back to the leadership with its plan, this time brandishing the statements out of Tokyo. Not only was Beijing's zone comparable to Tokyo's in its distance from the Japanese mainland. It also included the Senkaku/Diaoyu Islands, to underscore the point that they were Chinese territory. Xi Jinping, now ensconced as party chief and head of the military, displayed none of the hesitation of his predecessor. When presented with the plan by the PLA, he told it to go ahead. Beijing had its excuse ready to hand: it was not behaving unilaterally, it said, but simply responding to another Japanese provocation.

But again, Beijing overplayed its hand. The zone declared by the Chinese not only crossed into territory disputed with Japan but also comprised rocky island outcrops claimed by South Korea, the nation that China had been trying to lure out of the West's orbit. In response, Seoul expanded its own air defense zone to cover the same area, effectively thumbing its nose at China. Beijing had also made a technical error in the radio frequency it had demanded foreign airlines use for notification of their presence, making aviation in the area less safe. The United States sent B-52s flying through the area without notifying Beijing, to make its own point about the Chinese unilateral declaration. In the end, Beijing's tactical errors offered Washington a strategic windfall, for Seoul and Tokyo now had a reason to talk to each other again.

In some respects, the declaration of the air defense zone was at the low end of the spectrum of ways that Beijing could have pushed back against Tokyo in the simmering wake of the 2012 crisis over the islands. In the immediate aftermath of their nationalization, Washington had warned Beijing against taking any military action, but a coterie of U.S. intelligence officials, and regional leaders, reckoned that the Chinese had never taken that type of response off the agenda.

The Chinese had been integrating their navy and air force, a technically, and technologically, complex task, which would enable them to conduct joint operations; they had built and deployed long-range missiles; and they had also gained experience on the high seas far from China, conducting antipiracy operations in the Gulf of Aden. The Chinese military's long-standing efforts to sell the party leadership on the need for a strong navy with global reach had paid dividends. "In the '70s and '80s, they went down to the islands in the South China Sea and killed some Vietnamese and Filipinos and came back, leaving some small, dinky outposts behind," said Captain James Fanell, a naval officer of nearly three decades who had been tracking Beijing's fleet buildup for years. As a professional, he was impressed; as a U.S. naval officer, he was alarmed. "Now they have the ability to conduct continuous operations through the Miyako Strait [near Japan]."

In February 2013, with the diplomatic dust barely settled on China's declaration of the air defense zone, Fanell, by then the navy's top intelligence official for the Asia-Pacific, told his audience at an annual naval conference in San Diego that China had largely fabricated territorial claims in the South and East China Seas and was using them to seize the maritime rights of its neighbors: "Make no mistake: the PRC navy is focused on war at sea, and sinking an opposing fleet." Two years later, Fanell was back at the same conference, delivering an even more somber message about the East China Sea. China had long trained for an amphibious invasion of Taiwan. Now, Fanell said, the PLA's planning had been extended to include training for a "short, sharp war" with Japan, including seizure of the Senkaku/Diaoyu Islands.

Fanell's comments caused an uproar. Some intelligence officials disagreed with his assessment, and Fanell himself later insisted that he wasn't claiming that China was about to attack Japan, merely that it was fine-tuning the capability to do so. Still, such headline-grabbing remarks did not go down well with his superiors. Later that year, Fanell was removed from his position, following an investigation into an anonymous complaint that he had improperly discussed intelligence in the presence of foreigners.

Fanell was not alone in believing that China was seriously considering military action against Japan over the Senkaku/Diaoyu Islands. One retired regional leader with good connections in both China and Japan said Beijing had studied its options carefully: "They did a number of basic tabletop exercises to work out, if there was a conflict over the islands, whether China could prevail; I had many conversations with Chinese military planners at the time." In the end, he said, Beijing concluded that the "co-relation of forces was not with them." Unlike Japan, which has fought naval wars, China has fought only one, in 1895, which it lost. Chinese maritime capabilities are untested in battle, for all the hype about their new aircraft carriers. Beijing also weighed the fact that China was in striking distance of Japanese airfields. Whatever their calculation, the truth was that the Chinese had made huge strides as a military power and were far more advanced than where the United

States ten years earlier had expected them to be. "When they did not have that capability that they have now, they kept their mouth shut," said Fanell. "Now they do, and they are pushing back. Everyone thought I was hyperventilating and being Chicken Little-ish, but look what happened."

Perhaps the most salient factor in China's calculations was what might happen if it should lose to Japan. In Tokyo, a military loss would be disastrous, and the government would certainly fall. But that would be nothing compared with the hammer blow to China's national psyche should Japan prevail. "That would be terminal for the CCP," the former regional leader observed. "Regime change."

CHAPTER FIFTEEN

Freezing Point

It's really amazing some people still believe they have the moral high ground and credibility to accuse others, if we consider the Snowden revelations.

> —Cui Tiankai, Chinese ambassador on American accusations of Chinese spying

They used to think that China was underdeveloped; they felt guilty at this point. The voices that hated China were not heard, but now with China rising, they think they can say these things.

> —Bu Ping, Chinese historian

By the end of 2013, Yasuo Fukuda was one of many senior politicians worried Japan and China could stumble into an armed clash. "I told Chinese leaders we needed to have some kind of agreement to avoid a crisis," the former prime minister of Japan recalled. Fukuda didn't believe military conflict was inevitable or even likely, but he had heard enough discussion about the prospect, including from Chinese diplomats, to take the issue seriously. He was soon convinced that talking with Beijing officials lower in the chain of command wasn't getting him anywhere. "It was clear that no major decision would be taken unless I spoke to Xi Jinping personally."

Fukuda was not only a former prime minister himself but the son of one as well. From Beijing's perspective, he was respected for another reason: He hailed from the wing of the ruling conservative party that over time had become most in favor of good relations with Beijing. His father, Takeo Fukuda, had learned the hard way about the importance of China. In 1972,

Beijing had effectively killed his chances of taking over as prime minister after Richard Nixon's shock opening to Beijing. The elder Fukuda had close ties to Taiwan and had served in the puppet Chinese government in Nanjing in the war, which made him an unacceptable partner to Beijing.

Takeo Fukuda's luck had improved by the time he became prime minister in late 1976, just as China was emerging out of the dark days of Mao Zedong's rule. The pro-Taiwan holdouts in Japan had by then largely acclimatized to the new regional order. "That was only possible because of the goodwill my father had built up," his son said. "No one else could have done it." In 1978, the elder Fukuda and Deng Xiaoping signed the Peace and Friendship Treaty, an agreement that laid the foundation for a decade-long golden era in bilateral ties. Fukuda liked to recount that Japan and China had signed four major agreements in the postwar period and that "my family is responsible for two of the four." As prime minister, he had signed his own deal with Hu Jintao in 2008. "The position of the Fukuda family is that we have to promote—we are obliged to promote—friendly ties with China."

When Yasao Fukuda was conscripted into patching up ties with Beijing in early 2014, he was dealing with the scions of two other elite political families, both with their own firm views on bilateral relations. Neither Xi nor Shinzō Abe wanted antagonistic ties for their own sake, but neither leader would have said, as Fukuda did, that he felt obliged to promote good relations between the two countries, whatever the circumstances. By that time, both men were dug deeply into their respective positions. Xi had given himself, and, by definition, his diplomats, no room to move in the wake of the Senkaku/Diaoyu conflict. Abe was adamant that the days of kowtowing to China were over. By mid-2014, both men had been in power for well over a year and had still not met. Behind the scenes, however, the two leaders were mulling options that they could use to dial the tensions down.

Over the decades, Tokyo and Beijing had developed multiple channels of communication outside the formal dialogue between leaders. Both countries had friendship associations whose respective heads could carry messages back and forth, and Japanese business leaders often acted as intermediaries via Beijing's party-sanctioned industry associations. In the days when Chinese leaders granted audiences to visiting foreign executives, the businessmen were also a conduit to the very top of the system in Beijing. Factional warlords in the two ruling parties—the CCP in Beijing and the Liberal

Democratic Party in Tokyo—had also cultivated personal relationships to exchange ideas that were routed back into the bureaucracy. "Don't worry," Cui Tiankai, Beijing's ambassador to the United States since early 2013, told a White House official when reassuring him about Sino-Japanese ties. "The CCP and the LDP know how to talk to each other."

These catacombs of communication help explain why, in the words of an Obama administration official, "things never really went off the rails, when they could have." Whenever the hyper-nationalists in each country tried to push disputes to the fore—Japanese right-wingers by placing a lighthouse on one of the Senkaku/Diaoyu Islands, or the Chinese by dispatching flotillas of fishing and other boats to the area—the respective governments were able to stay in touch, either directly or through intermediaries, to quietly pull them into line. The confrontation over the islands in 2012, though, changed the calculus of both countries, probably for good.

Through Chinese eyes, the trouble was all Tokyo's doing. "Look at Tokyo's handling of Taiwan, the islands, and the history issue," a senior Chinese diplomat said. "The people were enraged by the Japanese government's change in position." From Tokyo's perspective, the rage was the product of the decades-long party campaign to burnish its patriotic luster with an unrelenting diet of anti-Japanese history and news. In the words of one historian in China, the party had raised young Chinese on a diet of "wolf's milk" and was now reaping the whirlwind. Needless to say, the party didn't appreciate this analysis. The liberal magazine that published the Chinese historian's essay in 2006, *Freezing Point,* was suspended by the authorities soon after.

The ballast that economic interdependency had provided to bilateral ties was also taking on water. Japanese companies, which had invested billions in China (second only to overseas Chinese from Taiwan and Hong Kong), had always hedged their business bets on the mainland. For the previous decade, they had pursued what they called a "China plus one" investment strategy to ensure they didn't put all their eggs into the mainland basket. If a Japanese company built a factory in China, it might decide to construct its next one in Vietnam or Malaysia. What began as a prudent business decision—to ensure that if production was cut off at a factory in one country for whatever reason, it could be ramped up elsewhere—soon became a political hedge as well.

The anti-Japanese riots in 2005 hadn't affected the basic pattern of Japanese investment in the region, nor did the backlash against Japan in 2010 after the jailing of the Chinese ship captain caught off the Senkaku/Diaoyu Islands. Throughout this period, the level of Japanese investment in China and in the rest of Asia remained on par. But after 2012, when scores of Japanese businesses and factories were attacked in the wake of the nationalization of the islands, there was an immediate and dramatic change in sentiment. Investment in China flatlined and even fell slightly, while Japanese investments in the rest of Asia nearly doubled.

By the time Fukuda stepped into the breach, then, the back channels had largely been closed off. The LDP and the CCP weren't talking to each other. Business investment was falling. In both countries, mutual loathing among the public had solidified. Fukuda's worry about war was not just a politician's sixth sense in operation. At the height of the crisis, Xu Caihou, then the country's top military leader, said Chinese forces "should be prepared for any possible military combat."

Fukuda jokingly described his role in Sino-Japanese ties as akin to a *ro-bashin,* a playful Japanese word describing a fussing, elderly neighborhood busybody who presses her advice on all, whether it is asked for or not. Caught between Xi and Abe, however, Fukuda needed all his diplomatic skills and credibility to bridge the gap. Working in his favor was the end-of-year summit in 2014 of Asia-Pacific leaders in Beijing, an event that China didn't want dominated by headlines about Xi as an ungracious host, refusing to meet his Japanese guest. Until then, Beijing had put all the familiar conditions on granting Abe a meeting: a commitment from Abe not to go to Yasukuni Shrine and an acknowledgment that the two sides were in dispute over the Senkaku/Diaoyu Islands. Abe refused on both counts.

At that point, Fukuda said, "the room to negotiate on both sides had become much narrower." He traveled to Beijing for talks in July 2014, a trip dubbed without irony a "stealth visit" by members of the Japanese press, even as they covered it feverishly. It was important nonetheless, because it cleared the way for lower-level officials to finally begin exploring ways to revive relations. "I think the Chinese were feeling remorseful about their behavior; they knew they had gone too far [in attacking Japan and allowing protests]," Fukuda recalled. "I told them that if they were interested in building good ties with the international community, this would not work." Fukuda returned to Beijing in late October, just before the regional summit, this time meeting with Xi.

Fukuda's belief that Beijing had been reflecting with remorse on its anti-Japan policy had more than a touch of wishful thinking. The Chinese didn't particularly regret the waves of ugly anti-Japan sentiment that had so alienated the Japanese public. The rift, however, was diplomatically inconvenient and commercially damaging. With Fukuda as a soothing intermediary and Beijing's periodic pragmatism to the fore, the two countries' officials had enough leeway to negotiate the face-saving statement both sides wanted.

The four-point agreement, announced days before Xi was due to greet more than a dozen regional leaders at the APEC meeting in Beijing, was a masterpiece of diplomatic obfuscation. The headlines hailed the declaration as a "joint statement." The respective Chinese- and Japanese-language versions, though, contained a number of semantic back doors that allowed each side to get its version past the most uncompromising elements in its system. Nowhere in the documents did Japan promise that its leaders would stay away from Yasukuni, nor did they acknowledge the existence of a sovereignty dispute over the Senkaku/Diaoyu Islands. While Tokyo's version cited "different views" on the islands, Beijing's described them as "different positions." Beijing's statement mentioned the islands, while Tokyo's focused on the seas around them. "In short," said Adam Liff, a U.S. academic who conducted a forensic trilingual examination of the documents, "while the spirit of these declarations may convey consensus, their letter does not."

The fact that the statement settled little between the two countries was obvious from the moment Xi greeted Abe in Beijing a week later. Wang Yi, the foreign minister, had indicated that Xi would meet the Japanese leader, but only out of courtesy, explaining, "China is the host, and there is a custom in China, which is that visitors are all guests." As it turned out, Xi barely extended the most basic courtesies in their brief encounter in the Great Hall of the People. Rather than waiting to greet Abe, as was customary for the host, Xi made Abe stand and wait alone in front of the cameras in the meeting room. When he eventually did appear, Xi extended a limp hand and looked briefly at the Japanese prime minister with a scowl, ignoring Abe's verbal greeting before turning to face the cameras with unconcealed distaste. Abe's expression, in the face of such an obvious slight, was half-bemused and half-resigned. Later, Richard Armitage, the former Pentagon and State official, joked that the two leaders "looked like they were smelling each other's socks."

The Japanese—even those who had little time for Abe—were furious at this snub. Sakutaro Tanino, a former ambassador to Beijing and one of the most prominent members of the Foreign Ministry's China school, said Abe had been "forced to move toward Xi as if he were an emperor." Fukuda, an old classmate of Tanino's, tried to calm down the retired diplomat, explaining, "Don't be so furious; Xi has to deal with public opinion."

That so many parties in both China and Japan believed that Xi, already emerging as China's most powerful leader in a generation, had to be careful about how he greeted Abe in public lest he earn the ire of the populace was telling. Certainly senior officials in Beijing expressed that view. A Chinese diplomat said at the time that Xi had been "courageous" to even meet with Abe. Xi himself encouraged such sentiment in meetings with foreign leaders, including Obama. As distasteful a slight as it was, Xi's behavior at least functioned as a signal from on high to cool things down. "Unless Xi moves," said Tanino, "others cannot do a thing." The intrusive Chinese coast guard patrols around the Senkaku/Diaoyu Islands settled into a routine. The threat of some kind of maritime incident remained, but the worries about something worse taking place were receding. Abe, however, hardly behaved like a man reassured.

A few months later, at the annual Davos retreat in the Swiss Alps, the Japanese prime minister appeared on a panel convened by the *Financial Times*. Asked if war between Japan and China was "conceivable," Abe didn't rule out a conflict. Instead, he drew upon the most inflammatory of historical parallels for his international audience, suggesting that the relationship between Japan and China in 2014 had an echo of Britain and Germany's rivalry a century earlier, on the eve of World War I. The British and Germans had, of course, been close trading partners, but that had not stopped them from falling into a lengthy, destructive conflict. Japan and China, Abe said, were in a "similar situation."

A few years and several Japanese prime ministers earlier, it had been Japan's turn to host the regional APEC summit in Yokohama. In 2010, among the many protocol problems that habitually beset an annual event with nearly two dozen national leaders was a seemingly trivial one. The heads of the nine nations at the summit who were negotiating a new regional trade pact, known as the Trans-Pacific Partnership, had gathered for a photograph before a meeting of their own, separate from the larger forum. The TPP, a deal first backed by George W. Bush and then taken up by Barack Obama, aimed to knit together regional economies by reducing tariffs and harmonizing their regulatory environments. Although Japan was not one of the then-nine countries involved in the negotiations, Prime Minister Naoto Kan, their host in the city, wanted to be included in the TPP photograph nonetheless. It was an awkward request, to which, after much debate, the United States and other Pacific countries acceded.

Kan's desire to be part of the TPP group photograph was a signal that Tokyo was having second thoughts about declining to take part in the trade deal. Japan's characteristic caution on any agreement that might force open its agricultural markets was starting to take a backseat to finding ways to fend off China. TPP, after all, was advertised as a way for the United States and regional nations to write the rules for trade and intellectual property protection in a region increasingly overshadowed by the Chinese economic juggernaut. Months before the Yokohama summit, Japanese trade officials had begun quietly sounding out the Americans about joining the negotiations. Mike Froman, then heading international economics in the White House, was supportive almost from the outset, because his instincts pulled him toward a bigger, grander agreement. "A light went off in his head," recalled one of his advisers, who said that Froman sensed that the administration could get a trade deal with Japan through Congress, something that would have been impossible even a decade earlier.

While trade talks between Washington and Tokyo had long ceased to have an existential character to them, the two sides had never grown to like each other. Many experienced officials in the office of the U.S. trade representative, which Froman would go on to lead in Obama's second term, were leery about inviting Japan into the TPP. After years of painfully grappling with Tokyo across the negotiating table, they worried that Japan and its familiar objections to farm imports and other foreign goods and services would grind the talks to a halt. U.S. officials pointed to Robert Zoellick, who headed America's trade negotiating body in George W. Bush's first term, as a high-profile case of someone who had soured on Japan. A seasoned international figure, Zoellick took over USTR in 2001 ambitious to transform economic ties with Japan. The officials in the agency dated Zoellick's disillusionment to an encounter with Japan's agriculture minister, Tsutomu Takebe, early in his time in office.

Takebe brought a PowerPoint presentation to the meeting with Zoellick, laying out in detail the Agriculture Ministry's case for Japan becoming self-sufficient in food. Japan's trading partners thought Tokyo's policy was delusional, as well as being a handy cloak for protectionism. As Zoellick tried to engage Takebe in a big-picture discussion of global trade and U.S.-Japan relations, Takebe would nod politely and then interrupt, insisting on resuming his lengthy presentation. "Yes, yes," he would say, "but back to page 3 . . ." One U.S. official remembers catching the eye of a Japanese counterpart across the table. Both sensed at that moment that Zoellick's goodwill toward Japan was being lost for good. "He felt they didn't act like a great power," said one of his advisers.

Zoellick had been taken aback the first time he noticed a Japanese minister speaking, only to watch as one of his bureaucrats stood up and pointed to the talking points the ministry had prepared, to keep the minister on track. Early in his career, Zoellick had also been struck with how U.S. diplomats had become in part aligned with their counterparts in Tokyo. He remembers going into the State Department during the administration of George H. W. Bush and finding that "the Japanologists and Sinologists divided into two camps and that with the Japanologists the talking points were shared with Japanese officials in advance."

Later, at a negotiating session with his global counterparts, the Japanese trade minister's habit of metronomically reading out the brief prepared for him by his bureaucrats prompted Zoellick to virtually tell him to shut up. We know you need your special deal on rice, Zoellick said. We will take care of that, so please stand aside. Zoellick wasn't alone at USTR in his views. "Within a year, everyone would be using the *f* word when talking about the Japanese," recalled one longtime U.S. trade negotiator.

"There is frustration in the American system if the counterpart you deal with is just a titular figure," Zoellick said, in criticism that echoed Henry Kissinger's complaints about dealing with Tokyo four decades earlier. "In the old days, we were used to dealing with the party barons in Japan to get things done, but it was very hard to get a strategic discussion." At the World Bank from 2007, Zoellick found partnering with the Chinese more stimulating and fruitful. With backing from top leaders, the bank worked with the cabinet's think tank in Beijing to produce a pioneering report on how China could break out of the stagnancy that trapped many developing countries after initial periods of breakneck growth.

Midway through the Obama administration's first term, however, Japan's perspective had changed. Political leaders and much of the bureaucracy in Tokyo saw a chance to leverage the TPP negotiations to push changes at home that their opponents were resisting. Using outside pressure to force reform within the country was a time-honored tactic in Japan. The Japanese had watched from the sidelines as regional nations secured trade pacts with the Americans and with one another. They were alarmed when the United States and South Korea managed to seal a bilateral deal. "The Japanese would always come into our office and say, Why are you spending all your time with the Koreans? You will never get a deal," said a senior U.S. trade negotiator. Later, the South Koreans would use similar arguments when Japan mulled joining TPP. "They were shocked," the U.S. official said. "They said you are wasting your time, but they knew that Japan might now have a veto over them getting in."

For the Americans, the key was Tokyo's change in negotiating strategy to address the complaints that had so frustrated the likes of Zoellick. "We told them, we are not negotiating the old-fashioned way, ministry by ministry," said Wendy Cutler, then a USTR deputy. "That way, you never had any sense you were negotiating with a real leader." In Abe, Japan had a leader strong enough to get around the balkanized bureaucracy and place responsibility for the negotiations into an office directly under his control. Mindful of the need to get Congress on its side, Washington began testing Tokyo on small but symbolic issues, such as insurance and car certification and the like. With both sides demonstrating their resolve, the Americans believed they could finally get Tokyo to move on agriculture. Tokyo, in turn, grew confident that Washington could overcome objections from the U.S. auto industry to do a deal with Japan.

Japan's commitment to join the TPP was at the time a transformative event. In trade terms, Japan's size instantly gave the deal more clout.

Collectively, the twelve countries in the partnership were responsible for 40 percent of global economic output. Within the Asia-Pacific, TPP had the potential to give regional economies an advantage over China by setting rules for investments by state-owned companies and lowering trade barriers among one another. It was a game changer for the United States and Japan as well, because for the first time since the war the two sides began to work together in harmony on trade. The same old problems—farm imports for Japan, and autos for the United States—remained difficult. On the modern cross-border issues that were the core of the TPP negotiations, however—intellectual property rights, patents and trademarks, and labor and environmental standards—Washington found that Tokyo was its best partner. Within the TPP, the United States and Japan were effectively negotiating a bilateral free trade deal alongside the other ten member countries, something that would have been unthinkable a few years earlier. Not only that, but they were doing so in a spirit of goodwill.

The TPP, and its positioning as a shield against China, were significant in transforming the relationship between Obama and Abe as well. Obama forged few warm personal relationships with world leaders in his eight years in the White House. Within the administration, his personal counsel was tightly held to a handful of confidants. Many of Obama's former advisers who remained outside the inner circle speak of the president with respect but rarely affection. In building their relationship, Obama and Abe faced barriers beyond personality, for they were ideologically at odds as well, a division that their camp followers in Washington and Tokyo often played up. Obama and his advisers' agitation over Abe's handling of history continued to cause resentment in Tokyo. The Japanese were shocked by the strength of comments that Obama made on the comfort women in South Korea in 2014, in a speech delivered just after departing Tokyo. The president's remarks, about the need for a full accounting of the "terrible, egregious violation of human rights" suffered by the women, came out of the blue even to his advisers.

History and partisan ideology aside, Obama was an unsentimental character whose misgivings about China by then far outweighed any reservations about Abe. Washington and Beijing had worked well together on climate change and during negotiations over Iran's nuclear program. There had been a spark of cooperation when Xi Jinping met

Obama at Sunnylands, the Palm Springs desert retreat, in mid-2013, bringing with him an idea for a bilateral compact with the United States clumsily
called a "new model of great-power relations." The White House was initially willing to countenance the idea, and both Joe Biden and Susan Rice,
the national security adviser, used the term in speeches. But it didn't take
long for the nascent understanding to fray. The Obama administration
soon got feedback from Asian capitals that Chinese diplomats had been
promoting their understanding with Washington as a deal that would set a
template for the region. "They immediately started going around Asia sort
of saying that the U.S. and China are doing a deal, and please, don't mess
things up, don't be pains in the ass," said a White House official. "We told
them, you can't do that. We have not signed up for that."

The Japanese unsurprisingly hated the Chinese idea of "great-power
relations" and complained vehemently when Biden and Rice appeared to
sanctify it. Any hint of a bilateral arrangement was anathema to Tokyo,
because it felt it would sideline Japan. But Washington soon dropped the
idea, even as China continued to mention it. Larger trends were already
pulling the United States and China inexorably in opposite directions.
Beijing's unilateral announcement in late 2013 of its control of the airspace
around the Senkaku/Diaoyu Islands was just one reminder among many
of the challenge from China, as was the military pressure it was continuing
to exert in the area. Dai Bingguo complained that the United States had
misunderstood Beijing's outreach. The "new model of great-power relations" that Americans saw as a way to constrain the United States "was
actually conceived with the aim in mind of constraining China," he told
one of his interlocutors in Washington. "It was developed with the idea to
promote a more moderate rise in China." Few in Washington, however,
were willing to believe such blandishments from China any longer.

One Obama administration official described the U.S.-China rivalry
as akin to a roughhouse game of water polo. The competition that spec-
tators could see above the surface, as vigorous as it was, concealed the
array of even dirtier tactics deployed beneath it as each side probed the
most sensitive parts of the other's systems to gain the upper hand. In
geopolitical terms, that included everything from cyber espionage and
theft, sabotaging naval vessels at sea, close-in spy flights, and bribery and
threats to U.S. allies in the region. Washington was convinced that Beijing was trying to undermine its postwar position in Asia and evict it

from the region altogether in the longer term. Beijing, in turn, was programmed to view Washington's pushback against its territorial claims and its military rebalance in favor of Asia as just one more round of the kinds of measures the West had used for more than 150 years to contain and weaken China.

Few things angered Obama and his administration more than what they claimed was the wholesale cyber theft of confidential U.S. business data by Chinese state-backed hackers. "He thought the Chinese were out to screw us," said one of Obama's advisers. Here, however, Washington's initial efforts to put Beijing on notice blew up embarrassingly. The first time that Obama registered his anger face-to-face with Xi, at the mid-2013 Sunnylands summit, coincided with Edward Snowden's leak of a torrent of top-secret documents from America's omnivorous electronic eavesdropper, the National Security Agency. The administration's careful distinction between ordinary spying (which everyone did) and China's theft of U.S. companies' proprietary information and technology for commercial exploitation (which the United States said Beijing did on an industrial scale) was smothered by the sensational revelations.

Snowden's documents detailed how the NSA had penetrated the networks of the Chinese telecommunications giant Huawei, the same company that Washington had barred from U.S. equipment markets on security grounds for its potential to create back doors into U.S. systems. "We have so much data [on Huawei] that we don't know what to do with it," one NSA official said, according to the documents. The leak did more than provide Beijing with an invaluable road map to the NSA's activities; it was a propaganda windfall as well. When the United States identified and charged in absentia five Chinese military officers for cyber hacking in 2014, the Chinese responded with derision. "It's really amazing some people still believe they have the moral high ground and credibility to accuse others, if we consider the Snowden revelations," said Cui Tiankai, China's ambassador to Washington.

The revelation in the Snowden documents that really touched a nerve in China was the fact that the NSA had managed to listen in to some of Hu Jintao's calls while he was party leader and president. Chinese scholars said that in Xi's next meeting with Obama after Sunnylands, on the sidelines of a nuclear summit in The Hague in early 2014, the Chinese president complained to Obama about the bugging of his predecessor.

For the Chinese, it was a delicious role reversal. The scholars were dismissive of U.S. allegations of Chinese cyber theft of corporate secrets. They argued that bugging their leadership was worse, because it "affects the dignity of the whole nation," adopting a tone that mixed indignation with exhilaration as Xi turned the tables on Obama.

With China breathing down their necks, Obama and Abe had every incentive to solidify their relationship and their countries' alliance. "They didn't have a warm personal relationship, but they developed a very productive relationship," Ben Rhodes observed. "Abe's agenda had a lot of connective tissue to our Asian strategy." In the wake of the White House's criticism of Abe's visit to Yasukuni Shrine in late 2013, Washington began working quietly to take the sting out of its rebuke. "We slathered him with love, and gave him nothing but respect," said one administration official. "We looked at everything we could to demonstrate real regard for Japan; we did not want to look like we were jamming them, just to drive home to him he will have set back his cause if he does not deal with this."

The United States also offered reassurance. During his visit to Japan in April 2014, Obama announced that the bilateral security treaty covered the Senkaku Islands, the first sitting American president to make such a statement. In return, the United States wanted a commitment from Abe to not engage in provocative behavior himself, either militarily or via any history-related issue. "We gave them what they wanted on the Senkakus," said Rhodes, "but privately the message was that we don't want you to precipitate any conflict." By early 2015, the two countries were ready to announce new defense guidelines giving Japan greater leeway to assist U.S. forces in battle, in Asia and beyond. They were also nearing a deal on TPP, which would give the administration's pivot to Asia a commercial sales pitch in the region.

In a high-profile April 2015 visit to the United States that included a historic address to Congress, Abe stopped first in Boston, where he had dinner at the home of Secretary of State John Kerry. While Obama had already spoken to Abe about history in Brisbane the year before, Kerry had now been designated within the administration to raise the issue with him again. A few days before his arrival, the *Boston Herald* ran an editorial that read as if it were dictated by the administration, citing the need for a strong, confident Japan to finally put its history problems to rest. Over the meal at his stately town house, which had been an Epis-copal convent in the nineteenth century, Kerry took a different tack with Abe from that used by previous officials. Instead of reciting Japan's mis-deeds, Kerry spoke at length about the United States' challenges in squarely facing its own demons. He used the example of the recently released movie *Selma,* an acclaimed account of the 1965 marches led by Martin Luther King in the segregated South to obtain voting rights for African Americans. Kerry's message was, if the United States could do it, then so could Japan.

In Washington, Obama escorted Abe to the Lincoln Memorial, the first of a number of gestures on both sides weighted with multiple levels of symbolism. Obama noted how the memorial honored a president "who believed great conflict had to be followed by reconciliation." For his part, Abe paid a visit alone to America's national military cemetery at nearby Arlington. As Obama framed it in their joint press conference, Abe's Arlington trip embodied the idea that "former adversaries can be-come powerful allies," one that could be harnessed in support of Sino-Japanese ties. Arlington had another meaning for Japanese conservatives like Abe, who compared it to Yasukuni Shrine, on the basis that both sites honored the war dead. If U.S. leaders could pay their respects to the fallen at Arlington, why shouldn't the Japanese do the same at Yasukuni? It was an argument that had never gained much traction in Washington.

Abe's most striking comments, though, received little notice. Stand-ing next to Obama, Abe announced that Japan wanted to work "hand in hand" with America "to spread basic values throughout the world, such as freedom, democracy, basic human rights, and the rule of law." No Japanese leader since Yasuhiro Nakasone, who enjoyed a close rela-tionship with Ronald Reagan, had gone as far in aligning Japan in such terms with the democratic West. In his brief first stint as prime minister, Abe had advanced the formation of a loose alliance among four democ-racies: Japan, the United States, India, and Australia. The Bush White House was divided on the idea; India was not enthusiastic. Kevin Rudd, then prime minister in Australia, was antagonistic to an arrangement he worried could hitch Canberra to poisonous Sino-Japanese relations. With little support from potential partners, Abe's initiative died.

But the times now suited Abe's idea. If nothing else, Abe was ideo-logically far removed from the administration of Yukio Hatoyama, which only a few years earlier had wanted to distance Tokyo from Washington to move closer to Beijing. Obama, too, was more receptive than his predecessor and willing to put his personal reservations about Abe aside to work more closely with the Japanese prime minister. "Obama does not do chemistry," said Mike Green, George W. Bush's former Asia adviser. "But he learned how to do face." For supporters of the alliance in Washington and Tokyo, the two leaders' mutual accommodation during Abe's weeklong state visit in April 2015 marked a turning point in regional geopolitics.

Abe had another reason to solidify ties with Washington. The massive parade that Beijing planned to mark the seventieth anniversary in September 2015 of the end of the war was the biggest that the Communist state had ever staged. It was also the first time that Beijing had marked the occasion with a public display of military hardware. In the months beforehand, Chinese diplomats had fanned out across the globe, pressing countries that had fought with China against Japan to send military units to march with the PLA through Tiananmen Square in the parade's finale. Wang Yi, the foreign minister, personally lobbied European and Asian ambassadors in Beijing, a sign of the importance the Politburo attached to the event.

It was an audacious pitch, to have serving soldiers from Western nations march through central Beijing side by side with a Chinese army that was all too clear about its mission in life: to banish Western interlopers from the region and humiliate the West's now ally, Japan. "Starting from 2012, they tried to play that card again, that Japan was trying to upset the postwar order and get around the verdict of [defeat]," said one of Obama's top advisers on Asia. "It was so clumsy. 'I hope our American friends will not forget we were allies. We still hope we can work together today,' they'd say. I always told them, We don't need any lectures on history."

The first serious attempt to build a foundation for historical reconciliation between Japan and China, of the kind that might have taken the sting out of the anniversary parade, had been launched by Abe himself. To take advantage of the thaw in relations on his visit to Beijing in 2006, the two governments announced the establishment of a panel of eminent scholars from both countries to try to find common ground on history. Bu Ping, a mainstream historian from the state think tank, the Chinese

Academy of Social Sciences, headed the panel nominated by Beijing. The Japanese historians were led by Shinichi Kitaoka, a Tokyo University professor with an extensive government and academic résumé. The two sides divided their work into three sections: the study of early contacts, back hundreds of years to early Chinese dynasties; the war; and the postwar period. In the words of one Japanese participant, the aim wasn't to identify winners and losers or to write a uniform account of the relationship. Rather, they sought to understand each other's positions and, wherever possible, build a common baseline for research. They were due to release a report two years later, just before the 2008 Beijing Olympics.

The two sides circled each other warily at the start. "The Japanese side said we should not politicize history," Bu said in 2015. "We also said they should not politicize history." The aim of the panel, or least that of the Japanese, was in fact to take history out of the political arena, which, of course, could be considered itself a highly political act. As one of the Chinese historians, Tao Wenzhao, observed, "When a politician raises history, both countries can say their historians are addressing it." Bu, as the leader of the Chinese delegation, had initially been cynical about the project, telling visitors that Beijing had agreed to the proposal only to give the two sides something to announce in connection with Abe's trip. The scholars from both countries, however, said that once the initial media glare was off them, they worked together in a professional and civil manner. "We found we had one thing in common," said Bu. "We both operated from an academic point of view." It wasn't until later, when it came time to publish their findings, that the problems started.

The two sides agreed on the history of earlier eras, publishing a joint paper on ancient and medieval times. On the war, they disagreed on the Nanjing Massacre—not on whether it had taken place but on the numbers of casualties, and related issues—and so ended up publishing separate papers. The divisions over Nanjing symbolized the much bigger underlying conflict that made history so difficult to grapple with: the hardening politicization of the war and memory in both countries, and the different ways in which each system handled these fissures, internally and with the outside world. In many respects, the heated debate over Nanjing in pluralistic Japan had been the trigger for a reassessment and repositioning of the incident in authoritarian China.

In the late 1960s and early 1970s, left-leaning historians and journalists in Japan published detailed accounts of the killings in books and major newspapers, illustrated with photographs of mutilated bodies and severed heads. The writers had interviewed Chinese survivors and retired soldiers in Japan, as well as combing through the transcripts of postwar trials in Tokyo and Nanjing. The Japanese research, ironically enough, was invaluable to Beijing in prosecuting its case against Tokyo on the issue. Within months, however, another set of Japanese writers mobilized to challenge the evidence, capped by the publication of an award-winning book, *The Illusion of the Nanjing Massacre*.

So divided were the warring camps in Japan that the media attached tabloid tags to identify them in shorthand, as the "great massacre faction" and the "illusion faction." In between these polarized camps was another group, the "middle-of-the-road" faction, which didn't dispute the massacre but questioned the official 300,000 death toll produced in the postwar war crimes trials in Nanjing. The divisions in Japan over Nanjing, and the war more generally, spilled into battles over the content of school textbooks in the early 1980s. In turn, the battles stirred up over the textbooks helped transform relations with China, and South Korea, into a running war over history from that time on. "Nanjing was a special issue for us," Bu said, "but both sides realized we had to discuss it, because of the media interest."

The two panels of historians debated the factors that triggered the slaughter, from ill-disciplined Japanese soldiers to a chaotic Chinese retreat, with citizens being caught up in fighting. On the numbers killed, the Chinese stuck resolutely to the figure first propagated in the postwar trials, of 300,000. The Japanese accepted that there had been mass killings but suggested the death toll was lower, ranging from 200,000 to 20,000. The lower figure reflected the conclusions of the "middle-of-the-road" faction, which included many professional historians who had tried to distinguish between civilian casualties and soldiers and sort through conflicting estimates of the death toll. For the Chinese, however, to even question the official figure was a display of bad faith. The 300,000 figure has been etched in concrete on the outside of the museum in Nanjing. As the death toll dictated by the party, the figure is politically untouchable in China. With no freedom to diverge from it, Chinese historians without exception fell into the "great massacre" school.

The differences over Nanjing were not surprising, because they reflected decades of discord in both countries. What was most telling was the area where the two panels fell out altogether. The most contentious divide was not over the war itself but over its aftermath. At the opening meeting, the Japanese scholars complained that the party had never educated young Chinese about postwar Japan's peaceful, democratic transformation and the apologies the country had made for the war. In private, Bu virtually conceded the point in discussions with American diplomats. Most Chinese, he acknowledged, still believed that the Japanese systematically denied their wartime history. To be called "pro-Japanese," he said, "remained an insult" in China. In public, the Chinese historians had little room to move in which to address the Japanese complaints on this topic.

After both sides had submitted their papers on the postwar period, the Chinese requested changes. They didn't want any mention of the 1989 military crackdown, though Japanese scholars considered the incident pivotal, the point at which the public began to sour on China. The Chinese were also hesitant to put their imprimatur on a document underlining Japan's peaceful postwar posture. They refused to allow any questioning of the findings of the Tokyo Tribunal, which tried and convicted Japanese war criminals. They did not want to draw attention to China's own postwar about-face of first rejecting apologies from Japan and later insisting on them. The list of objections went on and on.

Despite multiple Japanese requests, the release of the project's papers kept getting put off. Bu admitted the delay was at the request of the Beijing government. "We had the Olympics in 2008, and then in 2009 there were problems in Tibet and in Xinjiang," he said. "The government was a little bit worried that it would have some negative impact." In the end, the Chinese declined to release any of the findings on the postwar period. Even for a process that had started with so little promise, it was a depressing denouement. "The Chinese government will not show papers that offer a non-Chinese perspective to Chinese citizens," said Shin Kawashima, one of the Japanese historians.

In person, Bu Ping affected the modest dress and work style of a genial cadre. In conversation, he was much like an official as well, alternatively disarmingly frank and sinuously evasive, with an ability to acknowledge sensitive issues when they came up while also skirting around them. None of this was a surprise. As a senior historian in the

Chinese Academy of Social Sciences, Bu occupied a position controlled
by the party's Organization Department. His views about history thus
reflected the different directions he was pulled in, between his profession
as an academic and his career as an official.

While he conceded that the party had to do a better job in acknowledging the dark corners of its own history, he insisted that had nothing
to do with Japan. While Mao Zedong might have dismissed the need for
apologies, Bu said, the real problem was that Japan had changed its position, not China: "They used to think that China was underdeveloped;
they felt guilty at this point. The voices that hated China were not heard,
but now with China rising, they think they can say these things."

To illustrate the mind-set in Beijing on history, Bu conjured up a
Venn diagram with three interlocking circles, taking in scholarly study,
politics, and emotion. By the finish of the joint project, he had started to
question where he stood himself. "I am basically part of the academic
part of the diagram, but I also wondered whether my studies were also
impacted by extreme emotionalism," he said. "Germany and France took
fifty years after they started work on joint textbooks to come up with
one; maybe it will take us just as long."

In the end, the project built no sturdy bridges between the two countries' historians, let alone their governments and their peoples. That
much became obvious when the seventieth anniversary of the end of the
war came into clear sight.

In any country, democratic or authoritarian, popular culture, in books
and movies, is influenced by political factors, directly and indirectly.
Governments and the media in democracies can be harsh arbiters of
what passes for patriotism, as the often nasty debates in post-9/11 America illustrated. Still, in China the party has the ability to shape the parameters of what is allowed, and what is not, in a way unimaginable in
a democracy. The debate over the Nanjing Massacre in Japan was often
ugly, but it was also the product of a society with free speech. In China,
by contrast, the list of taboo topics is long and the ability to enforce them
formidable. They extend from discussions of powerful, well-connected
individuals, like top leaders and their families, to institutions like the
party itself and its right to rule, to issues of sovereignty, like Taiwan,
Tibet, and Xinjiang. With so many topics off the agenda, Chinese

journalists, writers, and filmmakers naturally gravitate to areas where they have the freedom to work and get paid for it. Ahead of the seventieth anniversary commemoration, no area of cultural output was freer, and better funded, than accounts of the war and Japan.

The party's Propaganda Department had long made it clear that artists had to restrict themselves to the black-and-white official narrative of the war: of brave, patriotic Chinese battling evil, demonic Japanese. Those who didn't saw their careers suffer. The party had firmly set this template a decade and a half earlier. In 2000, Jiang Wen, one of China's most famous actors and directors, had written and directed a satire, *Devils on the Doorstep,* about a small village that doesn't know how to deal with captured Japanese soldiers. The film was hailed at overseas film festivals on its release but was banned in China. The official ruling by state censors, which, unusually, was leaked in full, cited numerous problems with the film: the "common Chinese people" did not show sufficient hatred toward the Japanese; the cruelty of the Japanese was not presented strongly enough (one enemy soldier gave candy to a child); and "Japanese army songs are played often, putting a spin on the Japanese imperialists flaunting their strength, which may gravely hurt the feelings of the Chinese people."

In 2013, with Chinese movie producers readying their schedules for the anniversary two years later, the state film bureau approved sixty-nine television series and about a hundred films with anti-Japanese story lines. At one stage that year, forty-eight of the anti-Japanese-themed series were being shot simultaneously at the Hengdian World Studios, one of the country's filmmaking centers, in Zhejiang province, adjoining Shanghai. A Chinese university professor estimated that about 70 percent of the dramas on Chinese television consisted of wartime shows, inevitably focusing on Japan and its misdeeds.

Perhaps in an effort to find new plot points or fresh ways of displaying fealty to the cause, the deluge of films and television dramas displayed extraordinary license. In one, a Chinese soldier managed to bring down a Japanese plane by throwing rocks at it from the ground. Another Chinese hero, after managing to fend off bullets and attacks with a sword, tore a Japanese soldier in half with his bare hands. To underline his family's bravery, a character in one film declared his grandfather had been killed "by the Japanese devils when he was nine years old."

In a scene that seemed to tip public reaction from incredulity to outright mockery, a woman played by one of China's most famous actresses smuggled a grenade into a prison inside her vagina and made love with her Chinese prisoner boyfriend, before suddenly producing the weapon from its hiding place to blow up the Japanese guards. That was the final straw for the Propaganda Department, which was alarmed to see the anti-Japanese films being mocked online as "Resisting-Japan Bizarre Dramas." In a lengthy article in the official media, the department issued an edict for these projects to "respect historical facts" regarding Japan.

The flood of anti-Japanese movies and books in China ran in parallel with another wartime drama, just as familiar and shopworn, in Japan itself. A few weeks before China's military parade, Shinzō Abe was due to deliver an official message to mark the anniversary. Japan had apologized for the war many times in many forums, at home and overseas. On the seventieth anniversary, another expression of remorse was expected by Japan's enemies and allies alike. Abe was determined that it would be final.

Abe's statement had been in preparation for months. The White House had had its say, pressing Abe to make sure he met his neighbors' minimum benchmarks, in an effort to draw a line under the issue. Both Beijing and Seoul had made clear their bottom line for what the apology should include. They insisted that Abe admit imperial Japan had waged a war of aggression and been a colonial power. Anyone who had not been embroiled in Japanese domestic politics could be forgiven for wondering why this was ever in dispute, but the country's conservatives had always railed against this description of the Pacific War, which they regarded as one of self-defense against encroaching Western powers. If that was Japan's sin, they argued, shouldn't the Western countries apologize as well for their aggressive conquests of foreign lands?

Abe, though, had prepared for this moment. Once given to diplomatically reckless statements about the comfort women and the like, he now had his eyes on the bigger picture. In his second term, he had both tapped and constrained the nationalist elements in his party. He had done enough to placate his right wing. The Japanese scholars who had taken part in the joint history project, some of whom were advising him on his anniversary statement, had already declared that Tokyo had been the aggressor, giving him cover on that issue. Abe was determined to take Japan in a much more strategic direction. The complaints of his American friends and many of his bureaucratic advisers—that he was only helping China by backsliding on war apologies—now had more force.

His cabinet and the Foreign Ministry, as well as the White House and the State Department, didn't see the final text of Abe's statement until just before he delivered it on August 14, the eve of the anniversary of Hirohito's statement of surrender in 1945. In the end, Abe's statement ticked all the boxes, mollifying the Right at home and Japan's allies abroad. He spoke of how Western colonial powers had pushed Japan into isolation in the 1930s and down a disastrous road to war. He apologized for Tokyo's own aggression and colonialism. In conclusion, he added his own distinctive rider, that this would be the last time that Japan needed to say it was sorry: "We must not let our children, grandchildren, and even further generations to come, who have nothing to do with that war, be predestined to apologize."

On September 2, the date that coincided with Japan's formal surrender, Xi had his own say, with the military parade. Not every country had dismissed Beijing's invitation to its leaders to the event. South Korea's president, Park Geun-hye, attended, watching from pride of place under the portrait of Mao Zedong on the podium above the entrance to the Forbidden City. So, too, did Vladimir Putin, returning a favor to Xi Jinping, who had traveled to Moscow earlier in the year for Russia's celebratory victory parade. About thirty other heads of state or government were present, as were soldiers from countries such as Serbia, Cuba, Cambodia, and Fiji. The Western nations that had been the target of Beijing's lobbying to re-create their wartime alliances sent lower-level representatives, such as ambassadors or ministers handling veterans' issues. Marching through Tiananmen Square, a place freighted with memories of 1989 in the West, even if the military crackdown had in fact taken place in the boulevards nearby, was never going to pass muster in Western capitals.

Before the parade, there was speculation that Abe himself might visit Beijing as a gesture toward righting past wrongs and establishing future ties. In hindsight, such a visit was never likely. "We asked the Chinese whether the parade was going to be anti-Japanese," one of Abe's advisers said. "They said no, and then we said, 'What is the name of the parade?'" The parade's official title was the "Commemoration of 70th Anniversary of Victory of Chinese People's Resistance Against Japanese Aggression and World Anti-Fascist War." The Web site curating news about the event overflowed with venom about Japanese misdeeds, mixed with a grab bag of laudatory fare about CCP heroism: stories like "China's Last Comfort Woman Suing Japan Dies," followed by "The Truth About the Nanjing Massacre," "Japan Soldiers Rape, Kill New Mothers: Confession," and "Interview: China Makes Great Contribution to Global War Against Fascism: Thai Businessman."

Listing Japanese atrocities was by now to be expected. More telling was how the Propaganda Department placed front and center the party's role in Japan's defeat. That most of the fighting against the Japanese had been done by Chiang Kai-shek's Nationalist army was now recognized by an overwhelming number of historians outside the party's tightly controlled orbit. The party was effectively celebrating a victory in a war that it didn't actually win. It had moved slowly in acknowledging the Nationalists' role, but only as part of "joint cooperation" with the CCP. The tortured syntax used at the entrance to the exhibition in the museum on the outskirts of Beijing commemorating the war carefully skirted the central role of the Nationalists, not to say the role of Washington's atomic bombs, in defeating the Japanese. The foreword states that all Chinese "united under the banner of the Anti-Japanese United front initiated by the CCP and on the basis of the CCP-Kuomintang [Nationalist] cooperation." An entire wall at the museum, specially renovated for the seventieth anniversary, bolstered this message, featuring a diorama of the CCP's bases behind enemy lines.

The truth, of course, had been acknowledged by Mao Zedong decades earlier in meetings with the Japanese. Mao had thanked them for invading, because it had enabled the CCP to retreat from the superior Nationalist forces and regroup. Even then, it wasn't the Chinese that ultimately defeated Japan. Hirohito didn't mention China in his surrender speech, for a good reason: At the time that the United States dropped the two atomic bombs on Hiroshima and Nagasaki, large parts of China were still under Japanese occupation. When the surrender itself was signed on the U.S.S. *Missouri* in Tokyo Bay, China was represented at the ceremony, but so were Canada, the Netherlands, Australia, New Zealand, and the provisional French Republic. None of these countries claim today, as Xi did from the podium on Tiananmen Square, that they deserved the credit for "total victory against the Japanese militarist aggressors."

Seven decades later, the party presided over a nation that was on its way to becoming a genuine superpower, and its attitudes had changed accordingly. Chinese Foreign Ministry officials didn't dare echo Mao's sardonic statement thanking the Japanese for paving the way for the Communist victory in 1949. Instead of praising Japan's expressions of regret, Chinese officials now picked them apart, word by word, pointing to the telltale signs of right-wing influence and the unwillingness to take responsibility for the conflict. "If you read it, you don't know who was invading whom," one official remarked.

The Chinese mind-set was captured more coldly and succinctly in May 2016 after Barack Obama visited Hiroshima. Wang Yi, the foreign minister and the ministry's erstwhile leading Japan expert, was decidedly unsympathetic. "Hiroshima is worthy of attention. But even more so Nanjing should not be forgotten," he said. "The victims deserve sympathy, but the perpetrators could never shake off their responsibility."

Even at such a solemn moment, Wang had made China's feelings clear: Japan, forever more, should know its place. The Japanese had long complained about the "victor's justice" meted out by Western powers after the war. China saw victor's justice as the natural order of things. For Japan, that meant a life sentence with no parole.

Afterword

In the summer of 2016, I made an appointment to see Tong Zeng, a longtime anti-Japan activist, in his office in west Beijing. It wasn't the best of times to be discussing sensitive political topics in China. On coming to power four years earlier, Xi Jinping had inherited a tightly held, opaque political system. During his first term, he achieved a rare double: he made the system even less transparent and more intimidating. The party marginalized and investigated political enemies, jailed activist lawyers, and instructed academics, scholars, and the media in no uncertain terms to toe the line. A number of foreigners working in overseas-funded civil society groups were detained and forced to film Maoist-style confessions for the evening news before being deported. Anyone with a finger to the political winds in China was not lining up to talk to the Western press.

Tong had proved to be a canny operator since emerging in the early 1990s, agitating to change China's long-standing policy forgoing war reparations from Japan. A young master's graduate from Peking University, Tong had been at loose ends after being admonished for participating in the 1989 protests when he came across a story in the *People's Daily*. The small item, tucked away on the inside pages of the CCP organ, recounted how Poland had decided to seek war reparations from West Germany after the fall of the Berlin Wall. (Communist Poland had already received some money from the former East Germany.) In an essay written in 1991 titled "Lifting the Spirits of the Chinese," Tong advocated China doing the same with Japan. When no newspaper would publish it, he took his views to delegates at the annual meeting of the National People's Congress, China's pseudo-parliament, in Beijing. Even in the fetid post-1989 environment, when any extracurricular political activities carried grave risks, dozens of delegates he managed to pull aside supported him.

Soon after circulating a petition demanding reparations, Tong was visited by the Beijing police. In Tong's telling of the story, they satisfied themselves he didn't have a broader antiparty agenda and confided that they supported his mission. "My grandfather was killed by the Japanese," one policeman told him. Still, the authorities kept a close eye on him. Most years, during the NPC sessions, or at other sensitive moments, Tong says the authorities would "invite him to travel," giving him a free trip out of town so he could not cause any trouble. During the emperor's visit to Beijing in 1992, he was sent to Chongqing. Classed as an intellectual, Tong was picked up at airports by high-level officials and put up at good hotels. He would go sightseeing by day and do karaoke at night. "After I left to go back to Beijing, the local officials would thank me for behaving, as they would get a bonus if there were no incidents," he said.

Over the years, Tong adapted to these constraints and gradually built a space in which he could operate. Crafty and sinuous, with a finely tuned sense of when to press ahead and when to pull back, and, above all, keeping his focus on Japan's ill deeds rather than the party's shortcomings, Tong built a career out of campaigning for reparations that would endure for the next twenty-five years. Along the way, he managed to make a reasonable living through a consulting business, using his stature as a patriotic warrior to open doors for companies that wanted to list on the stock exchange. As for welcoming foreign journalists to his office, that was no problem, despite the icy political winds blowing through the capital in 2016. "Now is actually a good time for me to give interviews," he said.

With his focus on Japan, Tong was living in an alternate political universe from the rest of the country. Although he was campaigning against long-settled government policy on reparations, the police didn't come to his house to issue him warnings or drag him away in the early morning to detention. The local media, when they did discuss him, often referred to him as *tiaopi,* meaning naughty or mischievous. The authorities tolerated Tong's work, which for him amounted to a green light. "The government is not against us," he said. "And in China, if the government is not against you, they support you."

Over the previous quarter century, Tong and like-minded activists had helped organize numerous stunts, mostly by sending flotillas of fishing boats to the Senkaku/Diaoyu Islands at different times. He continued to petition the National People's Congress and to talk to the local media. Other like-minded activist groups, scattered over different parts of the country, but mainly in Beijing and around the coastal areas near the islands, endured nasty internal splits over money and the timing of campaigns, but their movement never disintegrated.

When I visited him, Tong said the campaign to extract money from Japan had reached a complicated "third stage." Initially, the activists had tracked down victims they could use to front claims for monetary damages. With the assistance of lawyers and civil society groups in Japan, they filed numerous cases in Tokyo, for everything from back pay for forced laborers during the occupation to damages for the seizure of assets. The cases were largely unsuccessful. Then, as relations with Tokyo deteriorated, the activists eyed opportunities closer to home by working through the Chinese legal system.

In 2014, after refusing such cases for decades, a Chinese court finally agreed to hear a claim against one of Japan's giant global trading houses, Mitsui. A Chinese family was demanding compensation for the loss of two coal carriers leased by Mitsui and then commandeered by the Imperial Navy during the late 1930s. One boat was sunk by a torpedo and the other lost at sea during a storm. After one of Mitsui's ships was impounded in China in April 2014 on court orders, the Japanese company quickly agreed to pay $29 million to settle the case.

The Chinese government called the Mitsui affair a simple business dispute that had been handled according to the law, unrelated to political battles over reparations and the like. In truth, the case was a milestone. It set a legal precedent but more important, given that the law is subservient to politics in China, a political one. Beijing had given the activists a tactical victory on their own doorstep, a decision that kept pressure on Japan and left the door ajar for further such cases to be brought in the future.

In Vladimir Putin's Russia, the Kremlin decided that if it couldn't control nationalist and patriotic groups, then it would make sure it was leading them. Beijing's approach was subtly different. The Chinese authorities led the anti-Japan movements from behind, camouflaging their support for the activists with bland statements about the law and past diplomatic practice. At the same time, the authorities kept the activists on a tight leash through the party's control of the courts and the press, to ensure that they could be yanked back into line at any time. The Chinese state does not need to display its sinews to remind people of its might. Most are all too aware of the party's power and have learned to keep their heads down or devise ways around it.

Tong and his staff at his small office in Beijing had long internalized the parameters of what was permissible, even as they tried to expand the boundaries within which they could work. Tong headquartered his consulting business in the Chinese capital. His group that lobbied for reparations, the Chinese Association for Claiming Compensation from Japan, however, had been discreetly registered in Hong Kong, at arm's length from the authorities in Beijing. His office always ran any statements about his work past the Propaganda Department and the Foreign Ministry before releasing them. Did they follow whatever instructions they were given? I asked. "Of course we do," his assistant assured me.

But endemic tensions remained between the government and activists nonetheless. The same week that I chatted with Tong, I met in Beijing with a retired senior Foreign Ministry official. Xu Dunxin was a former vice-minister who served as ambassador to Japan for five years beginning in 1993, a period when relations started their downward trend. Dapper and relaxed, Xu spoke with the confidence of someone who has held high office but in his case without the edge that often appears when Chinese hold forth on Japan. Born in 1934 in Yangzhou, near Nanjing, where he went to the same middle school as Jiang Zemin, he harbored a young boy's memories of the war and its hardships. "When I was young, aged four, I wore my shoes to bed, because I thought I might have to flee," he recalled. "That memory cannot be removed easily."

Throughout his career, Xu had a frontline view of the bitter rifts over China policy within Japan: between the right wing and the left wing, within the Right, and within the bureaucracy, academia, and think tanks. "They were not minor; they were huge," he observed. "There were forces in Japan who supported friendship; there were forces who opposed friendship." In China, by contrast, he maintained that officials, scholars, and citizens were unified on the most sensitive issues in the bilateral relationship—history, Taiwan, and the disputed islands. "We speak with one voice," he said, "while on the future of the relationship and on the issue of Japanese militarism, there are differences of opinion."

Xu was correct in describing what outsiders can see of the debate on Japan within China. The "one voice" to which he referred was drummed into schoolchildren from a young age and enforced politically throughout the system. Any official, scholar, or newspaper editor who persistently spoke out of turn would have had a very short career. The "new thinking on Japan" movement that had emerged in the early years of the twenty-first century had all but been snuffed out. That meant that whatever internal schisms were visible within China were inevitably on the other side of the ledger. The infighting that could be seen from the outside was directed not at the government for being too tough on Japan. Rather, it was aimed at the government—or more precisely the Foreign Ministry—for not being tough enough.

No visitor to Tong's offices in Beijing could have departed with any doubt about his views. Although he was careful not to make direct criticisms of Chinese diplomats himself, he handed visitors a laudatory biography of him written by a friend, which contained evidence enough of his opinions. *Tong Zeng: Messenger of Peace* was filled with venomous and deeply personal attacks against the Foreign Ministry and its senior cadres for being soft on Japan. Numerous top officials, including three retired and serving foreign ministers, were identified by name and criticized for being "venal," "corrupt," "passive," "foul-mouthed," "weak," "deficient," "humiliating," "servile," and "obsequious."

Tong's diaries, quoted in the book, include his disparaging assessment of Wang Yi, who, at the time Tong's thoughts were recorded, had yet to become foreign minister. They were not the sorts of things Tong would dare express in public these days. "Once upon a time, a man called Wang Yi wants to become an official. . . . To become a senior official, he simply needs to apply in the area of Sino-Japanese relations, provided he gives up his principles." The diaries depict Wang as an ambitious climber, willing to give up the Diaoyu Islands and nearby oil fields in the East China Sea just to get on with Japan. Chinese diplomats, the book declares, "inevitably become the servant, losing pride in the values of their native Asia after being in contact with the culture and civilization of the West."

The most scurrilous sections of *Tong Zeng: Messenger of Peace* targeted another Japan expert, Tang Jiaxuan, the foreign minister and later state councillor under Hu Jintao in the first decade of the twenty-first century. They accuse Tang—and they are, effectively, accusations, whether they are true or not—of having relatives who collaborated with the Japanese puppet regime in the 1930s in Nanjing. Worse, the book claims that more recently Tang and his family made money from business connections in Japan, facilitated by his "modest Japanese wife." "Come and see what foreign minister there is here," the author writes. "If he can represent the Chinese from the waist down, how can he speak on stage facing the world?"

When I asked a Chinese scholar whether Tang was in fact married to a Japanese woman, his reply was instructive. He said not "That's wrong" but rather "Impossible!" An official of Tang's seniority, after all, is not permitted under the party's rules to be wed to a foreigner. Tang could never have been promoted within the party if he had a Japanese wife, modest or otherwise. The claim in the biography was pure slander, and emblematic of the nasty undercurrents of the debate in China, and the dangers facing any official who dealt closely with Japan.

Xu and other Foreign Ministry officials had long carried the burden within the system of tamping down the kind of anti-Japanese zealotry displayed in the Tong biography. Beginning in the 1980s, when students at Peking University protested against a visit by the then Japanese prime minister to Yasukuni Shrine, to the nationalization of the Senkaku/Diaoyu Islands in 2012, the authorities' playbook had been much the same: tighten control of the media; praise patriotism while demanding that it be expressed rationally; send in the police in numbers, if the trouble spills into the streets; and dispatch the diplomats, if the problems occur in more elite forums, like campuses.

There were times when the authorities let the protesters have their heads, but they were eventually always pulled into line. "When this problem arises, I always go on the media and to universities to talk about what real patriotism is," Xu explained. "I tell them what's right and what's wrong, and I tell them, you are not supporting China; you are smearing China." Tong, at least when talking to me, maintained a similar position. "I am strongly against the nationalist campaigns against the Japanese as a whole," he said. "But if there is one country that the Chinese people are angry at, it is Japan."

Tong, however, played both sides of the street. He claimed to dissent from the nationalists while at the same time handing out books slandering Chinese diplomats for selling out their country to Japan. The biography attacking China's Japan experts that he handed out to visitors was published in English, and in Hong Kong, rather than in Chinese, in China, to minimize any trouble it could cause him at home. Tong's courage, like that of any survivor in the Chinese system, went only so far.

A few months after meeting Tong Zeng, I flew along from Los Angeles to Tokyo aboard Air Force Three, on the last overseas trip of Ash Carter, Obama's fourth, and final, secretary of defense. The itinerary of Carter's two-week trip in December 2016 took in the vast sweep of America's global military interests and all of the expectations that come with them. At each stop was a different ally or partner, some new and some decades old, each with a different set of needs, demands, and sensitivities to manage, now all the more complicated following the election weeks beforehand of Donald Trump. The itinerary was also a reminder that forging, building, managing, and sustaining alliances and other partnerships had been one of America's greatest skills in the postwar era.

The first stop of Carter's trip was Japan, from where he would proceed to India, Afghanistan, Bahrain, Baghdad, Israel, and Italy, ending in the United States' traditional ally, the United Kingdom. With such a crowded schedule, the Pentagon's traveling doctor walked the aisles of the plane on the first leg to Tokyo handing out sleeping pills to anyone who asked for them. In the small area where the press corps were seated, one wide-screen television tracked the plane's passage across the Pacific Ocean, while the other showed an NFL game live.

Before he set out, Carter had spoken at an annual defense conference held at the Ronald Reagan Library near Los Angeles. An Oxford-educated theoretical physicist, Carter was the most accomplished technocrat of his generation, rising to the top of the Pentagon as "the ultimate budget and acquisitions" guy, in the words of one profile. He delivered two speeches at the Reagan event. One was in acceptance of the Peace Through Strength award presented annually by the conference, which is sponsored mostly by arms contractors. "All part of team America," said Carter, approvingly, of his hosts. The other, longer speech was a *tour d'horizon* of U.S. global security interests and challenges.

Like most speeches at such expositions, Carter's speech first traversed Washington's most pressing frontline military engagements, first in Iraq and Afghanistan, then to a NATO facing a resurgent Russia, and finally in the Asia-Pacific. Always touted as the most important region of the world for the United States, the area usually got the least attention, because it was invariably the most peaceful. Measured by the military commitments on both sides, let alone by what is at stake, though, Japan is America's most important defense alliance, a fact not readily apparent to anyone following the day-to-day media coverage in the United States.

Carter's emphasis in his speech was similar to the views expressed by Obama in office, in stressing how Pax Americana had anchored "economic miracle after miracle" in Asia. "Populations are growing, education has improved, freedom and self-determination have spread, economies have grown more interconnected, and military spending and cooperation are both increasing," he said. Carter delivered a comparable message once he landed in Japan twelve hours later, although the focus was subtly different, not so much about U.S. military spending as about Japan's.

Carter spent his first morning in Japan on the *Izumo,* the largest naval vessel built by Japan since its surrender in the Pacific War, stationed at Yokosuka, south of Tokyo. For a defense secretary trying to highlight the pivot to Asia, or the rebalance, as the Pentagon preferred to call it, there could hardly have been a better symbol—a 248-meter-long vessel, commissioned in 2010 and completed in 2013 and stationed at a port that was America's largest overseas naval base.

Even better, the vessel had been built by the Japanese, an ally that has traditionally been reluctant to parade its military prowess. That reluctance was evident in the way that the boat was classified. The Japanese called the *Izumo* a "helicopter destroyer," a name that many naval experts thought cloaked the fact that the boat had the dimensions and capabilities of an aircraft carrier. The Chinese, naturally, had a darker view, noting that the *Izumo* was the "namesake of a Japanese cruiser used during the invasion of China in the early 20th century." (Japanese warships had in fact always been named after old administrative divisions of the country.)

The port where the *Izumo* was docked, Yokosuka, was itself a remarkable symbol of the longevity of the alliance between once bitter enemies. Founded in 1868 as imperial Japan's naval headquarters, the port was handed over to the United States after Tokyo's surrender in 1945. Since then, Yokosuka has been under American control as the base for the U.S. Seventh Fleet. In reality, these days it operates as a joint facility, befitting the growing intimacy of the alliance. For Pax Americana, the port is an invaluable resource, with a permanent skilled workforce who repair and maintain the ships. It is a facility that would be hard to replicate anywhere else in the world, let alone in Asia. As one U.S. naval officer sardonically noted, "We couldn't do this in Karachi."

Standing on the *Izumo*'s broad deck with Japan's top defense bureaucrat by his side, Carter stressed the single message that he carried throughout his trip: the strength of the alliance and its mutual benefits. "This is a two-way street," he said. "We provide enhanced security to one another." His Trump-appointed successor, General James Mattis, said much the same on his first trip as defense secretary, to Japan, in February 2017, calling the two countries' cost-sharing deal to pay for the stationing of U.S. troops a model for other nations.

The way that Carter and Mattis spoke about the Asia-Pacific was telling. They were both, in different ways, rebuking Trump for his charges of Japanese freeloading. They both represented the Pentagon's institutional view of the value of the alliance, no matter who was in the White House. But the fact that they felt the need to make such forthright statements reflected the existential dread gripping pro-U.S. governments in east Asia. America's allies and partners feared Trump represented not just a rollback of the pivot but the harbinger of something much more destabilizing, a withdrawal from the region altogether.

While the United States was a global superpower, China, for all its worldly ambitions, wanted only to extend its dominance to the countries, and seas, around it. As the Chinese often liked to remind their neighbors, the U.S. presence in Asia was a geopolitical choice. China's presence in Asia, by contrast, was a geopolitical reality. From the 1990s onward, China had systematically and largely successfully worked to settle its land borders with the fourteen states adjacent to it. The disputes on its maritime flank were more difficult to manage, and not just because Beijing's claims were so outlandish and conflicted with those of so many of its neighbors. To dominate Asia, China still had to marginalize the United States.

When I met Ben Rhodes, Obama's foreign policy communications chief, in the White House a month before Donald Trump was elected, he was not particularly concerned by China's advances in the South and East China Seas. "It should not be a test of American strength whenever China builds some outputs on the Paracels or harasses some fishing boats," he said. This, or course, was precisely China's calculation—that each of its actions on its own would not provoke an American response. Rhodes was unmoved by the criticism that the administration had been outmaneuvered by the Chinese. "Obama has always taken a more measured view than is sometimes expressed in this town. He has said that he expects that China is going to have some space. I think he even said they were going to be the biggest and most powerful country in the region. We have to kind of calibrate our approach on things that are clearly of concern to us, like freedom of navigation and the alliances. Those are our core interests," he said. "China is, in fact, pushing our allies closer to us."

Elsewhere in the administration, though, there was more angst about the American response to Beijing's rise in Asia. The Obama administration was caught short in early 2014, when the first reports emerged of China's dredging operations around the Spratly Islands, a collection of small islands and reefs contested by Beijing as well as Vietnam, Malaysia, the Philippines, Brunei, and Taiwan, in the South China Sea. "We collectively underestimated the magnitude of the operation," said one official. "At first it was novel, kind of like, 'What the hell are they doing?'" Before long, though, Beijing had built massive artificial islands in the area, featuring three-thousand-meter-long runways, deep harbors, and hangars reinforced to house dozens of jets and bombers. In the words of one U.S. military officer, "They look like major fighter bases in the making."

Subsequently, the administration's critics claimed, the decisions to sail U.S. naval ships through the areas claimed by China—freedom-of-navigation operations intended to uphold the right to sail through international waters—were tardy, infrequent, and poorly explained. While America's regional allies did look to the United States for leadership on the issue, as Rhodes said, they weren't always happy with what they saw. Asian diplomats complained privately that Obama and John Kerry were more focused on striking a deal on climate change with China than taking a stand in the South China Sea. The U.S. officials who did speak up—notably Admiral Harry Harris, who headed military operations in the Asia-Pacific—were warned to watch their words. In testimony to Congress, Harris had said that China was "clearly militarizing" the disputed waters. "You'd have to believe in a flat earth to think otherwise." The White House was not happy with Harris's forcefulness, which officials viewed as an effort to maneuver the president into a tougher position.

The White House, in turn, did toughen its line. By late 2015 and 2016, U.S. intelligence was warning that China was readying more construction in the South China Sea, this time at the Scarborough Shoal, near the Philippines. Chinese dredging ships were spotted near the reefs, along with naval vessels, all "red flashing lights" for an administration determined not to be caught short again. Remaining mute over construction in an area claimed by the Philippines, a U.S. treaty ally, was untenable. Washington remembered with bitterness that Beijing had reneged on the deal it had negotiated in the 2012 standoff between Manila and Beijing, when the Philippines' vessels left the Scarborough Shoal area, as agreed, while the Chinese vessels remained.

In a March 2016 meeting in Washington, Obama laid down a red line for Xi: We understand that we both have vital interests at stake, he told the Chinese leader, but the United States has obligations to its allies, and we take them seriously. It would be a historic tragedy, Obama added, if we were to fall into conflict in protecting these interests. The president wanted an understanding with Xi that Beijing would not try to turn the Scarborough Shoal into another Chinese island outpost. The timing of Obama's warning was significant, because in a few months an international court was scheduled to rule on Manila's challenge to Beijing's expansive claims in the South China Sea. Xi remained noncommittal in the meeting, but if China did have construction plans, they were, after Obama's warning, shelved.

Obama was almost always calm and cautious in his eight years as president, in public and in private, maddeningly so for his critics, many of whom thought the president needlessly cast aside military firepower as an instrument of diplomacy. In his public comments, Obama often dismissed anyone who pressed for military solutions as warmongers. In response, his critics claimed Obama was weak, or, more kindly, had overlearned the lessons of the second Iraq war to the point of paralysis in foreign policy. In Asia, they said, Obama spent too much time reassuring China rather than America's Asian allies.

The temperamental disconnect was especially pronounced with Tokyo, an ironic role reversal given that the United States had traditionally been typecast as the overbearing bully in the relationship, always demanding more of the reluctant, supposedly pacifist Japanese. It was a criticism that Obama's advisers resented. In truth, they said the record showed that

Obama had been steadfast in backing Japan and was the first U.S. president to publicly commit to defending the Senkaku Islands under the mutual defense treaty. "Obama takes hits for not being tough enough," said one of his advisers, "but he has always been unflinching in standing up for Japan." The crude way that Chinese propaganda organs reported on Obama's departure from office adds weight to this view. The *People's Daily* declared that America's "decaying credibility in east Asia" should have made it clear to Trump that Obama's pivot would "never pay off," especially where the Senkaku/Diaoyu Islands were concerned.

The pivot to Asia, though, ended with a whimper following the collapse of the Trans-Pacific Partnership. The military leg of the rebalance had been underwhelming. The economic leg didn't survive at all. In the 2016 election campaign, Trump trashed the agreement relentlessly, and Hillary Clinton, who had strongly supported it as secretary of state, ran a mile from the deal. In the end, Obama didn't even bother to push for a vote on Capitol Hill, and Trump formally dumped it within days of taking office. For Japan, it was a devastating outcome. "The U.S. withdrawal from T.P.P. was the biggest shock to the alliance since Nixon went to China," said Yoichi Funabashi, Japan's preeminent foreign policy commentator.

Japanese prime ministers have always tried to be among the first foreigners to call on a new American president, but they usually waited until after the inauguration. After Trump's election, Shinzō Abe was in New York barely a week later. He had good reason to be in a hurry. Compared with "no drama" Obama, Trump was unpredictable and volatile, potentially the worst kind of ally. His ideas about trade, and his belief that foreigners were taking advantage of the United States, were formed in the 1980s, when Japan was viewed as the economic enemy, not China. Trump's election had triggered panic in a Japan that already feared it was being slowly ground down by Beijing. However much Trump had criticized Japan over the decades, Tokyo had no choice but to work with whoever was in power in Washington. "We need America; we cannot handle China on our own," an adviser to Abe told me.

As with most visitors doing the rounds in Tokyo during the postelection period, I was regaled with the latest details of China's efforts to slowly strangle Japan's control over the Senkaku/Diaoyu Islands. By then, the Chinese coast guard was patrolling around the islands, just

outside the territorial waters, twenty-four hours a day, in three shifts.
Every ten days or so, one of the Chinese vessels would slip into Japanese
territorial waters around the islands. Only a few years earlier, the Japanese had viewed the Chinese boats as being of relatively low quality and
their sailors ill-disciplined. "They were always smoking on decks, and the
boats were rusting," one official said. That was no longer the case. The
Chinese patrols had quickly developed into highly disciplined operations. Like most items manufactured in China, the boats' quality had
improved. New vessels were coming off the production lines with the
speed that perhaps only China, as the proverbial workshop of the world,
could manage. In 2012, Japan had had about 50 coast guard vessels to
China's 40. Now the ratio was about 120 to 60 in China's favor. Elsewhere, with ever-increasing frequency, Japanese fighter planes were also
being scrambled to track Chinese jets in the Miyako Strait.

This trend, of more and better disciplined Chinese boats, some attached to the navy and some the highly militarized coast guard, was ominous for Japan. For many years, a Japanese diplomat in Tokyo's Beijing
embassy had been designated to call his Chinese counterpart each morning to protest the Chinese presence around the islands. When Chinese
boats made incursions into Japanese territorial waters, the complaints were
delivered with greater vehemence, and at higher levels. Over and over
again, the Japanese objected, but to no effect. China simply pressed ahead.

For Japan, China's brazen breaches of its sovereignty were humiliating. Imagine if Japan behaved in a similar manner in its own territorial
quarrels, Kazuhiko Togo, a retired senior diplomat, observed. Tokyo and
Seoul both claim the Dokdo/Takeshima Islands. Tokyo is also in dispute
with Moscow over the Northern Territories, at the tip of Hokkaido,
which Joseph Stalin's Red Army grabbed in the last days of World War II.
"If we had sent our coast guard ships to the islands disputed with Russia
and South Korea to demonstrate our claims, they would have sunk our
boats immediately," Togo said. "China has been doing it for three years,
and we have not sunk a thing. It is an impossible situation. The current
situation is a diplomatic disaster for us."

In the weeks leading up to Trump's swearing in, China was engaged
in almost daily military forays near the Senkaku/Diaoyu Islands region.
Its sole aircraft carrier, the *Liaoning*, led battleships through the Miyako
Strait, south of Okinawa, for its first voyage into the western Pacific. The

carrier battle group returned to port through the narrow Taiwan Strait, a message to Taipei's anti-reunification president to stay in line. In a show of force for the United States, Chinese bombers flew a number of missions over the Spratly Islands. In the words of James Fanell, the former naval intelligence officer, "The heat in the pool just keeps going up one degree at a time."

The sense of foreboding in Japan could easily be gauged from newspaper coverage during the period that Ash Carter was in Tokyo. Stories discussing the aging demographic were everywhere. One longtime American visitor to Japan recalled how he used to go to the top of the Skytree, the tallest structure in Tokyo, with its 360-degree view over the densely populated Kanto Plain, to remind himself of the coming crunch. In three decades or so, based on current projections, the equivalent of the thirty million population of greater Tokyo visible from the tower—about a quarter of the nation's current population—will have vanished.

After numerous fatal accidents involving aged drivers, some with dementia, one newspaper report recounted the government's efforts to persuade elderly people to surrender their licenses. Other headlines recorded the spike in nursing home deaths. Another, more poignant story, in the *Yomiuri Shimbun,* the mass-selling daily, detailed the upswing in the number of lonely elderly people finding solace in interactive stuffed animals. One of these gadgets, when patted on the back, took on the voice of a four-year-old to offer advice like "It's hot. You should drink a lot of water."

By the end of the Obama administration, Sino-Japanese relations had thawed only slightly from the deep freeze they went into in 2012. Xi Jinping and Shinzō Abe met on a number of occasions, largely because the Chinese leader couldn't avoid his Japanese counterpart at global and regional summits—at Hangzhou, at the G20 gathering in September 2016, and a few months later at the APEC meeting in Peru. The constant, deliberate slights, though, directed by each side against the other, as well as the dangerous jostling at sea around the disputed islands and in the air between their air forces, were evidence that the two countries were at best enjoying a kind of cold peace.

In June 2016, after a Chinese naval vessel in tandem with Russian destroyers entered what Tokyo claimed as its territorial waters around the Senkaku/Diaoyu Islands, the Foreign Ministry summoned the Chinese ambassador to lodge a protest. The manner of the summons seemed to be a deliberate, pointed replication of what the Chinese had done to Japanese diplomats, and those of other countries, whenever they wanted to make a point. Instead of waiting until normal business hours, the Japanese ordered the Chinese ambassador out of bed at 2:00 a.m. to come to the Foreign Ministry in Tokyo for an immediate dressing-down. The Japanese official who conveyed the message said the Chinese ambassador had been dragged in early in the morning because of the possible threat of a military clash. The intrusion of a naval vessel was inherently more dangerous than one from the coast guard. The Chinese ambassador noted the symmetry of the timing of the summons when he arrived at the Foreign Ministry, but waved it away.

A few months later, in August, there was another flurry of activity around the islands with the appearance of Chinese fishing and coast guard vessels. This time, the Chinese ambassador was beckoned for a reprimand after sunrise. The Chinese Foreign Ministry officials I met later the same day in Beijing were seething nonetheless. They complained that the Japanese had made the ambassador wait for eight minutes, alone and in front of the assembled media pack and their mass of cameras, before he was received for a lengthy lecture. In their eyes, it was a calculated humiliation.

The Chinese played the same game at the G20 meetings in Hangzhou. In the space of one day, Xi met with the leaders of South Korea, Germany, Spain, and the United Kingdom, on each occasion posing for a photograph with them, in accordance with protocol, in front of their flags. Abe, by contrast, was received in a smaller, shabby room without his country's flag. The *People's Daily* played up the contrast by running all five photographs on the same page, with the picture of Abe pointedly featured at the bottom of the page. China called it a "working meeting" rather than an "official meeting," which amounted to a diplomatic downgrade. As petty as it all sounded, Beijing went out of its way to make clear that it was doing no more than acceding to a Japanese request that a meeting take place. "They have to make Abe appear like a vassal," one of the prime minister's advisers told me.

As it had done for a number of years, in the summer of 2016, the Japanese embassy in Beijing sent out an e-mail to citizens who had registered with it as living in China. "August and September are months when public attention could easily turn to Japan," it said. "We ask all citizens to act cautiously and to avoid becoming embroiled in trouble through careless political statements." The statement was timed to coincide with the annual commemorations of the end of the war, when an ill-considered word from Japan could trigger uproar, either real or confected. But the fear of blowback was about more than just the anniversaries. As the diplomatic reprimands demonstrated, under Abe's leadership Japan had decided the only viable policy to pursue with China was firmness at every juncture. Tokyo's view was best summed up by one of Abe's advisers, who said that despite Japan's apologies, aid, and effort to build closer ties over four decades, "We got nothing!"

The Chinese, of course, felt much the same way. They believed they had been generous to Japan and likewise got nothing in return. At the Foreign Ministry in Beijing, the diplomat in charge of managing day-to-day relations with Tokyo was frank about the difficulties of his job. He pointed to one of China's current regional problems in the South China Sea, where Indonesia had been impounding foreign fishing boats, including Chinese vessels, caught in its territorial waters. The Indonesian maritime and fisheries minister, in a popular publicity stunt, had been packing the boats with dynamite and spectacularly blowing them up for television. Beijing had lodged protests but done little more. "If the Japanese had done that, the people would have been in the streets in China; if the Americans had done it, the general public would have maintained a different attitude; it is always more sensitive with Japan," the diplomat said. "The people say, Japan has been the worst to us in all of Chinese history; with Japan, you touch on the softest and most fragile part of Chinese psychology."

Certainly, it was always more sensitive with Japan, but in many ways China's own propaganda apparatus continued to guarantee that would be the case. The Chinese system never ceased to spew out anti-Japanese bile. One of Beijing's targets in 2016 was Shunji Yanai, who after retiring from the top position in Japan's Foreign Ministry became president of the International Tribunal for the Law of the Sea. When the Philippines brought a case against China, Beijing refused to participate in the proceedings and thus forfeited its ability to help nominate judges for the panel hearing the case. In Beijing's absence, Yanai, as the tribunal's president, was required to appoint the judges himself. When Beijing lost the case in 2016, the attacks on Yanai didn't come just in the form of faceless editorials in official newspapers. In an interview posted on the Foreign

Ministry's Web site a day after the ruling, Yang Jiechi, the state councillor for foreign affairs, claimed that Yanai was at the head of a conspiracy in the selection of judges and called him "a right-wing Japanese intent on ridding Japan of postwar arrangements. Anyone with good sense can see the tricks." That was just one of many assaults over the coming days, portraying Yanai as the rightist "manipulator" behind an "illegal" decision and someone who was close to Abe and pro-American.

Another target was Admiral Harris, whose hawkishness the Chinese linked to the fact that his mother was Japanese. "Some may say an overemphasis on the Japanese background about an American general is a bit unkind," said Xinhua, the official news agency. "But it is simply impossible to ignore Admiral Harris's blood, background, political inclination and values." Shortly before Christmas 2016, a shopping mall in Shenyang, in northeast China, erected likenesses of world leaders, including Barack Obama and Vladimir Putin. It also featured a statue of Abe, but with a Hitler mustache, bowing against the background of Chinese characters about the war. The mall, which said the statues had been erected to "enrich the shopping experience of customers," removed the Abe statue a few days later.

Obama's last bilateral meeting was with Abe in Hawaii, where the two men commemorated the casualties from the notorious Japanese attack on the U.S. naval base at Pearl Harbor. Months earlier, Abe had hosted Obama in Hiroshima. On one level, the two ceremonies illustrated how much shrewder Abe had become about managing the history wars. While he gave no indication of changing his revisionist views on the conflict and Japan's responsibility for it, he no longer made emotional, off-the-cuff, and damaging statements about the comfort women and the like. In their place, in Hawaii, he offered heartfelt tributes to the dead in both countries.

Abe's main focus in managing the history wars was assuaging the United States, followed by South Korea, where Japan had worked hard to address the comfort women issue. Abe had judged, probably correctly, that Beijing still wanted to receive apologies but wasn't willing to accept them. After his Pearl Harbor speech, the Chinese snarled from the sidelines. "Can a so-called victim-consolation trip to Pearl Harbor completely wipe away World War II history?" a government spokeswoman in Beijing asked. "I am afraid it's just wishful thinking on his part." As if to confirm Beijing's doubts, Japan's defense minister, Tomomi Inada, undid much of the good of Abe's Hawaii visit by going to Yasukuni Shrine a few days later. Inada had made her name as a supporter of numerous war revisionist movements, including those denying the Nanjing Massacre.

Abe's commitment to work closely with the United States at the time has stood in stark contrast with the hurly-burly elsewhere in Asia. The Philippines has flipped, for the moment, from a close U.S. ally to cultivating China following the election of a new anti-American president, Rodrigo Duterte, in 2016. The 2014 Thai military coup cooled relations with Washington. In Australia, long one of America's closest regional allies, political and business elites were deeply divided over moving closer to the country's chief economic partner, China, at the expense of the U.S. alliance. The Malaysian prime minister, Najib Razak, a onetime golf partner of Obama's, had been courting China, in part in anger at U.S. investigations implicating him in a money-laundering probe at a state investment fund. In South Korea, the impeachment of President Park Geun-hye, in December 2016, cleared the way for a more pro-China replacement.

None of these anti-American trends were set in stone. Trump, who has exhibited little concern over human rights, called Duterte both before and after his inauguration to invite him to the White House and also congratulated him on doing an "unbelievable job" in his war on drugs, which had seen about seven thousand vigilante murders. Equally, Trump seemed willing to set aside concerns about the Thai coup and make peace with Bangkok. Most Australians still favored strong ties with the United States. Ethnic Malays, who dominate the country's politics, remained deeply suspicious of China and their own ethnic Chinese citizens. And in Seoul, whoever is in power will have to deal with the threat from North Korea, an issue that Trump pledged to work on with China. Still, after more than four years in office, Abe, whom Ash Carter praised for his "leadership and statesmanship," represented the kind of stability that the United States craved in Asia and that now looked as if it was slipping away.

The web of American alliances and partnerships in Asia used to be referred to as a "hub and spokes" model, with the United States at the center of a series of bilateral relationships. This reflected not only American preeminence but also the fact that Washington often had better ties with Asian nations than they had with one another. The rise of China and the growth of intra-Asian trade, however, along with Obama's Asia pivot, fostered a whole new set of relationships that changed the regional security landscape. Instead of a single hub-and-spoke model, there were multiple coalitions, some involving the United States and many others exclusively within the region itself.

Japan had strengthened ties with India, Vietnam, the Philippines, and Australia and, in the shadow of Pyongyang's nuclear capability, managed to persuade South Korea to finally complete an intelligence-sharing agreement. There were multiple other bonds, in the form of dialogues and military exercises, between India and Australia, Australia and Singapore, Vietnam and India, Vietnam and the Philippines, and so on. In an interview aboard Air Force Three, Carter observed that the proliferation of new associations had been "part of the design" of the rebalance from the start. He said that he usually referred to these new relationships as "networks" rather than alliances, adding, "The word is chosen advisedly. We have encouraged relationships that do not involve us. When you see India and Australia and Japan exercising together, they got that concept from exercises organized by the U.S. in decades past. We created the template."

Prior to Trump's emergence, just about any scenario for the United States in east Asia assumed there would be broad continuity for the core elements of past policy, including trade liberalization and a commitment to alliances. In his campaign and his early months in office, Trump sent contradictory signals, in favor of retrenchment and every country fending for itself, leaning toward supporting allies like Japan once he gained office and trying to cultivate China's Xi Jinping.

In many ways, the split reflected the divisions on Trump's staff in his early months in the White House, between the economic nationalists and the mainstream globalists. One senior adviser, Stephen Bannon, called Trump's decision to withdraw the United States from the Trans-Pacific Partnership almost immediately after his inauguration "one of the most pivotal moments in modern American history." Once Abe had a chance to sit down with Trump, though, the U.S. president was more accommodating, at least on strategic issues. In part, that was because of pressure from advisers, such as his daughter Ivanka, who persuaded her reluctant father to stand by Obama's commitment for the United States to help defend the Senkaku Islands from attack. It was also the result, at times, of Trump's own vanities. When Trump was presented with a joint statement in February 2017 to be issued with Abe from the White House, a draft that the Japanese had largely authored on their own, he asked for just one change to the text. In place of "Donald Trump," the president said it should read "Donald J. Trump."

Even if Trump accepted that the United States, for the moment, had to abide by its treaty obligations to Japan and other regional allies, he never made the argument, during the campaign, or in office, as to why it should. On the question of the other "Thucydides trap"—the principle that it is dangerous to build an empire but more dangerous to let it go— Trump had seemed quite unconcerned; that was something for other countries to worry about. Far from fretting about Japan's ability to defend itself against China, Trump seemed to believe it would do fine, given its past record against its neighbor.

In an interview with the *Economist* in September 2015, at a time when few pundits and political professionals gave him a chance of winning the Republican primary, let alone the White House, Trump discussed Asia at length. He spoke of his angst at seeing thousands of imported Japanese cars unloaded at the port in Los Angeles—"just pouring off these ships, and I am saying to myself, we send them beef, it's a tiny fraction, and, by the way, they don't even want it." He declared Abe to be a "great leader" while decrying Caroline Kennedy, who was then the U.S. ambassador to Tokyo. "Who is our chief negotiator? Essentially it is Caroline Kennedy. I mean, give me a break. She doesn't even know she's alive." He complained about having to order four thousand Samsung television sets because he couldn't find any made at home, although he did give himself credit for driving a hard bargain on the purchase price.

When he got onto the subject of Japan and China, after making the usual protestations ("By the way, I love China. I love Japan"), Trump was asked what would happen if China started bullying its neighbors without the United States being there to protect them. He was unfazed at the prospect of leaving Japan on its own, casting his mind back to more than a century earlier, when Japan and China began to fall into conflict.

"If we step back, they will protect themselves very well," Trump said. "Remember when Japan used to beat China routinely in wars? You know that, right? Japan used to beat China, they routinely beat China. Why are we defending [them at all]?"

Acknowledgments

Writing books, as this project reminded me, requires extreme selfishness on the part of the author, while demanding exceptional generosity from everyone else. The subjects, and the targets, of the research, and family and friends, are all expected to fall into line, while the author goes about his, or her, business. Thus, it's only natural that there should be many people to thank for getting this book written and out the door.

First, the Woodrow Wilson Center for Scholars in Washington gave me a yearlong fellowship. There can be no better place to write a book. My only complaint is that the fellowship didn't last two years. Robert Daly, the director of the Kissinger Institute on China and the United Stsates, and Robert Litwak, who runs the scholars' program, offered every support and encouragement, as did Stapleton Roy, Shihoko Goto, and Sandy Pho. Robert Daly also read the manuscript. Chuck Kraus, at the Cold War International History Project, housed within the Wilson Center, was endlessly helpful. The project itself has built a treasure trove of invaluable documentation, and long may it last.

I am indebted to David Shambaugh, who first suggested filling an empty office at the Sigur Center for Asian Studies at George Washington University, and Bruce Dickson, who made it happen. Both have produced exceptional books of their own in recent years, and my time there was invaluable. While there, I also enjoyed chatting with Robert Sutter. David also made some valuable comments on the manuscript.

I would like to single out some great libraries and librarians. The Wilson Center library, led by Janet Spikes, with Michelle Kamalich and Katherine Wahler, was very helpful. It also benefits from access to the great Library of Congress. I returned for the first time in two decades to the library at the Foreign Correspondents Club in Tokyo and was thrilled to get my hands dirty leafing through their folders of dusty, sepia-edged newspaper clippings, just like the old days.

Finally, I would not have been able to do the necessary research for the book, including multiple trips to Japan and China, without the generous support of the Smith Richardson Foundation and its program officer, Allan Song. I am thankful for the foundation's help.

Thanks to various people who read all or some of the book as a work in progress, including Bob Suettinger, Alexis Dudden, Jim Mann, Steve Tsang, Bruce Jacobs, Jamil Anderlini, Isaac Kardon, Alex McGregor, and Jacob Schlesinger. Ezra Vogel, who is working on a China-Japan book of this own, and Rick Dyke, both steeped in the history of Sino-Japanese relations, took time to read the whole manuscript and made many worthwhile suggestions. Akio Takahara's close read was invaluable. Mike Green and Kurt Campbell were both supportive of the project from the beginning and also read slabs of the book. Likewise, Yoichi Funabashi, who has blazed a trail in reporting on Japan's relations with the United States and Asia, and Don Keyser offered pungent comments on an early draft and were generous with advice at the project's outset.

In the course of research, I would like to thank, in no particular order, Akihisa Nagashima, Andrew Krepinevich, Ash Carter, Ben Rhodes, Robert Hormats, the late Bu Ping, Charles Schmitz, Chen Jian, Chip Goodson, Chris Padilla, Chu Shulong, Dan Blumenthal, Dan Kritenbrink, Daniel Russel, David Loevinger, Dennis Wilder, Dennis Blair, Derek Chollet, Doug Paal, Evan Medeiros, Evans Revere, Glen S. Fukushima, Gui Yongtao, Hans Dieter Schweisgut, Hideaki Kase, Hidehiro Konno, Hitoshi Tanaka, James Fanell, Jeff Bader, Jeff Prescott, Jim Steinberg, Jin Linbo, Tong Zeng, Toshiya Tsugami, Victor Yuan, Wendy Cutler, Winston Lord, Xie Tao, Xu Dunxin, Yang Bojiang, Yang Yu, Yasuo Fukuda, Yuji Miyamoto, Zhou Yongsheng, Zhu Jianrong, Akitaka Saiki, Joe Donovan, Jon Huntsman, Kathleen Hicks, Katsuya Okada, Kazuhiko Togo, James Keith, Andrew Saibel, Kenichiro Sasae, Kevin Maher, Kuni Miyake, Kunihiko Makita, Larry Summers, Kevin Rudd, Liang Yanxiang, Liu Jiangyong, Ma Licheng, Matthew Goodman, Michael Schiffer, Nobukatsu Kanehara, Paul Giarra, Paul Keating, Qian Chengdan, Richard Armitage, the late Richard Solomon, Rust Deming,

Sadaaki Numata, Sakutaro Tanino, Seiji Maehara, Shi Yinhong, Rory MacFarquhar, Shintaro Ishihara, Stapleton Roy, Tatsumi Okabe, Tim Geithner, Andrew Shearer, and Ruan Congze.

Many people I spoke to for this book, especially but not only in China, did not want to be quoted by name, for obvious reasons, so I salute them in anonymity. Having said that, the Foreign Ministry in Beijing did make a number of retired and serving officials available to talk with me in August 2016, and I am grateful for that. The Japanese Foreign Ministry and a number of its diplomats were very generous with their time.

For their help, suggestions, chatter, introductions, referrals, hospitality, clarifying e-mails, writings, and so forth, I would also like to thank Hugh White, Frances Adamson, David Ellis, John Delury, Bud Cole, Cynthia Watson, Jeff Kingston, Stephen Harner, Keiko Iizuka, Wang Yingyao, Jane Perlez, Michael Thawley, Hiroyasu Izumi, Dimon Liu, Stephen Harder, Chris Buckley, Rowan Callick, John Garnaut, Xu Xiaonian, Boer Deng, Bill Breer, Go Eguchi, Masato Otaka, Yasuyuki Sugiura, Ryozo Kato, Chris Johnson, Narushige Michishita, Gary Bass, Ely Ratner, Tobias Harris, Kim Beazley, Cheng Li, Joerg Wuttke, Tony Abbott, Dinny McMahon, David McNeil, Martin Fackler, Ryosei Kokubun, Robert Tomkin, Daniel Twining, Gerry Curtis, Clyde Prestowitz, John Pomfret, Elizabeth Hague, Ben Goldberg, Kevin Nealer, Robin Harding, Bruce Miller, Evan Osnos, Gideon Rachman, Geoff Dyer, Tom Mitchell, Edward Luce, Eric Heginbotham, Liu Weimin, Takako Hikotani, Tamaki Tsukada, Richard Lawless, and David Lague. My former colleagues at the *Financial Times* Demetri Sevastopolo and Lucy Hornby were generous with advice, materials, and introductions. James Lamont was helpful in arranging time off from the paper to pursue the project. I would also like to pay tribute to the *FT,* which was a great home for fifteen years, in Shanghai, Beijing, London, and Washington.

Compared with many scholarly books on this and related topics, mine will feel like a will-o'-the-wisp effort. The authors whose books and papers helped pave the way include Robert Hoppens, Andrew Oros, He Yinan, Gilbert Rozman, Jessica Chen Weiss, Tag Murphy, Thomas Berger, Richard Bush, John Welfield, Kenneth Pyle, June Teufel Dreyer, Tsuyoshi Sunohara, Yang Daqing, Wang Zheng, Robert Eldridge, Shu Guang Zhang, Ming Wan, Michael Schaller, Robert Boynton, James

Reilly, Amy King (who also read the opening chapters), Sheila Smith, James Manicom, and Michael Yahuda.

For help in digging out nuggets and arranging interviews, thanks to Wang Suya in Beijing and Huang Yufan. In Japan, thanks to Chieko Tsuneoka, who has all but written many of the books about Japanese politics by foreigners; Taeko Kawamura; Hiroshi Oseda; and Naoto Okamura. In Washington, special thanks to Dong Mengyu and Han Bao, as well as to Lucy Song, Takao Kaka, and Aviva Liu.

For all the professed interest in China, books about the country and its politics still aren't an easy sell. The same goes even more for Japan. I am thankful once again to my agents, Gail Ross in Washington and Felicity Bryan in the UK, for putting their shoulders to the wheel to secure publishing deals, and to Rick Kot in New York and Thomas Penn in London for signing on and taking their job of editing seriously. Their efforts vastly improved the manuscript. Diego Núñez helped shepherd the book through the final stages along with the production team, Bruce Giffords, Nancy Resnick, Jason Ramirez, and Jeffrey Ward. Like most authors, I feel compelled to note, sadly, that the responsibility for any errors is mine alone.

Finally, I could not have done this without the love and support of my family. First, I owe a great debt to my wife, Kath Cummins, whose insights I often store away for possible future plagiarism. Thanks also to my children: to Cate for her endless encouragement, and to Angus for yelling at me to stay off Twitter and get back to writing. For authors, this is universally good advice.

Washington, D.C., April 2017

Notes

Preface

xv **the scene in the movie *Reservoir Dogs:*** The scene, ironically enough, was inspired by a 1987 Hong Kong movie, *City on Fire,* https://litreactor.com/columns/5-movies-that -influenced-quentin-tarantinos-reservoir-dogs.

xvi **"As Michael Green . . . notes":** Michael J. Green, *By More Than Providence: Grand Strategy and American Power in the Asia Pacific Since 1783* (Columbia University Press, 2017), 1.

xvi **Once, Beijing begrudgingly:** See Adam P. Liff, "China and the US Alliance System," *The China Quarterly,* 1–29, April 2017, https://www.cambridge.org/core/journals/china -quarterly/article/china-and-the-us-alliance-system/1FF369905B4A8110DC8693A3C8 A7857B/core-reader.

xvii **shut for a "system upgrade":** See Maura Cunningham, "Denying Historians: China's Archives Increasingly Off-Bounds," *Wall Street Journal,* Aug. 19, 2014, http://blogs .wsj.com/chinarealtime/2014/08/19/denying-historians-chinas-archives-increasingly-off -bounds/.

Introduction

2 **Xi veered off script:** Based on interviews with people in the meeting and officials briefed on its contents.

3 **the Athens and the Rome of east Asia:** A. Doak Barnett, *China and the Major Powers in East Asia* (Brookings Institution Press, 1977), 90.

3 **Japan and China have demanded:** June Teufel Dreyer makes a similar point in her book *Middle Kingdom and the Empire of the Rising Sun: Sino-Japanese Relations, Past and Present* (Oxford University Press, 2016).

3 **"interdependence and autonomy":** See Akira Iriye, ed., *The Chinese and the Japanese: Essays in Political and Cultural Interactions* (Princeton Legacy Library, 1980), 3.

5 **"thinking about how to kill Americans":** Jeffrey Goldberg, "The Obama Doctrine," *Atlantic,* April 2016, http://www.theatlantic.com/magazine/archive/2016/04/the-obama -doctrine/471525/.

5 **"The globalists gutted":** Michael Wolff, "Ringside with Steve Bannon at Trump Tower," *Hollywood Reporter,* Nov. 18, 2016.

6 **"It is not only true":** "Security Experts on China's Rise, Shifting US Political Tides," *Nikkei Asian Review,* May 31, 2016, http://asia.nikkei.com/Politics-Economy/International -Relations/Security-experts-on-China-s-rise-shifting-US-political-tides?n_cid=NARAN012.

6 **Americans viewed Japanese economic power as a threat:** The poll, conducted by Gallup for the Chicago Council on Foreign Relations in 1990, found that 63 percent of

Americans saw Japanese economic power as a "critical threat" to U.S. interests over the coming decade, compared with 33 percent for the Soviet military.

6 **Since 1990, the U.S. economy:** Thanks to Arthur Kroeber for these calculations, which compare the size of the economies in 1990 and 2015, measured in U.S. dollars.

6 **"If you are number one":** Personal interview.

7 **If China surpasses the U.S. economy:** Kevin Rudd, Alastair Buchan Memorial Lecture, Arundel House, Dec. 16, 2013.

7 **"This is a people":** "Friend or Foe? A Special Report on China's Place in the World," *Economist,* Dec. 4, 2010.

7 **"since the 1648 Peace of Westphalia":** George Packard, "The United States–Japan Security Treaty at 50," *Foreign Affairs* 89, no. 2 (2010).

8 **"unpleasant reality":** Kenneth Pyle, "The U.S.-Japan Alliance in the 21st Century," Nov. 13, 2012, National Bureau of Asian Research, http://www.nbr.org/research/activity .aspx?id=296.

8 **"an unnatural intimacy":** Quoted in ibid.

9 **"I don't think we understood":** Bartholomew Sparrow, *The Strategist: Brent Scowcroft and the Call of National Security* (Public Affairs, 2015), 473.

9 **"The Americans like the Chinese":** Personal conversation.

10 **Beijing favors Potsdam:** See "China's Recovery of Nansha Islands Part of Post-war International Order," Xinhua, April 23, 2016, http://news.xinhuanet.com/english /2016-04/23/c_135306016.htm.

11 **"The international community":** See Amy King's excellent paper "Where Does Japan Fit in China's 'New Type of Great Power Relations'?," *Asan Forum,* March 20, 2014, for a discussion of this issue.

11 **"In Some Respects, to Do Nothing":** Yinan He, *The Search for Reconciliation: Sino-Japanese and German-Polish Relations Since World War II* (Cambridge University Press, 2009), 263. Ironically, the Chinese book was inspired by the Japanese book by Shintaro Ishihara, *The Japan That Can Say No.*

11 **"more cooperative":** Zbigniew Brzezinski, "America's New Geostrategy," *Foreign Affairs* 66, no. 4 (Spring 1988), 696–97.

11 **"headed for divorce":** See Niall Ferguson's blog of Aug. 30, 2009, http://www.niallfer guson.com/journalism/finance-economics/chimerica-is-headed-for-divorce.

11 **The term Safire invented:** William Safire, *Full Disclosure* (Doubleday, 1977).

13 **"whether Japan can accept":** http://theory.people.com.cn/n/2013/0307/c136457 -20709154-2.html.

13 **"but has to be politically":** Comments from a private paper provided to the author by Yun Sun, of the Stimson Center in Washington, based on her interviews with Beijing policy makers and scholars about Chinese views of Japan.

14 **"In east Asia we have no tradition":** Personal interview.

14 **"You know we have a treaty":** Jesse Johnson, "Trump Rips U.S. Defense of Japan as Too Expensive, One-Sided," *Japan Times,* Aug. 6, 2016; see also Linda Sieg, "Trump Candidacy Stirs Alliance Angst in Japan," Reuters, March 20, 2016.

15 **the so-called Thucydides trap:** See Graham Allison, "The Thucydides Trap: Are the U.S. and China Headed for War?," *Atlantic,* Sept. 24, 2015.

Chapter One: China, Red or Green

19 **"We had a surprise announcement":** Kissinger and Ushiba, Memorandum of Conversation, Sept. 8, 1971, item KT00348, Digital National Security Archive.

20 **"Every time the Japanese ambassador":** Kissinger's complaint about being served Wiener schnitzel can be found in a number of places, with slightly different wording. See Michael Schaller, "The Nixon 'Shocks' and U.S.-Japan Strategic Relations, 1969–74" (U.S.-Japan Project: Diplomatic, Security, and Economic Relations Since 1960, working paper 2, National Security Archive); also an interview with Ambassador Richard A.

Ericson Jr., in the Association for Diplomatic Studies and Training Foreign Affairs Oral History Project, 1972, http://www.adst.org/OH%20TOCs/ERICSON,%20Richard%20A.toc.pdf. In this version, Kissinger complains he is being served "Austrian food."

22 **"Kissinger was a mere passenger":** Marvin Kalb and Bernard Kalb, *Kissinger* (Little, Brown, 1974), 221.

22 a **"stomachache":** Douglas Brinkley and Luke Nichter, *Nixon Tapes* (Houghton Mifflin Harcourt, 2014), 196.

22 **"But in a Japanese cultural context":** Rust Deming, interview in the Association for Diplomatic Studies and Training Foreign Affairs Oral History Project, interviewed by Charles Stuart Kennedy, Dec. 8, 2004, page 37, http://adst.org/wp-content/uploads/2013/12/Deming-Rust-M.oh1_.pdf.

22 **"stick it to the Japanese":** Schaller, "Nixon 'Shocks' and U.S.-Japan Strategic Relations." This excellent paper helped inform much of my thinking on this period.

22 **"When are you going to dump us":** Personal interview.

23 **"We leapfrogged them":** Personal interview; see also Lord's interview with the Association for Diplomatic Studies and Training Foreign Affairs Oral History Project, http://www.adst.org/OI I%20TOCs/Lord,%20Winston.pdf.

23 **Chinese patriots grappling:** See Barnett, *China and the Major Powers in East Asia*.

23 **"the first truly large-scale migration":** Ibid., 91; see also Marius P. Jansen, *Japan and China: From War to Peace, 1894–1972* (Rand McNally College Publishing, 1975).

24 **"We should sever all relations":** Quoted in John Welfield, *An Empire in Eclipse: Japan in the Postwar American Alliance System* (Athlone Press, 1988).

25 **"If Japan falls":** Richard M. Nixon, "To the Japanese People," *Contemporary Japan* 22, no. 7–9 (1953): 369–71.

25 **"Yesterday's militaristic enemy":** John Dower, "The San Francisco System: Past, Present, Future in U.S.-Japan-China Relations," *Asia-Pacific Journal* 12, no. 8 (2014); also at http://www.japanfocus.org/-John_W_-Dower/4079/article.html.

25 a **bilateral security pact:** James Chace, *Acheson: The Secretary of State Who Created the American World* (Simon & Schuster, 1998), 318–19. The United States suspended its obligations to New Zealand under the ANZUS Treaty in the 1980s in a dispute over a ban on U.S. ships visiting New Zealand ports.

26 **"Much like rare metals":** See Shu Guang Zhang, *Beijing's Economic Statecraft During the Cold War, 1949–1991* (Johns Hopkins University Press, 2014).

26 **"whether it was red or green":** Quoted in Robert Hoppens, *The China Problem in Postwar Japan: Japanese National Identity and Sino-Japanese Relations* (Bloomsbury Academic, 2015).

26 **The United States had kept the emperor Hirohito:** Thomas Berger, *War, Guilt, and World Politics After World War II* (Cambridge University Press, 2012).

27 **"Japan [has been turned] completely":** See Jianwei Wang and Xinbo Wu, "Against Us or with Us? The Chinese Perspective of America's Alliance with Japan and Korea" (Asia/Pacific Research Center, May 1998).

28 **"hide its light and bide its time":** The phrase *taoguang yanghui* is literally translated as "hide light, nurture obscurity."

28 **"We would still be in the mountains":** The first quotations of Mao and Zhou are contained in Zhang, *Beijing's Economic Statecraft During the Cold War;* the second Mao quotation can be found on many Internet bulletin boards and is also contained in J. Chester Cheng, ed. and trans., *Documents of Dissent: Chinese Political Thought Since Mao* (Hoover Institution Press, 1980). See also Michael Lewis, ed., *"History Wars" and Reconciliation in Japan and Korea: The Roles of Historians, Artists, and Activists* (Palgrave Press, 2017), 4.

29 **"This came from Mao's mouth":** Personal interview.

29 the *People's Daily:* This is based on a search of the *People's Daily* online database, conducted in July 2015.

30 **"pragmatic with pragmatists":** Simon Leys, "The Path of an Empty Boat: Zhou Enlai," in *The Burning Forest: Essays on Chinese Culture and Politics* (Henry Holt, 1985).

30 **"a deft talent":** Quoted in Jonathan Spence, "The Mystery of Zhou Enlai," *New York Review of Books,* May 28, 2009.

30 **He calculated that Tokyo's business chieftains:** Zhang, *Beijing's Economic Statecraft During the Cold War.* This book has an excellent account of this period.

30 **"ministers of foreign affairs":** This quotation and the time line for trade ties come from ibid.

31 **"You are about to be hanged":** See Dan Kurzman, *Kishi and Japan: The Search for the Sun* (Ivan Obolensky, 1960), 235.

32 **one of the "Japanese invaders":** *People's Daily,* July 6, 1949.

32 **"In a literal sense":** Michael Schaller, "America's Favorite War Criminal: Kishi Nobusuke and the Transformation of U.S.-Japan Relations," *This Is Yomiuri,* Aug. 1995; "The CIA and Japanese Politics," *Asian Perspective* 24, no. 4 (2000): 79–103.

33 **"We were financing a party":** Tim Weiner, "C.I.A. Spent Millions to Support Japanese Right in 50's and 60's," *New York Times,* Oct. 9, 1994.

33 **"I had a deep relationship":** Ibid.

33 **"Jap Premier Golfs with Ike":** See the report here: https://www.youtube.com/watch?v=a_6ecRRyE1M.

33 **Eisenhower secretly approved:** For details about the CIA program, see Weiner, "C.I.A. Spent Millions to Support Japanese Right in 50's and 60's"; Schaller, "America's Favorite War Criminal"; "The CIA and Japanese Politics."

33 **"The 'mainland' lobby":** CIA, "The China Problem in Japanese Politics," May 1, 1964, item JT00032, Digital National Security Archive.

34 **"was a poor area":** Zhang, *Beijing's Economic Statecraft During the Cold War,* 135.

34 **Tanzan Ishibashi, an economist:** I am indebted to Rick Dyke for this section, and for his pointing out Ishibashi's importance.

34 **"had hurt the feelings":** This comes from research by Amy King: "The Origins, First Use, and Logic of That Peculiar Chinese Foreign Policy Phrase," Feb. 15, 2017, Wilson Center, https://www.wilsoncenter.org/blog-post/hurting-the-feelings-the-chinese-people.

35 **"To hell with Red China":** Eisenhower and Kishi, Memorandum of Conversation, Jan. 19, 1960, item JU00032, Digital National Security Archive.

36 **"In the summer of 1960":** Welfield, *Empire in Eclipse.*

36 **"fascist thug and feudal clown":** See Erik Esselstrom, "The 1960 'Anpo' Struggle in the *People's Daily,*" Japan Focus, *Asia-Pacific Journal,* Dec. 17, 2012, http://www.japanfocus.org/-Erik-Esselstrom/3869/article.html.

37 **At one stage, John F. Kennedy:** Welfield, *Empire in Eclipse.*

37 **Japanese diplomats conducted secret talks:** "Japan, China Held Top-Secret Talks on Normalizing Ties in 1964," *Japan Times,* Jan. 4, 2015, http://www.japantimes.co.jp/news/2015/01/04/national/history/japan-china-held-top-secret-talks-in-1964-on-normalizing-relations/#.VYxll09VhBc.

37 **By 1971:** Amy King, *China-Japan Relations After World War Two: Empire, Industry and War, 1949–1971* (Cambridge University Press, 2016), 2.

37 **"no intention in the near future":** Nixon and Kishi, Memorandum of Conversation, April 4, 1969, item JU10154, Digital National Security Archive.

38 **"act hastily and believes":** President's Daily Brief, Dec. 23, 1970, https://www.cia.gov/library/readingroom/docs/DOC_0005977865.pdf.

38 **Tokyo's "prime objective":** President's Daily Brief, Feb. 25, 1971, https://www.cia.gov/library/readingroom/docs/DOC_0005992499.pdf.

38 **Zhou Enlai pointedly announced:** President's Daily Brief, March 23, 1971, https://www.cia.gov/library/readingroom/docs/DOC_0005992543.pdf.

Chapter Two: Countering Japan

41 **"'Getting to know you'":** Quoted in Stephen Sestanovich, "The Long History of Leading from Behind," *Atlantic,* Jan./Feb. 2016.

42 **"must be petrified of the Japanese":** Brinkley and Nichter, *Nixon Tapes,* 197.

43 **"The man who wanted to sleep":** Quoted in Ian Buruma, "Can He Take Back Japan?," *New York Review of Books,* Nov. 6, 2014.

43 **"The truth is that neither I":** Henry Kissinger, *White House Years* (Little, Brown, 1979), 324.

43 **"Kissinger always thought":** Personal conversation with Richard Solomon, who passed away in March 2017; Winston Lord expressed similar sentiments in an interview and also here: www.adst.org/OH%20TOCs/Lord,%20Winston.pdf, around 122.

44 **"The idea was to get a sense":** Personal interview.

44 **on Kissinger's, and Chinese, attitudes toward Japan:** See Gary Bass, *The Blood Telegram: Nixon, Kissinger, and a Forgotten Genocide* (Vintage, 2014), xvi.

45 **"You are rearming the Japanese militarists":** Kissinger and Zhou, Memorandum of Conversation, July 9, 1971, item KY00303, Digital National Security Archive.

45 **"I believe that we have got to":** Brinkley and Nichter, *Nixon Tapes,* 305.

45 **"pro-Japanese chieftains":** Kissinger and Zhou, "The President's Visit," Memorandum of Conversation, Oct. 21, 1971, Digital National Security Archive.

46 **"We are very clear about history":** Kissinger and Zhou, "The President's Visit," Memorandum of Conversation, Oct. 22, 1971, Digital National Security Archive.

46 **"tribal," "peculiar," "difficult":** Ibid. "Your Japan Visit—Scope Paper," June 1972, item JU01548, Digital National Security Archive.

46 **"narrow" and "strange":** Brinkley and Nichter, *Nixon Tapes,* 305.

46 **"The Japanese are capable":** Kissinger and Zhou, "The President's Visit," Memorandum of Conversation, Oct. 22, 1971.

47 **victim of "Soviet hegemony":** Wang and Wu, "Against Us or with Us?"

47 **"essential for the preservation of peace":** President's Daily Brief, Dec. 12, 1972.

47 **"The worst outcome":** Kissinger, Memorandum of Japan meeting, Sept. 7, 1971, item KT00347, Digital National Security Archive.

47 **"My philosophy is that":** Personal communication from Fred Bergsten, then on the Treasury staff.

48 **"Connally said this morning":** Japan-U.S. Joint Committee on Trade and Economic Affairs, U.S. Relations with Japan and China, Sept. 7, 1971, item KA06400, Digital National Security Archive.

48 **"Kissinger go home!":** Fukuda and Connally, Memorandum of Conversation, Nov. 11, 1971, item JU01464, Digital National Security Archive.

49 **"I did everything":** Welfield, *Empire in Eclipse,* 295.

49 **"The PRC has come back":** Kissinger and Fukuda, Memorandum of Conversation, June 11, 1972, item JU01559, Digital National Security Archive.

50 **"man of the rickshaw class":** See Jacob M. Schlesinger, *Shadow Shoguns: The Rise and Fall of Japan's Postwar Political Machine* (Simon & Schuster, 1997), 57.

50 **Tanaka fused personal charisma:** See R. Taggart Murphy, *Japan and the Shackles of the Past* (Oxford University Press, 2014), 279, for an extended comparison between Tanaka and Johnson.

50 **"Tanaka is someone":** Schlesinger, *Shadow Shoguns,* 74.

50 **"But I advise you to collect":** Kissinger and Tanaka, Memorandum of Conversation, June 12, 1972, item JU01612, also numbered JU01561, Digital National Security Archive.

50 **"You only talked with them":** Kissinger and Mao, Memorandum of Conversation, Feb. 17, 1972, item KT00677, Digital National Security Archive.

51 **"In my heart, I am glad":** Kissinger and Tanaka, Memorandum of Conversation, June 12, 1972, item JU01612, Digital National Security Archive.

51 **"are mean and treacherous":** Seymour Hersh, *The Price of Power* (Summit Books, 1983), 381–82.

51 **"simply too dangerous":** Michael Green and Benjamin Self, "Japan's Changing China Policy," *Survival* 38, no. 2 (Summer 1996).

52 **"Underlying all the pro-China arguments":** Sadako Ogata, "Japanese Attitude Toward China," *Asian Survey* 5, no. 8 (Aug. 1965).

52 **"They are going to want":** Brinkley and Nichter, *Nixon Tapes,* 358.

52 **"Many years of contradictory evidence":** "People's Republic of China Attitude Towards Japan," State Department Briefing Paper, Aug. 1972, item JU01588, Digital National Security Archive.

53 **"This is an extremely sensitive problem":** Kissinger and Fukuda, Memorandum of Conversation, June 12, 1972, item JU01561, Digital National Security Archive.

54 **"The Japanese view of Americans":** Personal interview.

54 **"passion for secrecy":** Quoted in Schaller, "Nixon 'Shocks' and U.S.-Japan Strategic Relations."

Chapter Three: Five Ragged Islands

55 **In the Chinese telling:** "Excerpt of Mao Zedong's Conversation with Japanese Prime Minister Kakuei Tanaka," Digital Archive, Wilson Center, http://digitalarchive .wilsoncenter.org/document/118567.

56 **"Well, have you finished your quarrel?":** *Yomiuri Shimbun,* Sept. 27, 1972.

57 **"Japan and China severed":** Charles Smith, UPI article, *Mainichi Shimbun,* Sept. 27, 1972.

58 **"Three Main Rules of Discipline":** Welfield, *Empire in Eclipse,* 319.

59 **too strong an apology would upset:** *Asahi Shimbun,* March 6, 2015.

59 **"exchange opinions regarding":** Informal talks between Ōhira and Ji, Digital Archive, Wilson Center, http://digitalarchive.wilsoncenter.org/document/121231.pdf?v =d41d8cd98f00b204e9800998ecf8427e.

60 **"If you look at the normalization process":** Personal interview.

60 **"A minority had opposed":** "Sino-Japanese Normalization," 1972, record of second meeting between Prime Minister Tanaka and Premier Zhou Enlai, http://digitalarchive .wilsoncenter.org/document/121227.

60 **"Tanaka's initiative to visit China":** Quoted in Xuanli Liao, *Chinese Foreign Policy Think Tanks and China's Policy Towards Japan* (Chinese University Press, 2006), 145.

61 **"Tanaka was not controlled":** "Japan's Normalization of Relations with the PRC" (National Security Council background paper, Aug. 1972), item JU01594, Digital National Security Archive.

61 **"The Taiwanese will cause little troubles":** See "Sino-Japanese Normalization, 1972," Digital Archive, Wilson Center, http://digitalarchive.wilsoncenter.org/collection/262 /sino-japanese-normalization-1972, for the records of the conversations between Chinese and Japanese leaders during this period.

62 **Tokyo, however, looked at Taiwan:** Thanks to Steven Tsang for making these points.

62 **"We have felt an emotional attachment":** U.S. Office of the White House, "Meeting Between Henry Kissinger and Foreign Minister Ohira," 1972, http://search.proquest.com /docview/1679117136?accountid=29118.

63 **"No accountant would be able":** Kissinger and Mao, Memorandum of Conversation, Feb. 17, 1973, item KT00256, Digital National Security Archive.

64 **"Fine. We need not":** Yang Daqing, "Was There a 'Tacit Agreement' Between China and Japan in 1972?," *Sources and Methods,* Wilson Center, March 27, 2017, www.wilsoncenter .org/blog-post/official-records-and-diplomatic-implications.

64 **"The Senkakus, uninhabited and unimportant":** "The Senkaku Islands Dispute: Oil Under Troubled Waters?," May 1971, Directorate of Intelligence, CIA.

65 **"There is a high probability":** Quoted in Robert D. Eldridge, *The Origins of U.S. Policy in the East China Sea Islands Dispute: Okinawa's Reversion and the Senkaku Islands* (Routledge, 2014), 111.

65 **"The Chinese government":** Ibid., 120.

65 **"400 million tons was the equivalent":** Ibid., 111.
66 **"Japan would turn to China":** Kissinger and Takezo Shimoda, Memorandum of Conversation, May 21, 1969, item KC00014, Digital National Security Archive.
67 **"About those G__damn islands!":** Ryukyu Islands, June 7, 1971, item KA05887, Digital National Security Archive.
67 **"had been a defense against charges":** Personal interview.
67 **"But that is nonsense":** https://history.state.gov/historicaldocuments/frus1969 -76v17/d115.
68 **"a very badly needed shock":** Eldridge, *Origins of U.S. Policy in the East China Sea Islands Dispute,* 223.
68 **"What position are we involved in?":** Ibid., 222.
68 **"running amok":** *Mainichi Shimbun,* May 5, 1972.
68 **"This is an offense":** Frederick H. Marks, UPI report, *Mainichi Shimbun,* March 27, 1972.
69 **"Can we steer them":** State Department Staff Meeting, Attached to Decision Memorandum Dated Feb. 4, 1974, item KT01017, Digital National Security Archive.
70 **"The thought suddenly crossed":** See Liu Xiaohong, *Chinese Ambassadors: The Rise of Diplomatic Professionalism Since 1949* (University of Washington Press, 2001), 138–42.
71 **"The incident has nothing":** Geng Biao was a close associate of Xi Zhongxun's and helped his son Xi Jinping get a job with the PLA in the late 1970s.
71 **"It was unthinkable":** Nobuyuki Sugimoto, *Daichi no hoko* [Roar of the earth] (PHP Institute, 2006). I also met and discussed these issues with Sugimoto when he was the Japanese consul general in Shanghai in 2004.
72 **"We wanted China to become".** Personal interview.
72 **"He kneels, though he need not":** Written by the *Der Spiegel* journalist Hermann Schreiber and quoted at *Tearing the Iron Curtain Apart,* Polish History Museum, 1989, https://www.google.com/culturalinstitute/beta/u/0/exhibit/QR__NrJC.

Chapter Four: The Golden Years
78 **"We must admit":** These paragraphs about Deng's trip to Japan draw in part on an excellent chapter on the visit in Ezra Vogel's *Deng Xiaoping and the Transformation of China* (Belknap Press of Harvard University Press, 2011).
78 **"had made foreign policy subordinate":** See Allen Whiting, *China Eyes Japan* (University of California Press, 1989), 86–87.
79 **"I used to be referred to":** The quotations from the meetings between Nakasone and his delegation with Chinese leaders come from the Wilson Center archive, https://www .wilsoncenter.org/publication/more-friends-foes-sino-japanese-relations-1984.
79 **his unabashed nationalism:** See Karel van Wolferen, *The Enigma of Japanese Power* (Macmillan, 1989), 150, for this description of Nakasone.
81 **"shadow shogun":** See Schlesinger, *Shadow Shoguns.*
84 **"little brother Japan":** Doc. R037408, Digital Archive, Wilson Center, http://digitalarchive .wilsoncenter.org/document/119548.
84 **"The historical friendly":** Doc. R037811, Digital Archive, Wilson Center, http:// digitalarchive.wilsoncenter.org/document/118849.
84 **comments about the United States:** Doc. R037698, Digital Archive, Wilson Center, http://digitalarchive.wilsoncenter.org/document/119553.
85 **he told the U.S. press:** Don Oberdorfer, the veteran *Washington Post* correspondent who interviewed Nakasone and wrote the articles, has an amusing account of the interpretation snafu in the *International House of Japan Bulletin,* No. 16–20, 1996–2000, No. 2, 1977; http://www.nytimes.com/2012/09/17/world/asia/anti-japanese-protests -over-disputed-islands-continue-in-china.html.
85 **A State Department cable:** "The Chinese Attitude Towards Japan's Defense Policies," Sept. 1984, item JT00490, Digital National Security Archive.

86 **resisting Japan remained a bedrock source:** See Christopher R. Hughes, "Japan in the Politics of Chinese Leadership Legitimacy: Recent Developments in Historical Perspective," *Japan Forum* 20, no. 2 (2008): 245–66.

86 **reported that the Education Ministry:** The initial Japanese press reports would turn out to be misleading. The Education Ministry had not in fact approved the revisionist textbooks; they had simply been submitted to the ministry.

86 **"cultivate the Japanese spirit":** Quoted in Yinan He, "Remembering and Forgetting the War: Elite Mythmaking, Mass Reaction, and Sino-Japanese Relations, 1950–2006," https://ir.cas2.lehigh.edu/sites/ir.cas2.lehigh.edu/files/YinanHe_RememberingForgettingWar.pdf, 53.

86 **Education Ministry had struggled for years:** See Hiroshi Mitani, "The History Textbook Issue in Japan and East Asia: Institutional Framework, Controversies, and International Efforts for Common Histories," in *East Asia's Haunted Present: Historical Memories and the Resurgence of Nationalism,* ed. Tsuyoshi Hasegawa and Kazuhiko Togo (Praeger Security International, 2008), 85.

87 **"Japan is being painted unfairly":** *Tokyo Shimbun,* Aug. 17, 1994.

87 **"This entire issue is so sensitive":** Cable from U.S. embassy in Seoul, Oct. 1982, item JA01033, Digital National Security Archive. The official in question was Shigeru Tokinoya.

87 **The affair erupted:** He Yinan has an excellent paper that covers this period: "Remembering and Forgetting the War."

88 **"corrosion by decadent ideas":** Quoted in ibid.

88 **"Are the officials of the Japanese Ministry":** Quoted in Whiting, *China Eyes Japan,* 49.

89 **"We were treated by the party":** Thanks to Rick Dyke for this anecdote from Sugimoto's book. Sugimoto's memoirs, a bestseller in Japan, came about in tragic circumstances. When he was consul general in Shanghai in 2004, Sugimoto was forced to rush back to Tokyo for consultations after one of his staff committed suicide. The staff member had been caught in a classic "honey trap," seduced and compromised by a Chinese intelligence officer. In Tokyo, Sugimoto discovered in a routine medical check that he had lung cancer. His book was written in a rush, in the final few months of his life in 2004.

89 **"The reception orchestrated for Hu":** Department of Defense cable, Sept. 1984, item JT00490, Digital National Security Archive.

89 **Hu's speeches . . . were written:** First reported in the *People's Daily,* July 26, 2004, http://bj.people.com.cn/GB/14563/2665593.html.

89 **"We invited about three hundred":** Personal interview.

89 **Hu's supporters defended him:** Commentary about Hu Yaobang, including the debate about his invitation to Japanese students, can be found at a Web site established by his supporters, http://www.hybsl.cn.

90 **Blue Storm Society:** See Schlesinger, *Shadow Shoguns,* 76. Also, personal interview with Shintaro Ishihara.

90 **They were thrilled when the *People's Daily:*** I am indebted to Robert Hoppens, *China Problem in Postwar Japan,* for much of my understanding of this group.

91 **"just like a peasant":** Ibid., 118.

91 **Far from settling the controversy:** Personal interview with Ishihara; Hoppens makes similar points.

92 **The conservative push to make Yasukuni:** Sheila Smith's *Intimate Rivals: Japanese Domestic Politics and a Rising China* (Columbia University Press, 2015) has an excellent section on the history of both Yasukuni and Japan's leading veterans' organization, the Japan War-Bereaved Families Association (Nippon Izokukai), both of which I have drawn on for this section.

93 **"Overturning the verdicts":** Hasegawa and Togo, *East Asia's Haunted Present,* 123.

94 **"specifically dedicated to the imperialist aggression":** *People's Daily,* April 20, 1974.

94 **"a complete resettlement":** Hasegawa and Togo, *East Asia's Haunted Present,* 124.

94 **"The new devils"**: Quoted in Masao Miyoshi, *Japan in the World* (Duke University Press, 1993), 64.

95 **protests continued to break out:** See Whiting, *China Eyes Japan,* 66–73; Hasegawa and Togo, *East Asia's Haunted Present,* 124–29.

95 **"If I continue to visit"**: Hasegawa and Togo, *East Asia's Haunted Present,* 128.

95 **"He was saying, it takes"**: Personal interview.

96 **"Neither God nor man"**: See Smith, *Intimate Rivals,* 80.

96 **his head "up in the clouds"**: Whiting, *China Eyes Japan,* 158.

96 **"According to my understanding"**: Personal interview.

Chapter Five: Japan Says No

98 **Clyde Prestowitz, a longtime trade negotiator:** Clyde Prestowitz Jr., *The Betrayal of American Prosperity: Free Market Delusions, America's Decline, and How We Must Compete in the Post-Dollar Era* (Free Press, 2010), 101; also, personal interview.

99 **"It is more important"**: See Mike Smith's oral history for the Association for Diplomatic Studies and Training, http://www.adst.org/OH%20TOCs/Smith,%20Michael%20B.toc.pdf, 85; also, personal interview.

100 **"No major US manufactured export"**: Memorandum for the President, Dec. 18, 1981, item 00931, Digital National Security Archive.

100 **"Watching the United States suddenly lose"**: Kenneth Pyle, "The Future of Japanese Nationality: An Essay in Contemporary History," *Journal of Japanese Studies* 8, no. 2 (Summer 1982): 223–63. The *Asahi* commentator was Yukio Matsuyama.

100 **"For them, the name of the game"**: See the unofficial translation of Shintaro Ishihara and Akio Morita, *The Japan That Can Say No,* http://www.csse.monash.edu.au/~jwb/japanno.txt.

101 **"The President was delighted"**: Eisenhower and Kishi, Memorandum of Conversation, Jan. 19, 1960, item JU00032, Digital National Security Archive.

102 **Eisenhower secured the first:** John Kunkel, *America's Trade Policy Towards Japan: Demanding Results* (Routledge, 2003), has a good chronicle of trade disputes and deals.

102 **"I have a list"**: U.S. National Security Council, "Meeting Between Henry Kissinger and Prime Minister Tanaka," 1972, http://search.proquest.com/docview/1679116793?accountid=29118.

102 **"grain, enriched uranium"**: U.S. Assistant to the President for National Security Affairs, "Highlights of My Second Visit to Japan," 1972, http://search.proquest.com/docview/1679045642?accountid=29118.

103 **"Every US administration in the past 20 years"**: U.S. Department of Defense, "Japanese Defense Efforts for Visit of Prime Minister Suzuki to U.S.; Includes Talking Points," 1981, http://search.proquest.com/docview/1679151192?accountid=29118.

103 **"The Americans were always asking us"**: Welfield, *Empire in Eclipse,* 251.

103 **"merchant nation"**: See Pyle, "Future of Japanese Nationality," 228.

104 **"Precisely because the times"**: U.S. Department of Defense Deputy Assistant Secretary for East Asia and Pacific Affairs, MEMCON of Meeting between Secretary of Defense Weinberger and Japanese Foreign Minister Masayoshi Ito, March 23, 1981, 1530-1645, Pentagon Rm 3E912 Attached to Cover Memorandum, 1981, http://search.proquest.com/docview/1679151854?accountid=29118.

104 **"we could face defeat"**: U.S. Department of Defense Deputy Assistant Secretary for East Asia and Pacific Affairs, Meeting between the Secretary of Defense and Japanese Prime Minister Zenko Suzuki, May 8, 1981, 2:30–3:30 p.m., Blair House, http://search.proquest.com/docview/1679142113?accountid=29118.

104 **described the U.S.-Japan relationship as an "alliance"**: See U.S. Department of Defense Deputy Assistant Secretary for East Asia and Pacific Affairs, "Resignation of Japanese Foreign Minister Ito," 1981, http://search.proquest.com/docview/1679152273?accountid=29118.

105 **"The Japanese expect that by 1975"**: Zbigniew Brzezinski, *The Fragile Blossom: Crisis and Change in Japan* (Harper Torchbooks, 1972), 105–7.

106   **Tokyo hadn't added any firepower:** Green and Self, "Japan's Changing China Policy."

106   **the Chinese and the Japanese began exchanging intelligence:** Bureau of Intelligence and Research, "Japan's Evolving Security Role," June 27, 1984, http://search.proquest.com /docview/1679151902?accountid=29118.

106   **In the spirit of subterfuge:** Robert Gates, *From the Shadows* (Simon & Schuster, 1996), 123.

107   **"The desk officer":** Per Mike Smith's oral history, 89.

108   **"You know the old Confucian statement":** See the interview of Gaston Sigur for the Association for Diplomatic Studies and Training Foreign Affairs Oral History Project, http://www.adst.org/OH%20TOCs/Sigur,%20Gaston%20J.toc.pdf.

108   **"The real import barriers":** Memorandum for Secretary Regan, from Marc E. Leland, March 3, 1981, National Security Archives, Document No. 00844.

109   **"a share of the benefit":** Kunkel, *America's Trade Policy Towards Japan,* 72.

109   **Reagan appeared to doze off:** Clyde V. Prestowitz Jr., *Trading Places: How America Allowed Japan to Take the Lead* (Charles E. Tuttle, 1988), 18.

109   **"voluntary restraints":** U.S. Department of State Bureau of East Asian and Pacific Affairs Office of Japanese Affairs, "General Foreign Policy, Automobiles, Defense, North-South Alexander Haig–Masayoshi Ito Meeting of March 23, 1981," 1981, http://search .proquest.com/docview/1679151361?accountid=29118.

109   **"foreigner's concubine":** Pyle, "The Future of Japanese Nationality," 253.

110   **"He told Mr. Abe":** See Bill Breer, interview for the Association for Diplomatic Studies and Training Foreign Affairs Oral History Project, http://www.adst.org/OH%20TOCs /Breer,%20William%20T.toc.pdf.

110   **"The semiconductor agreement":** Personal interview.

111   **"among the most dramatic events":** Douglas Irwin, "The U.S.-Japan Semiconductor Trade Conflict," National Bureau of Economic Research, Jan. 1996.

112   **"If I had remained a movie director":** The *Playboy* interview is quoted in "The Man Who Would Be Warlord," *Foreign Policy,* Nov. 1, 2013.

112   **"I feel . . . the Japanese people":** An online English-language translation of the original Japanese version of *The Japan That Can Say No* can be found here: http://www.csse .monash.edu.au/~jwb/japanno.txt.

113   **"I suspect your America bashing":** Quoted in Ryuzo Sato, *The Chrysanthemum and the Eagle: The Future of U.S.-Japan Relations* (New York University Press, 1995), 57.

114   **Americans viewed the threat:** "The Perceived Threat: A *Newsweek* Poll," *Newsweek,* Oct. 9, 1989.

114   **"The red menace is dead":** Walter Russell Mead, "Bashing Japan as an Evil Enemy May Make Good Politics, but the Targets Are Tired of It and Are Striking Back," *Los Angeles Times,* Feb. 16, 1992.

114   **A 1992 Pentagon document:** Patrick Tyler, "U.S. Strategy Plan Calls for Insuring No Rivals Develop," *New York Times,* March 8, 1992.

114   **"Remember, this was when the U.S. had troops":** Personal interview.

115   **"one of the hard-liners":** The Nye quotation comes from a personal interview. Morell declined to be interviewed, and the CIA refused a Freedom of Information request for a copy of the report.

116   **"took its place beside":** Welfield, *Empire in Eclipse,* 286.

116   **"Labour unions organize strikes":** Wolferen, *Enigma of Japanese Power,* 25.

117   **"One-party autocracy":** "Our One-Party Democracy," *New York Times,* Sept. 8, 2009, http://www.nytimes.com/2009/09/09/opinion/09friedman.html?_r=0.

117   **"a mighty industrial economy":** Quoted in Robert Ross and Changbin Jiang, eds., *Re-examining the Cold War: U.S.-China Diplomacy, 1954–1973* (Harvard University Asia Center, 2003), 380.

119   **"The consistent talking point":** Personal interview.

119 **China's share of global exports:** See WTO data. Also *China 2030,* the report produced jointly by the World Bank and the State Council's Development Research Center, refers cryptically to this on p. 14.

119 **"The Chinese were smart":** Personal conversation. Nishimiya died tragically of a heart attack before he could take up the ambassador's post in Beijing.

120 **"When the U.S.":** Personal interview.

Chapter Six: Asian Values

124 **"I was never present":** Personal interview.

124 **personally attacked by dogs:** Interviews with officials present during the meetings.

125 **"the weakest link":** Qian Qichen, *Ten Episodes in China's Diplomacy* (HarperCollins, 2005), 150.

125 **"We used Japan as a stalking horse":** Personal interviews.

125 **"It was a good letter":** Personal interview. Looking back, Bader told me that such goodwill "looks like the Jurassic ages" these days.

126 **"That must have been tough":** Personal interview.

127 **"We were the victorious state":** Personal interview.

128 **"filtering the emotion":** Robert Thomson, "An End to Asia's Long Winter," *Financial Times,* Oct. 22, 1992.

128 **he had overruled his security detail:** Personal interviews with Japanese officials on the visit.

129 **"strategically available":** Personal interview.

129 **"biggest mistake":** See Zheng Wang, *Never Forget National Humiliation: Historical Memory in Chinese Politics and Foreign Relations* (Columbia University Press, 2012), 96.

129 **two letters written by Jiang:** Ibid.

130 **"the rehabilitation, re-evaluation, and revision":** Quoted in ibid., 101.

130 **"even to the children":** Ibid., 98.

130 **divided into two camps:** Ibid., 124.

130 **national sites to serve as "demonstration bases":** Ibid., 105–6.

131 **"the non-celebration of anniversaries":** Simon Leys, "The Art of Interpreting Nonexistent Inscriptions Written in Invisible Ink on a Blank Page," *New York Review of Books,* Oct. 11, 1990.

132 **"China's relinquishing of such claims":** See the discussion of this issue in Kazuko Mori, "New Relations Between China and Japan: A Gloomy, Frail Rivalry," *Modern Asian Studies Review* 2 (March 2007). An English translation is also posted on the Internet.

132 **mocked in China as "mumbo-jumbo":** Ibid., 33.

132 **"We were proud":** http://t.qq.com/p/t/423425129150343#p=2&select=1&time=1416398520&mid=442314094489068&format=1.

132 **labeled simply as "traitors":** http://club.china.com/data/thread/1011/2755/91/96/9_1.html.

133 **When Washington asked Japan for logistics assistance:** See Takashi Oka, *Policy Entrepreneurship and Elections in Japan: A Political Biography of Ozawa Ichiro* (Routledge, 2011), 33.

134 **"military march music":** Yoichi Funabashi, *Alliance Adrift* (Council on Foreign Relations Press, 1999), 120.

134 **akin to a tortoise:** Takashi Oka, "Japan Peers out of Its Shell," *Christian Science Monitor,* March 22, 1991.

134 **"We will be sweating with you":** The various conversations can be found at U.S. White House, "Meeting with Prime Minister Toshiki Kaifu of Japan," 1990, http://search.proquest.com/docview/1679142237?accountid=29118; U.S. National Security Council, TELCON with Toshiki Kaifu, Prime Minister of Japan, Sept. 13, 1990, http://search

.proquest.com/docview/1679143489?accountid=29118; U.S. White House, "Meeting with Prime Minister Toshiki Kaifu of Japan," 1990, http://search.proquest.com /docview/1679143467?accountid=29118.

134   **"Basically, Baker didn't like the Japanese":** Personal interview.

135   **"We are not going to allow":** This story comes from Matt Goodman, who served in the Treasury and the White House and overseas over a number of administrations. He is now at the Washington think tank, the Center for Strategic and International Studies.

135   **"tin cup" missions:** A number of Geithner's colleagues told me of this nickname, but Geithner himself, when contacted, said that all such entreaties for Japan to cough up money for the war were called "tin cup" operations and that the moniker didn't apply to him personally.

135   **"There was something ridiculous":** Timothy F. Geithner, *Stress Test: Reflections on Financial Crises* (Broadway Books, 2014), 41.

135   **"We ended up with a $60 billion war":** Cheney was speaking at the Reagan National Defense Forum, Dec. 3, 2016.

135   **"This is the only":** Personal interview.

136   **"At the negotiating table":** Qian, *Ten Episodes in China's Diplomacy,* 146, 74.

136   **rapid military victory in the Gulf War:** Michael Armacost, *Friends or Rivals? The Insider's Account of U.S.-Japan Relations* (Columbia University Press, 1996), 99.

137   **"Business ought to bear":** These anecdotes come from Schlesinger, *Shadow Shoguns,* 180, 254.

137   **"Somewhere along the way":** Oka, *Policy Entrepreneurship and Elections in Japan,* 48.

138   **The new Japan Ozawa envisaged:** Ibid., 49.

138   **"Yes, the day before he goes there":** Robert G. Gilpin Jr., "The United States and East Asia in the New World Order," *International House of Japan Bulletin* 17, no. 1 (Winter 1997).

138   **"They always said":** Personal interview.

138   **"With Japan, something akin":** Cited in Kunkel, *America's Trade Policy Towards Japan,* 163.

139   **"like a glacier breaking apart":** Don Oberdorfer, *The Changing Context of U.S.-Japan Relations* (Japan Society, 1998), 9.

139   **proselytizers of "Asian values":** This characterization is based on Alan Dupont, "Is There an 'Asian Way'?," *Survival* (Summer 1996).

141   **"America sends its young off":** Funabashi, *Alliance Adrift,* 284.

141   **"to define its interests":** Joseph Nye, "The Nye Report: Six Years Later," *International Relations of the Asia-Pacific* 1, no. 1 (2001): 95–103.

142   **"a strange, anomalous joining":** Pyle, "U.S.-Japan Alliance in the 21st Century."

142   **Tokyo had been obsessed with "Japan bashing":** An entire book has been written on the history of so-called Japan bashing. See Narelle Morris, *Japan Bashing* (Routledge, 2011).

142   **"I've been to Japan twice":** http://adst.org/wp-content/uploads/2013/12/Deming -Rust-M.oh1_.pdf.

Chapter Seven: Apologies and Their Discontents

144   **"Does the United States see China":** The transcript of this meeting was released by the Clinton Library in Jan. 2016; http://clinton.presidentiallibraries.us/items/show/ 47988.

147   **"The U.S. will lose its share":** Robert Suettinger, *Beyond Tiananmen* (Brookings Institution, 2003), 187.

147   **"It was amateur hour":** Personal interview.

148   **Lee had only spent ten days:** Thanks to Nick Frisch for this nugget.

149   **first for the parliament:** Now called the Legislative Yuan.

149 **to avoid being "swallowed alive":** See Nancy Bernkopf Tucker, *China Confidential* (Columbia University Press, 2015), 473; Lee Teng-hui, *Creating the Future* (Taiwan: Government Information Office, 1992), 102.

150 **Lee called the Nationalists "an alien regime":** Bruce Dickson and Chien-min Chao, eds., *Assessing the Lee Teng-hui Legacy in Taiwan's Politics* (Routledge, 2002), 224–25; see also Bruce Jacobs and I-hao Ben Liu, "Lee Teng-hui and the Idea of 'Taiwan,'" *China Quarterly,* no. 190 (June 2007): 375–93; the "alien regime" is literally "a regime that came to Taiwan from the outside."

150 **"Whether those formulaic perceptions":** Suettinger, *Beyond Tiananmen,* 217.

150 **Lee's campaign to overturn:** Nancy Bernkopf Tucker, *Strait Talk* (Harvard University Press, 2009), 207–12.

150 **White House's reversal was "mere sophistry":** Qian, *Ten Episodes in China's Diplomacy,* 244.

150 **"I hate our China policy!":** Barton Gellman, "U.S. and China Nearly Came to Blows in '96," *Washington Post,* June 21, 1998.

151 **"grave consequences":** Personal interviews; see also Gellman, "U.S. and China Nearly Came to Blows in '96."

151 **"deformed test tube baby":** Some of the insults were compiled on ccn.com, http://www.cnn.com/SPECIALS/1999/china.50/inside.china/profiles/lee.tenghui/.

152 **"Supporting the Taiwan regime":** Qian, *Ten Episodes in China's Diplomacy,* 244.

152 **The virtuosic U.S. military performance:** Roger Cliff et al., *Shaking the Heavens and Splitting the Earth: Chinese Air Force Employment Concepts in the 21st Century,* http://www.rand.org/content/dam/rand/pubs/monographs/2011/RAND_MG915.pdf.

152 **"[The Chinese] were blind":** Personal interview with Carter who also recounted Perry's comments to Chi.

152 **"Beijing should know":** Suettinger, *Beyond Tiananmen,* 258.

153 **A focus on advanced technology:** Cliff et al., *Shaking the Heavens and Splitting the Earth: Chinese Air Force Employment Concepts in the 21st Century.*

153 **deeper lesson from the Taiwan crisis:** Dickson and Chao, *Assessing the Lee Teng-hui Legacy in Taiwan's Politics,* 220.

154 **"If I was an international psychiatrist":** See the BBC documentary *Nippon, Risen Sun* at about the twenty-sixth minute.

155 **"We can apologize":** Yukio Okamoto recounted Takeshita's words in a speech to the Foreign Correspondents' Club in Tokyo on May 26, 2015. The speech is posted on YouTube.

155 **"If it leaked":** Personal interview.

156 **"The trouble with you":** Armacost, *Friends or Rivals?,* 120.

156 **"Hashimoto could have made trouble":** Personal interview.

156 **"loss of the war":** See Berger, *War, Guilt, and World Politics After World War II,* 181–83.

157 **"The . . . Prime Minister might have":** Quoted in Kazuhiko Togo, ed., *Japan and Reconciliation in Post-war Asia: The Murayama Statement and Its Implications* (Palgrave Macmillan, 2013), 14.

157 **move would not be "unreasonable":** "Harold Brown's Conversation with Japanese Defense Minister Kanemaru," U.S. Department of Defense, Secret, Memorandum of Conversation, Nov. 8, 1978.

158 **"reluctant realists":** See Green and Self, "Japan's Changing China Policy."

158 **"cork in the bottle":** See Bonnie Glaser and Brittney Farrar, "Through Beijing's Eyes: How China Sees the U.S.-Japan Alliance," *National Interest,* May 12, 2015.

158 **"The people who think China":** Personal interview.

159 **"I was not so motivated":** Susan V. Lawrence and Emily MacFarquhar, "The New Look in Beijing: Jiang Zemin Comes to New York as China and the United States Slowly Mend Frayed Relations," *U.S. News & World Report,* Oct. 23, 1995, 70.

159 **ushering his uncle:** An online memorial site for Jiang Shangqing can be found here: http://dangshi.people.com.cn/GB/144964/145332/8891463.html.

159   **On the hundredth anniversary:** http://news.sina.com.cn/c/2011-04-11/053022268920.shtml.

159   **according to Gilley, Jiang showed few signs:** See Bruce Gilley, *Tiger on the Brink: Jiang Zemin and China's New Elite* (University of California Press, 1998), 17–20.

160   **Jiang's father was a collaborator:** See *Epoch Times,* Aug. 22, 2014, http://www .theepochtimes.com/n3/879977-anything-for-power-the-real-story-of-chinas-jiang-zemin -introduction/.

160   **none dismissed it out of hand:** This reflects my personal conversations with a number of Chinese scholars.

160   **his "three no's" policy:** Jim Mann, "Clinton 1st to OK China, Taiwan '3 No's,'" *Los Angeles Times,* July 8, 1998.

160   **"more disciplined" on Taiwan:** Seth Faison, "U.S. Trip Is Everything Jiang Expected," *New York Times,* Nov. 3, 1997, https://partners.nytimes.com/library/world/110397us -china-assess.html.

161   **"The joint communiqué":** Kazuo Sato, "The Japan-China Summit and Joint Declaration of 1998: A Watershed for Japan-China Relations in the 21st Century?," Jan. 1, 2001, Brookings Institution, https://www.brookings.edu/research/the-japan-china -summit-and-joint-declaration-of-1998-a-watershed-for-japan-china-relations-in-the-21st -century/.

161   **"Tang and Wang said":** Personal interview.

162   **"President Jiang is from":** See the *Asahi Evening News,* Dec. 16, 1998, for a long ac- count of the negotiations.

162   **"Isn't this a finished problem?":** Nicholas Kristof, "Burying the Past: War Guilt Haunts Japan," *New York Times,* Nov. 30, 1998.

162   **Obuchi did offer Jiang a written apology:** Sato, "Japan-China Summit and Joint Declaration of 1998."

163   **"I don't think the idea":** Personal interview.

163   **Tang himself came under pressure to resign:** Ming Wan, *Sino-Japanese Relations: Interaction, Logic, and Transformation* (Stanford University Press, 2006), see footnotes 86–89.

163   **"You want me to bow down":** According to officials present at the meeting.

164   **he looked to the United States:** Thanks to Wang Yingyao on this point.

164   **"offend the Japanese people":** Hisahiko Okazaki, "China Refuses to Let History Be," *Japan Times,* Nov. 7, 2000.

164   **"The following question":** The exchange can be found here: http://news.ifeng.com /history/zhongguoxiandaishi/detail_2011_12/22/11499623_1.shtml.

164   **"How can they say":** Quoted in Agence France-Presse, Oct. 17, 2000.

165   **"They didn't realize":** Personal interview.

Chapter Eight: Yasukuni Respects

170   **Ma attacked the leftist throwbacks:** See Peter Hays Gries, "China's 'New Thinking' on Japan," *China Quarterly* 184 (Dec. 2005): 831–50. I have drawn on this article for some of the reaction to Ma's articles. Other material comes from interviews with participants in the debates, including Ma; Shi Yinhong; and, on an anonymous basis, executives from Phoenix Television, the *People's Daily,* and a number of other scholars.

171   **"We cannot forget history":** See Gries, "China's 'New Thinking' on Japan."

171   **"Japan has not returned":** See ibid.

172   **Ma . . . began receiving death threats:** This account comes from conversations with people with firsthand knowledge of the events.

172   **"Nineteen eighty-nine":** Personal interview.

174   **"Bonjin, Gunjin, Henjin":** The "bland man" was Keizō Obuchi, and the "military man" was Seiroku Kajiyama.

174   **won her a prize:** See Oka, *Policy Entrepreneurship and Elections in Japan,* 105.

174 **Tokyo's ambassador to Beijing:** See Tang Jiaxuan, *Heavy Storm and Gentle Breeze: A Memoir of China's Diplomacy* (HarperCollins, 2011), in particular the chapter titled "The Tortuous Road of Sino-Japanese Relations."

175 **visit the shrine on August 13:** Ibid.

176 **"I am not a right-winger":** Personal interviews with the officials who briefed Koizumi.

177 **"He didn't tell me":** Personal interview.

178 **"It would be better":** Personal interviews.

178 **"I cannot tolerate his visit":** Hasegawa and Togo, *East Asia's Haunted Present,* 136.

178 **"No, No! Listen, China":** Willem van Kemenade, *China and Japan: Partners or Permanent Rivals?,* Nov. 2006, Netherlands Institute of International Relations, https://www.clingendael.nl/sites/default/files/200611_cdsp_paper_kemenade.pdf.

179 **"The early China school people":** Personal interview.

179 **"Why is North America":** Personal interview.

180 **"The China school are turncoats":** Personal interview.

180 **"The people entrusted":** *Japan Times,* Dec. 1998.

181 **"The younger generation":** Personal interview.

181 **"diplomatic version of *Rashomon*":** James Przystup has a good account of this period in his regular updates of Sino-Japanese relations. See http://csis.org/files/media/csis/pubs/0202qjapan_china.pdf.

182 **"it was better not to be involved":** Discussions with Japanese diplomats at the meeting; also, Japanese press reports.

182 **"China policy should not be":** Personal interview.

185 **His family's mining company:** See "Aso's Slave Link Under Scrutiny," *Japan Times,* April 25, 2006; "The War According to Aso Co.," *Japan Times,* June 26, 2007.

186 **"The majority of LDP voters":** "FM Aso Comments; Advertisements for Himself?," Feb. 8, 2006, WikiLeaks.

186 **"What image did I have":** Zhanlue Duihua [Strategic Dialogues], Dai Bingguo, Hui Yilu, Renmin Chubanshe [People's Press], Shijie Zhishi Chubanshe [World Knowledge Press], March 2016.

187 **"Although Dai did not avail himself":** "Japan-China: China Trying to 'Wall Off' Yasukuni?," Feb. 23, 2006, WikiLeaks.

187 **"For Beijing the issue":** "Ambassador's Lunch with VFM Yachi, March 2, 2006," March 3, 2006, WikiLeaks.

188 **Chinese scholars joked later:** "China-Japan Relations: PRC Scholars Expect Continued Difficulties," Aug. 16, 2006, WikiLeaks.

188 **"shrug off the historical constraints":** See Tang, *Heavy Storm and Gentle Breeze,* 45.

189 **"There is no solution":** "Japanese Readout: Dai Bingguo Uncompromising on Yasukuni, Seeks 'Positive' Signals from Japan," Feb. 13, 2006, WikiLeaks. The quotation is from Hiroyasu Izumi, the head of the ministry's China division.

189 **"The Japanese became":** Personal interview.

Chapter Nine: History's Cauldron

191 **Bush was mindful of the region's success:** The one obvious exception is Bush's highly derogatory comments about North Korea and its leaders. He was also critical of Kim Dae-jung's "sunshine" policy toward North Korea.

191 **"Clinton had to call me six times":** This is from an administration official with first-hand knowledge of the conversation.

191 **"Did I say something wrong?":** Dennis Wilder, speaking at a symposium at the Brookings Institution, Jan. 24, 2017.

192 **"immoral and dangerous":** Ted Galen Carpenter, "President Bush's Taiwan Policy: Immoral and Dangerous," Cato Institute, March 31, 2004, http://www.cato.org/publications/commentary/president-bushs-taiwan-policy-immoral-dangerous.

193   **Hu effectively confirmed:** Based on interviews with people with firsthand knowledge of the conversations.

194   **"Not the slightest":** Edward Beauchamp, ed., *History of Contemporary Japan Since World War II* (Routledge, 1998), 140.

194   **were "rank revisionism":** "President Rejects Apology to Japan," *New York Times,* Dec. 1, 1991.

194   **lead-up to the fiftieth anniversary:** Hasegawa and Togo, *East Asia's Haunted Present,* 213–15.

195   **"Even if a dispute":** See the chapter by David Straub in *East Asia's Haunted Present: Historical Memories and the Resurgence of Nationalism,* ed. Tsuyoshi Hasegawa and Kazuhiko Togo (Praeger Security International, 2008), 212.

196   **"World War II bound China":** See Funabashi, *Alliance Adrift,* 440–42, for the details of these visits; I also discussed the encounters with Pentagon officials involved in arranging the visits and the debriefing for the Japanese that followed.

196   **"Terrible! But there is no comparison":** Funabashi, *Alliance Adrift,* plus conversations with Pentagon officials.

197   **"a scheme developed":** "Japanese Economics Officers on Minister Nikai Visit, Auto Parts, IPR in China," March 10, 2006, WikiLeaks.

197   **"If these views are heard":** "Ambassador Schieffer Discusses Yasukuni, Japan-China Relations with China's Ambassador Wang Yi," June 15, 2006, WikiLeaks.

198   **any interference from the United States:** "China Watchers Pin Hopes for Improved Japan-China Relations on Next Prime Minister," Feb. 15, 2006, WikiLeaks.

198   **many Japanese critics of China:** "LDP's Nakagawa and Kyuma on DPRI, China, Iran, and Beef," March 29, 2006, WikiLeaks.

198   **Pentagon official lamented:** Personal interview.

198   **"You couldn't put the China relationship":** Personal interviews with former Pentagon and NSC officials.

198   **what it called "sensitive" information:** "Japanese Officials in Seoul Discuss History Issue," March 22, 2006, WikiLeaks.

199   **"would have likely been in jail":** Alexis Dudden, *Troubled Apologies Among Japan, Korea, and the United States* (Columbia University Press, 2008), 94–95.

199   **Park would later rationalize:** See John Delury, "The Kishi Effect: A Political Genealogy of Japan-ROK Relations," *Asian Perspective* 39, no. 3 (2015): 447.

199   **the bilateral agreement:** "Korea-Japan Ties Burdened by Baggage," *Asia Times,* Nov. 22, 2013.

201   **Seoul's decision to "break the deal":** "Japan-ROK Relations: Strong Emotions Won't Shake Firm Common Ground," Feb. 22, 2006, WikiLeaks.

201   **a handful of themes dominated coverage:** Quoted in Richard Samuels, *Securing Japan: Tokyo's Grand Strategy and the Future of East Asia,* Kindle ed. (Cornell University Press, 2007), 3332.

201   **"The public loves to see":** "No Joy in Arranging Hu Visit to Japan," April 24, 2008, WikiLeaks.

201   **"fundamentally incapable of behaving":** Wu Xinbo, "The End of the Silver Lining: A Chinese View of the U.S.-Japanese Alliance," *Washington Quarterly* 29, no. 1 (2005).

202   **officials and scholars privately expressed anger:** Based on off-the-record discussions in China at the time.

202   **"the bright side of the U.S.-Japanese alliance":** Wu, "End of the Silver Lining."

202   **"The United States will not be happy":** Peter Alford, "Abe's Views Damning," *Australian,* Aug. 29, 2006.

203   **"Have any Japanese prime ministers":** *Toward a Beautiful Country* (Bungei Shunju, 2006), 69.

203   **"They are using anti-Japanese sentiment":** "Admiral Fallon's Meeting with Chief Cabinet Secretary Abe Shinzo," Sept. 6, 2006, WikiLeaks.

204 **Dai and Yachi and their teams negotiated:** These details come from Zhanlue Duihua [Strategic Dialogues], Dai Bingguo, Hui Yilu, Renmin Chubanshe [People's Press], Shijie Zhishi Chubanshe [World Knowledge Press], March 2016.

204 **"they were not war criminals":** "Japan's PM Rejects WWII 'War Criminal' Label," Agence France-Presse, Oct. 6, 2006.

205 **"There is no evidence":** "Japanese PM Denies Wartime 'Comfort Women' Were Forced," *Daily Telegraph,* March 3, 2007, www.telegraph.co.uk/news/worldnews/1544471 /Japanese-PM-denies-wartime-comfort-women-were-forced.html.

206 **reexamine the Kono Statement:** Nakayama had to resign from the cabinet in 2008 after saying that the Japanese "did not like or desire foreigners" and that Japan was "ethnically homogenous." http://www.japantimes.co.jp/news/2008/09/29/national /gaffe-prone-nakayama-quits-cabinet/#.Vyy5ZfkrI2y.

206 **"Some say it is useful":** Hiroko Tabuchi, "Japan's Abe: No Proof of WWII Sex Slaves," Associated Press, March 1, 2007.

206 **"disturbing indication he is willing":** "Comfort Women: Keeping It Low Key," March 19, 2007, WikiLeaks.

206 **"The prime minister knows too much":** "PM Abe, Others Have Now 'Got the Message' on Comfort Women," March 30, 2007, WikiLeaks.

206 **"Abe's body language":** "PM Abe Tries to Defuse Comfort Women Issue in Advance of U.S. Trip," April 24, 2007, WikiLeaks.

206 **he had been personally offended:** Conversations with individuals who spoke to Abe about this matter.

207 **Kim Jong Il's abduction program:** Robert Boynton, *The Invitation-Only Zone: The True Story of North Korea's Abduction Project* (Farrar, Straus & Giroux, 2016), is a great account of this story.

208 **A note was attached:** "Official Receives Bomb Threat," *Japan Times*, Sept. 11, 2003, http://www.japantimes.co.jp/news/2003/09/11/national/official-receives-bomb-threat/# .Vyz-nPkrI2w.

208 **"When I see politicians":** Abe, *Toward a Beautiful Country,* 3.

209 **"Why can't Asia be more":** This remark, and numerous other details about Rice and Hill and the six-party talks, come from personal interviews with numerous administration and State Department officials, as well as Japanese officials. Neither Hill nor Rice agreed to be interviewed.

210 **"Give me the Bosnian Serbs":** Christopher R. Hill, *Outpost: Life on the Frontlines of American Diplomacy: A Memoir* (Simon & Schuster, 2014), 227.

210 **"Do you have any idea":** Ibid.

210 **"His view was that policy":** Personal interview.

210 **"We needed a confident Japan":** Condoleezza Rice, *No Higher Honor: A Memoir of My Years in Washington* (Crown, 2011), 526–27, 649.

210 **"assistant secretary for North Korea":** Based on discussions with White House officials at the time.

211 **"If you feel so strongly":** Personal interview.

Chapter Ten: The Ampo Mafia

212 **"Hu grabbed my arm":** Personal interview.

213 **"Japanese companies":** "EAP A/S Hill's Meeting with Asian DG Sasae on Asian Issues," April 21, 2006, WikiLeaks.

213 **a cup and a straw:** See James Manicom, *Bridging Troubled Waters: China, Japan, and the Maritime Order in the East China Sea* (Georgetown University Press, 2014), which was very helpful in this chapter. The anecdote about the straw comes from *Nihon Keiza Shimbun,* July 5, 2004.

214 **"maritime rights and interests":** See Manicom, *Bridging Troubled Waters,* 129.

214 **"our mobile national territory":** "For China Boss, Oil Rigs Are a 'Strategic Weapon,'" *Wall Street Journal,* Aug. 29, 2012. Wang later returned to head CNPC, or PetroChina, which may explain his politically loaded comments.

214 **The initial talks starting:** "DDG Qiu on Japan-China Dialogue," May 11, 2006, WikiLeaks.

215 **The worker was sentenced to life:** "Dumpling Poisoner Faces Stiff Sentence," *Japan Times,* July 30, 2013.

215 **"In China, once Hu Jintao":** "Sino-Japanese Relations After PM Fukuda's Resignation," Sept. 5, 2008, WikiLeaks.

216 **"Did you think about":** See Richard Bush, *The Perils of Proximity: China-Japan Security Relations,* Kindle ed. (Brookings Institution Press, 2010), 1967.

216 **the hawks in Beijing had then assailed him:** Personal interview.

217 **"Now we are in the center":** "Sen. Lieberman's Meetings with Japanese Politicians," June 3, 2008, WikiLeaks. The fact that Asō was speaking with Lieberman, a noted hawk, might have influenced his playing up the China threat.

217 **"Sea of Peace, Cooperation and Friendship":** See Smith, *Intimate Rivals,* for a comprehensive account of the East China Sea talks.

217 **"We thought we had a fair deal":** Personal interview.

218 **With a population of 1.3 billion:** "Advance Arrangement of East China Sea Agreement," June 26, 2008, WikiLeaks.

218 **"That was a deal breaker":** Personal interview.

218 **"People like him":** Personal interview.

218 **"The Chinese negotiators":** Personal interview.

220 **"an immense, neglected military dump":** Gavan McCormack, "Obama vs. Okinawa," *New Left Review* 63 (July–Aug. 2010).

221 **"Many of the problems":** Personal interview.

221 **"My reaction was":** Personal interview.

221 **Hatoyama's nickname was "the alien":** "The 'Alien' Vows to Tame Power of the Civil Service," *Financial Times,* Jan. 27, 2009.

221 **the new prime minister had summoned:** "Yukio Hatoyama Does the Impossible; Now for the Hard Part," *Daily Telegraph,* Sept. 1, 2009. Hatoyama told this story to the article's author, Paul Carter, who was then on his staff.

222 **U.S. campaign against a Japanese-led regional monetary fund:** Paul Blustein's book *The Chastening* (Public Affairs, 2001), on the IMF and the Asian crisis, has an excellent account of this episode, on p. 163.

222 **"China was opposed to it":** Personal interview.

222 **"The probability [is that] we could not":** "Memorandum for Deputy Secretary Summers, Under Secretary Lipton, From Timothy F. Geithner," Oct. 31, 1997, Department of the Treasury.

222 **"He was entirely reassuring":** Personal interview.

223 **"They overloaded the system":** Personal interview.

224 **"In the U.S.":** Personal interview.

224 **The bilateral conversations:** "EAP Assistant Secretary Kurt Campbell's Meeting with Foreign Minister Katsuya Okada," Sept. 21, 2009, WikiLeaks.

224 **"would end in failure":** "EAP Kurt Campbell's Meeting with MOFA DG Akitaka Saiki," Sept. 21, 2009, WikiLeaks.

225 **"Gates was very, very blunt":** Personal interview.

225 **his plan for a new Asian community:** For these thoughts, I had the benefit of reading in advance a chapter of a new book by Daniel Sneider, *The New Asianism: Japanese Foreign Policy Under the Democratic Party of Japan.*

225 **"The U.S. was doing a rebalance":** Personal interview.

225–26 **"Imagine the Japanese response":** "A/S Campbell, GOJ Officials Discuss PM Hatoyama's Comments on U.S./China/South Korea," Oct. 15, 2009, WikiLeaks; also, interviews with Japanese officials.

226 **"mindblower":** Personal interview.

227 **"The message they were sending":** "Japan's Ex–Prime Minister Yukio Hatoyama Answers His Critics," *Financial Times,* July 20, 2016.

227 **"deliberately sabotaged by a de facto alliance":** Murphy, *Japan and the Shackles of the Past,* 352.

227 **"We miscalculated":** Personal interview.

228 **"A lot of people were shocked":** Personal interview.

Chapter Eleven: The Rise and Retreat of Great Powers

230 **Qi was so annoyed:** For Qi's speech, see this reference: http://cul.sohu.com/20151206 /n429904484.shtml. This section is also based on interviews with people directly involved in the study session on great powers.

231 **"nine great powers":** See Liu Xiaobo, "Behind the Rise of Great Powers," trans. Josephine Chiu-Duke, *Guernica,* Jan. 1, 2012.

231 **China had only just entered:** Gordon Chang's book *The Coming Collapse of China* was published around this time, with his theory in part based on the threat posed by WTO entry.

232 **"The documentary does not":** Personal interview.

232 **"avoiding the propaganda":** Liu, "Behind the Rise of Great Powers."

232 **"Most of them occur":** Ibid.

232 **"Many issues in Japan's century":** This is a caption from episode seven of the series.

233 **"to let people know":** Personal interview.

233 **"Top Ten Traitors":** http://www.xici.net/d31058506.htm.

234 **"the relatively fair":** Personal interview.

235 **"You can see from the Internet":** Personal interview.

235 **"These critics cannot":** Personal interview.

235 **"peaceful rise":** This section is based on my interviews with Zheng Bijian and some of his critics in 2005. See "From the Friendship Hotel, a Message of Amity," *Financial Times,* Sept. 3, 2005; also see the excellent article on this policy debate by Bonnie S. Glaser and Evan Medeiros, "The Changing Ecology of Foreign Policy-Making in China: The Ascension and Demise of the Theory of 'Peaceful Rise,'" *China Quarterly* 190 (June 2007): 291–310.

236 **"a curious and atypical path":** See Glaser and Medeiros, "Changing Ecology of Foreign Policy-Making in China."

237 *jumin* **(military),** *gumin* **(shareholders), and** *wangmin* **(netizens):** See Linda Jakobson and David Knox, "New Foreign Policy Actors in China," Stockholm International Peace Research Institute Policy Paper 26, Sept. 2010.

238 **"frequency, duration, complexity":** Christopher H. Sharman, "China Moves Out: Stepping Stones Toward a New Maritime Strategy," Center for the Study of Chinese Naval Affairs, Institute for National Strategic Studies, *China Strategic Perspectives* 9 (April 2015).

238 **China finally had the strength:** David Lague, "China's Hawks Take the Offensive," Reuters, Jan. 17, 2013.

239 **"Because of the nature of geography":** See Thomas Mahnken and Dan Blumenthal, *Strategy in Asia: The Past, Present, and Future of Regional Security* (Stanford Security Series, 2014), in particular the chapter by Toshi Yoshihara, "Chinese Maritime Geography," 43–53.

239 **"Chinese aircraft can bomb":** The quotations in this paragraph come from Lague, "China's Hawks Take the Offensive."

240 **"You were my teacher":** Henry M. Paulson, *Dealing with China: An Insider Unmasks the New Economic Superpower* (Twelve, 2015), 240.

241 **"To the Japanese, China is":** "Nicchu Gyakuten—Bocho suru Chugoku no Shinjitsu" [China has taken Japan's place: The truth about a growing/rising China], *Nihon Keizai Shinbunsha,* May 2010, 3.

241 **"most significant landmark":** Yuan Peng, "Xunqiu Zhongmei Yatai liangxing hudong" [Seeking good ties between China and the United States in Asia-Pacific], *Guoji Anquan Yanjiu,* no. 1 (2013).

241 **Instead, China emphasized:** See King, "Where Does Japan Fit in China's 'New Type of Great Power Relations'?," for an excellent discussion of China's view of Japan's weakness.

242 **Hu welcomed him in the Great Hall of the People:** "Hu Meets General Secretary of the DPJ," Xinhua, Dec. 11, 2009.

243 **Campbell suggested to Ozawa:** "DPJ Secretary-General Ozawa Desires Strong U.S.-Japan Relations; Expresses Concern Regarding China," Feb. 9, 2010, WikiLeaks.

243 **"the specter of the Japanese liberation army":** Murphy, *Japan and the Shackles of the Past,* 336.

244 **He'll tell you he supports:** "Assistant Secretary Campbell's February 2 Meeting with Minister of State for Okinawa Maehara," Feb. 8, 2010, WikiLeaks.

244 **From the record of their conversation:** "DPJ Secretary-General Ozawa Desires Strong U.S.-Japan Relations."

244 **A courtly, urbane character:** By contrast, once he was posted to Washington, Cui sometimes struggled to handle blunter U.S. officials, like Susan Rice. He usually addressed Ms. Rice as "Ma'am."

245 **"If you are asking for the emperor":** Mari Yamaguchi, "China Official's Royal Audience Stirs Ire in Japan," Associated Press, Dec. 15, 2009.

245 **"golden opportunity":** Martin Fackler, "In Japan, U.S. Losing Diplomatic Ground to China," *New York Times,* Jan. 23, 2010.

246 **"We offered to have talks":** Personal interview.

246 **"I have never understood":** Personal interview.

246 **"Maybe the bureaucracy":** Personal interview.

246 **Hu was still vulnerable:** "MOFA China Division Director on Japan-China Relations," March 4, 2005, WikiLeaks.

247 **"The real reason":** Personal interview.

247 **headline on the WikiLeaks cable:** "No Joy in Arranging Hu Visit to Japan."

Chapter Twelve: China Lays Down the Law

249 **"These islands might be pieces of dirt":** Personal interview.

249 **map produced by the Nationalists:** Because it was the Nationalist government that produced the first map, before its leaders fled to Taipei, Taiwan in theory makes the same claim as China.

250 **"indisputable sovereignty":** See Michael M. Swaine and M. Taylor Fravel, "China's Assertive Behavior—Part Two: The Maritime Periphery," *China Leadership Monitor,* no. 35 (2011): 1–29.

250 **Chinese state planted flags:** See ibid.

251 **"I love BP":** Madame Fu's visit was first reported in detail by Bill Hayton in his book *The South China Sea: The Struggle for Power in Asia* (Yale University Press, 2014), 136–37, and was confirmed by BP executives. See also Bill Hayton, "China Is Trying to Outflank Vietnam Within ASEAN," *National Interest,* May 16, 2016.

252 **"Because we were weak":** Robert Gates, *Duty: Memoirs of a Secretary at War* (Alfred A. Knopf, 2014), 416.

252 **"This effort has largely succeeded":** Simon S. C. Tay, *Asia Alone: The Dangerous Post-crisis Divide from America* (John Wiley & Sons, 2010), 14, 58.

252 **statesmen like Lee Kuan Yew:** See Fareed Zakaria, "Culture Is Destiny: A Conversation with Lee Kuan Yew," *Foreign Affairs,* March/April 1994, https://paulbacon.files .wordpress.com/2010/04/zakaria_lee.pdf.

253 **"China tells us that countries":** See Graham Allison and Robert Blackwill, *Lee Kuan Yew: The Grand Master's Insights on China, the United States, and the World,* with Ali Wyne (Belfer Center Studies in International Security, 2013).

254 **"The Japanese ambassador was coming":** See Jeffrey Bader, "Obama Policy Toward China and Asia" (speech at Harvard Fairbank Center, Dec. 14, 2011), https://www .youtube.com/watch?v=cbNyiYJDXuY.

255 **postponed the visit of the Dalai Lama:** "Ambassador Bader and FM Yang Discuss the President's China Trip, Trade Friction, Taiwan, Iran, Af/Pak," Sept. 16, 2009, WikiLeaks.

256 **"We were about 40 vans down":** "America: A Fearsome Foursome," *Financial Times,* Feb. 3, 2010.

256 **"gunfight at the OK Corral":** See Bader, "Obama Policy Toward China and Asia."

256 **"sent inconsistent signals":** Medeiros, interview by Bonnie Glaser, *ChinaPower* (podcast), Sept. 29, 2016, http://chinapower.csis.org/podcasts/, at about twenty-eight-minute mark.

256 **"There was a belief":** See Bader, "Obama Policy Toward China and Asia."

256 **Beijing's labeling of an issue:** Michael D. Swaine, "China's Assertive Behavior—Part One: On Core Interest," *China Leadership Monitor,* no. 34 (2010).

257 **South China Sea as a "core interest":** "Chinese Military Seeks to Extend Its Naval Power," *New York Times,* April 23, 2010, http://www.nytimes.com/2010/04/24/world /asia/24navy.html?_r=0. The story is slightly ambiguously worded as to whether the Chinese told Bader and Steinberg that the South China Sea was a "core interest."

257 **"We had had lots of discussions":** Personal interview.

257 **a statement claiming "indisputable sovereignty":** John Pomfret, "Beijing Claims 'Indisputable Sovereignty' over the South China Sea," *Washington Post,* July 31, 2010.

257 **"No internal or public Chinese document":** "The Core of the Issue," *Beijing Review,* Aug. 29, 2013, http://www.bjreview.com.cn/print/txt/2013-08/26/content_562998_2.htm.

257 **"I immediately said":** Hillary Clinton, interview by Greg Sheridan of *Australian,* Nov. 8, 2010, https://2009-2017.state.gov/secretary/20092013clinton/rm/2010/11/150671.htm.

258 **"They are easier to intimidate":** Gates, *Duty,* 417.

258 **"He reacted volcanically":** Bader, "Obama Policy Toward China and Asia."

258 **Yang took aim:** The details of this meeting are reconstructed from conversations with people in the room.

258 **"China is a big country":** There are two versions for what Yang said here. The second, slightly less colorful, has him saying, "China is a big country, bigger than any other countries here."

259 **Okada raised his hand:** Personal interview with a number of people in the meeting, including Okada; see also Jeffrey Lewis, "Did Yang Jiechi Lose It?," *Arms Control Wonk,* May 25, 2010, http://www.armscontrolwonk.com/archive/202747/did-yang-jiechi -lose-it/.

259 **one of China's first barbarian handlers:** See James Mann, "Does China Have Any Friends Left in the Obama Administration?," *New Republic,* Aug. 26, 2010.

260 **Dai published a lengthy article:** "Zhongguo guowu weiyuan Dai Bingguo: Jianchi zou heping fazhan zhi lu" [State Councillor Dai Bingguo: Adhere to the path of peaceful development], Dec. 6, 2010.

260 **At the White House, Tom Donilon:** David Sanger, *Confront and Conceal: Obama's Secret Wars and the Surprising Use of American Power* (Broadway Books, 2012).

261 **"There was an internal debate":** Bader, "Obama Policy Toward China and Asia."

261 **"lift the Chinese people out of poverty":** Dai Bingguo, "China's Peaceful Development Is Good for America," *Wall Street Journal,* May 9, 2011.

262 **tapes of the incident:** See the footage carried by *Japan Probe,* http://www.japanprobe .com/2010/11/05/senkaku-footage-leaked-on-to-internet-shows-chinese-trawler-ramming -japanese-patrol-boat/.

262 **"I was targeted by China":** Personal interview.

263 **"minor fender bender":** William Wan, "Boat Collision Sparks Anger, Breakdown in China-Japan Talks," *Washington Post,* Sept. 20, 2010.

264 **"Did we back down?":** Personal interview.

265 **embargo on the export of rare earths:** Amy King and Shiro Armstrong, "Did China Really Ban Rare Earth Metals Exports to Japan?," *East Asia Forum,* Aug. 18, 2013, http://www .eastasiaforum.org/2013/08/18/did-china-really-ban-rare-earth-metals-exports-to-japan/.

265 **Chinese officials privately told:** Interviews with U.S. officials.

Chapter Thirteen: Nationalization

270 **"I don't like Communism":** Ishihara's speech can be found on the Heritage Foundation Web site at https://www.youtube.com/watch?v=b90cZQOOAnw.

270 **Ishihara's address triggered a chain reaction:** This section on the handling of the 2012 crisis over the islands is based on interviews with officials in Japan, China, and the United States. Also helpful was the book by the Japanese journalist Tsuyoshi Sunohara, *Anto: Senkaku kokuyu-ka* [Hidden struggle: Nationalization of the Senkakus] (Shincho-sha, 2013).

272 **"Ishihara raised the bar":** Personal interview.

274 **CCP is much like the deep national security state:** See Mike Lofgren, *The Deep State: The Fall of the Constitution and the Rise of the Shadow Government* (Viking, 2016), for a description of this phenomenon.

274 **accused of conspiring with Zhou Yongkang:** "Disgraced Officials Zhou Yongkang and Bo Xilai Formed 'Clique' to Challenge Leaders," *South China Morning Post,* Jan. 15, 2015.

274 **"not only greedy financially":** "Chinese President Accuses Fallen Top Officials of 'Political Conspiracies,'" *South China Morning Post,* Jan. 2, 2017.

275 **Paulson had tried to leverage his relationship:** Jane Perlez, "Henry Paulson on 'Dealing with China,'" *New York Times,* April 24, 2015.

275 **"You know, Director":** Personal interview.

276 **"China never said yes":** Personal interview.

276 **"China's response was":** Personal interview.

276 **"Sasae [of the Foreign Ministry] believes that China":** "U.S. Urged Japan to Consult with China Before 2012 Senkakus Purchase," *Japan Times,* Jan. 31, 2016.

277 **"We never imagined that Japan":** Quoted in Jessica Chen Weiss, *Powerful Patriots: Nationalist Protest in China's Foreign Relations* (Oxford University Press, 2014), 205.

278 **"Can I shout":** See the Lai See column in the *South China Morning Post,* Sept. 21, 2012, quoting *Caixin* magazine.

278 **"No one would doubt":** quoted in "Beijing Mixes Messages over Anti-Japan Protests," September 16, 2012.

279 **Western newspapers credulously reported:** See Mark Kitto, "What Really Happened to Xi Jinping," *Prospect,* Oct. 31, 2012.

279 **Xi reappeared, with the state media announcing:** Jonathan Fenby, "The Missing Mr. Xi and the Price of Official Secrecy," *New York Times,* Sept. 17, 2012.

279 **His role in heading up the party group:** The Taiwanese media mentioned Xi's role in Sept. 2012, but nothing definitive was reported until the following year. http://phtv .ifeng.com/program/jqgcs/detail_2012_12/27/20577385_0.shtml.

279 **"Given our clear commitments":** Personal interview.

280 **"We assess that the Chinese":** See https://wikileaks.org/clinton-emails/emailid/7487.

280 **"You have to avoid":** Personal interview.

280 **"Their main pitch was":** Personal interview.

281 **"If this thing got out of control":** Personal interview.

281 **"While the US is scurrying":** "China Avoids Diaoyu Mediation Attempts by US Delegation," *Global Times,* Oct. 24, 2012.

281 **"'We appreciate your neutrality'":** "U.S. Not Neutral About Japan, Armitage Told Beijing," *Wall Street Journal,* Nov. 29, 2012.

281 **The crisis and its aftermath:** "Niwa: Japan-China Ties Face Worst Crisis in 40 Years," *Asahi Shimbun,* Oct. 21, 2012; also quoted here, http://chinamatters.blogspot.com/2012 /10/us-learns-hard-lessons-of-asia-pivot.html.

282 **"Both sides are saying"**: Campbell's comments were made in a conversation with Susan Shirk, on June 7, 2013, in an event broadcast on University of California Television.

284 **"strategic reassurance"**: Steinberg himself claims his speech, and the phrase, were known in advance; no one raised any objection to it.

284 **"That [phrase] caused a lot of anger and angst"**: Personal interview.

284 **"They did not want it"**: Personal interview.

285 **"It was a shorthand code"**: Personal interview.

285 **"Rarely in history"**: Kurt M. Campbell, *The Pivot: The Future of American Statecraft in Asia* (Twelve, 2016), 121.

285 **"I always encourage the U.S."**: Personal interview.

287 **"No one wanted to send"**: Personal interview.

287 **"All China is doing"**: "US Strategists Face Dilemma over South China Sea," *Financial Times*, July 9, 2014.

287 **"If there's anyone who knows"**: Ely Ratner, "Learning the Lessons of Scarborough Reef," *National Interest*, Nov. 21, 2013.

287 **"demonstrated that U.S. efforts"**: Ibid.

288 **"The purpose of isolating"**: See "Reforming Chinese Diplomacy Through Innovation," May 25, 2014, http://www.imir.tsinghua.edu.cn/publish/iis/7237/20140614134840 011604362/ReformingChineseDiplomacyThroughInnovation.pdf.

Chapter Fourteen: Creation Myths

289 **The president was in Brisbane:** The account of the Brisbane meeting comes from three people in the room at different times and officials briefed on the meeting.

290 **"We just could not have a situation"**: Personal interview.

293 **"Our families have been united"**: This story was told to John Garnaut during his research for his (as yet unpublished) book on Chinese elite politics.

293 **Xi's father never fired a shot:** Jia Juchen, *Xi Zhongxun zhuan* [Biography of Xi Zhongxun], vol. 1 (CCCPC Party Literature Publishing House, 2013); Jia Juchen et al., *Xi Zhongxun zhuan*, vol. 2 (CCCPC Party Literature Publishing House, 2013).

293 **far from repudiating Mao:** See Andrew J. Nathan, "Who Is Xi?," *New York Review of Books*, May 12, 2016.

294 **"There are two Xi Jinpings"**: Andrew Higgins, "For China's Next Leader, the Past Is Sensitive," *Washington Post*, Feb. 13, 2012.

294 **"talks like Mao and acts like Deng"**: I first heard this line from Chris Johnson, the former chief China analyst for the CIA, now at the Center for Strategic and International Studies in Washington.

294 **"extraordinary contribution in creating"**: *Takungpao*, July 8, 2014, http://news .takungpao.com/mainland/focus/2014-07/2585020.html.

294 **Xi Zhongxun had personally approved:** *Beijing News*, July 6, 2015, http://epaper .bjnews.com.cn/html/2015-07/06/content_585877.htm?div=0.

295 **"By no means can the terrible crimes"**: Kurzman, *Kishi and Japan*, 141.

296 **Chōshū was to the Meiji Restoration:** Thanks to Tobias Harris for this formula.

297 **"This prefecture is the source of war criminals"**: The prime ministers listed by Liu were Itō Hirobumi, Aritomo Yamagata, Tarō Katsura, Masatake Terauchi, Giichi Tanaka, Nobusuke Kishi, Eisaku Satō, and Shinzō Abe. Naoto Kan was also born in Yamaguchi, but wasn't mentioned.

297 **Privately, reactions in China:** The comments in this paragraph come from personal conversations.

297 **Chinese academic based in Japan:** Jane Perlez, "China Is Said to Be Holding a Professor Based in Japan," *New York Times*, Oct. 1, 2013, http://www.nytimes.com/2013/10/02 /world/asia/china-is-said-to-be-holding-professor-over-his-activities-in-japan.html?_r=0.

298 **Japanese prime ministers would try to avoid:** Funabashi, *Alliance Adrift*, 117–20.

298 **"Look at that"**: Personal interview.

299   **"We have not learned":** Personal interview.

300   **"You would need a microscope":** This is from two people in the meeting. Russel himself said he couldn't recall making this comment.

300   **"spectacle of a Japanese government":** See Tessa Morris-Suzuki, "Japan and the Art of Un-apologising," *East Asia Forum,* July 16, 2014.

301   **"It was sort of like":** Personal interview.

301   **"The Japanese told us":** Personal interview.

301   **"Their image at the start":** Personal interview.

302   **"Abe believes that the lectures":** Personal interview.

302   **"Look at the right side":** Personal interview.

302   **"And then, my government":** "Remarks by Prime Minister Shinzo Abe on the Occasion of Accepting Hudson Institute's 2013 Herman Kahn Award," Sept. 25, 2013, http://japan.kantei.go.jp/96_abe/statement/201309/25hudson_e.html.

302   **"It's unlike any diplomacy":** "6 Takeaways from the New Hillary Clinton Emails," NPR, Jan. 29, 2016, http://www.npr.org/2016/01/29/464936930/6-takeaways-from-the-new-hillary-clinton-emails.

303   **"I go to see Abe":** Steve Clemons, "The Geopolitical Therapist: A Conversation with Vice President Joe Biden," *Atlantic,* Aug. 26, 2016.

304   **"If there were no assertive":** Personal interview.

304   **"That was one reason":** Personal interview.

304   **"I have said to Abe privately":** Personal interview.

304   **"They want to get":** Personal interview.

305   **a vast part of the airspace:** See Eric Heginbotham, "China's ADIZ in the East China Sea," *Lawfare,* Aug. 24, 2014, for an excellent account of such zones in the sea off China and Japan.

305   **"The magistrates are free":** "U.S., Japan Wrong to Blame China for Air Zone," Xinhua, Nov. 26, 2013.

307   **"Now they have the ability":** Personal interview.

307   **"Make no mistake":** Sam Roggeveen, "Blunt Words on China from US Navy," *Lowy Interpreter,* Feb. 5, 2013.

307   **a "short, sharp war":** "Naval Intel Officer Warns of Future China Conflict," *Washington Free Beacon,* Feb. 2, 2015.

307   **"They did a number of basic":** Personal interview with the retired leader.

308   **"When they did not have":** Personal interview.

308   **"That would be":** Personal interview.

Chapter Fifteen: Freezing Point

309   **"I told Chinese leaders":** Personal interview.

311   **Through Chinese eyes, the trouble:** I interviewed both Li Datong, the editor, and Yuan Weishi, the historian, for my previous book, *The Party.*

311   **"Look at Tokyo's":** Personal interview.

312   **Investment in China flatlined:** Taken from a presentation by Hiroyuki Ishige, chairman and CEO of the Japan External Trade Organization (JETRO), "Progress of Asia-Pacific Economic Integration and the Role of the U.S. and Japan," June 14, 2016.

312   **"should be prepared":** *Washington Free Beacon,* quoting Xinhua, Sept. 18, 2013.

313   **"while the spirit of these declarations":** Adam Liff, "Principles Without Consensus: Setting the Record Straight on the 2014 Sino-Japanese 'Agreement to Improve Bilateral Relations'" (working paper, Nov. 8, 2014), http://www.adamphailliff.com/documents/Liff2014_PrinciplesWithoutConsensus.pdf.

314   **"forced to move toward Xi":** Personal interview, here with Tanino.

314   **Xi had been "courageous":** Personal communication.

315   **"A light went off":** Personal interview.

316   **"Yes, yes":** Personal interview.

316   **"He felt they didn't act":** Personal interview.

316   **"the Japanologists and Sinologists":** Personal interview.

316   **"There is frustration in the American system":** Personal interview.

319   **"They immediately started going around Asia":** Personal interview.

319   **"was actually conceived":** Personal interview with former officials who had spoken to Dai.

320   **"We have so much data":** "Targeting Huawei," *Der Spiegel International*, March 22, 2014, http://www.spiegel.de/international/world/nsa-spied-on-chinese-government -and-networking-firm-huawei-a-960199.html.

320   **"It's really amazing":** "Cyber Crime: Hacked Off," *Financial Times*, May 23, 2014.

321   **"affects the dignity":** Personal conversation with one of China's top international rela- tions scholars. I have no independent confirmation from either Obama's or Xi's office.

321   **"We slathered him":** Personal interview.

322   **"former adversaries can become powerful allies":** The press conference transcript can be accessed here: https://www.whitehouse.gov/the-press-office/2015/04/28/remarks -president-obama-and-prime-minister-abe-japan-joint-press-confere.

323   **"Starting from 2012":** Personal interview.

324   **divided their work into three sections:** Kawashima Shin, "The Three Phases of Japan- China Joint History Research: What Was the Challenge?," *Asian Perspective* 34, no. 4 (2010): 19–43.

324   **"When a politician raises history":** "PRC-Japan History Dialogue: Comfort Woman Issue Low Profile but Much Controversy Remains," March 19, 2007, https://wikileaks .org/plusd/cables/07BEIJING1841_a.html.

324   **Bu, as the leader:** See "PRC-Japan History Dialogue: Comfort Women Issue Low Profile but Much Controversy Remains," May 19, 2007, WikiLeaks; https://wikileaks .org/plusd/cables/07BEIJING1841_a.html; also, personal interview with Bu Ping.

325   **"great massacre faction":** For an excellent account of the evolving disputes in both countries over Nanjing, see Daqing Yang, "A Sino-Japanese Controversy: The Nanjing Atrocity as History," *Sino-Japanese Studies* 3, no. 1 (1990), http://chinajapan.org/articles /03.1/03.1.14-35yang.pdf.

325   **"middle-of-the-road" faction:** See David Askew, "New Research on the Nanjing Inci- dent," *Asia-Pacific Journal* 2, issue 7 (2004), http://apjjf.org/-David-Askew/1729/article .html.

326   **To be called "pro-Japanese":** WikiLeaks op cit.

326   **"The Chinese government will not":** Shin, "Three Phases of Japan-China Joint His- tory Research."

327   **"I am basically part of the academic part":** Bu Ping passed away in August 2016 from a cancer-related illness. One of the Japanese participants in the history project, Akio Takahara of Tokyo University, in lamenting Bu's death, said, "We lost another rare 'moderate' in today's China."

328   **The official ruling by state censors:** The document was posted on China Copyright and Media on Oct. 17, 2002, edited by Rogier Creemers, https://chinacopyrightandmedia .wordpress.com/2012/10/17/devils-on-the-doorstep-an-interesting-look-into-film-censorship/. It also appeared on *China Digital Times*.

328   **70 percent of the dramas:** See "China World of Anti-Japan Films," Reuters, Aug. 23, 2013; "China's Television War on Japan," *New York Times*, Feb. 9, 2014.

329   **"Resisting-Japan Bizarre Dramas":** See "China's Bizarre Anti-Japanese TV and Movie Kitsch Backfires," *Washington Times*, May 21, 2015; "Anti-Japan Plays Must Not Play with Facts," *China Daily*, May 23–24, 2015.

330   **"We asked the Chinese":** Personal interview.

331   **"total victory against the Japanese":** Frank Ching, "How China Tried to Rewrite History with Military Parade," *EJ Insight*, Sept. 8, 2015.

332   **"If you read it":** Personal interview.

Afterword

334 **"My grandfather was killed"**: Personal interview.

334 **"Now is actually a good time"**: Personal interview.

335 **Chinese government called the Mitsui affair**: See Lucy Hornby, "Mitsui OSK Settles to Free Ship Impounded in China," *Financial Times,* April 23, 2014; "Japan's Mitsui Pays China to Release Seized Ship," Reuters, April 24, 2014.

337 **"Once upon a time, a man"**: Liu Bai, *Tong Zeng: Messenger of Peace* (Mistral, 2015), 249–63.

340 **"namesake of a Japanese cruiser"**: Xinhua, Aug. 7, 2013.

341 **to settle its land borders:** With the possible exception of India, China was largely successful in this endeavor.

342 **"They look like major fighter bases"**: Thomas Shugart, "China's Artificial Islands Are Bigger (and a Bigger Deal) Than You Think," *War on the Rocks,* Sept. 21, 2016, https://warontherocks. com/2016/09/chinas-artificial-islands-are-bigger-and-a-bigger-deal-than-you-think/.

344 **"decaying credibility in east Asia"**: "Meddling in the Diaoyu Islands Doomed to Be a Bad Deal for Washington," *People's Daily,* Feb. 7, 2017.

344 **The U.S. withdrawal:** Funabashi was speaking at a conference organized by the Sasakawa Foundation at the Willard Hotel in Washington on May 2, 2017.

345 **"If we had sent our coast guard ships"**: Personal interview.

346 **"The heat in the pool"**: Bill Gertz, "How China Wins the South China Sea War (Without Firing a Shot)," *National Interest,* Jan. 10, 2017.

347 **Chinese played the same game:** "President Xi Parties Like an Ancient Sinocentrist," *Nikkei Asian Review,* Sept. 16, 2016.

347 **"August and September are months"**: Ken Moriyasu, "China's Need to Show Strength at Home Stirs Up Trouble at Sea," *Nikkei Asian Review,* Aug. 11, 2016.

349 **"a right-wing Japanese"**: See "News Analysis: Shunji Yanai, Manipulator Behind Illegal South China Sea Arbitration," *People's Daily,* July 17, 2016; "China Puts Japan in Cross Hairs with Blistering, Sustained Attack over Alleged Role in Sea Ruling," *Japan Times,* Aug. 2, 2016.

349 **"Some may say"**: Quoted in "A U.S. Admiral's Bluntness Rattles China, and Washington," *New York Times,* May 6, 2016.

350 **"unbelievable job"**: Transcript at *The Intercept,* http://theintercept.com/2017/05/23 /read-the-full-transcript-of-trumps-call-with-philippine-president-rodrigo-duterte/.

351 **When Trump was presented:** The text of the statement can be found at https://www .whitehouse.gov/the-press-office/2017/02/10/joint-statement-president-donald-j-trump -and-prime-minister-shinzo-abe.

352 **In place of:** Personal interviews.

352 **"If we step back"**: "*The Economist* Interviews Donald Trump," *Economist,* Sept. 2, 2015. Thanks to David Rennie for pointing out this transcript.

Index

Abbott, Tony, 289–90, 291
Abe, Shintaro, 81, 83, 110
Abe, Shinzō, 8, 14, 35, 83, 179, 202–8, 211,
    219, 265, 289–92, 305
    on comfort women, 205–7, 300,
        318, 349
    on democratic values, 322–23
    and history wars, 300–304, 318, 321,
        349–50
    life story of, 294–97
    and North Korean abductions, 208, 210
    on postwar "victor's justice," 204–5, 332
    return to office, 283, 285, 292, 299–304
    and Sino-Japanese relations, 35, 181, 288,
        310, 312, 313–14, 329–30, 346–50
    Toward a Beautiful Country, 202–3
    U.S. visits of, 302, 318, 321–23, 324, 344,
        349–50, 352
    and Yasukuni Shrine, 187–88, 202, 203,
        204, 289, 302–4, 312, 321, 322
Afghanistan, U.S. war in, 176, 184, 223,
    283, 340
Akiba, Takeo, 201, 247
Akihito, Emperor, 93, 124–28, 129, 153, 180,
    245, 334
Albania, 35
Albright, Madeleine, 124
Amaya, Naohiro, 103–4, 109, 120, 136
Anami, Koreshige, 174–75, 176, 181–82
Aquino, Benigno, 288
Armacost, Michael, 156
Armitage, Richard, 243, 249, 280–81,
    302, 314
Asahi Shimbun, 100, 272, 304
Asakai, Koichiro, 38

ASEAN, 226, 248–49, 250, 252–54,
    257–60, 261, 284
Asia:
    changing diplomatic landscape in, 51, 60,
        222, 243, 252–57, 350–51
    China's rise to power in, 241, 242,
        252–58, 285–88
    Chinese cultural influence in, 125, 252
    and cold war, 21, 26, 32, 84
    "C-shaped encirclement" of China in,
        238–39
    economic growth in, 340
    financial crisis (1990s), 222
    Japanese apologies in, 154–55, 164
    Japanese economic effect in, 142, 222
    Nixon's travels to, 42
    Pan-Asian union, 13, 138, 139–43
    Pax Americana in, xv–xvi, 4–7, 10, 13, 15,
        21, 42, 99, 101, 305, 340, 341
    Sinocentric order in, xvi, 7, 23, 252–54
    Soviet encroachment in, 84, 104, 105, 106
    and T.P.P., 315, 317–23, 344, 351
    U.S. influence waning in, 139, 252–53,
        342, 344, 350–51
    U.S. military presence in, xvi, 4, 5, 6, 7, 8,
        11, 14, 25, 28, 42, 66, 115, 140, 142, 151,
        153, 220, 224–25, 226–27, 339
    U.S. pivot to, 7, 223, 254–57, 283–85,
        341, 344, 350–51
    U.S. policy on, 191, 254–58, 340, 341–42,
        350–51
    Western embargo in, 28, 60
    Western misunderstanding of, 25, 109
"Asian values," 12, 129, 130–31,
    139–40, 253

Asia-Pacific Economic Cooperation
 (APEC), 222, 267–69, 276–77,
 284–85, 313, 314–15, 346
Asia-Pacific summits, 177–78, 312
Asia That Can Say No, The (Mahathir and
 Ishihara), 140
Asō, Tarō, 185–86, 187–88, 217, 219, 254–55
Australia, 10, 25, 206, 222, 322, 350, 351

Bader, Jeff, 125–26, 221, 226, 255–57, 258,
 259, 261
Bai Jingfan, 171
Baker, James, 8, 134–36
Bannon, Stephen, 5, 351
Barmé, Geremie, 130
Beijing Olympics (2008), 216, 240, 324, 326
Berlin Wall, fall of, 114, 132, 186, 333
Biden, Joe, 287, 302–3, 304, 305, 319
Blair, Dennis, 275
Bo Xilai, 196–97, 198, 273–75, 279
Bo Yibo, 273
BP, and South China Sea, 250–51
Brandt, Willy, 72
Brock, William, 100
Brzezinski, Zbigniew, 11, 105
Bu Ping, 309, 323–24, 326–27
Bush, George H. W., 95, 98, 106, 124, 125,
 134, 145, 190–91, 194, 195, 259
Bush, George W., 114, 189, 190–94, 197–98,
 207, 243, 283, 290, 315
Bush (H. W.) administration, 133–36, 316
Bush (W.) administration, 115, 190,
 192–94, 198, 207–11, 275, 285,
 291, 302, 316, 323

Cairo conference (1943), 10, 11
Calderón, Felipe, 267, 268–69
Campbell, Kurt, 128, 129, 224–26, 243–44,
 257–58, 276, 280, 282, 283–84, 285,
 286, 299, 302
Carter, Ashton, 152, 339–41, 346, 350, 351
Carter, Jimmy, 102, 105
Carter administration, 11, 105, 157
CCP, *see* Chinese Communist Party
Cheney, Dick, 135, 211, 302
Chen Shui-bian, 191–92
Chiang Ching-guo, 149
Chiang Kai-shek, xiv, 20, 25, 34, 61, 62, 63,
 65, 130, 149, 179, 249, 293, 331
Chi Haotian, 152, 195–96

China:
 air defense zone, 305–8, 319
 anti-Western mission of, 245–46, 323
 as ascending superpower, 2, 5, 6–7, 10, 97,
  128, 129, 189, 228–29, 230–32, 235,
  240, 252–57, 265, 285, 309, 319, 332
 Beijing Olympics (2008), 216, 240,
  324, 326
 Boao Forum, 177
 Boxer Rebellion (1899–1900), 95
 British burning of Summer
  Palace (1860), 95
 "capitalism with Chinese
  characteristics," 235
 CCTV, 231–33
 censorship in, 60, 73, 171, 234–35,
  255–56, 327–28, 339
 "China threat theory," 236
 Chunxiao/Shirakaba gas field, 217
 civil war in, 28–29, 61, 149, 293
 and cold war, *see* cold war
 Communism in, *see* Chinese
  Communist Party
 "C-shaped encirclement" threats to,
  238–39
 cultural influence of, 3, 23, 53, 57, 62,
  125, 252
 Cultural Revolution, 56, 69, 84, 131,
  235, 293
 currency issues in, 83–84, 118, 119
 cyber theft in, 275, 319, 320–21
 death of panda in, 264
 disintegration of, 3, 23
 disputes within, 259–60
 economic growth of, 4, 6–7, 28, 36, 77,
  82–84, 87, 138, 140–41, 146, 154, 177,
  195, 231, 237, 240, 241–42, 245,
  268, 315
 economic problems of, 87–88, 240
 as energy exporter, 115
 foreign policy of, 28, 233, 235, 237–39,
  251–52, 253, 259–60
 Gang of Four, 69–70, 73, 169
 Great Leap Forward in, 35, 131
 and Gulf War, 136
 hereditary rule of, 294
 historical record in, xvi–xvii
 and history wars, *see* history wars
 imperial times in, 2, 57, 186, 234, 297
 and international class struggle, 132

and international law, 315, 318, 319–21, 335, 343, 348–49

Internet in, 132, 170, 171, 172, 184–85, 204, 218, 233–35, 237, 320–21, 349

isolation of, 128

and Japan, *see* China and Japan

and Korea, 199, 208–9

and Long March, 293

as managed economy, 115–16, 233

markets in, 13, 81, 84, 87, 96, 116, 119, 147, 184

and meetings in Cairo and Potsdam, 10, 11

military strategies of, 85, 153, 201–2, 236, 238–40, 251 52, 257, 262, 277, 278, 280, 282, 299, 302, 306–8, 314, 319, 320, 345, 346–47

nationalism in, 4, 93, 132, 154, 170–71, 173, 195, 213, 237, 263–64, 274, 277–78, 280–81, 287, 311, 338

and Nixon, 15, 19–23, 41–54

nuclear capability of, 154, 160, 247, 259

oil industry in, 213–14, 275

and Pacific War, *see* Pacific War

patriotic education campaign in, 130–32, 170, 185

Pax Sinica in Asia, xvi, 7, 23, 252–54

"peaceful rise" of, 235–37, 251, 260, 327

People's Republic (PRC), 29, 49, 63

population of, 218

post-Mao generation of leaders, 80–82, 87, 125, 151, 165

regional dominance sought by, xvi, 7, 9, 12–14, 23, 45, 91, 143, 157, 189, 201–2, 228, 230–32, 238–39, 252–58, 285–88, 305–8, 323–29, 341–42, 347

Republic of, *see* Taiwan

and revolution (1949), 21, 24, 28, 61, 179, 249, 273, 292–93

and San Francisco Treaty (1951), 10–11, 21

and Senkaku/Diaoyu Islands, 64–74, 79, 129, 154, 239, 261–62, 268–73, 275–76, 277–82, 292, 299, 303, 305–7, 310–14, 344–47

Shanghai Gang, 182

Sichuan earthquake, 217

sovereignty of, 217–18, 246, 256, 273, 280, 282, 327

and Soviet Union, 26, 53, 61, 70, 106, 120, 153, 278

state media in, 170, 172

student/public protests, 87, 94–95, 96, 129, 160, 185, 201, 204, 233–34, 235, 245, 246, 264, 277–78, 333, 338

technology in, 82, 85, 153

territorial claims of, xvii, 2, 10, 64–74, 129, 214, 238, 249–54, 256–58, 261–66, 285–88, 294, 305–8, 320, 341–45

Tiananmen Square protests (1985), 94–95, 96

Tiananmen Square protests (1989), 87, 129, 131, 136, 145, 146, 147, 169, 171, 172–73, 195, 273, 326, 330, 333

"Top Ten Traitors" of, 233–35, 246

tributary system in, 13–14

"two thirty-years" period of, 293–94

and United Nations, 37, 68, 136, 184

War of Liberation (civil war), 28–29

Western sanctions against, 125, 128, 136, 145, 147

and World Trade Organization, 183, 231

Yan'an revolutionary base, 292–93

China and Japan:

alliance of, 141, 203

anti-Japanese activism in China, 94–95, 203, 233–34, 311–12, 313, 329, 335, 338, 348

China-Japan Friendship Hospital, 83

China's Japan strategy, 29–31, 34–38, 47, 61, 132, 164, 171, 173

China's push for dominance, 13–14, 23, 157, 185, 189, 197, 201–2, 228, 231–32, 238–39, 241–47, 262, 292, 327

Chinese boat captain detained, 262–64, 265, 312

Chinese cultural infuence, 3, 23, 53, 57, 62

commercial ties, xiii–xiv, 6, 48, 72, 184, 212, 265, 310, 311–12, 315–18

complexities of relationship, 2–4, 6, 13, 24, 35, 42, 51–53, 71, 72, 132, 177, 292–94, 312–14, 333, 336, 346–49

diplomatic ties, 33–34, 48, 49, 52, 93, 124, 129, 242, 245

disputes, xiv, 2–4, 6, 9, 10, 27, 196–97, 213, 214–16, 234, 238, 252, 261–65, 336, 346–47

and East China Sea, 212, 213–14, 217–19, 234, 246, 251, 292

China and Japan *(cont.)*
  and "first island chain," 238–39
  fishing treaty, 30
  Freezing Point essay, 311
  geopolitics as influence on, 9, 83, 93,
    319, 323
  "Guidelines of Internal Propaganda,"
    60–61
  and history wars, *see* history wars
  Ishihara's Heritage Foundation speech,
    270–72
  Japanese aid program (1972), 72, 82–84,
    96, 97, 162, 181, 348
  and Japanese apologies, *see* history wars
  Japanese "China school" experts, 161,
    179–82, 314
  Japanese occupation of China, 2, 9,
    28–29, 31, 42, 62, 86, 162, 176, 196,
    234, 270, 331, 338
  and Japanese territorial expansion, 24,28
  Japanese textbooks, 86–87, 88, 94, 173
  Japanese war orphans stranded
    in China, 80
  and Japan's decline, 247
  Japan's dominance in, 44–45, 189
  and Japan's technology, 77–78, 203
  market economy status granted to
    China, 197
  military ties of, 106
  Nanjing Massacre, *see* Nanjing Massacre
  and Nixon, 37–38, 41–44, 45–47, 49
  normalization agreement, 63
  and Pacific War, *see* Pacific War
  and Pan-Asian union, 13
  peace treaty (1978), 69, 70–71, 73–74, 84,
    174, 310
  and poisoned dumplings, 213, 214–16
  possibility of war, 4, 5, 270, 307–8, 309,
    310, 312, 314, 321, 347–48
  rapprochement of, 52–53, 73, 81–82,
    85–86, 90, 125–26, 164, 179, 187,
    203–5, 216, 219–20, 247, 310–13,
    321–22, 323–24
  rare-earths trade, 265
  reversal of fortunes, 6, 23–24, 85, 130
  roots of discord, 85–86, 97, 130, 201–2,
    292, 310–14
  and Senkaku/Diaoyu Islands, 64–74, 79,
    261–62, 268–73, 275–76, 277–82, 292,
    297, 299, 303, 305–7, 310–14, 344–47

  shared Asian identity of, 3–4, 13, 23, 53,
    57, 62, 72, 79, 118, 172
  Sino-Japanese Wars, 9; First (1894–95),
    241, 297; Second (1937), 131, 176, 292
  "Three Alls" policy, 60
  and Tiananmen Square protests, 326
  trade agreements, 25, 30, 36, 37, 72,
    88, 203
  and two Chinas, 53–54, 61–62, 158
  and U.S. embargo, 31, 60
  and U.S.–Japan treaties, 27, 30, 202
  and World War II, *see* Pacific War
  and Yasukuni Shrine, 93–97, 184, 188,
    193, 303–4
China and Taiwan, 6, 7, 38, 199, 218, 336
  Chinese claim on Taiwan, 43, 61–62, 256
  Chinese threats to Taiwan, 147, 150–53,
    154, 157–58, 183, 202, 236, 238,
    239, 346
  civil war edict repealed, 149
  and one-China policy, 145, 148–49, 192
  and reunification, 149, 153
  two Chinas, 53–54, 58, 158, 160
China and United States:
  annual ministerial dialogue of, 261, 317
  China's cultivation of U.S., 36–37, 164
  and China's rise to power, 254–58, 291,
    341–42
  China's wish to remove U.S. influence, 13,
    220, 245–46, 278, 320, 323, 341
  Chinese–U.S. air crash (2001), 191
  and Clinton administration, 144–47,
    150–51
  economic rivalry, 7, 9, 101, 116,
    117, 319
  and freedom of the seas, 342
  human rights issue, 146–47, 255, 318
  Nixon's outreach to China, 15, 19–23, 37,
    41–45, 53–54, 56, 67, 68, 310
  normalization of relations (1979), 251–52
  and Pacific War, *see* Pacific War
  parallels with Japan–U.S. relations,
    115–20
  in Scarborough Shoal, 283, 286–88, 343
  and Taiwan, 144–45, 148–53, 179
  U.S. bombing of Chinese embassy,
    Belgrade, 185, 191
  U.S. recognition of China, 38
  U.S. trade embargo, 31, 60
China That Can Say No, The, 11, 132

China Youth League, 90, 183
Chinese Communist Party (CCP), 11,
    129, 338
  anniversary of, 240
  and CNOOC, 213–14
  and cold war, 20–21, 179
  Eight Immortals of the revolution, 273
  government controlled by, 9, 12–13, 73,
    117, 130, 145, 146, 172, 186, 231, 258
  history wars overlooked by, 60–61
  history wars rekindled by, xv, 49, 127
  internal schism in, 273–75
  and Japan, 29, 31–32, 34, 35, 36, 60, 63,
    85–86, 130, 159, 169–73, 174, 183,
    195, 310
  and Kuomintang, 331
  nationalism in, 73, 131, 154
  National People's Congress, 333–35
  and Pacific War anniversary, 323, 331
  party congress (1980s), 87–88, 272; (2012),
    273–74, 278
  patriotism as ideological tool, 90, 131–32
  and People's Daily, 29, 169–70
  and PLA, 151–52, 153, 157, 236, 237–38,
    250, 257, 305
  Politburo, 87–88, 230–31, 237, 259, 274,
    278, 293
  president as party chief, 242, 268
  propaganda of, xiv, 88, 90, 96, 170, 172,
    204, 235–37, 260, 299, 329, 344,
    348–49
  and revolution (1949), 21, 292–93
  rise to power, 28, 32, 231, 235, 245, 257
  and Taiwan, 25, 199
  and territorial sovereignty, 2, 250,
    275–76, 306, 308
  and two Chinas, 61, 179
  United Front Department, 277
Chinese Nationalists, 26, 61, 148, 293
  and Cairo meeting, 11
  exile in Taiwan, 25, 26, 61, 62, 130, 199,
    249; see also Taiwan
  and Nixon's outreach to "Red China,"
    20–21
  and Pacific War, xiv, 331
  and South China Sea, 249
Christopher, Warren, 146–47, 150
Churchill, Winston, 208, 271
Chu Shulong, 230, 234–35
CIA, 32–33, 38, 61, 64, 106, 108, 115

Clinton, Bill, 123, 142–43, 144, 145–47, 150,
    152, 160, 162, 191, 194, 195, 255
Clinton, Hillary, as secretary of state, 7, 129,
    224, 248, 254, 257, 258, 259, 267, 269,
    279–80, 283–84, 302, 344
Clinton administration, 115, 128–29, 138,
    140–43, 144–47, 148, 150–51, 157,
    224, 276
cold war:
  and Communism, 23, 25, 31, 32, 35, 36,
    179–80, 236
  end of, 7, 114, 128, 141, 186
  and Japan, 7–8, 25–27, 32, 34, 52, 60, 78,
    84–85, 99, 101, 103, 120, 142
  and "Red China," 20–21, 25, 27, 32,
    35, 37
  and Soviet Union, xvi, 6, 20, 21, 25–27,
    32, 42, 47, 51, 80, 84, 85, 101, 114,
    120, 236
  and trilateral relationship, 84
Confucian ideals, 12, 23, 26, 57, 108, 117,
    139–40
Connally, John, 47–48
Cui Tiankai, 3, 13, 244–45, 297, 309,
    311, 320
Cutler, Wendy, 223, 317

Dai Bingguo, 7, 186–87, 203–4, 257,
    260–61, 263, 264, 276, 279, 305, 319
Dai Xu, 230, 238, 239
Dalai Lama, 255–56
Deming, Rust, 22, 138–39
Deng Xiaoping, 144, 246
  CCP criticisms of, 87–88
  comeback of, 70
  death of, 151
  economic reforms of, 90, 128, 169, 170,
    235, 273, 293
  and Gang of Four, 69, 73
  on "hiding China's light," 28, 231,
    260, 261
  legacy of, 293–94
  political career of, 84
  purged by Mao, 69
  and Senkaku/Diaoyu Islands, 71, 73
  and Sino-Japanese relations, 77–79,
    81–82, 84, 96, 124, 216, 310
  and student protests, 96, 129, 273
  on Taiwan reunification, 153
  U.S. trip of, 77–79

Diaoyu Islands, *see* Senkaku/Diaoyu Islands
Doihara, Kenji, 92
Dokdo/Takeshima Islands, 345
Donilon, Tom, 260, 283–84
Dulles, John Foster, 10, 26, 34
Duterte, Rodrigo, 288, 350

East Asia Summit (2005), 222
East China Sea:
    in China's air defense zone, 305, 307
    Japanese-Chinese joint development of,
        212, 213–14, 217–19, 246
    oil and gas reserves in, 213–14, 219, 337
    territorial disputes in, 158, 213–14, 234,
        251, 292, 294, 305–8, 342
Eisenhower, Dwight D., 33, 35, 36,
    101–2
Eisenhower administration, 10, 26, 34
Europe, xiv, 21, 43, 112, 209
European Union, 197

Fallows, James, 116
Falun Gong, 159–60
Fanell, James, 306–8, 346
Fan Shuzhi, 233–34
Friedman, Thomas, 117
Froman, Mike, 315
Fu Hao, 70, 71
Fukuda, Takeo, 48–50, 53, 70,
    174, 309–10
Fukuda, Yasuo, 174–75, 178, 212, 215,
    216–17, 219, 309, 310, 312–14
Fukuzawa, Yukichi, 24
Fu Ying, 250–51, 286–87

G7/G20 meetings, 108, 346, 347
Gao Wenqian, 289, 294
Gates, Robert, 225, 227, 251–52, 258
Geithner, Tim, 135, 222
Germany, 114, 208, 232, 333, 347
    Nazi Party in, 43, 59, 72, 104
Gingrich, Newt, 145–46, 147
gold standard, abandonment of, 19, 47
Gore, Al, 144, 146
Gotoda, Masaharu, 33, 95, 126
Great East Asia Co-prosperity Sphere, 12
Green, Michael, xvi, 190, 193–94, 198, 209,
    302, 304, 323
Gregson, Chip, 220–21, 298
Guam, U.S. military in, 220, 228

Gulf of Aden, antipiracy operations in, 306
Gulf War, 132–36, 137, 152, 192

Hadley, Stephen, 191, 280
Haig, Alexander, 41–42
Hainan Island, 191
Harris, Harry, 342–43, 349
Hashimoto, Ryutaro, 156, 157, 161, 298
Hatoyama, Ichirō, 34–35
Hatoyama, Yukio, 13, 35, 212, 219–28, 239,
    242, 245–46, 263, 268, 281, 322
Heritage Foundation, 269–70
Hersh, Seymour, 51
Hill, Christopher, 190, 193, 209–11
Hirohito, Emperor, 26–27, 70, 79, 93,
    330, 331
    death of, 124
history wars, 9–11, 88–97
    comfort women, 10, 154, 200, 205–7, 291,
        300, 318, 326, 329, 331, 349
    Japanese apologies for atrocities and war,
        xv, 4, 9, 10, 28, 58–60, 62, 72, 73, 79,
        82, 131–32, 154–58, 161–64, 171, 176,
        188, 200, 208, 300–301, 326, 348
    Japanese atrocities (1930s and 1940s), xiv,
        xvii, 2, 9–10, 26, 29, 46, 60, 88, 124,
        131, 154, 176, 200, 304, 321–22,
        324–25
    Japanese invasion and occupation of
        Asian nations, 87, 154
    Japanese invasion and occupation of
        China (1930s and 1940s), 2, 9, 28–29,
        31, 42, 62, 86, 162, 176, 196, 234, 270,
        331, 338
    Japanese territorial reach, 23, 311
    Marco Polo Bridge clash, 131, 175–76, 294
    moving away from, 187, 189, 193–94, 198
    Nanjing Massacre, 9, 29, 70, 71, 95, 97,
        112, 131, 245, 304, 324–26, 327,
        332, 350
    as obstacle to postwar settlement, 10, 28,
        52–54, 58, 60–61, 63–64, 72, 73, 87,
        96–97, 143, 154, 171, 178–79, 187, 189,
        193, 205, 211, 321, 324–27
    and reparations from Japan, 9, 10, 25, 27,
        45–46, 58, 63–64, 73, 82–83, 96, 97,
        131–32, 156, 199–200, 333–36
    revisionist views of, xv, 13–14, 26–27, 86,
        130–32, 189, 205–7, 216, 300–301,
        325–27, 349

Sino-Japanese panel on, 323–27
Sino-Japanese wars, 9, 131, 176, 241,
    292, 297
and South Korea, 198–201, 291, 318, 349
and trilateral relations, 196–97
U.S. interests damaged by, 303
U.S. stoking memories of, 42, 45, 46, 192,
    198, 290–92, 304
and Yasukuni Shrine, 91–94, 176, 178–79,
    188, 192–93, 196–99
Holbrooke, Richard, 120
Hormats, Robert, 22, 114–15, 267–69
Hosokawa, Morihiro, 155
Howard, John, 193, 206
Hu Jintao, 182–84, 230–31, 236
    advisers of, 7, 89, 186, 187, 257, 261, 337
    and Sino-Japanese relations, 89–90,
        183–84, 193, 203, 204, 212, 215–16,
        217, 222–23, 228, 242–44, 268–69,
        276–77, 305, 310
    and Sino-U.S. relations, 210, 243, 320
    and succession, 1–2, 182, 244, 294
    and Yasukuni Shrine, 190, 192–93
Hummel, Arthur, 69
Hussein, Saddam, 128, 133, 135
Hu Yaobang, 80–82, 87, 88–90, 95–96, 183,
    235, 273, 292–93

Ikeda, Hayato, 37, 51
Inada, Tomomi, 349–50
India, 23, 322, 351
Indonesia, territory of, 348
International Monetary Fund, 119, 222
International Tribunal for the Law of the
    Sea, 348–49
Iran, nuclear program in, 223, 318
Iraq, U.S. invasion of, 114, 128, 132–36, 152,
    184, 190, 192, 283, 339, 343
Ishibashi, Tanzan, 34
Ishihara, Shintaro, 91, 112–14, 132, 268,
    269–72, 276, 280
Israel, Japanese attack on Lod Airport,
    48–49
Itō, Hirobumi, 296
Ito, Masayoshi, 104
Izumo, 340–41

Japan:
    agricultural markets of, 315–16, 317–18
    air defense zone of, 305–6, 319

apologies from, see history wars
Asia-Pacific role of, 138, 139–43,
    222, 351
atomic bombs dropped on, xiv, 8, 27, 114,
    174, 194–96, 331
and Australia, 206, 222, 322, 351
Blue Storm Society, 90–91, 113
and China, see China and Japan
Clinton's visit to, 194, 195
and cold war, 7–8, 25, 32, 34, 52, 60,
    84–85, 99, 101, 103, 120, 142
conservatives in, 8, 27, 32–34, 36, 50, 62,
    64, 86, 92–94, 116, 126, 157, 173, 180,
    202, 206, 210, 217, 223, 243, 329
constitution of, 8, 24, 25, 42, 79,
    203, 228
democracy in, 31–32, 42, 46, 72, 91, 99,
    116, 141, 195, 203, 239, 322, 326, 327
Democratic Party of (DPJ), 219, 227–28,
    242–45, 262–63, 268, 272, 281
diffuse power in, 43
economic decline of, 4, 6, 7, 128, 138–39,
    154, 240, 241–42, 245–47, 268
economic growth of, 4, 6, 8, 12, 21, 37,
    42, 45, 50, 77–78, 80, 91, 99–105, 114,
    118–19, 137, 139, 142
education in, 3, 23, 78, 86–87, 88, 94
emperor worship in, 46, 91
flag and national anthem of, 137, 155
as global power, 5, 114, 189
and history wars, see history wars
Imperial Army of, 29, 42, 45, 58, 60, 86,
    95, 154, 205
independence of (1951), 24–25
influence in nineteenth century, 23–24
keiretsu system of, 117
Kono Statement (1993), 205–7
and Korea, 199–201, 207–8, 209–10, 297
Liberal Democratic Party (LDP), 32–33,
    48, 52, 58, 62, 69, 73, 86, 91–92, 96,
    116, 129, 134, 136–37, 138, 139, 155,
    156, 172, 173, 174, 178, 180, 182, 186,
    198, 202, 219, 221, 225, 227, 242, 268,
    310–11
as managed economy, 110–11, 115
and Meiji Restoration (1868), 23,
    248, 296
military/militarism of, 14, 15, 24, 25,
    27–28, 42–43, 45–46, 47, 63–64, 77,
    80, 84–85, 91, 94, 101, 103–13, 133–36,

Japan *(cont.)*
  138, 140, 157, 158, 162, 170, 202, 203,
    205, 221, 223, 228, 232, 253, 288,
    298–99, 307, 321, 337, 340
  MITI, 103, 109, 116, 120, 135–36
  modernization in, 3, 23, 44, 78, 84,
    232–33, 241, 296
  nationalism in, 4, 73, 90–93, 112, 115,
    126, 138, 156, 175, 185, 202, 206, 213,
    263–64, 268, 272, 301, 311
  and North Korea, 141–42, 207–10
  nuclear weapons in, 223
  and Okinawa, 220
  and Pacific War, *see* Pacific War
  and Pan-Asian union, 13, 138, 139–43
  population decline in, 64, 242, 247, 346
  protectionism of, 48, 316
  Red Army terror group, 48–49
  security policy of, 133–34, 141, 184, 281, 299
  Self-Defense Agency (1970), 80
  and Senkaku/Diaoyu Islands, 65–74, 79,
    239, 261–62, 268–73, 275–76, 277–82,
    292, 299, 303, 305–7, 310–14, 344–47
  Socialist Party, 52, 137, 138, 155
  and South China Sea, 259, 348
  sovereignty of, 8, 10, 25, 67, 68, 70–71,
    218, 263, 268, 280, 345
  and Soviet Union, 60, 105–6
  strengths and weaknesses of, 241–42, 268
  and Taiwan, 27, 37, 45, 49, 59, 62–63,
    72–73, 157–58, 184, 310, 311
  technology in, 77–78, 82, 84, 97, 98,
    99–100, 110, 113, 115, 197, 203, 241, 265
  territorial claims of, 10, 12, 23, 24, 28, 34,
    49, 62, 64–74, 87, 158, 186, 199,
    261–66, 288, 291, 330, 345
  Tokyo Tribunal, 8, 29, 92–93, 180, 199,
    204, 300–301, 326
  and tsarist Russia, 23
  and United Nations, 138, 154, 184, 189, 234
  Yasukuni Shrine, *see* Yasukuni Shrine
Japan and United States:
  alliance of, 104–5, 106, 108, 115, 135,
    142–43, 189, 195, 202, 225–26, 253,
    264, 285, 299, 340–41, 344
  and "Ampo mafia," 220, 227
  anti-Americanism in Japan, 100, 136,
    137, 225
  and China as trading partner, 21–23, 25,
    28, 37, 125, 141–42

and China's rise to power, 253,
    285, 288
  defense treaties, xiv, xvi, 7–9, 10–11, 14,
    25–27, 33, 35–36, 43, 66, 78, 80, 115,
    142, 155, 157–58, 195, 200, 202, 220, 227,
    228, 264, 279–82, 295, 299, 301, 344
  in economic competition, 7, 11, 84,
    100–104, 114, 118–20, 135, 136, 142,
    317–18
  from enemies to allies, 32, 35, 233,
    340, 344
  exchange rate, 111–12
  and Gulf War, 132–36, 137
  Ishihara's Heritage Foundation speech,
    269–72
  Japan's dependency, 13, 14, 15, 37, 52–53,
    91, 105, 120, 140, 221, 288, 343
  language barriers, 22, 109
  in Nixon administration, 19–21, 22,
    37–38, 45–47
  and North Korea, 211
  in Obama administration, 221, 254–55,
    311, 315, 317, 323, 339–41, 343–44
  parallels with China–U.S. relations, 115–20
  Plaza Accord, 111–12, 118–19
  in post-cold-war world, 137–43
  and racism, 24, 113–14, 135
  in Reagan administration, 108–12
  and San Francisco Treaty (1951), 10–11,
    21, 25, 26, 157
  and Taiwan, 148, 157–58, 202
  and trade, 20, 21, 22, 30, 66, 67–68, 80,
    84, 98–101, 106–12, 115–17, 138, 139,
    143, 223–24, 315–18
  U.S. military in Japan, 25, 26, 28, 31, 47,
    66, 98–99, 102–6, 115, 140, 142,
    220–22, 288, 340–41
  U.S. outreach to China, 15, 19, 21–22, 38,
    53–54
  U.S. postwar occupation of Japan, 8, 10,
    24–25, 27, 31, 33, 34, 79, 91–92,
    137, 203
  weaning Japan away from U.S., 30, 220,
    223, 228, 245–46, 323
  on Western ideas vs. Asian traditions,
    23–24, 43, 46
Japan That Can Say No, The (Ishihara and
    Morita), 113–14, 132
Japan War-Bereaved Families Association,
    92, 156

Jiang Qing, 69
Jiang Shangqing, 159
Jiang Zemin, 123–24, 126, 127, 129, 132, 152, 158–65, 175, 191, 273, 336
anti-Japanese stance of, 158–59, 160, 162, 169, 178, 183
and history issues, 126, 130, 161–62, 176–77, 178
Japan visits by, 160–65, 172, 176–77, 180, 200, 216
in retirement, 182, 246–47
rise to power, 159–60
U.S. visits by, 146, 160
and Yasukuni Shrine, 126, 192–93
Jiao Guobiao, 234
Jin Linbo, 60, 61, 158
Jin Xide, 297
Ji Pengfei, 55, 59
Johnson, Lyndon B., 50
Johnson, U. Alexis, 33, 54, 67

Kaifu, Toshiki, 125, 133–35, 298
Kan, Naoto, 262, 263, 264, 265–66, 268, 315
Kanemaru, Shin, 157
Kase, Hideaki, 180
Kato, Koichi, 123, 141, 180, 186, 202
Kennan, George F., 8
Kennedy, David, 68
Kennedy, John F., 37, 102
Kerry, John, 300, 321–22, 342
Kim Dae-jung, 161, 163, 200
Kim Il Sung, 25
Kim Jong Il, 177, 207–8, 211
Kim Jong Un, xiii, 211, 286
Kimura, Heitarō, 92
Kishi, Nobusuke, 31–37, 49, 51, 83, 90, 102, 202, 204, 294–95, 297, 301
Kissinger, Henry A., 8
and Clinton, 144–45
meetings with Japanese diplomats, 19–21, 41, 50–51, 53, 62, 66, 102, 141, 210, 316–17
and Senkaku/Diaoyu Islands, 55, 65–69
visits to China, 8, 15, 20–23, 36, 37, 38, 41–54, 63, 65, 67, 68, 145
White House Years, 66
Kitaoka, Shinichi, 324
Koizumi, Junichiro, 180, 183–84, 190, 204
apologies offered by, 208

departure from office, 185–86, 187–88, 189, 201, 210, 219, 225, 247, 268, 303
and Yasukuni Shrine, 173–79, 184, 187–88, 190, 192–93, 196, 198, 200, 303
Konno, Hidehiro, 14, 72, 98, 120
Kono, Yohei, 205–7
Korea, 6, 207–10
civil war in, 25, 80, 209
and Japan, 24, 62, 207–8, 297
see also North Korea; South Korea
Korean War, 30, 196, 199, 278

Lee Kuan Yew, 12, 139, 155, 252–53
Lee Teng-hui, 145, 147–52
Leys, Simon, 30, 131
Liang Yunxiang, 215, 234
Libby, Lewis "Scooter," 114, 302
Li Changchun, 172–73
Li Keqiang, 289
Lin Biao, 61
Li Peng, 95, 144, 146–47
Liu Huaqiu, 151
Liu Jiangyong, 158, 296–97
Liu Xiaobo, 232, 233
Li Zhaoxing, 185
Loevinger, David, 118–19
Lord, Winston, 23, 44

MacArthur, Douglas, 8, 34, 79, 85
Machimura, Nobutaka, 185
Maehara, Seiji, 242–43, 262–64
Makita, Kunihiko, 89, 95, 155, 156
Malaysia, 140, 342, 350
Ma Licheng, 170–73, 234
Manchuria, Japanese takeover of (1930s), 24, 34, 58, 199, 301
Mansfield, Mike, 139
Mao Zedong, 270, 274, 327
brutal court politics and purges, 29–30, 59, 69, 78, 81, 159, 169, 273, 310
collected works of, 235
and Communists, 24, 35, 130, 249, 294
death of (1976), 29, 69
disastrous plans of, 28–30, 35, 56
Great Proletarian Cultural Revolution, 56, 69, 235, 293
and his father, 57
and Japanese diplomats, 26, 28, 30, 54–58, 132
and Japanese invasion, 331, 332

Mao Zedong *(cont.)*
  and Kissinger, 19, 43, 50, 63
  and Long March, 293
  power of, 28, 29, 61, 63, 233
  and revolution (1949), 28, 179, 249, 293
  and Tanaka, 55–58
  and Zhou, 19, 28, 29–30, 59, 61
Marxism, 130, 232
Mattis, James, 341
Medeiros, Evan, 256, 286–87
Middle East:
  Japanese influence in, 23
  oil from, 133
  U.S. military resources in, 105
  U.S. policy on, 191, 285
Miyake, Kunihiko, 179, 181, 245, 304
Miyako Strait, 238, 307, 345
Miyamoto, Yuji, 7, 212, 216
Mohamad, Mahathir, 140
Mondale, Walter F., 194, 195
Morell, Mike, 115
Morita, Akio, 100, 113
Mulford, David, 135
Murata, Ryohei, 157
Murayama, Tomiichi, 154, 155–57,
  164, 176
Murphy, Tag, 227

Nagashima, Akihisa, 228, 272, 276, 277,281
Nakasone, Yasuhiro, 74, 79–85, 89, 94,
  95–97, 106, 108, 114, 134, 155, 188, 322
Nakayama, Nariaki, 206
Nanjing Massacre, 9, 29, 70, 71, 95, 97, 112,
  131, 245, 304, 324–26, 325–26, 327,
  332, 350
New Zealand, U.S. treaty with, 25
Nikai, Toshihiro, 196–97
Nishimiya, Shinichi, 119, 189, 197, 269
Niwa, Uichiro, 263, 267, 271, 281–82
Nixon, Richard M., 25, 36
  and China-Japan relations, 37–38, 41–44,
    45–47, 49
  outreach to China, 15, 19–23, 37, 41–45,
    54, 56, 67, 68, 310
Nixon administration, 102
  gold standard abandoned, 19, 47
  and Japanese diplomats, 19–21, 22, 37–38
  outreach to China, 15, 19–23, 36, 41–54,
    66–67, 145
"Nixon shocks," 47–48

Noda, Yoshihiko, 268–69, 271–72,
  275–77, 280
North Korea, 148, 153, 181, 299
  Japanese citizens kidnapped by, 207–10
  nuclear capacity of, xiii, 6, 141–42,
    207–11, 286
  six-party talks on, 208–11
  and South Korea, 6, 209–10, 256,
    292, 350
Nye, Joseph, 140–42, 280

Obama, Barack, xiii, 195, 267
  and Asia-Pacific region, 5–6, 283, 284,
    289–92, 315, 340, 342–45
  leadership style of, 285, 318, 343, 344
  meetings with Chinese, 1–2, 314,
    320–21, 343
  meetings with Japanese, 219, 220,
    222–23, 291–92, 318–23, 332, 349–50
Obama administration, 115, 126, 135,
  223–28, 240, 245, 298
  and Asia policy, 254–57, 280–88,
    290–92, 299–305, 315–23, 341–45, 346
  and cyber theft, 275, 319, 320–21
  meetings with Chinese, 1–2, 275, 319
  meetings with Japanese, 221, 254–55, 315,
    317–18
  pivot to Asia, 7, 223, 254–57, 283–85,
    341, 344, 350–51
  and Senkaku/Diaoyu Islands, 321, 344
  and Sino-Japanese relations, 311, 323,
    339–41, 343–44
Obuchi, Keizō, 161–63
Ogata, Sadako, 52
Ōhira, Masayoshi, 59, 62, 63, 72
Okada, Katsuya, 224–25, 248, 258–59
Okazaki, Hisahiko, 178, 180
Okinawa, 23, 37, 65, 66–68, 115, 201–2, 214,
  220–22, 223, 224–25, 226–27, 228, 305
Ozawa, Ichirō, 136–39, 143, 219,
  242–46, 262

Paal, Douglas, 124, 125
Pacific War:
  anniversaries of, 154, 155, 184–85, 194,
    291, 323–32, 328–32, 348
  Chinese deaths in, 24, 56, 196, 259
  Chinese parade for end of, 323–24,
    329, 330
  Chinese victory claims for, xiv, 331

Devils on the Doorstep (film) on, 328
end of, xiv, 2, 9, 114, 174, 180, 195, 331
films and television dramas about, 328–29
Japan as Axis power in, 43, 104
Japanese apologies for, 28, 58–60, 79, 82,
    154, 155–58, 161–64, 176, 177, 188, 208,
    329–30
Japanese brutality in, 46, 154, 196, 208,
    220, 304, 331
Japanese reparations for, 27, 156, 199
Japanese responsibility for, 26, 27, 70, 86,
    91, 171
Japanese surrender in, 2, 4, 9, 10–11, 24,
    27, 31, 53, 54, 62, 94, 131, 143, 156, 159,
    174–75, 180, 195, 232, 330, 331, 340
Japanese territorial claims in, 24, 330
Japanese view of, 329–30
legacy of, xiv, 26
Pearl Harbor attack, 31, 186, 194,
    349–50
revisionist history of, 26, 86, 331
San Francisco Treaty (1951), 10–11,
    21, 157
U.S. B-24 relic from, 195–96
war crimes tribunal, 8, 29, 92–93, 180,
    199, 204, 300–301, 326
and Yasukuni Shrine, 92, 193
Pal, Radhabinod, 180
Paracel Islands, 69, 249
Park Chung-hee, 199–200, 301
Park Geun-hye, 290, 291, 301, 302, 303,
    330, 350
Paulson, Hank, 240, 275
Pax Americana, xv–xvi, 4–7, 10, 13, 15, 21,
    42, 99, 101, 305, 340, 341
Peace of Westphalia (1648), 7, 14
People's Daily, 29, 32, 36, 90, 93, 159,
    169–73, 234, 267, 278, 333, 347
People's Republic of China (PRC), 29, 49, 63
Perry, William, 140–41, 151, 152–53, 196
Philippines, 305, 351
    and China's rise, 253, 258, 285–88,
        343, 350
    and South China Sea, 251, 258, 285–88,
        306, 342, 343
    U.S. treaty with, 25, 343
Plaza Accord, 111–12, 118–19
Potsdam Conference (1945), 10
Putin, Vladimir, xiii, 290, 330, 335
Pyle, Kenneth, 8, 142

Qian Chengdan, 230–31, 232–33
Qian Qichen, 124–25, 128, 136, 144, 150,
    152, 160
Qi Shiyong, 230–31
Qu Yuan, 57

Razak, Najib, 350
Reagan, Ronald, 100, 102, 104, 108, 109,
    255, 322
Reagan administration, 102–3, 106–12
Ren Xuean, *The Rise of Great Powers*, 231–33
Republic of China, *see* Taiwan
Rhodes, Ben, 290, 291, 292, 321,
    341–42
Rice, Condoleezza, 209, 210–11
Roy, Stapleton, 54, 147
Rudd, Kevin, 226
Rusk, Dean, 43
Russel, Daniel, 276, 299–300
Russia, 290, 330, 335, 339, 345; from 1922
    to 1991, *see* Soviet Union
    and North Korea, 209
    and Sino-Japanese relations, 346
    and South Korea, 199
    tsarist, 23
Ryukyu Islands, 23, 64

Safire, William, *Full Disclosure,* 11–12, 13
Saiki, Akitaka, 224–25
San Francisco Treaty (1951), 10–11, 21, 25,
    26, 157
Sasae, Kenichiro, 201, 204, 213, 271, 276
Satō, Eisaku, 22, 37–38, 49, 51, 61, 66,
    103, 297
Scarborough Shoal, 283, 286–88, 343
Schieffer, Tom, 187–88, 189, 197–98
Schmitz, Charles, 67, 68
Scowcroft, Brent, 8–9
Senkaku/Diaoyu Islands, 64–74, 335
    international treaty on, 321
    Japan's nationalization of, 305, 312
    new "three no's" policy, 282
    oil in, 64, 65, 67, 213
    territorial disputes over, 2, 64–65, 67–71,
        72–74, 154, 239, 261–64, 266, 268–73,
        275–76, 277–82, 288, 299, 305–7,
        310–14, 319, 344–47
    U.S. target practice on, 64, 66
September 11 attacks, 175, 184, 190, 192,
    283, 327

Shangri-La Dialogue (2010), 251–52
Shen Dingli, 236–37
Shi Yinhong, 171, 189, 234
Shultz, George P., 110
Sigur, Gaston, 98–99, 108
Singapore, 139, 252–53, 258, 351
Smith, Mike, 107, 108
Snowden, Edward, 309, 320–21
Solomon, Richard, 43
Song·Minsoon, 210
Sonoda, Sunao, 70, 71, 103
Sony Corporation, 100, 113, 117
South China Sea, territorial disputes in, 69,
    214, 248–53, 254, 256–59, 260,
    285–88, 294, 306–7, 342–44, 348
Southeast Asia, xiii, 4–5, 10, 24, 42
    and APEC, 222, 267–69, 276–77,
        284–85, 313, 314–15, 346
    ASEAN, 226, 248–49, 250, 252–54,
        257–60, 261, 284
    and China's rise, 253, 257
    fishing grounds in, 249–50, 251, 253,
        262, 270, 282, 286, 311
    oil and gas claims in, 251
    South China Sea claims, 248–54
South Korea, 193, 225, 330, 347, 350
    air defense zone of, 305, 306
    and Chinese threat, 157
    as democracy, 199, 200
    and Dokdo/Takeshima Islands, 345
    economic position of, xiii, 4, 7, 87,
        135, 201
    global trade with, 5, 317
    and history issues, 198–201, 291,
        318, 349
    and Japanese apologies, 154, 155, 157, 161,
        188, 200
    Japanese disputes with, 290–91, 292
    Japanese economic ties to, 187, 201
    Japanese rule in, 62, 87, 199–200
    and North Korea, 6, 209–10, 256,
        292, 350
    and U.S.–Japan security treaty (1965),
        157–58, 200
Soviet Union, 66, 103, 116; before 1922 and
    after 1991, see Russia
    and China, 26, 53, 61, 70, 106, 120,
        153, 278
    and cold war, see cold war
    encroachment in Asia, 84, 104, 105, 106

implosion of, 114, 133, 186
    and Japan, 60, 105–6
Spratly Islands, 342, 346
Stalin, Joseph, 186, 345
Steinberg, James, 256–57, 280,
    284, 288
Sugimoto, Nobuyuki, 71, 88–89
Summers, Larry, 113, 222
Suzuki, Hideji, 298
Suzuki, Zenkō, 103, 104, 105–6

Taiwan, xiii, 85, 143, 148–53, 327
    and China, see China and Taiwan
    as democracy, 144–45, 148, 149,
        150, 199
    diplomatic isolation of, 20–21, 37, 62–63,
        68, 91, 160
    economic growth of, 4, 153
    global trade with, 5, 145
    independence of, 157, 160, 192, 238
    Japanese control of (1895), 24, 62,
        186, 199
    Japanese economic ties with, 27, 37, 45,
        49, 62–63, 184
    Nationalist exile in, 25, 26, 61,
        62, 130, 199, 249; see also Chinese
        Nationalists
    and Nixon's outreach to "Red China,"
        20–21
    and one-China policy, 148–49, 192
    as Republic of China, 10, 26, 63
    and revolution (1949), 21
    and Senkaku/Diaoyu Islands, 64–74, 239
    and Sino-Japanese relations, 61–63,
        310, 311
    and South China Sea, 342
    "three no's" U.S. policy on, 160, 162
    and two Chinas, 53–54, 58, 62, 144, 148,
        157–58, 160
    and United Nations, 38, 68, 149
    U.S. arms sales to, 251–52, 256
    and U.S.–Japan security treaty, 157–58
    U.S. military in, 25, 151, 153
    U.S. strategic ambiguity on, 151, 179–80,
        191–92, 255
Taiwan Strait, 346
    U.S.–China confrontation in (1996),
        152–53, 158, 160, 183
Takeshita, Noboru, 155
Tanaka, Hitoshi, 169, 177, 179, 189

Tanaka, Kakuei, 41, 50–51, 53–54,
     69, 81, 174
  apology offered by, 58–60
  diplomatic tactics of, 73, 74, 91, 180
  and Mao, 55–58
  and Ozawa, 136–37
  poem by, 57–58
  and trade deficit, 102
  visit to Beijing, 55–64, 69, 71–73
Tanaka, Makiko, 174–75
Tang Jiaxuan, 161–63, 169, 174–76, 177, 184,
     185, 186, 188, 277, 337–38
Tanino, Sakutaro, 126–27, 153–54, 155–56,
     161, 163, 182, 314
Tay, Simon, *Asia Alone*, 252–53
Thucydides trap, 15, 352
Tibet, China's claims on, 256, 259,
     326, 327
Togo, Kazuhiko, 246, 345
Tōjō, Hideki, 38, 92
Tong Zeng, 333–39
Tong Zeng: Messenger of Peace, 337–39
Trans-Pacific Partnership (TPP), 315,
     317–23, 344, 351
Treaty of Shimonoseki, 62
trilateral relationship:
  changes in (1990s), 128–32
  and cold war, 84
  complexity of, xv, 2, 9, 11–15, 35, 41,
     51, 85
  interdependence of, 15, 84, 85, 93, 120,
     189, 192
  security issues in, 103–6
  trade issues in, 106–13
  and Yasukuni Shrine, 196–97
Truman, Harry S., 194, 195
Trump, Donald J.:
  election of, 12, 341, 345
  as president, xiii, 341–42, 344, 350, 351–52
  presidential campaign of, xvi, 5, 6, 14–15,
     344, 351
  and U.S.–Japan security pact, 14, 341, 352

United Kingdom, 10, 11, 95, 339, 347
United Nations, 38, 149, 184–85, 222
  and China, 37, 68, 136, 184
  and Gulf War, 136
  and Japan, 138, 154, 184, 189, 234
  and law of the sea, 214, 250
  and Senkaku/Diaoyu Islands, 65, 68, 213

United States:
  and air defense zones, 306–7
  Asian relations with, *see* Asia
  atomic bombs dropped by, xiv, 8, 27, 114,
     174, 194–96, 331
  capitalist system of, 118
  and China, *see* China and United States
  declining economy of, 102
  declining powers of, 6, 21, 77, 84, 240,
     256, 285
  and democratic values, 322
  dominant power of, 4, 5, 107, 120, 133,
     135, 156, 228, 232, 341
  economic growth of, 6, 118, 138
  and financial crisis (2008), 118, 232, 240,
     255, 282
  gold standard abandoned, 19, 47
  and "great-power relations," 319
  and Gulf War, 132–36, 137, 152, 192
  imperialism of, 29, 42, 61
  and Japan, *see* Japan and United States
  McCarthyism in, 31, 179–80
  and meetings in Cairo and Potsdam,
     10, 11
  military presence of, xvi, 4, 5, 6, 7, 8, 11,
     14, 42, 66, 220, 339
  National Security Agency, 320–21
  national security as first priority, 51, 99,
     107, 110–11, 114, 143, 194, 198
  and Pax Americana, xv–xvi, 4–7, 10, 13,
     15, 21, 42, 99, 101, 305, 340, 341
  Pentagon in, 110–11, 128, 140–41, 198,
     227, 284, 341
  and racism, 7, 11, 24, 46, 113–14, 117, 147
  and regional geopolitics, 323
  and Senkaku/Diaoyu Islands, 65–69,
     239, 292, 306, 321, 344
  September 11 attacks on, 175, 184, 190,
     192, 283, 327
  and six-party talks on Korea, 208–10
  technological advances in, 128
  trade deficit in, 21, 77, 102, 110, 111, 118
  as uncultured interloper, 12, 24, 125
  value of the dollar, 21, 102, 109, 112
  war on terror, 115, 223
Ushiba, Nobuhiko, 19–20

Vietnam, 305
  and China's rise, 253–54, 258
  and Japan, 226, 351

Vietnam *(cont.)*
  and South China Sea, 250–51, 258–59,
    306, 342
  U.S. diplomatic ties to, 254
Vietnam War, 7, 21, 66, 151, 199, 224, 226

Wang Pin, 281
Wang Qishan, 240
Wang Yi, 89, 161, 175, 176, 197–98, 204, 218,
  304, 313, 323, 332, 337
Wang Yilin, 212, 214
Watanabe, Michio, 114
Weinberger, Caspar, 99, 103, 104, 105
Wen Jiabao, 182–83, 216, 228, 236,
  265–66, 268
Wolferen, Karel van, *The Enigma of Japanese
  Power,* 116, 117
Wolfowitz, Paul, 114
World Bank, 119, 317
World Trade Organization, 183, 231
World War I, 24, 314
World War II:
  China as U.S ally in, 25
  end of, xiv, 2, 9, 10
  in Europe, xiv, 21
  in the Pacific, *see* Pacific War
  U.S. victory in, 156

Xi Jinping, 244–45, 288, 290, 292–95, 351
  Abe's life compared to, 294–95
  on "China Dream," 12
  and Pacific War anniversary, 330, 331
  and postwar international order, 11
  rise to power, xvii, 1–2, 183, 244, 270–71,
    272–73, 274, 275, 293–94, 333
  and Sino-Japanese relations, 310, 312–14,
    330, 346–47
  and territorial disputes, 3, 276, 279, 343
  U.S. visit of, 318–19, 320–21
Xinjiang, Chinese problems in, 326, 327
Xiong Guangkai, 190, 196
Xi Zhongxun, 293–94
Xu Caihou, 312
Xu Dunxin, 96–97, 127, 336–37, 338

Yachi, Shotaro, 187–88, 198–99,
  203–4
Yanai, Shunji, 348–49
Yang Jiechi, 248, 255, 258–60, 261, 277,
  279, 280–81, 287, 349
Yan Xuetong, 6, 237
Yasukuni Shrine, Tokyo, 90–94, 96–97,
  126, 157, 186, 220, 313, 338
  Abe's visits to, 187–88, 202, 203, 204,
    289, 302–4, 312, 321, 322
  August 15 visits to, 94, 175
  China's obsession about, 93–97, 184,
    187–88, 193, 197–98, 246,
    303–4, 350
  Class A war criminals enshrined in,
    92–94, 184, 198, 200, 204
  Koizumi's visits to, 173–79, 184, 187–88,
    190, 192–93, 196, 198, 200, 303
Yokosuka (Japanese port), 340–41
Yoshida, Shigeru, 25–26, 34, 50
Yugoslavia, breakup of, 209, 210

Zeng Qinghong, 172
Zhan Qixiong, 265
Zhao Ziyang, 80–82, 83, 87, 90
Zheng Bijian, 235–37
Zhou Enlai, 28, 56, 218
  and Chiang, 61
  death of, 69
  and Japan strategy, 29–31, 34, 45, 47, 49,
    59, 60–61, 73, 132, 172
  and Kissinger, 8, 19, 43, 45, 46–47, 61, 67
  and Senkaku/Diaoyu Islands, 64–65,
    68, 74
  and South China Sea, 249
  and Taiwan, 38, 61, 63
  and Tanaka, 56, 59–64, 73, 74
  travel to Japan, 44–45
Zhou Yongkang, 274–75
Zhou Yongsheng, 234
Zhu Jianrong, 132, 297–98
Zhu Rongji, 163–65, 176, 177,
  182–83
Zoellick, Robert, 8, 315–17